THE ELGAR COMPANION TO THE OECD

ELGAR COMPANIONS TO INTERNATIONAL ORGANISATIONS

The Elgar Companions to International Organisations series comprises original reference works on individual organisations within the international arena. In addition to detailing the historical background of the organisation in question, each book examines the respective rules, procedure, and capacity for law-making of that organisation. They examine the impact the organisation has had on a particular field of law, and the role that it plays in the wider world. Designed for use by specialists in the field and for more general reference, the books represent the insight and analysis of teams of experts.

For a full list of Edward Elgar published titles, including the titles in this series, visit our website at www.e-elgar.com.

The Elgar Companion to the OECD

Edited by

Fabrizio De Francesco

Senior Lecturer in Public Policy, School of Government and Public Policy, University of Strathclyde, UK

Claudio M. Radaelli

Professor of Comparative Public Policy, School of Transnational Governance (EUI), Italy and Professor of Public Policy, University College London, UK

ELGAR COMPANIONS TO INTERNATIONAL ORGANISATIONS

Edward Elgar
PUBLISHING

Cheltenham, UK • Northampton, MA, USA

Published by
Edward Elgar Publishing Limited
The Lypiatts
15 Lansdown Road
Cheltenham
Glos GL50 2JA
UK

Edward Elgar Publishing, Inc.
William Pratt House
9 Dewey Court
Northampton
Massachusetts 01060
USA

A catalogue record for this book
is available from the British Library

Library of Congress Control Number: 2023941685

This book is available electronically in the **Elgar**online
Political Science and Public Policy subject collection
http://dx.doi.org/10.4337/9781800886872

ISBN 978 1 80088 686 5 (cased)
ISBN 978 1 80088 687 2 (eBook)

Printed and bound by CPI Group (UK) Ltd, Croydon, CR0 4YY

Contents

Figures

Contributors

Fayçal Ait Abdellouhab is a Consultant at the World Bank, Policy Leader Fellow (2021–2022) at the School of Transnational Governance (EUI), Italy, and a Former Senior Tax Inspector and Tax Auditor, General Directorate of Taxes, Ministry of Finance, Algeria.

Marco Amici is a post-doc researcher in Public Management at the Department of Management & Law, University of Rome Tor Vergata, Italy.

Peter Carroll is a Professor at the Faculty of Business, University of Tasmania, Australia.

Denita Cepiku is a Professor of Public Management at the Department of Management & Law, University of Rome Tor Vergata, Italy.

Alice Chessé is a PhD candidate at the Department of Political Science, McGill University, Canada.

Thomas Conzelmann is a Professor of International Relations at the Faculty of Arts and Social Sciences, Maastricht University, The Netherlands.

Anthony J. S. Craig is a Research Associate at the School of Government and Public Policy, University of Strathclyde, United Kingdom and a cyber threat analyst in the Scottish Government.

Fabrizio De Francesco is a Senior Lecturer in Public Policy at the School of Government and Public Policy, University of Strathclyde, United Kingdom.

Mauricio I. Dussauge-Laguna is a Professor-Researcher at the Public Administration Division, Centro de Investigación y Docencia Económicas (CIDE), Mexico and a Visiting Researcher at the Center for Asian and Pacific Studies (CAPS), Seikei University, Japan.

Sotiria Grek is a Professor of European and Global Education Governance at the School of Social and Political Science, University of Edinburgh, United Kingdom.

Magdaléna Hadjiisky is a Senior Lecturer in Political Science at the *Institut d'Etudes Politiques*, and a member of the Research Unit SAGE (*Sociétés, Acteurs en Gouvernement en Europe*) of the Université de Strasbourg, France.

Saltanat Janenova is a Lecturer in Public Policy, School for Policy Studies, University of Bristol, United Kingdom.

Stefanie Khoury is a Visiting Research Fellow, Centre for Climate Crime and Justice, School of Law, Queen Mary University of London, United Kingdom / Adjunct Assistant Professor, Department of Global Development Studies, Queens University, Kingston (ON), Canada.

Colin Knox is a Professor of Public Policy at the Graduate School of Public Policy, Nazarbayev University, Kazakhstan and Emeritus Professor of Public Policy, Ulster University, United Kingdom.

Matthias Kranke is a post-doctoral researcher at the Institute of Political Science, University of Kassel, Germany.

Markku Lehtonen is a Researcher at the Faculty of Humanities, Pompeu Fabra University, Barcelona, Spain; a Researcher at the Institute for Government and Public Policy (IGOP), Universitat Autònoma de Barcelona, Spain and a Researcher at the Department of Social Sciences and Philosophy, University of Jyväskylä, Finland.

Matthieu Leimgruber is an Associate Professor of Modern and Swiss History at the History Department, Research Center for Social and Economic History, University of Zurich, Switzerland.

Bob Lingard is a Professorial Fellow in the Institute for Learning Sciences and Teacher Education at Australian Catholic University and Emeritus Professor at the University of Queensland, Australia.

Martin Marcussen is a Professor of Political Science at the Department of Political Science, University of Copenhagen, Denmark.

Leslie A. Pal is the Founding Dean of the College of Public Policy, Hamad Bin Khalifa University, Doha, Qatar.

George Papaconstantinou is a Professor of International Political Economy, School of Transnational Governance, European University Institute, Italy.

Fabiola Perales-Fernández is a PhD in Public Policy by the Centro de Investigación y Docencia Económicas (CIDE), Mexico.

B. Guy Peters is Maurice Falk Professor of American Government at the Department of Political Science, University of Pittsburgh, United States of America.

Osmany Porto de Oliveira is a Tenured Assistant Professor at the Department of International Relations, Federal University of São Paulo (Unifesp), Osasco, Brazil and Coordinator of the International Public Policies Laboratory (Laboppi).

Claudio M. Radaelli is a Professor of Comparative Public Policy at the School of Transnational Governance, European University Institute, Florence, Italy and Professor of Public Policy, University College London, United Kingdom.

Matthias Schmelzer is a post-doctoral researcher at the Friedrich-Schiller University Jena, Germany and works at Laboratory for New Economic Ideas.

Diane Stone is a Professor of Global Policy, School of Transnational Governance, European University Institute, Italy.

Jarle Trondal is a Professor of Political Science at the Department of Political Science and Management, University of Agder, Norway and Professor of Political Science, University of Oslo, ARENA Centre for European Studies, Norway and Senior Fellow, University of California, Berkeley, Institute of European Studies, United States of America.

Francesca Pia Vantaggiato is a Lecturer (Assistant Professor) in Public Policy at the Department of Political Economy, King's College London, United Kingdom.

Amy Verdun is a Professor of Political Science at the Department of Political Science, University of Victoria, BC Canada and Visiting Professor, Institute of Political Science, Leiden University, The Netherlands.

Joren Verschaeve is a Doctor in Political Science and Associated Post-doctoral Researcher at the Ghent Institute for International and European Studies (GIES), Ghent, Belgium; and Programme Manager at the Environmental Coalition on Standards (ECOS), Brussels, Belgium.

David Whyte is a Professor of Climate Justice at the Centre for Climate Crime and Justice, School of Law, Queen Mary University of London, United Kingdom.

Ulrike Zeigermann is an Assistant Professor of Social Science Sustainability Studies at the Institute of Political Science and Sociology, University of Wuerzburg, Germany.

1. Introduction to *The Elgar Companion to the OECD*

Fabrizio De Francesco and Claudio M. Radaelli

Established in the aftermath of the Second World War to support the Marshall plan for the reconstruction of Europe, the Organisation for Economic Co-operation and Development (OECD) is now an international organisation that advises 48 members, accession and partner countries. To facilitate international cooperation and coordination, the OECD has no funds as it is not an international development bank and, in comparison with other international institutions, has a only a limited toolbox of legal instruments (Clifton and Díaz-Fuentes, 2014; Pal, 2012). At the same time, this international organisation shapes the political discourse and policy agenda of so many countries by relying on its knowledge and policy norms about what works in tackling a huge range of wicked and transnational issues. In turn, 'what works' and 'for whom' are contested terms – thus, the OECD policy paradigms and discourse have been challenged by university researchers and civil society organisations. In any case, the position of this international organisation in the global competition for ideas, policy instruments, reform agendas, and indicators remains remarkable. How is this possible, given that it does not have the power of money and the power of regulating?

This Companion allows the reader to answer this question and gain knowledge of what the OECD does, why, and to what effect in a range of policy domains. It provides a state-of-the-art knowledge on the OECD, focusing on its evolution and structure, its role in the transnational formation of policies and its impact at the domestic level. Our aim is not only to contribute to a greater understanding of the OECD and its methods of governance (Martens & Jakobi, 2010), but also to provide a comprehensive reference text for public managers, academics, independent researchers and students interested in this international organisation.

We achieve this goal through a multi- and inter-disciplinary approach. We wish to give our readers a single reference point on the advancement of the studies in several disciplines such as development, economics, education and social policy, history, international political economy, international relations, global public policy, public administration, and socio-legal studies. With our contributors, we provide a mix of scholarly reviews of the state of knowledge as well as original empirical analyses. And those interested in policy diffusion and transfer, as well as global and international policy, will find several elements of interest in this book.

THE CONTRIBUTIONS

As mentioned, among the international organisations, the OECD is peculiar in not relying on instruments of substantial power such as regulation, enforcement, and financial aid. Indeed, the OECD is recognised for its soft power based on its knowledge, expertise, indicators and policy standards. As the result of intensive networking and research involving academics, policy makers, ambassadors and practitioners, the OECD and its publications generate a common knowledge of, and language for, policy reform. Knowledge, performance measurement, policy appraisals and epistemic communities legitimate the establishment of transnational governance norms and standards. Through best practices, peer review and policy benchmarking, the OECD is acknowledged as a transnational institution for policy evaluation. Accordingly, the definitions attributed to this international organisation are disparate: 'transnational evaluator' (Mahon and McBride 2009), 'editor' of policy ideas and contents (Sahlin-Andersson 2001) and 'orchestrator of global knowledge networks' (Porter and Webb 2008; Carroll and Kellow 2011). Notwithstanding the many definitional terms, scholars tend to agree on how the OECD operates. It shares information and knowledge and then, in a delicate balance of the preferences of member states, establishes norms and standards on policy domains. Precisely because of its position in global governance, the OECD role is also contested in terms of accountability and, in diametrically different ways, irrelevance. Finally, the OECD role, influence and accountability must be appraised in the context of a world where other international organisations shape the circulation and diffusion of policy ideas, standards, and indicators of best practice. The OECD is not alone. It is in competition with other providers of similar 'products'.

Arguably because of the absence of harder forms of power for enforcing international norms, until few years ago the OECD was considered the 'forgotten institution of global governance' (Woodward, 2004, p. 124). This is now counter-balanced by the rising attention on the impact of this international organisation on domestic policy – a phenomenon visible in several disciplines. For instance, the impact of the OECD-generated benchmark on international student assessment (PISA) has been widely acknowledged, explained and also contested among education studies. Political scientists assessed its role in employment and social policies. Taxation and regulation are also other domains through which the OECD (together with the International Monetary Fund's tax policy division and the World Bank) is as pivotal actor in transgovernmental and transnational networks defining standards of good practice and approaches to policy design. Other scholars instead of considering the impact on public policies, have looked inside the OECD, exploring it with the models and tools suitable for any international organisation. These studies opened up its institutional-organisational black box and explored the decision-making processes that led to the definition of global policy standards, and, from the organisational perspective, autonomy and legitimation via knowledge and expertise. Also relevant in this domain is the interplay between the OECD bureaucracies and the delegates from the member states.

This volume brings these perspectives together to achieve a fine-grained analysis, considering the internal *modus operandi*, the bureaucratic relationships inside and outside the organisation, the impact on public policies and the member states. We do so by leveraging different disciplines and methodologies to provide an analytical portray of the OECD as a transnational policy maker, idea broker and standard setter. Hence, the Companion consolidates the research trajectory and the empirical findings of different disciplines.

To achieve this goal, the Companion proceeds in five parts. The first is a systematic overview of the ways the OECD has been examined through different disciplinary lenses. Precisely, we offer the lenses of history, international political economy, socio-legal studies, and organisational studies. Matthieu Leimgruber and Matthias Schmelzer analyse the historical evolution. They do so by combining the analytics of the OECD modes of governance (basically, ideas, peer-review, and data generation) with the essential steps of the historical trajectory. The reference to modes of governance and working methods reverberates throughout the Companion, including in the chapter dedicated to the discipline of international political economy. There, Alice Chessé and Amy Verdun argue that the knowledge produced by the OECD can be distinguished between two types of structural power: creative and regulative. To enhance its creative power, the OECD classifies and shapes meanings through activities of production and legitimation of policy ideas as well as conceptual and normative frameworks. To enhance its regulatory power, the OECD relies on epistemic communities that distil knowledge and lessons from varieties of policy appraisal and cross-country benchmarking exercises. Stefanie Khoury and David Whyte bring a novel perspective, by examining the regulative power of the Guidelines on Multinational Enterprises. To address corporate violations of human rights and other corporate responsibility standards, the Guidelines require national governments to oversee the voluntary adherence of multinational corporations. Their analysis of a data set of complaint outcomes related to the Guidelines shows that this international regime of self-regulation is weak and ineffective. Through the lens of political science, Magdaléna Hadjiisky tackles this puzzle:

> how can we analyse politics in an organisation that does its best to stay away from politics? Could the OECD have succeeded in serving in a policy advisory capacity without getting mixed up in politics? Does the centrality of expertise in its activities and legitimisation mean that the OECD has no means of exercising political authority over its members?

Hadjiisky shows how politicisation is reduced or muted. This is done via an on-going process of negotiation and the continuous co-optation of elite segments of national executives. These processes and methods of governance enhance the legitimacy of the OECD, empowering the organisation to select policy frames, solutions and practices over others.

The final lens of the first part of the Compendium deploys a public management performance perspective to open the organisational box. Denita Cepiku and Marco Amici assess whether the public management ideas, standards and practices endorsed by the OECD are actually applied inside the organisation's activities in order to prove an effective and efficient management of resources. They conclude that the OECD still needs to fully develop a comprehensive performance management system allowing for the possibility of external auditing, and enhancing accountability and external communication.

The second part provides a closer analysis of the different roles of the OECD as an international bureaucracy which draws on several organisational models as well as tools of soft governance to engage with other international organisations and national authorities. Martin Marcussen and Jarle Trondal show that, with the expansion in terms of geographical and topical scope, the organisational structure of the OECD is at risk of organisational overstretch and fragmentation. Although it is a dynamic organisation able to adjust to the external stimuli by taking on new challenges, in a sense the OECD is still in the making and in search of an adequate organisational model. Diane Stone provides another perspective on the current challenges taken by the OECD as an organisation that interacts within an ecosystem of other international organisations, national authorities, as well as various communities of stakeholders. She concludes that the OECD remains a formal international organisation which works with 'member countries' and does not yet have resources and perhaps the vision to act as a transnational policy player.

Turning to the instruments of governance, the Compendium explores peer-review, benchmarking, and networking. Thomas Conzelmann looks at peer-review in policy sectors as different as economics, development policy, money laundering, and corruption control. This comparative analysis allows him to pin down the variety in the design of peer-review "governance instruments", resulting in a differentiate impact on domestic policies. It also allows him to remark the substantial indirect effects of peer reviews. Although not directly triggering domestic policy change, peer-reviews provide a structure for forming transnational policy networks which in turn are venues for the injection of new ideas and best practices, and for the consolidation of standards and norms. The final two chapters of this part are dedicated to networking and benchmarking indicators. Matthias Kranke overviews the experience of the OECD in designing and governing comparative policy metrics. Indicators, rankings and benchmarks are forms of soft governance capable of sharpening policy goal precision, reinforcing mechanisms of naming and shaming, and elicit the response of governments – for example to justify the worsening position on a ranking. Francesca Vantaggiato's contribution is centred on networks. She provides an analysis of how the OECD has been effective in recognising a gap between design and implementation of regulatory reforms adopted by member states on the basis of recommended best practice. She envisions the possibility of networks of economic regulators establishing a closer collaboration with the OECD Regulatory Policy Committee, to cover both agenda setting (where the OECD has a pivotal role) and implementation (which is in the hands of regulators).

The third part of this book amalgamates knowledge of the OECD as a transnational policy maker in several policy sectors such as international development, education, environment, regulatory reform, international taxation, and economic policy. Let us start with economic policy. As Papaconstantinou rightly says, economic policy has been, historically, and still is today the *raison d'être* of this organisation. In turn, economic policy paradigms have changed over the decades, with the OECD having to manage the slow but steady evolution of economic policy norms with specific policy appraisal and recommendations to member states on their economic reforms, both in the macro-economy and in the micro-economy – where the work of the OECD Economics Department ties in with the advice on regulatory reforms. Economists also feature in many other departments of the OECD, such as Tax Policy and Administration; Financial and Enterprise Affairs; Employment, Labour and Social Affairs; Environment; Science, Technology and innovation; and Trade and Agriculture. Understanding what is the brand of economics that the OECD stands for, then, requires granular analysis. Papakonstantinou explains that nowadays the OECD's economic principles incorporate concerns about sustainable growth and social inclusion. It is however to be determined how these additional goals can be achieved, reform by reform, instrument by instrument.

Verschaeve provides an account of the evolution of the Development Assistance Committee (DAC) also by relating the readers to the growing body of literature dedicated to this institution. He remarks that the recent scholarly interest in the DAC is somewhat misplaced. This is because the DAC needs to be studied within the broader institutional context of the OECD as the challenges of international development require stronger horizontal integration for tackling the wicked issue of climate change and other international threats.

On education, arguably one of the clearest success stories of the OECD (in terms of impact on the global agenda), Grek and Lingard track down the interplay between education science and public policy, and the rise of global performance indicators. With a kind of 'policy by numbers' approach, the Programme for International Assessment (PISA), supplemented by national and thematic policy reviews, has enabled the OECD to frame reform options at the national level and to establish its role in the global policy space for education. On environment too – Lehtonen demonstrates – the OECD has proceeded by trying to lead on the emergence of new environmental reform ideas and norms. Environmental policy is a delicate area for the

OECD since for many years the organisation has been championed the growth of the Gross Domestic Product as the alpha and omega of all public policies. In this context, the environment structures of the OECD have been the place where the balance between different narratives of growth has been struck. The OECD impact in the field of environmental and climate reforms will depend on the influence of the organisation on countries like China, India and Brazil, as well as on this role in the wider global coordination of climate policies.

Regulation reform – covered by De Francesco and Radaelli – has gradually grown as a fundamental domain, from the early days where regulation was seen in the context of public management reforms to the current success of the OECD indicators of regulatory governance. In this policy too we find the OECD engaged with a tricky balance between policy ideas of de-regulation and a norm of 'regulatory quality' that does not hinge on the quantity of rules. In this domain, the interplay between the OECD officers of the Regulatory Policy Committee and the delegates of the member states has been key – with a constant dialogue oriented to the production of reliable indicators and the consolidation of best practice. Regulation has also grown on the list of OECD policy priorities, taking an important part in how the organisation assesses the economic outlook of countries and the resilience of public administrations. As for taxation, Ait Abdellouhab and Radaelli track down a complex evolution of policy priorities, from the exclusive concern with mitigating international double taxation to the much more political issues of international tax competition, tax havens, and global compliance with norms of fair tax competition. Today the OECD is engaged with the emerging dilemmas of how to secure effective and fair taxation of digital services.

The fourth part is a review of how the role of the OECD is perceived from the perspective of its member and non-member states. Here our choice is eclectic. The Compendium illustrates the relationship between the OECD and Australia and Mexico (for the member states) and Brazil and Kazakhstan (for the non-member states). Peter Carroll and Perales-Fernández and Daussage-Laguna present two contrasting cases of member states: While Australia has often been an influential provider of OECD ideas – and Carroll focuses on the key example of international taxation, Mexico has been on the receiving end of OECD policy recommendations. For this reason, Mexico is also an exemplar of how OECD reform advice travels and diffuses – consequently, Perales-Fernández and Daussage-Laguna mobilise the policy transfer and policy diffusion literature.

Turning to non-member states, transfer and diffusion also feature in the case of Brazil, handled by Osmany Porto; but as much as transfer operates both in the march towards accession to the OECD, there is also political resistance. Looking at environmental policies, Osmany Porto evaluates the complex relationship between the OECD and Brazil. Not a candidate for accession nor a partner, Kazakhstan has however a long relationship with the OECD, from 2008 to the present day. This country is a paradigmatic case of countries seeking membership to gain wider international legitimacy and be seen as part of the club of virtuous systems. Knox and Janenova focus on a key dimension for a post-soviet Republic: Public governance. For a non-democratic system seeking accession to the OECD, public governance is tricky, leaving room for some degrees of mimicry. By this, Knox and Janenova mean that whilst organisational re-structuring along the lines of the OECD has taken place, in other fields like policy evaluation the government has only rhetorically endorsed the OECD principles and best practice.

The final fifth part is dedicated to the new emerging issues on the agenda of the OECD in the last decade. No doubt the OECD has been leading on (new) public management debates for a long time, Les Pal shows. Today, the emerging issue is how to widen the public govern-ance agenda to include key public services. Education and health are the most obvious cases. But – Pal carries on – there is also the emerging issue of what good governance means when it comes to equity and inclusion and delivering on the social policy missions embraced by the OECD. Essentially this has brough about an expansion of the portfolio, but the OECD is still a follower rather than a leader in the new global discourse on public governance.

Guy Peters casts his analysis on a wide territory of governance reforms. Peters explains the dynamics of public management doctrines inside the OECD since the 1990s. Like Pal, he sees an expansion – perhaps a mission creep – in the portfolio of policy issues. Often seen as cham-pion of the new public management in the past, today the position of the OECD on governance has to cope with rising challenges, including the fiscal challenge and the contestation brought about by populist leaders and illiberal democracies.

Cyber-security is definitively an emerging issue for an organisation that has not tradition-ally focused on security issues in international politics. However, Anthony Craig argues, the OECD was almost pre-destined to enter the global debate because cyber-technologies have wide implications for the quality of governance (extensively discussed by Peters), democ-racy, the economy, and global development in a world that seems to have become a place of 'unpeace' (Leonard, 2021).

Sustainability is an emerging issue that ties in with several established OECD policies and norms – Zeigermannn shows. In a sense, the organisation has been both a policy taker and a policy shaper in this field. The overriding objective has been the alignment with the Sustainable Development Goals and, most challenging for the OECD, the embedding of the goals in the various policy areas where the organisation has an important say in terms of policy advice and assistance to countries. The changes have been incremental, but steadily the OECD has learned the importance of multi-disciplinary initiatives and cooperation with the United Nations – Zeigermann concludes.

In a nutshell, these five parts are five different lenses on the OECD in contemporary, global and transgovernmental policy making. The discursive and policy role of the OECD is reflected in the capacity to innovate and reforms itself, in the impact on policy sectors and member states, in its ability to anticipate emerging policy issues and withstand contestation in the public sphere.

REFERENCES

Carroll, P. and Kellow, A. (eds). (2011). *The OECD. A Study of Organisational Adaptation*. Edward Elgar.
Clifton, J. and Díaz-Fuentes, D. (2014). 'The OECD and "The Rest": Analyzing the Limits of Policy Transfer.' *Journal of Comparative Policy Analysis: Research and Practice*, *16*(3), 249–265.
Leonard, M. (2021). *The Age of Unpeace: How Connectivity Causes Conflict*. Bantam Press.
Mahon, R. and McBride, S. (eds). (2008). *The OECD and Transnational Governance*. University of British Columbia Press.
Mahon, R. and McBride, S. (2009) 'Standardizing and Disseminating Knowledge: The Role of the OECD in Global Governance', *European Political Science Review*, 1(1), 83–101.
Martens, K. and Jakobi, A. P. (2010). *Mechanisms of OECD Governance: International Incentives for National Policy-Making?* Oxford University Press.
Pal, L. (2012). *Frontiers of Governance: The OECD and Global Public Management Reform*. Palgrave Macmillan, 1–283.

Porter, T. and Webb, M. (2008) 'Role of the OECD in the Orchestration of Global Knowledge Networks' in R. Mahon and S. McBride (eds) *The OECD and Transnational Governance*, Vancouver: UBC Press, 43–59.

Sahlin-Andersson, K. (2001) 'National, International and Transnational Constructions of New Public Management', in T. Christensen, and P. Lægreid (eds) *New Public Management: The Transformation of Ideas and Practice*, Aldershot, England: Ashgate, 43–72.

Woodward, R. (2004). The Organisation for Economic Cooperation and Development: Global Monitor. *New Political Economy*, *9*(1), 113–127.

PART I

DISCIPLINES

2. The historical transformations of the OECD

Matthieu Leimgruber and Matthias Schmelzer

This chapter presents a framework for understanding the history of the Organization for Economic Co-operation and Development (OECD) and its predecessor, the Organization for European Economic Co-operation (OEEC), from 1948 to the present. We start by introducing the Organizations' three key modes of governance. The main part of the chapter proposes a periodization linking mandates of successive Secretary-Generals with deeper transformations of the organization's set up, tasks, and overall outlook. The conclusion discusses the OECD as a (geo)political platform, as an expert think tank, and as an identity-generating club.[1]

IDEAS, PEERS, AND NUMBERS: OECD MODES OF GOVERNANCE

In the terminology proposed by Robert W. Cox and Harold K. Jacobson (1974, pp. 5–6), the OECD can be described both as a 'forum organization', providing a framework in which member countries exchange views, negotiate common initiatives and agreements, and collectively legitimate their policies, and a 'service organization' collecting, standardizing and disseminating information and data. However, in contrast to many international organizations, for the most part the OECD did not rely on legal or financial means to achieve and implement agreements. While these did play a role for the OEEC in the 1950s – notably in the context of Marshall Plan aid, and both European Payments Union (EPU) and European Productivity Agency (EPA) activities – the OECD mostly relied on soft power mechanisms, by shaping ideas and preferences.

Three mechanisms are particularly important for the organization's role in global governance: production of policy ideas, policy evaluation, and data generation (Carroll and Kellow, 2011; Leimgruber and Schmelzer, 2017a; Mahon and McBride, 2008; Schmelzer, 2016; Trondal et al., 2010). First, in internal reports, hundreds of annual routine or one-off studies, public statements and speeches, the OECD produces policy ideas, develops scenarios, sets agendas, defines guiding principles and narratives, frames topics and cause-effect-relationships, and maps what is going on in member countries' economies and societies. By introducing new questions, perspectives, guiding concepts, or policy proposals, OECD officials use the organization's committee structure, expert conferences, and seemingly objective language to advance and diffuse their agenda – and thus exercising some autonomy from member countries.

Second, the OEEC/OECD – as an organization of international civil servants engaged with national counterparts – has from the onset been engaged in policy evaluation, coordination, and harmonization. Even though financial incentives did play a role in the early years of the

---

[1]   The themes in this chapter are developed in more detail in Leimgruber and Schmelzer, 2017a.

OEEC, and some legally binding agreements were adopted, the procedure of multilateral surveillance developed since the 1950s became one of the hallmarks of the OECD. These involved processes of 'confrontation', 'examination', and 'peer review'. While the resultant recommendations did not directly force governments to change their policies, they often strengthened factions within national institutions by providing authoritative endorsement to specific economic policies. Governments could thus use the OECD in the logic of what international relations scholars have described as a two-level game to muster international backing in national controversies. The OECD also worked as a forum for its member countries to prepare common positions that they would then collectively advance in other international organizations such as the GATT, the UN, or the IMF.

The third governance mechanism, data generation, describes the OECD's capacity to develop and standardize statistical concepts and to assemble large sets of comparable quantitative data and long-term time series. The production of data in turn proved crucial in shaping both the OECD organizational procedures and its identity. Starting to work on a new area, the OECD synthesized existing academic work and transferred it into a comparative perspective, allowing comparisons between countries and over time, then internationalized existing data, and finally used rankings, benchmarking, and indicators. The publication of OECD rankings was a test of the performance of its member states that sparked public debates and furthered a policy process of convergence towards what the ranking constructed as best practice.

While these mechanisms – ideas, peers, and data – help us to understand the *actual* specificities of OECD work, a closer analysis of the OECD's historical trajectory (see Table 2.1 below) reveals *other* important roles and modes of action. We now turn to each of these three historical phases.

RECONSTRUCTION, LIBERALIZATION AND PRODUCTIVITY: THE OEEC AND THE LEGACY OF THE MARSHALL PLAN (1948–1961)

Assessments of the OEEC often tend to oscillate between the self-congratulatory perspective of insiders and dismissive scholarly remarks. As reported in 1956 by a US bureaucrat involved in the European Recovery Program: 'In corridor and dining room conversations ... among national representatives and Secretariat officials ... it has often been boasted that the [OEEC] is the most successful of the many postwar experiments in international organization' (Gordon, 1956, p. 1).

This view clearly obviated the OEEC's crisis-ridden evolution, but it still demonstrates a perspective prominent at that time. It is in stark contrast to assessments by some historians. Alan Milward, for example, has described the OEEC history as a process of 'depoliticization', resulting in nothing more than a mere 'forum for registering international agreements made elsewhere, increasingly of a minor kind' – a 'transition to honest statistical toil' (Milward, 1987, p. 207). While this perspective might capture the OEEC's legacy as evaluated considering early American plans for European integration, it ignores crucial soft-power functions that came to define OEEC (and then OECD) work until today. The OEEC was faced with two organizational crises: in the early 1950s, when the Marshall Plan, for which it had been founded, ended; and in the late 1950s, when the OEEC was unable to resolve inner-European trade disputes, which led to its re-foundation.

Table 2.1   The OEEC/OECD trajectory, 1948–2021

Periodization	1948–1961		1961–1984		1984–2021		
Secretary-generals	**Marjolin** (FRA) 1952–55	**Sergent** (FRA) 1955–60	**Kristensen** (DK) 1961–69	**van Lennep** (NL) 1969–84	**Paye** (FRA) 1984–96	**Johnston** (CAN) 1996–2006	**Gurria** (MEX) 2006–21
Perimeter	Western European (including colonies) and North Atlantic		Triadic (North Atlantic and Pacific)		«Global»		
Members	(n = 18) Western European Marshall Plan beneficiaries (and their colonies) Yugoslavia joined as an observer in 1955 then became an associate member in 1961		(n = 24) USA, Canada (1961), Japan (1964), Finland (1968), Australia (1971), New Zealand (1973)		(n = 38) Mexico, Czech Republic, Hungary, Korea, Poland, Slovakia (1994–2000), Chile, Colombia, Costa Rica, Estonia, Israel, Latvia, Lithuania, Slovenia (2010–2021)		
Core areas of work	Reconstruction, liberalization of payments and trade, European Productivity Agency (EPA), "economic NATO"		Economic growth, stabilizing Bretton Woods, development aid	Stabilizing liberal capitalism, environment, integration in G7 system	Liberalization, deregulation, Multilateral Agreement on Investment (MAI), Jobs Study	Managing globalization, financial governance, development, long-term problems	
Economic philosophy	Interventionist, increasingly Keynesian microeconomic		Keynesian consensus, macroeconomic demand side management	First focus on social and ecological steering of growth, then increasingly supply side microeconomic	Neoliberalism, Washington Consensus	Rethinking of neoliberalism, inclusive globalization	
Raison d'être	Reconstruction, European integration, Atlantic cooperation		Economic Cold War, coordinating capitalist rich countries vis-à-vis the Communist bloc and the global South	Stabilizing economic relations among capitalist countries; rethinking quantitative growth paradigm	Deepening liberalization, managing the transformation of formerly Soviet countries	Stabilizing economic relations among member countries and with BRICS; rethinking free market growth paradigm	

The trajectory of the OEEC was set in the context of postwar reconstruction, the intensification of the Cold War, and diverging conceptions of Western European integration. It began with the Marshall Plan. Because ad-hoc and bilateral US postwar aid had not prevented worsening scarcities of food, housing, raw materials, and fuel, dwindling international liquidity paralysed trade, and widespread social unrest and strong communist parties swamped many European countries, the US intervened with a more coordinated approach. In June 1947, Secretary of State George Marshall stated that longer-term US aid in the form of the European Recovery Program (ERP) would be conditional on effective European cooperation in devising a common reconstruction plan.

In July 1947 – after it had become clear that the Soviet Union and its satellites could not join this deliberately Western and Cold War program – France and Great Britain invited 16 other West European countries to a conference, which led to the foundation of the OEEC in April 1948. Even though the US was not a member until 1961, its influence went far beyond that of many OEEC members. The OEEC headquarter was set up in Paris as part of a deal between France and Britain, and in 1949 the OEEC moved into the Château de la Muette in the 16th *arrondissement*.

While US and French authorities attempted to give the new organization supranational powers, these efforts were successfully obviated by Britain, Sweden, and Switzerland, who promoted the foundation of a merely intergovernmental institution, foreclosing any transfer of sovereignty to the supranational level. As put by Milward (1987, pp. 168, 208), the US initiated the OEEC 'as the first stage in the political and economic integration of Western Europe, the embryonic hope for a Western European government'. Yet the OEEC did not become the executive branch of the United States of Europe. After it was decided that decisions would have to be taken unanimously, French Planning Commissioner Jean Monnet and his associates lost interest and pursued integration in the context of the Schuman-Plan (Kaiser et al., 2009).

The OEEC's first Secretary-General Robert Marjolin (1911–86) was a French politician and economist who had been involved in Charles de Gaulle's wartime government-in-exile and closely collaborated with Jean Monnet (Heiniger, 2014). Even though he was unable to transform the OEEC into the executive of European integration he, alongside Monnet, had hoped for, Marjolin passionately led the OEEC in its first years and developed new strategic directions, in particular the promotion of long-term growth. In its early years, the intergovernmental structure of the OEEC laboured to propose a common recovery plan and an agreement on the distribution of US aid. Delegates and experts in the organization managed to draft yearly plans and to oversee the distribution of ERP funds. Furthermore, under US pressure, the OEEC continuously liberalized intra-European trade and, through the European Payments Union (EPU) helped to rebuild currency convertibility (Griffiths, 1997b).

By the end of the Marshall Plan, the OEEC had been transformed from a standing political conference with a small staff and an unstable political agenda into an established European bureaucracy. Until the mid-1950s, 13 'vertical committees' (coal, electricity, oil, iron and steel, machinery, textiles, chemical products, non-ferrous metals, timber, pulp and paper, food and agriculture, maritime transport, inland transport) formed the core of the OEEC's coordination efforts. Their meetings provided technicians, civil servants, and many industrialists with opportunities for exchanges of views and the harmonization of outlooks and policies. Alongside these vertical committees, several horizontal ones (economic, trade, intra-European payments, overseas territories, as well as productivity and applied research) discussed broader issues of economic cooperation. With the re-foundation of the OECD, the work of the vertical committees was considerably reduced.

When the Marshall Plan aid was phased out, the OEEC lost its original *raison d'être*: European integration was pursued through competing routes such as the European Coal and Steel Community (ECSC), and, in the wake of the Korean War, several countries, most importantly the US and Britain, shifted their focus to NATO. This triggered an intense debate about the future of the OEEC. Proposals to either use NATO instead of the OEEC as the channel to distribute a blend of economic aid and military assistance, or to amalgamate the OEEC and the Council of Europe almost dealt a lethal blow to the organization. This first crisis was resolved not only by turning the OEEC into the '"economic arm" of NATO' – even if both organizations collaborated closely – but also by opening up new areas of activity (Leimgruber and Schmelzer, 2017a, p. 32). For example, the OEEC championed the standardization of international economic statistics and became an important site for transatlantic norms production and governance through the European Productivity Agency (EPA) and by coordinating growth policies. During its existence between 1953 and 1961, the EPA, which worked as a semi-autonomous OEEC body and accounted for 40 per cent of its budget, sent over 3000 specialists and hundreds of farmers to the US to spread the 'productivity gospel' (Boel, 2003). Furthermore, the OEEC played an important role in colonial affairs. In the organization's understanding, the African and Asian colonies of its members were part of the OEEC, and its Overseas Territories Committee coordinated the Colonial powers' common interests, trade issues, and early development aid (Hongler, 2019; Schmelzer, 2014, 2015a).

However, under the leadership of the second Secretary General René Sergent (1904–84), a French financial diplomat, the OEEC became entangled during the mid-1950s in an unsuccessful attempt to form a pan-European free trade area as an alternative to a restrictive customs union. The resulting standoff between two rival blocs of member countries – intergovernmentalists and supranationalists – paralysed its work. The looming feud within the Western European alliance intensified when the ECSC, with tacit US support, established the European Economic Community (EEC) in 1957 with common external tariffs (Giauque, 2002; Patel, 2020). This antagonism culminated in the break-up of the OEEC's Ministerial meeting in December 1958, which gave a final blow to an organization whose last two years were characterized by the continuous crisis and dissolution of its Secretariat (Griffiths, 1997a; Schmelzer, 2016).

PLANNING, DEVELOPMENT, AND COLD WAR COMPETITION: THE 'TEMPLE OF GROWTH' IN ITS FIRST DECADE (1961–1969)

In sharp contrast to its official historiography, the OEEC was not transformed into the OECD merely because the success of the intra-European trade and payments schemes had made the former superfluous. Rather, a decade after its foundation, the OEEC was, as couched in an internal British report, 'precarious in the extreme – impossible to kill but very difficult to keep alive' (cited in Leimgruber and Schmelzer, 2017a, p. 34). As the OEEC was entangled in its failing attempt to agree on a trade agreement, a new field of transnational governance was increasingly discussed among policymakers and experts: the need for closer Atlantic cooperation to counter the Soviet economic offensive and to cope with the emergence of the Global South. NATO was caught unprepared to meet the Soviet offensive on the economic front of the Cold War, notably in the decolonizing world. Further, the rich countries lost their majority, and thus their ability to dominate, the United Nations around 1960. In this context the idea emerged to transform the OEEC into an Atlantic organization, with the US and Canada as full members, that would focus on two tasks: the coordination of Western responses to the business cycle to boost economic growth, and the setting up of aid programs to counter communist influence in developing countries (Schmelzer, 2016).

Again, the US government was the key driving force behind the foundation of the OECD. The US estimated that a 'revitalized' OEEC could solve two pressing problems, namely – how to increase aid flows from Western European partners and how to prevent an imminent 'trade war' between the Six and the Seven. Solving these problem, American experts argued, was key to increase Western growth rates in the Cold War standoff with the Soviet Union. Indeed, in the 1960s, growth became the defining policy goal of the OECD. It was the first aim in its Convention, which prompted countries 'to achieve the highest sustainable economic growth', and growth has since then featured prominently at all Ministerial meetings. One could interpret this focus as the 'organizational ideology' of the OECD, which has been described by one of its most influential directors as 'a kind of temple of growth for industrialized countries – growth for growth's sake was what mattered' (cited in Schmelzer, 2016, p. 17). At its first Ministerial meeting in 1961, the OECD passed an ambitious growth target – to increase the combined Gross National Product (GNP) of its member countries by 50 per cent until 1970. Accordingly, the OECD steered the work of most of its committees towards increasing their specific contribution to reaching this growth target – from manpower, to agriculture, to science or education (Schmelzer, 2015b, 2016; Ydesen, 2019).

The OEEC had already established itself as an international stronghold of demand-oriented Keynesian policies while at the same time upholding the importance of free trade and price stability. Until the mid-1970s, the OECD further strengthened this outlook and was accordingly known as 'the house that Keynes built' (Sullivan, 1997, p. 50). In line with what John Ruggie (1982, p. 355) described as 'embedded liberalism', the OECD 'Keynesian consensus' around high growth rates was based on a combination of international competition and free-market policies on the one hand, and Keynesian demand management and economic planning on the other ('Keynes at home, Smith abroad'). Danish economist Thorkil Kristensen (1899–1989), the first Secretary General of the OECD, strongly influenced its outlook to become an avant-garde think tank with a 'catalytic role', in which the Secretariat focused on providing innovative ideas that could be picked up by member countries if they became interested (Schmelzer, 2013).

During the 1960s, the OECD was also highly influential and instrumental in making development aid a normal function of modern states. It set some of the key norms, standards and benchmarks in this field, most importantly with regard to what counts as public overseas development aid. By constituting itself as a donors' club, the Development Assistance Committee (see also Chapter 12) created a closed forum in which the interests of the Western rich countries could be articulated vis-à-vis the Global South and the Soviet Union (Schmelzer, 2014).

RESPONDING TO CRISES AND STABILIZING INTRA-CAPITALIST RELATIONS: THE OECD DURING THE 'LONG 1970s' (1969–1984)

In the late 1960s, the OECD became entangled, under the label of the 'problems of modern society', in a lively debate about the negative and unintentional side-effects of economic growth. The driving force behind this new perspective was a group of scientists and bureaucrats who were either working in the OECD Secretariat or were members of the OECD's Committee for Science Policy. Even though neglected by historical research and in the public memory, this group proved instrumental in launching the Club of Rome. By introducing the critique of quantitative growth and ecological questions into the epistemic space of the OECD at a very early stage, this group had a strong influence on the overall outlook of the organization in the early 1970s. However, the Keynesian and neoclassical economists within the Economics Department fervently opposed this critique, and, after the onset of economic stagflation and the oil crisis, OECD governments realigned the organization's focus to the short-term problems of increasing output and reflating the world economy (Schmelzer, 2017).

In contrast to Kristensen's research-oriented outlook, the second Secretary-General Emile van Lennep (1915–1996), a well-connected Dutch financial diplomat, strengthened the OECD's role in policymaking and policy-cooperation, streamlined and restructured the work of its directorates, and used the Secretariat to influence member countries through both hard and soft power governance mechanisms (Leimgruber and Beroud, 2014). However, this reorientation brought only mixed results. During the collapse of the Bretton Woods system and the economic turmoil and energy shortages of the early 1970s, the OECD on the one hand gained in prominence, as multifaceted crises and the related problem of 'interdependence' moved international economic questions to the forefront of governmental agendas. This was especially evidenced by the OECD being the first international organization to create an Environment Directorate in 1971, by the 1974 foundation, under the OECD umbrella, of the International Energy Agency, or its recurring role in countering threats posed by UNCTAD proposals of a New International Economic Order (Borowy, 2019; Graf, 2018; Türk, 2014). Yet, with the creation of the G7 in 1975 (France, Japan, the UK, the US, West Germany, Italy, and Canada from 1976 onwards) the OECD was relegated to a second tier in the international governance structure (Mourlon-Druol, 2012; Mourlon-Druol and Romero, 2014).

Besides the short-lived demoting of the quantitative growth paradigm, the 1970s witnessed a reorientation of the ideological outlook of the organization. While the OECD had long been a 'bastion of Keynesianism' that was 'either ignoring or stoutly opposing monetarist views' (Ron Gass, cited in Schmelzer 2016, p. 322), it gradually shifted perspectives and became a strong advocate of supply-side economics and neoliberal policy prescriptions. This transformation is often attributed to an expert group under the chairmanship of US economist Paul McCracken, whose 1977 report sparked a conflict between Keynesian 'macroeconomists', who promoted improved demand management, and 'structuralists', who advocated monetary and wage restraint and supply-side instruments. From the mid-1970s onwards the organization ceased to recommend fiscal policies aimed at fine-tuning the business cycle and only focused on medium-term macroeconomic goals related to growth, inflation, and employment (Dow, 1990; Gayon, 2019; Mahon and McBride, 2008). In a similar vein, with its 1979 *Interfutures* study, the OECD presented an official refutation to Club of Rome's *Limits to Growth* (Andersson, 2019). Faced with declining growth rates, the OECD started to consider social expenditures as an obstacle to growth, discussed the 'crisis of the welfare state', and increasingly promoted the privatization of social services (Leimgruber, 2013). Building on its long-standing work on the *Code for the Liberalization of Capital Movements*, the OECD also emerged as an advocate for the liberalization of capital movements and financial markets (Abdelal, 2007; Cammack, 2019; Gayon, 2010). In most of its policy areas market solutions prevailed.

The transformation from 'Keynesian' planning to a 'neoliberal' market-oriented policy framework was, however, a complicated process that was also driven by changing member states' interests. Various proposals generally attributed to these diverging policy schools overlapped and complemented each other during the 1970s: structural policies, and in particular 'positive adjustment policies', were developed from 1977 onwards by Keynesian economic advisers to President Jimmy Carter and German economists advocating the social market approach as a microeconomic complement to reflationary and interventionist macroeconomic policies (Beroud, 2021). The competition among international organizations for 'neoclassical' pre-eminence also played a role (Chwieroth, 2010).

FROM WARDEN OF GLOBALIZATION TO 'SUNSET ORGANIZATION'? THE OECD AND THE END OF THE COLD WAR (1984–PRESENT)

During the 1980s and 1990s, the OECD became a prominent promoter of liberal economic reforms, in particular in the areas of labour and social policies, public management, deregulation and privatization (Armingeon, 2004; Leimgruber, 2013; Mahon and McBride, 2008). By 1984, the promotion of global liberalization for products, services, investment, and capital moved to the core of the OECD's agenda. This date marked not only the coming of a new Secretary-General, Jean-Claude Paye (born 1934), a French economist and diplomat, but also some fundamental shifts on the level of key OECD personnel. By the mid-1980s positions incompatible with neoclassical economics had been ousted from the Secretariat and the organization fully embraced supply-side recipes. The OECD's new blueprint was, according to an internal memo, '[to] cut budgets, eliminate labor market rigidities, strengthen competition, free international trade, rationalize production, exploit all new technologies, refrain from demand management, strengthen the personal responsibility of individuals and families and reduce generous social security benefits' (cited in Leimgruber and Schmelzer, 2017a, p. 41).

In the 1990s the liberalization of trade, finance, and investment moved centre stage, as did, in the field of environmental policies, the focus on economic instruments and markets for environmental costs. In particular under the new Secretary-General, Canadian politician and lawyer Donald Johnston (1936–2002), the OECD became a 'champion of more open flows of goods, services and capital as a vehicle for increasing world economic growth and welfare' and played 'a particularly important role [...] in support of the globalization process' by launching – yet again – an 'OECD growth project' (Donald Johnston, in OECD, 2000, p. 5). One of the key efforts to deepen this globalization drive was the so-called Multilateral Agreement on Investment (MAI). Negotiated within the OECD between 1995 and 1998, this initiative failed due to widespread protests by civil society groups and then a broader anti-globalization movement challenging corporate-led liberalization of trade and finance (Jackson and Sanger, 1998; Woodward, 2004, pp. 34–41).

Both the end of the Cold War and the relative economic sluggishness of OECD members in comparison to the much faster growth rates achieved by non-OECD economies proved unsettling. Founded as a Cold War institution asserting the hegemony of Western donor countries in North-South relations, the OECD was ill equipped to face the multipolar world of globalization and the growing geopolitical weight of 'the Rest'. To counter its eclipse as a purveyor of universal claims, the OECD admitted 'emerging' partners such as Mexico (1994) and South Korea (1996), as well as the most advanced economies in 'transition' from planned economy to free market capitalism (see Table 2.1 above). Informal, and then official contacts with the USSR and Russia, notably on development aid, had also begun by the late 1980s (Carroll and Kellow, 2021).

Former Mexican foreign and finance minister José Angel Gurría (born 1950) became Secretary-General of the OECD in 2006. Gurría presided over a second wave of admissions (see Table 2.1 above) and focused on tightening the OECD's relations with key emerging economies such as Brazil, China, India, Indonesia, and South Africa through the so-called 'Enhanced Engagement' program. However, faced with the rise of other international for a, most importantly the G20, the influence of the OECD on these countries was rather weak, not least due to the OECD's reputed 'Westerness' and because it had little to offer to new players. This further undermined the OECD area's former economic predominance. As stated by Judith Clifton and Daniel Díaz-Fuentes (2014): 'the organization needs the emerging economies, but do they need the OECD?' The OECD, the quintessential Western international organization, has thus been characterized not without irony by Singaporean diplomat Kishore Mahbubani (2012) as a 'sunset organization'.

In the 1990s, the OECD had already started to study and discuss inequalities – an issue that had largely been neglected during preceding decades. While the 2008 report *Growing Unequal* underscored the polarization of income distribution in most OECD countries, the 2009 OECD Ministerial Council also declared that '"green" and "growth" can go hand-in-hand' and called for a 'Green Growth Strategy in order to achieve [both] economic recovery and environmentally and socially sustainable economic growth'. Furthermore, building on older work which was taken up again in the 1990s, the OECD developed social indicators, published a *Society at a Glance* series, and in 2011 finally issued the *Your Better Life Index*, a multidimensional and interactive database. The OECD has thus not only opened up its membership to newly emerging markets, but – in particular since the economic crisis of 2008 – it has also taken a more open-minded and economically heterodox approach to policy (Carroll and Kellow, 2011; Clifton and Díaz-Fuentes, 2011; Dale et al., 2016; Jacobs, 2020).

CONCLUSION AND PERSPECTIVES

Given this unsettled history packed with fundamental reorientations, what is the *raison d'être* of this elusive organization? On the most general level, the OECD can be characterized as a 'warden of liberal capitalism', a forum and think tank designed for the defence, promotion, and monitoring of capitalist economies and a place to deal with the internal contradictions of liberal capitalism through specific modes of 'cooperation'. As the problems and the conceptions of liberal capitalism have changed, the specific functions of the OECD cannot be defined *a priori*, which contributes to its open-ended status. Three other dimensions are key to understand the historical trajectory of the OECD.

The OECD as Expert Think Tank and an Experts' Forum

The Organization worked as an expert think tank and an expert's forum. These two functions have continuously increased in importance throughout the history of the organization – from a minor characteristic in the OEEC to a definitive one after the end of the Cold War. Relying on 'soft power' mechanisms, the OECD has aimed at shaping the ideas and preferences of member countries through the production, standardization, diffusion, and legitimation of policy norms and expertise.

One of OECD's key contributions to global governance was the provision of a generally acceptable framing of issues and cause-and-effect relationships, the creation of convincing narratives, and the production of powerful models and metaphors, all of which enabled civil servants to perceive social facts and political problems in a convergent way (Morgan, 2012). This rationalization of an international bureaucratic space in a Weberian sense was a process of socialization that contributed to a culture of a shared Western administrative expertise and bureaucratic camaraderie. This process of socialization also encompassed contacts with academics, notably in the field of economics.

Relatedly, the practices of 'cooperation' enshrined in the name of the OECD contributed to the permeability of national bureaucracies. Soft-power modes of governance such as multilateral surveillance and peer review, the collective evaluation of (partly sensible) economic knowledge and economic policymaking information among bureaucrats helped not only in advancing a certain form of transparency among Western industrialized countries, but also in the internationalization of policymaking.

Of particular importance in this regard is the authority of economic expertise. While not many economists were engaged in the early OEEC and its committees – which were largely a meeting place for bureaucrats, politicians, and industrialists – from the 1960s onwards economics became the lead discipline within the organization. Relatedly, economic approaches increasingly came to expand on to and to dominate all other policy fields the organization dealt with – education and environment being examples of this process (Schmelzer, 2016). The OECD's authority in public debates derives to a large degree from the authority of economic expertise, which in the case of the OECD is framed as detached from national interests and thus devoid of a particular economic ideology. And in this regard the OECD's key task was and is to define good economics and the ruling norms of adequate government behaviour, not only for its member countries but also increasingly for the entire globe.

These developments have, however, not remained unchallenged. The early 1970s internecine conflicts around economic growth and environmental questions between two factions of the Secretariat, or the organization's shift in economic ideology from a roughly Keynesian framework to a supply-side orientation are two examples of such dynamics (Gayon, 2019; Schmelzer, 2012).

To fulfil its expert function, the OECD has used various strategies. Starting from the standardization of national income accounting in the early 1950s, the organization developed into a hub for the collection, harmonization, and presentation of supposedly neutral and reliable statistics (Godin, 2005; Schmelzer, 2016). From the late 1960s onwards, the OECD also strove to become *the* expert on long-term issues so as to anticipate global and interconnected newly emerging problems (Andersson, 2019). The OECD's publications – ranging from expert reports to its bi-annual *Economic Outlook*, or of member *Country reports*, to its monthly

Observer magazine – are also an important part of the OECD's self-portrayal as an expert organization (Gayon, 2009; Hongler, 2019).

The OECD as (Geo)political Platform

While the OECD was an important geopolitical actor throughout its history, its predecessor – the OEEC – never fulfilled the role it was designed for in 1948, to serve as the incubator for the United States of Europe. In this regard the OEEC/OECD is often strikingly ignored by European studies, who tend to bypass this organization in their accounts of early European integration. Yet the OECD soon took on another related role: up until 1989 (and possibly beyond) it was *the* grouping representing the economic interests of the capitalist West. Studies that consider not only the sanitized language of OECD publications, but also archival documents, in particular those from national archives of its larger member countries, demonstrate the overarching significance of the Cold War in the history of the OECD, an organization founded to coordinate the interests of Western capitalist countries vis-à-vis *both* the communist East and the decolonizing countries in the Global South.

Around 1960, when rich countries were losing their majority at the UN, this function was important not only to advance a common view on development issues, but also to coordinate Western global relations in a platform that shut out nations from both the Global South and the communist bloc, also with regard to broader international fora such as the IBRD/World bank or the UN. As stated in a 1964 British dispatch, the DAC was, '[an] essential organ in which, untrammeled by hysterical speeches from the Afro-Asian bloc or subversive maneuvers from behind the Iron and Bamboo curtains, the Western Powers can study the real substance of aid problems in all objectivity and think out a coordinated line to take at New York and Geneva'. (cited in Schmelzer, 2016, p. 224)

Already during the OEEC period, the organization's work had been dominated by France, Britain, and – even though officially only an associated member – the US. From the 1960s onwards, the OECD formalized the exclusion of smaller member countries from its key committees (e.g., DAC, or the EPC's WP3) and strengthened informal meetings among the Group of Five (France, Japan, UK, US, West Germany) that shaped the organization's work in its core areas such as international demand management, balance of payments issues, and development policies. Whereas up to the mid-1970s these negotiations took place – next to the G10 and to bilateral channels – within and through the OECD structure, with the foundation of the G7 in 1975, the OECD lost in importance. With the post-1989 rise of emerging market economies unwilling to join this organization – widely perceived as a Western Club – the geopolitical function of the OECD as a kind of Cold War economic NATO continued to be eroded.

The OECD as an Identity-generating Club of the West

The OECD has been described as a 'paradigmatic example of an identity-defining international organization' (Porter and Webb, 2004, p. 44). While some of its founders intended the OEEC to become the nucleus of European integration, the organization did not fulfil this function. However, during the 1950s and from the 1960s onwards, it became *the* organization defining the community of highly 'developed' or 'advanced' capitalist countries on the 'mental maps' of officials, and increasingly the wider public. This also meant that the OECD was founded as an imagined community of 'developed' countries with a common 'mission'.

The notion of 'like-mindedness' was key to all negotiations about new member countries throughout the OECD's history. This initial uncertainty was also revealed in the different names that were discussed, such as 'Organization for Atlantic Economic Cooperation' or 'Atlantic Economic Organization (A.E.O.)'. Besides the fact that such 'NATO-like' denominations would have upset its neutral members, it was clear to all concerned that the OECD essentially brought together the core countries of 'the West' (Leimgruber and Schmelzer, 2017b). It was founded as the 'economic conscience of the free world' that guarded the principles of liberal capitalism and the interests of this imagined community of countries (George W. Ball, cited in Schmelzer, 2016, p. 259f.).

The future of this identity of 'OECD countries' – which became widely used to denote the rich industrialized nations from Western Europe, North America, and the Pacific (Japan, Australia and New Zealand, with the US at the hinge of this trans-oceanic triad) – is uncertain due to shifts in membership and geopolitics. The same tension surrounds the widespread understanding of the OECD as a 'Rich Man's Club' and a 'Donors' Club' – an identity that has always been complicated by the membership of European peripheral countries such as Portugal, Spain, Greece, and Turkey that resulted largely as a historical relic from the Marshall Plan era.

Since for the demarcation of a community of countries the non-members – or the 'other' – is highly important, we can see that with the end of the Cold War and the rise of newly emerging market economies the OECD lost two key identity-defining markers. Since the 1990s, the OECD no longer encompasses *all* the core economies of global capitalism and struggles to find a new identity beyond the Cold War vision of representing rich capitalist countries and the (post)colonial idea of representing the major developed economic powers.

LITERATURE

Abdelal, R. (2007). *Capital Rules: The Construction of Global Finance*. Harvard University Press.

Andersson, J. (2019). The future of the Western world: The OECD and the Interfutures project. *Journal of Global History*, *14*(1), 126–144. https://doi.org/10.1017/S1740022818000384 accessed 16 April 2023.

Armingeon, K. (2004). OECD and national welfare state development. In K. Armingeon and M. Beyeler (eds), *The OECD and European Welfare States* (pp. 226–241). Edward Elgar.

Beroud, S. (2021). *Beyond the Great Depression? The Transformation of Western Economic Policies, 1969–1985*. PhD dissertation, University of Geneva.

Boel, B. (2003). *The European Productivity Agency and Transatlantic Relations, 1953–1961*. Museum Tusculanum Press.

Borowy, I. (2019). Before UNEP: Who was in charge of the global environment? The struggle for institutional responsibility 1968–72. *Journal of Global History*, *14*(1), 87–106. https://doi.org/10.1017/S1740022818000360 accessed 16 April 2023.

Cammack, P. (2019). The OECD and the world market: Antecedents of deep marketization. *Globalizations*, *16*(6), 804–818. https://doi.org/10.1080/14747731.2018.1560184 accessed 16 April 2023.

Carroll, P. and Kellow, A. (eds). (2011). *The OECD. A Study of Organisational Adaptation*. Edward Elgar.

Carroll, P. and Kellow, A. (2021). *The OECD: A Decade of Transformation: 2011–2021*. Walter de Gruyter.

Chwieroth, J.M. (2010). *Capital Ideas: The IMF and the Rise of Financial Liberalization*. Princeton University Press.

Clifton, J. and Díaz-Fuentes, D. (2011). *La Nueva Política Económica de la OCDE ante el cambio en la Econom a Mundial*. http://mpra.ub.uni-muenchen.de/33043 accessed 16 April 2023.

Clifton, J. and Díaz-Fuentes, D. (2014). The OECD and 'The Rest': Analyzing the limits of policy transfer. *Journal of Comparative Policy Analysis: Research and Practice*, 16(3), 249–265.

Cox, R.W. and Jacobson, H.K. (1974). The framework for inquiry. In R.W. Cox and Jacobson, Harold K., *The Anatomy of Influence: Decision Making in International Organizations* (pp. 1–36). Yale University Press.

Dale, G., Mathai, M.V. and Oliveira, J.P.D. (eds). (2016). *Green Growth: Ideology, Political Economy and the Alternatives*. Zed Books.

Dow, J.C.R. (1990). The Organization of Economic Cooperation and Development. In J.A. Pechman (ed.), *The Role of the Economist in Government: An International Perspective* (pp. 255–278). Harvester.

Gayon, V. (2009). Un atelier d'écriture internationale: L'OCDE au travail. Éléments de sociologie de la forme 'rapport.' *Sociologie du Travail*, 51(3), 324–342.

Gayon, V. (2010). *L'OCDE au travail. Contribution à une sociologie historique de la 'coopération économique internationale' sur le chômage et l'emploi* [Thèse pour l'obtention du doctorat en science politique, Université Paris Dauphine].

Gayon, V. (2019). Debating International Keynesianism: The sense of the acceptable and the neoliberal turn at the OECD. *Annales. Histoire, Sciences Sociales*, 72(1), 113–156. https://doi.org/10.1017/ahsse.2018.21 accessed 16 April 2023.

Giauque, J.G. (2002). *Grand Designs and Visions of Unity: The Atlantic Powers and the Reorganization of Western Europe, 1955–1963*. University of North Carolina Press.

Godin, B. (2005). *Measurement and Statistics on Science and Technology: 1920 to the Present*. Routledge.

Gordon, L. (1956). The Organization for European Economic Cooperation. *International Organization*, 10(1), 1–11.

Graf, R. (2018). *Oil and Sovereignty: Petro-Knowledge and Energy Policy in the United States and Western Europe in the 1970s*. Berghahn Books.

Griffiths, R. (1997a). 'An act of creative leadership': The end of the OEEC and the birth of the OECD. In R. Griffiths (ed.), *Explorations in OEEC History* (pp. 235–256). OECD.

Griffiths, R. (ed.). (1997b). *Explorations in OEEC History*. OECD.

Heiniger, A. (2014). Robert Marjolin. *Biographical Dictionary of Secretaries-General of International Organizations*. www.ru.nl/fm/iobio accessed 16 April 2023.

Hongler, P. (2019). *Den Süden erzählen: Berichte aus dem kolonialen Archiv der OECD (1948-1975)*. Chronos.

Jackson, A. and Sanger, M. (1998). *Dismantling Democracy: The Multilateral Agreement on Investment (MAI) and Its Impact*. James Lorimer.

Jacobs, M. (2020). *Beyond Growth: Towards a New Economic Approach*. OECD.

Kaiser, W., Leucht, B. and Rasmussen, M. (eds). (2009). *The History of the European Union: Origins of a Trans- and Supranational Polity 1950–72*. Routledge.

Leimgruber, M. (2013). The Embattled Standard-bearer of Social Insurance and Its Challenger: The ILO, the OECD and the 'crisis of the welfare state', 1975–1985. In S. Kott and J. Droux (eds), *Globalizing Social Rights: The International Labor Organization and Beyond* (pp. 293–309). Palgrave MacMillan.

Leimgruber, M. and Beroud, S. (2014). Emile van Lennep. *Biographical Dictionary of Secretaries-General of International Organizations*. www.ru.nl/fm/iobio accessed 16 April 2023.

Leimgruber, M. and Schmelzer, M. (2017a). From the Marshall Plan to global governance: Historical transformations of the OEEC/OECD, 1948 to present. In M. Leimgruber and M. Schmelzer (eds), *The OECD and the International Political Economy Since 1948* (pp. 23–61). Palgrave Macmillan.

Leimgruber, M. and Schmelzer, M. (eds). (2017b). *The OECD and the International Political Economy Since 1948*. Palgrave Macmillan.

Mahbubani, K. (2012). The OECD: A classic sunset organisation. *Global Policy*, 3(1), 117–118.

Mahon, R. and McBride, S. (eds). (2008). *The OECD and Transnational Governance*. University of British Columbia Press.

Milward, A.S. (1987). *The Reconstruction of Western Europe, 1945–51*. University of California Press.

Morgan, M.S. (2012). *The World in the Model: How Economists Work and Think*. Cambridge University Press.

Mourlon-Druol, E. (2012). *A Europe Made of Money: The emergence of the European Monetary System*. Cornell University Press.

Mourlon-Druol, E. and Romero, F. (2014). *International Summitry and Global Governance: The rise of the G7 and the European Council, 1974–1991*. Routledge.

OECD. (2000). *OECD Annual Report*. OECD.

Patel, K.K. (2020). *Project Europe: A History*. Cambridge University Press.

Porter, T. and Webb, M. (2004). The role of the OECD in the orchestration of global knowledge networks. *International Studies Association Annual Meeting, Montreal*.

Ruggie, J.G. (1982). International regimes, transactions, and change: Embedded liberalism in the postwar economic order. *International Organization*, 36(2), 379–415.

Schmelzer, M. (2012). The crisis before the crisis: The 'problems of modern society' and the OECD, 1968–74. *European Review of History*, 19(6), 999–1020.

Schmelzer, M. (2013). Thorkil Kristensen. *Biographical Dictionary of Secretaries-General of International Organizations*. www.ru.nl/fm/iobio accessed 16 April 2023.

Schmelzer, M. (2014). A club of the rich to help the poor? The OECD, 'development', and the hegemony of donor countries. In M. Frey, S. Kunkel, and C. Unger (Eds.), *International Organizations and Development, 1945 to 1990* (pp. 171–195). Palgrave Macmillan.

Schmelzer, M. (2015a). Entwickelter Norden, unterentwickelter Süden? Wissenseliten, Entwicklungshilfe und die Konstruktion des Westens in der OEEC und OECD. *Comparativ*, 25(5), 18–35.

Schmelzer, M. (2015b). 'Expandiere oder stirb.' Wachstumsziele, die OECD und die Steigerungslogik wirtschaftlicher Expansion. *Geschichte und Gesellschaft*, 41(3), 355–393.

Schmelzer, M. (2016). *The Hegemony of Growth. The OECD and the Making of the Economic Growth Paradigm*. Cambridge University Press.

Schmelzer, M. (2017). 'Born in the corridors of the OECD': The forgotten origins of the Club of Rome, transnational networks, and the 1970s in global history. *Journal of Global History*, 12(1), 26–48.

Sullivan, S. (1997). *From War to Wealth: Fifty Years of Innovation*. OECD.

Trondal, J., Marcussen, M., Larsson, T., and Veggeland, F. (2010). *Unpacking International Organisations. The Dynamics of Compound Bureaucracies*. Manchester University Press.

Türk, H. (2014). The Oil Crisis of 1973 as a challenge to multilateral energy cooperation among Western industrialized countries. *Historical Social Research*, 39(4), 209–230.

Woodward, R. (2004). The organisation for economic cooperation and development. *New Political Economy*, 9(1), 113–127.

Ydesen, C. (2019). *The OECD's Historical Rise in Education: The Formation of a Global Governing Complex*. Palgrave Macmillan. https://public.ebookcentral.proquest.com/choice/publicfullrecord.aspx?p=6000761 accessed 16 April 2023.

3. International political economy

Alice Chessé and Amy Verdun

INTRODUCTION

How can we understand the role of the Organization of Economic Co-operation and Development (OECD) in the global economic system? To answer this question, we critically review how the OECD has been analysed in the field of International Political Economy (IPE). In North American universities, IPE is traditionally taught as a subfield of International Relations (IR), which in turn is a field in Political Science. From time to time, there are discussions about whether the study of IPE differs on each side of the Atlantic (Verdun 2003) with United States (US) scholars being keen on producing more generalised theories, and European scholars having a more diverse range of theoretical and disciplinary approaches. In this tradition, IPE tools are used to focus on issues at the intersection of politics and economics – such as trade, monetary policy, and industrial policy – but also in areas where this intersection is less immediate – such as social policy, governance and identity issues (Jones and Verdun 2003; Cohen 2008). In the 20th century, the debates were dominated by North American and European scholars. More recently IPE has engaged more comprehensively with global issues and included a larger number of scholars from the Global South (Deciancio and Quiliconi 2020).

IPE scholars have stressed that the OECD is at the core of the so-called liberal international order (LIO) that has characterised relations among Western countries since the Second World War (Ikenberry 2011). Yet despite its central role, relatively little work has been done to understand how the organisation contributes to maintaining the global economic system compared to other International Economic Organizations (IEOs) such as the World Trade Organization (WTO), the International Monetary Fund (IMF) and the World Bank, or International Organizations (IOs) with similar membership, such as the European Union (EU). It has remained the '"forgotten institution" of global governance' (Woodward 2009: 124).[1] To make sense of this lacuna, we revisit the intellectual debates on why countries cooperate through IOs that took place in early North American IPE. We argue that the OECD has been in one of the blindspots of the young field as scholars did not develop analytical tools to grasp the role played by knowledge in legitimating the liberal international order. The OECD plays an important role in the creation and maintenance of a working consensus over the norms, ideologies, and practices that constitute the LIO, and this role is largely underappreciated by mainstream American IPE. This situation only started to change after the end of the Cold War as the scholarship on IOs expanded beyond IR debates over international cooperation, towards the development of an interdisciplinary study of global economic governance.

---

[1] To illustrate this point, one of the first book length studies of the OECD only came out in the 21st century (Woodward 2009). Furthermore, the otherwise excellent *Handbook of International Organization* (Routledge) edited by Bob Reinalda only discusses the OECD in less than half a page (Reinalda 2013: 37).

Expanding on the work of one of the founders of IPE (Cohen 2008), the late Susan Strange, we suggest that the OECD's main role in global economic governance is epistemic. Strange (1994) has contributed importantly to our understanding of the role of knowledge in international cooperation, through her important concepts of the 'knowledge structure' and 'structural power' (Mytelka 2000; Haggart 2019). This work has been echoed in a growing scholarship in the last ten to 20 years on transnational knowledge networks (see Sending 2019; and Stone 2020), and the structural power of the policy scripts they produce and diffuse through IOs such as the OECD (Broome and Seabrooke 2021). Following these works, we refine the concept of knowledge structure to analyse the structural power of the OECD, which we identify as being both creative and regulative. This analytical elaboration on the structural power of the OECD in the global economic system then helps illuminate contemporary debates over the crisis of the LIO.

The remainder of the chapter is structured as follows. Section two provides a historical background on classic IPE debates on institutionalised cooperation. Section three looks at what we call the creative power of the OECD by looking at how it has generated new ideas and policy paradigms. The next section examines the regulative power of the OECD by examining policy learning and standard-setting in selected cases. Section five then tries to bridge the gap between IR scholarship on institutionalised cooperation and scholarship on global governance by turning to more recent developments, around the socalled crisis of the Liberal International Order. Finally, in our conclusion, we offer some answers to the questions we set ourselves to review and propose avenues for future scholarship on the IPE of the OECD.

THE OECD IN IPE: A BRIEF INTELLECTUAL HISTORY

There have been various debates in IR on why states cooperate through international institutions. The first debate, between 'Realism and Liberalism' focused on the motivations of actors. The Realist tradition advanced the view that actors in the international arena are primarily self-interested, seek power and will engage in conflict to achieve their goals of national security in an anarchical international system. The Liberal view assumed that actors understand themselves as part of a community interested in an orderly international system that would ensure human rights, law, economic order. The second debate in the 1960s between 'Traditionalism and Behaviouralism' was mostly focused on research methodologies. New Behaviouralists argued that, just as natural sciences, social science research should be subject to hypothesis testing, causality and the ability to falsify findings, as opposed to the methods used by traditional approaches to IR coming from the humanities. In the 1970s, the third debate between neorealism and neoliberalism (or liberal institutionalism), merged the tenets of the previous two debates, as neorealism recast realist principles with specific hypotheses relying on more sophisticated methods. Likewise, neoliberalism or liberal institutionalism argued that international cooperation among states is possible if international institutions are properly designed. This third debate marked the origin of modern IR and American IPE, and centred around the possibility of institutionalised cooperation through IOs in an anarchic international system. Finally, the fourth debate in the 1980s–1990s opposed rationalist (positivist) approaches that stress the possibility for the researcher to observe facts objectively, to reflectivist approaches that argue that researcher and researched are part of the same social world and difficult to disentangle (constructivism), emphasising instead the role of history, context, interpretation, knowledge, norms and rules.

These debates provide important context about the differences in the field on institutionalised cooperation. Indeed, the relative lack of theoretical analyses of the OECD in IPE reflects the stronger emphasis on materialist and rationalist approaches in the discipline since its creation at the expense of a focus on ideas, norms and knowledge (LeBaron et al. 2021; Lake et al. 2021). This way of approaching world politics led scholars to view the OECD as a largely 'impotent' organisation (Woodward 2010). Indeed, the OECD does not rely on the governance tools traditionally identified by dominant IR theories to explain cooperation between states. Neither does it have coercive mechanisms enabling the collective use of force such as those depicted in UN peacekeeping missions, the financial leverage necessary to provide material incentives such as aid conditionality and loans of the World Bank or the IMF, or the legal capacity to make binding commitments as the WTO can. Instead, the OECD depends on 'soft' modes of governance that essentially involve the production and diffusion of knowledge in transnational knowledge networks through idea production, policy evaluation and data generation for policy-making (Mahon and McBride 2008; Martens and Jakobi 2010; Niemann and Martens 2018). Scholars agree that its influence in global economic governance 'depends critically on the OECD's identity as an unbiased expert source of knowledge and advice' (Porter and Webb 2008: 52). Thus understanding its role in the global economic system requires to address seriously the role of knowledge and institutionalised expertise in global governance.

Early IPE theories in the 1970s did not consider knowledge and expertise as important factors of institutionalised cooperation in world politics. Instead, scholars focused on whether IOs could facilitate cooperation between states through the provision of material incentives able to alter actors' rational cost/benefit calculations in a political environment characterised by the absence of a centralised authority with monopoly over the legitimate use of force, or what IR scholars referred to as 'anarchy'. The young discipline was largely polarised between two dominant perspectives. On the one hand, neorealist scholars considered that IOs were merely *instruments* (or *resources*)[2] in the hands of their most powerful member states and did not make any significant difference in world politics. (Neo)liberal and institutionalist scholars on the other hand, conceived of IOs as *forums* that could facilitate the making of reciprocally binding commitments among member states (Keohane 1984). In the 1970s and 1980s, neorealists and (neo)liberals debated *hegemonic stability theory* (HST), whether the material dominance of a hegemonic state was necessary to ensure institutionalised cooperation among sovereign states. In the context of what was then perceived as a systemic shift in the distribution of material capabilities in the global system, with a perceived decline of the US relative to the Soviet Union, IPE scholars discussed whether the power shift could potentially trigger the outbreak of a hegemonic war. To many, systemic stability was only possible under the leadership of a hegemon both willing and able to pay the costs involved in the creation and maintenance of international institutions to conserve their hegemonic domination over the international system at a relatively lower cost than coercion (Gilpin 1981).

In that view, the OECD was created to further the geopolitical interests of the US, the hegemon, by coordinating the policies and interests of its allies against the Soviet Union. Created in 1948 as the Organisation for European Economic Cooperation (OEEC), it was

---

[2]   This typology of three ontologies of IOs as actors, forums or resources has been popularised by Ian Hurd in his introductory textbook (2011).

meant to administer the Marshall Plan (see Leimgruber and Schmelzer 2017 and Chapter 2 in this volume). The young organization was an important component of Truman's containment strategy in the early Cold War, and it was largely considered as the 'economic NATO' (Caroll and Kellow 2011) to help contain the spread of communism in Western Europe. In 1961, the US became a member state and it has played a major influence in the organisation ever since, notably over its budget and informal negotiations at the Council level, despite the unanimity rule that regulates decision-making in its various committees (Clifton and Díaz-Fuentes 2011). In sum, for realists, the OECD was created and maintained to further the strategic interests of the American hegemon in Western Europe.

While the US has played a significant role in the organisation, its impressive resilience in the face of repeated institutional crises cannot solely be explained by US dominance (Carroll and Kellow 2011). In the late 1970s, liberal and institutionalist scholars argued that IOs created after 1945 could actually perform some of the functions traditionally fulfilled by hegemonic leaders to facilitate international cooperation. To them, IOs are *forums* that reduce the material costs of cooperation and provide collective goods for the benefit of all member states (Keohane 1984). As a result, every member state has a rational interest in institutional maintenance, as long as IOs are efficiently designed in such a way as to grant material incentives to comply with multilateral rules. John Ikenberry further added that once created, international institutions become 'sticky' and tend to perdure even in the face of major systemic changes, because institutional costs reduce over time. They also help expand the core of hegemonic followers by coopting new states into preserving the institutional status quo. To him, this institutional stickiness explains the resilience of the 'liberal international order' under the benign US liberal hegemony since 1945 (Ikenberry 2011).

In this sense, the OECD is a core institution of the liberal international order that has helped buy the cooperation of states in the Western community by giving all member states exclusive privileges and material benefits in exchange for compliance with principles such as the free movement of goods and capital, multilateralism and liberal democracy (Lake et al. 2021: 229). For instance, its Trade Committee played an important role in negotiating trade concessions such as the removal of quantitative restrictions among OEEC countries and the preparation of negotiations over tariff barriers that would be conducted at the GATT/WTO (Wolfe 2008). Likewise, its Codes of Liberalization of Capital Movement and of Current Invisible Operations have also played an important role in pushing for global financial liberalization since the 1970s (Porter 2010). As a result, the organisation contributed to expanding the liberal international order beyond the narrow club of early Cold War US allies, by increasing the material benefits of integration for outsider countries such as Japan or Finland, and after the end of the Cold War, Central and Eastern European countries that used to be affiliated to the Soviet Block. In sum, for liberal institutionalists, the OECD contributed to expanding the zone of liberal peace by providing incentives to comply with rules and principles of the LIO.

Only in the 1990s did knowledge start to play a central role in IPE theories of institutionalised cooperation. To many, the resilience of IOs after the end of the Cold War was not just a result of member states' cost-benefit calculations. Rather, it had to do with how IOs shape actors' perceptions and interpretations of their own identities and interests in the global economic system. Reflexive theories rapidly gained in popularity stressing that IOs are *actors* in their own right and on their own terms rather than instruments or forums (Barnett and Finnemore 2004). They are part of a network in which states and non-state actors together shape global governance, a loose framework of regulation over global economic affairs relying on 'the exercise of authority across national borders as well as consented norms and rules beyond the nation state, both of them justified with reference to common goods or transnational problems' (Zürn 2018: 3–4). Scholars now study how IOs are entangled in complex webs of overlapping, symbiotic or conflicting authority that involve different kinds of non-state and state actors (Strange 1996: 99) and through which they influence the global economic system by shaping knowledge about the world economy.

These new theoretical approaches have provided productive ways to conceive of the role of the OECD in world politics due to the unique structure of the organization as a 'global policy network' (Carroll and Kellow 2011; Pal 2012). Michael Zürn qualifies the organisation of a 'politically assigned epistemic authority', a transnational or international institution that does not make binding decisions, but rather rules through interpretations grounded in technocratic and legal expertise (Zürn 2018: 53, 81). In other words, the organisation shapes what Susan Strange called the 'knowledge structure' of the global economy, in that it defines 'what knowledge is discovered, how it is stored, and who communicates it, by what means to whom and on what terms' (Strange 1996: 121). It does so through two main modes of governance: one that involves the *creation* of knowledge, and the other one that involves the *regulation* of knowledge through processes of policy evaluation, coordination and harmonization (Schmelzer 2016; Haggart 2019). The next two sections discuss each of these modes of governance respectively.

THE CREATIVE POWER OF THE OECD: KNOWLEDGE CONSTRUCTION AND HEGEMONIC CONSENSUS

The OECD contributes to forging an epistemic consensus about the legitimacy of the core rules and norms of the liberal international order by producing knowledge about appropriate policymaking. In that sense, it legitimates the knowledge structure of the global economy by producing beliefs which 'shap[e] the terms on which we engage with the world' (Haggart 2019: 32). This process of knowledge production and legitimation corresponds to what OECD scholars call the 'meditative' mode of regulation of the OECD (Mahon and McBride 2008), as an arena 'where all kinds of experiences can be transmitted and compared, where ideas are generated and shared' and whose activities are 'mainly framed as discussions among experts about what is the best way or ways of doing something' (Jacobsson 2006: 208). It involves the OECD Secretariat's power to classify, fix meanings, and diffuse norms (Mahon and McBride 2008: 7) through activities of production, legitimation, and dissemination of policy ideas, conceptual frameworks, expertise, and values (Schmelzer 2016: 17).

For constructivists, these meditative activities play an important role in the first stages of the international norm life cycle (Finnemore and Sikkink 1998). In the process of norm emergence, the OECD often acts as a normative entrepreneur in articulating and diffusing new ideas about appropriate policies. In its early years, the OECD has acted as an 'ideational artist' (Marcussen 2004) as its first Secretary-General, Kristensen, had the ambition to make it an 'ideational agent' capable to 'think the unthinkable', and to 'speak truth to power' (Ron Gass, quoted in Schmelzer 2016) by proposing innovative policy ideas capable of shaking the political establishment for better social and economic outcomes. Some of these ideas effectively led to important normative changes in global economic governance, in particular until the late 1980s, as the OECD's soft mode of governance and expertise provided a leverage in comparison with other IOs often paralysed by Cold War politics. In the late 1940s and early 1950s, it played a particularly important role in the area of development economics in shaping the policy paradigm of Keynesianism (Schmelzer 2016) and in anchoring embedded liberalism as the normative compromise around which post-WWII international order was established (Ruggie 1982).

In the 1970s, the OECD was in the vanguard of the shift towards neoliberalism and the embrace of price stability programs. In 1978, a committee of independent economists close to the Mont-Pelerin Society and gathered by the OECD published the McCracken report, entitled *Towards Full Employment and Price Stability*, one of the earliest articulations of anti-inflationary policies by an IO (Keohane 1978). Following the publication of the McCracken report, Rawi Abdelal showed that the OECD acted as an institutional entrepreneur on financial liberalisation in the 1980s. Technical discussions between OECD economists and members states' national representatives within the OECD Committee on Capital Movements and Invisible Transactions (CMIT) led member countries to accept a degree of financial liberalisation much deeper than what they were initially ready to commit (Abdelal 2007; Howarth and Sadeh 2011).

This role of a normative entrepreneur is made possible because the OECD creates a shared sense of identity among its members who perceive each other as part of a group of like-minded developed market economies. The OECD is a 'paradigmatic example of an identity-defining international organization' for states that 'seek to identify themselves as modern, liberal, market-friendly and efficient', aspiring to represent the ideal modern state (Porter and Webb 2008: 43). Furthermore, critical scholars stress that IEOs shape hegemonic knowledge about the world economy, by producing paradigms and ideologies that are taken for granted as neutral facts and parameters guiding policymakers' behaviour (e.g., Cox and Jacobson 1973). The OECD is more than a creative think tank; it also produces a 'common policy culture' (Wolfe 2008: 41) around a 'liberalizing agenda' (Ougaard 2010: 35) among the people who attend its activities. Since its creation in 1961 the OECD has maintained an 'underlying belief in open markets and trade as the basis for peace' as its unquestioned ideological core (Wolfe 2008: 50), a common denominator across the varieties of liberalism represented in its publications (Mahon 2011; Gayon 2022).

For instance, the polluter pays principle (PPP) emanated from the OECD Environment Committee under the leadership of Jim MacNeill in 1972. While this constituted an important normative innovation, it also helped limit the changes that the concept of PPP would bring to global economic governance. Indeed the PPP constituted a technocratic compromise between environmental regulations and free international markets, constitutive of an early articulation of a liberal form of environmentalism (Bernstein 2001: 51). It was notably instrumental in legitimising the idea that environmental protection and economic growth were compatible, hence diluting the radical ecological critique articulated in the 1972 *Limits to Growth* Report published by the Club of Rome (see Schemlzer 2016). In sum, the OECD plays an important role in producing the commonsensical representation of the global economy. Its epistemic creativity then works as a compromise by proposing reforms to a set core of liberal principles that stay untouched, at best redefining hegemonic knowledge rather than transforming it (Bernstein 2001: 15).

In sum, the legitimation function of the OECD includes both the creation of new ideas, paradigms and policies and the maintenance of a hegemonic consensus over the core rules and principles of the global economic order. However, many have expressed scepticism regarding how much ideational creation is really at play at the OECD since the end of the Cold War. For Marcussen (2004), now the organisation has become more of an 'ideational arbitrator', playing an important role in policy regulation more so than in ideational creation. The next section discusses this 'inquisitive' mode of regulation (Jacobsson 2006; Mahon and McBride 2008).

THE REGULATIVE POWER OF THE OECD: POLICY LEARNING AND STANDARD-SETTING

Since the end of the Cold War, the OECD has played a more important role at the level of its committees by influencing transnational policymaking through practices of deliberation and socialization of member and partner countries' bureaucrats (Marcussen 2004). It has governed the economy through the regulation of knowledge produced elsewhere, more so than through the creation by its Secretariat of new knowledge about the world economy. We call this form of structural power *regulative* to differentiate it from power of ideational *creation* discussed in the previous section. These regulative espitemic activities encompass the formal and informal rules governing the standardisation and dissemination of policy knowledge (cf. Haggart 2019: 32). For constructivist scholarship, then the OECD is now more active in the later stages of the international norm life cycle, namely norm cascade, diffusion and internalisation by national policymakers (Finnemore and Sikkink 1998). The OECD global policy network socialises member countries bureaucrats into a certain working culture 'because its committees and other subsidiary bodies bring together on a regular basis staff from a much wider range of policy domains than just economics, so the social "glue" it encourages help provide an important degree of coherence in the system of global governance' (Carroll and Kellow 2011: 1–2; also Pal 2012). It contributes to the creation of a transnational bureaucratic culture around everyday governance practices of monitoring, standard-setting and benchmarking.

These activities make the OECD an important actor of transnational policy transfer through mechanisms of policy learning and emulation (Dobbin et al. 2007). Leslie Pal (2012) showed that these mechanisms have played an important role in the transnational transfer of policies of New Public Management since the 1980s. Here the working methods of the OECD committees, notably its activities of multilateral surveillance through peer review (Schäfer 2006; Porter and Webb 2008; see also Chapter 9 in this volume) have been key to incite policy change through the effects of international comparisons. As Clifton and Díaz-Fuentes (2014: 251) argue the OECD has a 'unique' way of operating: policies are created through dialogue and exchange between OECD staff and national policy representatives. Once a mutual agreement is reached, the transfer of policy occurs through technical reports. Its work of compilation of data also standardises knowledge about best policymaking practices and makes possible the production of international rankings of government performance. These rankings and standards in turn constitute important tools for diverse actors to incite policy change at the national level (see Cooley and Snyder 2015; Kelley and Simmons 2020). For instance, Jason Sharman showed how this form of power was at play in the OECD's policy on tax evasion by making national fiscal policies more 'legible' at the global level, successfully standardising fiscal administration through the work of the OECD Committee on Fiscal Affairs (Sharman 2012: 28). Furthermore, by publishing data on national fiscal policies in blacklist, the OECD project on Harmful Tax Competition incited policy compliance through mechanisms of naming and shaming (Sharman 2009). Kudrle (2010) concludes that the OECD 'has served far more as a transmitter than a generator of ideas' over international tax policy (Kudrle 2010: 76).

One of the most remarkable recent influences of the OECD on policy learning and standard-setting across the globe, is perhaps illustrated by a case study pertaining to the field of high school education. In 1999, the OECD launched a Programme for International Student Assessment (PISA), which measures the ability of students at 15 years of age (9th graders) in reading, mathematics, science and other relevant skills. Its formal aims were to assess 'aspects of preparedness for adult life' (OECD 2000: 3). The attraction was that a common standard was created that could compare learning outcomes in high school students across a variety of countries. It provided evidence-based data that could be used for benchmarking, comparison and policy change. Member countries were eager to use the outcomes to see where their country 'ranks', but also within countries, and where strengths and weaknesses lay within its educational system (Morgan and Shahjahan 2014). The PISA study has generated a lot of attention, in policy circles and in academic literature (Hopfenbeck et al. 2018), not least because the results of the tests challenged some established ideas about the relationship between economic and educational development (Sellar and Lingard 2013: 717). Given that the various PISA rounds have generated data at the country level and over time, the tempta-tion is to make broad statements about quality of education and to make the necessary policy changes to improve a country's performance (Volante, Fazio and Ritzen 2017; Kelley and Simmons 2020).

Some argue that the OECD contributed to this tendency by publishing league tables (Hopfenbeck et al. 2018: 347). In the EU, PISA led to an interest in policy cooperation in Higher Education which eventually triggered the change-over, through a bottom-up process, from a very diverse landscape to a much more standardised system referred to as the Bologna Process (Haskel 2009). The increasingly strong performance of China, especially in compar-ison to some leading advanced economies, such as Germany and the US, has given further credence to the reputation of the growth of China as a world power. At the same time, scholars have been critical to point to an increasing 'exam culture' and pressure on student performance in cities and states such as Shanghai, where PISA scores were high (Tan and Reyes 2018). The outstanding performance of China has however continued into the next edition in 2020 when the scores from China came top in all three categories. Again, scholars have scrutinised these exceptional performances and pointed to the result not being representative, because only the four wealthiest states of China (Beijing, Shanghai, Jiangsu and Zhejiang) participate. The strong increase between 2015 and 2020 is also a concern to some (Gruijters 2020). Yet voices point to a growing dominance of China as a superpower, with these rankings being yet another metric to make that point. In so doing, China has improved its standing in the above-mentioned knowledge structure. In sum, the OECD has contributed to standard setting in a number of areas, and education is one such example. Countries such as China, in a race to win global superpower status, have appeared to ensure that they 'show off' their dominance by doing well on these standards.

THE OECD AND THE CRISIS OF THE LIBERAL INTERNATIONAL ORDER

As our discussion has showed, the scholarship on the role of the OECD in global governance has tended to focus on policy change as its main object of study and it has slid away from early IPE debates about how IOs affect broader relations of power in the global economic system. In this last section, we try to bridge the gap between traditional American IPE debates over institutionalised cooperation introduced in section 1, and global governance scholarship on transnational policy change introduced in sections 2 and 3. In order to make sense of how IOs adapt to current challenges to the LIO, a closer look at the OECD would help illuminate how everyday practices of global policymaking structure enduring relations of power in the global economic system.

The OECD has been seen as a core institution of the LIO that fosters a transnational consensus about the legitimacy of its core 'international economic philosophy' (Schmelzer 2016: 17). The LIO has been taken for granted as something that advanced economies (ergo OECD countries) aspired to. For neo-Gramscians, the OECD 'develop[s] and organize[s] the global hegemonic leadership of the community of industrialized market democracies' (Ougaard 2010: 45–6). The production of this shared sense of identity constitutes and maintains relations of domination in the global economic system, notably between the Global North and the Global South (see Cox and Jacobson 1973). OECD membership has historically identified the Global North and the richest countries of the world economy (Clifton and Díaz-Fuentes 2015) and during much of the Cold War the organisation has been the 'warden of liberal capitalism and the West' (Schmelzer 2016: 29). This assumption was of course never fully unchallenged. For instance, during the Cold War a number of OECD countries were left unaligned (e.g., Austria, Ireland, and various Scandinavian countries). Still, in the period following the end of the Cold War the LIO seemed much more stable: a number of European member states joined the EU and countries such as China gradually integrated into the LIO. Cooperation via the OECD expanded and some forms of coordination were particularly salient such as the PISA study discussed prior.

However, in recent years, the LIO seems to have come under threat. In a recent Special Issue of the journal *International Organization*, the editors identify the challenges to the LIO as coming both from inside, with the spread of transnational right-wing populism, and from outside the LIO, with the emergence of new rising powers outside of the core of Western countries (Lake et al. 2021; also Luce 2017). The OECD has been working actively on both the internal and external challenges to legitimate the foundations of the LIO. Internally, the election of Donald Trump as the 45th President of the United States in 2016 and the decision of the United Kingdom to leave the EU revealed that one of the most pressing political economic challenges to the neoliberal form of the LIO came from its asymmetric distributive effects. Indeed, nationalist movements and populist parties have flourished in a context of widening income inequality within advanced societies that could be traced back to the lack of fairness in reaping the fruits of economic globalisation. Populism has also advanced an anti-elitist rhetoric, including disdain for established institutions and knowledge, which has led to a growth in conspiracy thinking and anti-establishment movements. Liberalism has also intrinsically contained its own critics. In recent years the public has become more sceptical of technocracy and high-level governance like the OECD.

The OECD has proved relatively successful in managing these internal challenges to the LIO. As an international organisation, the OECD has been much less in the spotlight than other international organisations, such as the World Trade Organization or the United Nations (see Zürn 2018). In a sense the OECD benefits from being an organisation that does not have hierarchical rule at its core, where no executive power is demonstrated. As the criticism on the liberal order has been mostly voiced by populist or nationalist politicians and their supporters, much less by bureaucracies or elites themselves, the work of the OECD has continued. In fact, during the COVID-19 pandemic, organisations such as the World Health Organization and the OECD were valuable sources of knowledge exchange (OECD 2020).

It is rather on the external challenges to the LIO that criticism on the OECD has concentrated, focusing on its narrow 'club-like' membership, its Western origins, and its tendency to be biased towards the norms and values of the original membership (Clifton and Díaz-Fuentes 2015). In the early 2000s it selected a few countries (Brazil, China, India, Indonesia, and South Africa (BRICS)) to make closer linkages to, through its 'Enhanced Engagement Programme'. The new program is meant to integrate rising economies and BRICS countries through pragmatic engagement in the everyday working methods of the organisation – its peer review and surveillance system – rather than through traditional membership enlargement (Clifton and Díaz-Fuentes 2015). The goal of these outreach activities is to enlarge and strengthen the hegemonic core consensus of the global economic system (Ougaard 2011). Yet Clifton and Díaz-Fuentes (2014) find varied success in the ability for the OECD to succeed in transferring policy to these emerging non-Western countries, and that the OECD faces considerable struggle to be noticed by these countries.

CONCLUSION

This chapter discussed how the field of IPE makes sense of the role the OECD plays in the global economic system. We identified two strands of scholarship, one originating in American IPE debates on institutionalised cooperation and another one in global governance research. A critical reading of both scholarships highlights that the organisation shapes and sustains an epistemic consensus around the core norms, principles and practices that constitute the LIO. We argued that an important shortcoming of current OECD research in IPE came from a lack of engagement between these two scholarships. Indeed, the organisation does not rely on the governance tools traditionally highlighted by IPE theories of institutionalised cooperation, namely, material incentives or binding commitments. As a result, scholars of global governance have tended to focus on its effects on national and transnational policymaking, but they have rarely analyzed how its soft mode of governance shapes the power structure of the global economic system. A better understanding of the role of the OECD in the global economic system then requires IPE scholars to analyse how expertise shapes and legitimates the knowledge structure of the global economy. We proposed that a deeper engagement with the works of Susan Strange could contribute to such developments by identifying how the OECD modes of governance through policy knowledge creation and regulation enact structural power in the global economy (Broome and Seabrooke 2021; see also Mytelka 2000). Two avenues of future research, empirical and theoretical, would help further bridge this gap.

At the empirical level, further research on the OECD would help understand the interplay between material and non-material sources of the resilience of the LIO (Lake et al. 2021). First, it would help uncover the colonial history of IPE. Indeed, the OECD is key to understanding how post-1945 IOs have shaped the history of colonialism and decolonisation considering the central role the OECD played in the North-South dialogue. Second, further research on the OECD could help understand how global governance institutions address existential global threats like climate change, pandemics and global economic crises that require a multidisciplinary approach to global policy problems. It is also a key window into the making of hybrid governance that mixes both public and private interests notably through the transnationalisation of managerial governance practices.

At the analytical level, further research on the OECD would help address several gaps in IPE. First, the OECD could illuminate how IOs are constructs that rest on social foundations notably by uncovering the political effects of institutionalised expertise in global governance. Second, research on the OECD would help analyse the distributive effects of institutionalised cooperation, by conceptualising how IOs provide club goods that sustain inequalities and exclusion in the ILO. Finally, further analysis of the OECD could look at the ambivalent role IOs play in fighting but also preserving systemic inequalities in the international order, between the Global North and the Global South, but also gendered and racial inequalities, through engagement with recent development in decolonial and feminist IPE. Tackling these issues would require what LeBaron et al. call an 'engaged pluralism' in IPE (2021: 292) able to foster conversations with theoretical perspectives traditionally marginalized in the field. This would ultimately contribute to decenter the IPE of global governance and institutionalised cooperation.

ACKNOWLEDGEMENTS

The authors wish to thank Frédéric Mérand for bringing them together, as well as the editors of this volume for helpful comments on an earlier version of this chapter. Furthermore, we would like to acknowledge the financial support generously provided by the Social Sciences and Humanities Research Council of Canada. Authors' names are listed in alphabetical order.

REFERENCES

Abdelal, Rawi. 2007. 'Privilege and Obligation: The OECD and Its Code of Liberalization.' In *Capital Rules: The Construction of Global Finance*, edited by Rawi Abdelal, 86–122. Harvard, MA: Harvard University Press.

Barnett, Michael N. and Martha Finnemore. 2004. *Rules for the World: International Organizations in Global Politics*. Ithaca, NY: Cornell University Press.

Bernstein, Steven. 2001. *The Compromise of Liberal Environmentalism*. New York, NY: Columbia University Press.

Broome, André and Leonard Seabrooke. 2021. 'Recursive Recognition in the International Political Economy.' *Review of International Political Economy* 28(2): 369–81.

Carroll, P.G.H. and Aynsley J. Kellow. 2011. *The OECD: A Study of Organisational Adaptation*. Cheltenham, UK: Edward Elgar.

Clifton, Judith and Daniel Díaz-Fuentes. 2011. 'The OECD and Phases in the International Political Economy, 1961–2011.' *Review of International Political Economy* 18(5): 552–69.

Clifton, Judith and Daniel Díaz-Fuentes. 2014. 'The OECD and "The Rest": Analyzing the Limits of Policy Transfer.' *Journal of Comparative Policy Analysis: Research and Practice* 16(3): 249–65.

Clifton, Judith and Daniel Díaz-Fuentes. 2015. 'From "Club of the Rich" to "Globalization à la Carte"? Evaluating Reform at the OECD.' In *Rising Powers and Multilateral Institutions*, Dries Lesage and Thijs van de Graaf (eds), 60–78. Basingstoke: Palgrave Macmillan.

Cohen, Benjamin J. 2008. *International Political Economy: An Intellectual History*. Princeton, NJ: Princeton University Press.

Cooley, Alexander and Jack L. Snyder (eds) 2015. *Ranking the World: Grading States as a Tool of Global Governance*. Cambridge: Cambridge University Press.

Cox, Robert W., and Harold K. Jacobson. 1973. *The Anatomy of Influence: Decision-Making in International Organization*. New Haven, CT: Yale University Press.

Deciancio, Melisa and Cintia Quiliconi. 2020. 'Widening the "Global Conversation": Highlighting the Voices of IPE in the Global South.' *All Azimuth* 9(2): 249–65.

Dobbin, Frank, Beth Simmons, and Geoffrey Garrett. 2007. 'The Global Diffusion of Public Policies: Social Construction, Coercion, Competition, or Learning?' *Annual Review of Sociology* 33 (1):449–72.

Dunlop, C.A. and C.M. Radaelli. 2018. 'The Lessons of Policy Learning: Types, Triggers, Hindrances and Pathologies.' *Policy and Politics* 46(2): 255–72.

Finnemore, Martha, and Sikkink, Kathryn. 1998. 'International Norm Dynamics and Political Change'. *International Organization* 52(4): 887–917.

Gayon, Vincent. 2022. *Épistémocratie: Enquête Sur Le Gouvernement International Du Capitalisme*. Paris: Raisons d'agir.

Gilpin, Robert. 1981. *War and Change in World Politics*. Cambridge: Cambridge University Press.

Gruijters, Rob J. 2020. 'How (Un)representative are China's stellar PISA results?' NORRAG Blog, 18 Feb., https://www.norrag.org/how-unrepresentative-are-chinas-stellar-pisa-results-by-rob-j-gruijters accesssed 17 April 2023.

Haggart, Blayne. 2019. 'Taking Knowledge Seriously: Towards an International Political Economy Theory of Knowledge Governance.' In *Information, Technology and Control in a Changing World: Understanding Power Structures in the 21st Century*, Blayne Haggart, Kathryn Henne and Natasha Tusikov (eds), 25–51. Basingstoke: Palgrave Macmillan.

Haskel, Barbara G. 2009. 'Weak Process, Strong Results: Cooperation in European Higher Education.' In *Innovative Governance in the European Union: The Politics of Multilevel Policymaking*, Ingeborg Tömmel and Amy Verdun (eds), 273–88, Boulder and London: Lynne Rienner.

Hopfenbeck, Therese N., Jenny Lenkeit, Yasmine El Masri, Kate Cantrell, Jeanne Ryan and Jo-Anne Baird. 2018. 'Lessons Learned from PISA: A Systematic Review of Peer-Reviewed Articles on the Programme for International Student Assessment.' *Scandinavian Journal of Educational Research* 62(3): 333–53.

Howarth, David and Tal Sadeh. 2011. 'In the Vanguard of Globalization: The OECD and International Capital Liberalization.' *Review of International Political Economy* 18(5): 622–45.

Hurd, Ian. 2011. *International Organizations: Politics, Law, Practice*. 1st edn Cambridge: Cambridge University Press.

Ikenberry, G. John. 2011. *Liberal Leviathan: The Origins, Crisis, and Transformation of the American World Order*. Princeton, NJ: Princeton University Press.

Jacobsson, Bengt. 2006. 'Regulated Regulators: Global Trends of State Transformation.' In *Transnational Governance: Institutional Dynamics of Regulation*, Marie-Laure Djelic and Kerstin Sahlin-Andersson (eds), 205–24. Cambridge: Cambridge University Press.

Jones, Erik and Amy Verdun. 2003. 'Introduction: Political Economy and European Integration.' *Journal of European Public Policy* 10(1): 81–83.

Kelley, Judith Green and Beth A. Simmons (eds) 2020. *The Power of Global Performance Indicators*. Cambridge: Cambridge University Press.

Keohane, Robert O. 1978. 'Economics, Inflation, and the Role of the State: Political Implications of the McCracken Report.' *World Politics* 31(1): 108–28.

Keohane, Robert O. 1984. *After Hegemony: Cooperation and Discord in the World Political Economy*. Princeton, NJ: Princeton University Press.

Kudrle, Robert T. 2010. 'Tax Policy in the OECD: Soft Governance Gets Harder.' In *Mechanisms of OECD Governance: International Incentives for National Policy-Making?*, Kerstin Martens and Anja P. Jakobi (eds), 75–97. Oxford: Oxford University Press.

Lake, D., Martin, L., and Risse, T. 2021. 'Challenges to the Liberal Order: Reflections on International Organization.' *International Organization* 75(2), 225–57.

LeBaron, Genevieve, Daniel Mügge, Jacqueline Best, and Colin Hay. 2021. 'Blind Spots in IPE: Marginalized Perspectives and Neglected Trends in Contemporary Capitalism.' *Review of International Political Economy* 28(2): 283–94.

Leimgruber, Matthieu and Matthias Schmelzer (eds), 2017. *The OECD and the International Political Economy since 1948.* Basingstoke: Palgrave Macmillan.

Luce, Edward. 2017. *The Retreat of Western Liberalism.* New York: Atlantic Monthly Press.

Mahon, Rianne. 2011. 'The Jobs Strategy: From Neo-to Inclusive Liberalism?' *Review of International Political Economy* 18(5): 570–91.

Mahon, Rianne and Stephen McBride (eds) 2008. *The OECD and Transnational Governance.* Vancouver: UBC Press.

Marcussen, Martin. 2004. 'The Organization for Economic Cooperation and Development as Ideational Artist and Arbitrator: Reality or Dream?' In *Decision Making within International Organizations*, Bob Reinalda and Bertjan Verbeek (eds), 90–105. London: Routledge.

Martens, Kerstin and Anja P. Jakobi. 2010. 'Introduction: The OECD as an Actor in International Politics.' In *Mechanisms of OECD Governance: International Incentives for National Policy-Making?*, Kerstin Martens and Anja P. Jakobi (eds), 1–30, Oxford: Oxford University Press.

Morgan, Clara and Riyad A. Shahjahan. 2014. 'The Legitimation of OECD's Global Educational Governance: Examining PISA and AHELO Test Production.' *Comparative Education* 50(2): 192–205.

Mytelka, Lynn K. 2000. 'Knowledge and Structural Power in the International Political Economy.' In *Strange Power: Shaping the Parameters of International Relations and International Political Economy*, Thomas C. Lawton, James N. Rosenau, and Amy C. Verdun (eds), 39–56, Aldershot, UK: Ashgate.

Niemann, Dennis and Kerstin Martens. 2018. 'Soft Governance by Hard Fact? The OECD as a Knowledge Broker in Education Policy.' *Global Social Policy* 18(3): 267–83.

OECD. 2000. Measuring Student Knowledge and Skills: The PISA 2000 assessment of reading, mathematical and scientific literacy. Paris: OECD.

OECD. 2020. The Territorial Impact of COVID-19: Managing the crisis across levels of government. Paris: OECD, 94 pages, available at: https://read.oecd-ilibrary.org/view/?ref=128_128287-5agkkojaaa&title=The-territorial-impact-of-covid-19-managing-the-crisis-across-levels-of-government&_ga=2.155827384.2097223841.1632945201-2045516522.1632763884 accessed 17 April 2023.

Ougaard, Morten. 2011. 'A New Role for the OECD? The "Enhanced Engagement" Strategy toward Emerging Economies.' In *Governing the Global Economy: Politics, Institutions, and Economic Development*, Dag Harald Claes and Carl Henrik Knutsen (eds), 91–109. London: Routledge.

Ougaard, Morten. 2010. 'The OECD's Global Role: Agenda-Setting and Policy Diffusion.' In *Mechanisms of OECD Governance: International Incentives for National Policy Making*, Kerstin Martens and Anja P. Jakobi (eds) Oxford: Oxford University Press.

Pal, Leslie A. 2012. *Frontiers of Governance: The OECD and Global Public Management Reform.* Basingstoke: Palgrave Macmillan.

Porter, Tony. 2010. 'The OECD and Global Finance: The Governance of New Issues, New Actors, and New Financial Frontiers.' In *Mechanisms of OECD Governance: International Incentives for National Policy-Making?* Jens Martens and Anja P. Jakobi (eds), 98–118. Oxford: Oxford University Press.

Porter, Tony and Michael Webb. 2008. 'Role of the OECD in the Orchestration of Global Knowledge Networks.' In *The OECD and Transnational Governance*, Rianne Mahon and Stephen McBride (eds), 43–59. Vancouver: UBC Press.

Reinalda, Bob (ed) 2013. *Routledge Handbook of International Organization.* London: Routledge.

Ruggie, John G. 1982. 'International Regimes, Transactions, and Change: Embedded Liberalism in the Postwar Economic Order.' *International Organization* 36(2): 379–415.

Schäfer, Armin. 2006. 'A New Form of Governance? Comparing the Open Method of Co-ordination to Multilateral Surveillance by the IMF and the OECD.' *Journal of European Public Policy* 13(1): 70–88.

Schmelzer, Matthias. 2016. *The Hegemony of Growth: The OECD and the Making of the Economic Growth Paradigm*. Cambridge: Cambridge University Press.

Sellar, Sam and Bob Lingard. 2013. 'The OECD and Global Governance in Education.' *Journal of Education Policy* 28(5): 710–25.

Sending, Ole Jacob. 2019. 'Knowledge Networks, Scientific Communities, and Evidence-Informed Policy.' In *The Oxford Handbook of Global Policy and Transnational Administration*, Diane Stone and Kim Moloney (eds), 383–400. Oxford: Oxford University Press.

Sharman, Jason C. 2009. 'The Bark *Is* the Bite: International Organizations and Blacklisting.' *Review of International Political Economy* 16(4): 573–96.

Sharman, Jason C. 2012. 'Seeing like the OECD on Tax.' *New Political Economy* 17(1): 17–33.

Stone, Diane. 2020. *Making Global Policy*. Cambridge: Cambridge University Press.

Strange, Susan. 1994. *States and Markets*. 2nd edn, New York: Continuum.

Strange, Susan. 1996. *The Retreat of the State: The Diffusion of Power in the World Economy*. Cambridge: Cambridge University Press.

Tan, Charlene and Vicente Chua Reyes. 2018. 'Shanghai-China and the Emergence of a Global Reference Society.' *The PISA Effect on Global Educational Governance*. L. Volante (ed), London: Routledge, Chapter 5, https://doi.org/10.4324/9781315440521 accessed 17 April 2023.

Verdun, Amy. 2003. 'An American/European Divide in European integration Studies: Bridging the Gap with International Political Economy.' *Journal of European Public Policy* 10(1): 84–101.

Volante, L., Fazio, X., and Ritzen, J. 2017. 'The OECD and Educational Policy Reform: International Surveys, Governance and Policy Evidence.' *Canadian Journal of Educational Administration and Policy* 184, 34–48.

Wolfe, Robert. 2008. 'From Reconstructing Europe to Constructing Globalization: The OECD in Historical Perspective.' In *The OECD and Transnational Governance*, Rianne Mahon and Stephen McBride (eds), 25–59. Vancouver: UBC Press.

Woodward, Richard. 2009. *The Organisation for Economic Co-operation and Development*. London: Routledge.

Woodward, Richard. 2010. 'The OECD and Economic Governance: Invisibility and Impotence?' In *Mechanisms of OECD Governance: International Incentives for National Policy-Making?* Kerstin Martens and Anja P. Jakobi (eds), 53–74, Oxford: Oxford University Press.

Zürn, Michael. 2018. *A Theory of Global Governance: Authority, Legitimacy, and Contestation*. First edition. Oxford: Oxford University Press.

4. Corporate consensus and the OECD's human rights mechanism

Stefanie Khoury and David Whyte

INTRODUCTION

The Organisation for Economic Cooperation and Development's (OECD) Guidelines on Multinational Enterprises (hereafter, 'the Guidelines') are unique insofar as they are 'the only corporate responsibility instrument formally adopted by states' that is truly global (Černič, 2010, p. 70). The Guidelines were first adopted in 1976 and have since been amended five times, the latest in 2011 (Bonucci and Kessedjian, 2018). The Guidelines set an obligation for member states to establish National Contact Points (NCPs) that have responsibility for addressing issues of implementation in specific instances. NCPs are non-judiciary mechanisms that have existed since 1984, although the Specific Instance Mechanism itself was only introduced in the Guidelines' 2000 revision. Most NCPs fall into government departments: e.g., the UK NCP is based in the Department for International Trade and Development and is typically overseen by a mix of representatives of business, trade unions and non-governmental organisations (NGOs) (see, e.g., UK NCP, n.d.).

The Guidelines cover the following areas: general policies (containing specific recommendations about corporate compliance); disclosure of information; human rights; employment and industrial relations; environmental protection; combating bribery, solicitation and extortion; consumer interests; science and technology; competition; taxation. The standards of conduct set out by the Guidelines are based upon a selection of international instruments, including: the Universal Declaration of Human Rights (UDHR); the International Convention on Civil and Political Rights and Political Rights (ICCPR); the International Convention on Economic, Social and Cultural Rights (ICESCR); the International Labour Organization's (ILO) Declaration on Fundamental Principles and Rights at Work; the Convention on Combating Bribery of Foreign Public Officials in International Business Transactions; the United Nations (UN) Convention against Corruption; the Rio Declaration on Environment and Development; the Convention on Access to Information, Public Participation in Decision-making, and Access to Justice in Environmental Matters; and International Organization for Standardization (ISO) standards, such as the Standard on Environmental Management Systems (OECD, 2011, pp. 32, 44, 49 and 50).

There is no other standing international mechanism available to lodge complaints *directly* against transnational corporations (TNCs) that has legal force obliging signatory governments. As such it is, in theory, a unique gateway to an international grievance mechanism for victims and survivors. Governments adhering to the OECD Guidelines must establish an NCP and have an obligation to ensure the procedural integrity of NCPs in terms of visibility, accessibility, transparency and accountability. NCPs are, however, independent of one another, with roles of mediation and conciliation between stakeholders. Participation in the NCP process is voluntary. Despite being open to individuals, human rights complaints to NCPs using the

Guidelines are mainly made by NGOs and trade unions concerned with labour rights (OECD, 2016). Indeed, only a very small minority of cases are taken by other parties. This may be due to questions of accessibility, as NGOs and Trade Unions may have the necessary administrative and technological know-how that individuals or local communities may not – including the most basic accessibility based on language. Indeed, NCPs have been widely criticised for their lack of visibility and accessibility.

In this chapter we analyse a data set of complaint outcomes made using the OECD Guidelines procedure in order to assess their ability to resolve conflicts over alleged corporate human rights violations. This data is analysed in more detail elsewhere (Khoury and Whyte, 2017 and Khoury and Whyte, 2019).

THE GUIDELINES AS 'CONSENSUS BUILDING'

The establishment of the Guidelines stemmed directly from the demands of developing countries during the 1960s and 1970s to limit the role of TNCs as conduits for the political aspirations of the most powerful governments (Murray, 2001). Developed nations supported the Guidelines as a means to protect their corporations from interference by host states. The 1976 Declaration on International Investment and Multinational Enterprises – to which the Guidelines belong – was adopted to give foreign corporations treatment 'consistent with international law and no less favourable than that accorded in like situations to domestic enterprises' (OECD, 1976). This political-historical context is commonly referred to as the 'post-war consensus': a period of social compromise in many OECD member states following World War II that saw a shift towards the establishment of social protections in the form of expanded regulatory mechanisms and a social welfare safety-net. In political and historical analyses, this is a shorthand description of a myriad of highly complex and differentiated processes of investments and protections for investors that is typically over-simplified and can be balanced for not paying attention to the grossly uneven development across different national contexts. Nonetheless, the idealised notion of a 'post-war consensus' has been a weather vane concept to the most influential policy makers and analysts.

This dominant mode of regulation that emerged in the post-war consensus was a 'co-operative' model, in which a series of fundamental, pluralist commitments are shared between the state and the 'regulated' party (Tombs and Whyte, 2010). It is based upon the idea that power in modern social orders is dispersed rather than concentrated, that a variety of interests can be mobilised to influence the formal political agenda, and that social change occurs best through the securing of common interests (Tombs and Whyte, 2013). In other words, this pluralist or consensus view of regulation assumes that mutually beneficial coincidence of interests amongst apparently antagonistic parties can be reached via relatively little or no state intervention. Whether consciously or not, both consensual/co-operative models of regulation, and neo-liberal approaches to regulation with emphases on self-regulation, provide a closely coherent theoretical justification for currently dominant strategies of regulation; or, as Tombs (2016) puts it, regulation without enforcement.

The framework of this pluralist socio-economic consensus is etched into the principles that inform the work of the OECD, with the core aim of the Guidelines to ensure 'mutual confidence between enterprises and the societies in which they operate …' It is an interesting choice of terms. Mutual confidence rather than dispute resolution. The Chair of the Business and

Industry Advisor Committee to the OECD (BIAC) has characterised the aim of the Guidelines as 'balanc[ing] public policy to promote an open international investment climate with a business commitment to responsible conduct' (Quadvlieg in BIAC, 2015). He explicitly notes the Guidelines are a reference document – in other words, something to consider but with no real obligation to fulfil.

The Guidelines' commentary emphasises that obligations upon corporations are *voluntary*, whilst also emphasising the binding responsibility on signatory states as part of their commitment to national laws and practices. The founding concepts and principles thus assert that:

> Obeying domestic laws is the first obligation of enterprises. The Guidelines are not a substitute for, nor should they be considered to override domestic law and regulation. While the Guidelines extend beyond the law in many cases, they should not and are not intended to place an enterprise in situations where it faces conflicting requirements. However, in countries where domestic laws and regulations conflict with the principles and standards of the Guidelines, enterprises should seek ways to honour such principles and standards to the fullest extent which does not place them in violation of domestic law. (OECD 2011, p. 17)

Thus, where domestic law is lacking or too weak to ensure compliance with the Guidelines' standards, the default position is self-regulation: that corporations should 'seek ways to honour such principles' themselves. The principle underpinning the Guidelines is that corporate compliance should be ensured by a process of remedy in which complainants seek review by the appropriate NCP.

The NCP is not envisaged as a judicial mechanism that will make judgements about corporate actions, even if there are obvious breaches of the Guidelines. Rather, the Guidelines note: '[t]he NCP will offer a forum for discussion and assist the business community, worker organisations, other [NGOs], and other interested parties concerned to deal with the issues raised in an efficient and timely manner' (Ibid.). This role for NCPs is fully supported by business and industry, particularly those in the business community who are not keen on enforcement or those who do not wish to be bound by 'unrealistic' expectations set by the Guidelines: 'the MNE Guidelines are deliberately not legally enforceable as they are intended to stimulate responsible behavior, not to trigger legal disputes'; moreover '… They also protect business from unrealistic expectations from stakeholders. Expectations that go clearly beyond the Guidelines will not easily be considered justified' (BIAC, 2015). Thus, the Guidelines define a partnership between the state and the corporation meant to stimulate responsible behaviour; the NCP is not intended to be an enforcement mechanism.

The NCP's regulatory approach emphasises techniques of persuasion, bargaining and compromise between stakeholder groups as the most successful strategy. It is therefore best described as a 'compliance'/'consensus' approach which encourages self-regulation, whereby corporations are responsible for monitoring and enforcing their own legal compliance as part of minimalist regulatory framework (Pearce and Tombs, 1990). 'Self-regulation' – a model of regulation where corporations are trusted to monitor and observe their own legal compliance – in fact constitutes the dominant approach to the 'regulation' of harmful business activities in OECD countries (Tombs and Whyte, 2015).

In the discussion that follows, we explore the concrete realities of the Guidelines' consensus approach, by presenting a detailed and original analysis of the outcome of cases that seek resolution through the Specific Instance Mechanism.

COMPLAINTS HEARD BY NCPs, 2002–2016

The analysis presented here is based upon a total of 403 cases sent to NCPs across all OECD countries for resolution and recorded by the Trade Union Advisory Committee (TUAC) to the OECD and the NGO OECDWatch from the introduction of the Specific Instance Mechanism in August 2002 to August 2016 (see Figure 4.1 below). This data includes a large majority of cases initiated under this procedure, with the largest single category of cases relating to human rights abuses (OECDWatch, 2014). This data is therefore relatively robust as an indication of the overall activity of the Specific Instance Mechanism: the two datasets constitute a relatively comprehensive and respected source of data on human rights cases (for a more in-depth discussion of those sources see, Ruggie and Nelson, 2015).

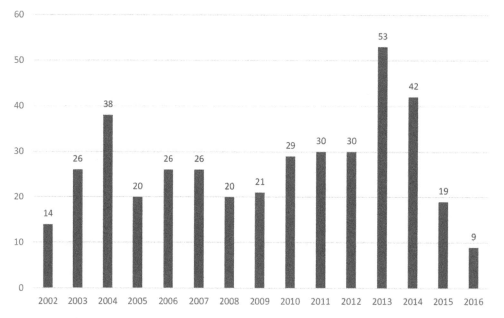

Note: Our analysis was delimited to cases from August 2002 to August 2016. For this reason, the number of cases for the years 2002 and 2016 do not take into account the total number of cases for these years but only cases from August to December 2002 and January to August 2016.

Figure 4.1   *Cases lodged with NCPs August 2002–August 2016*

From the initial 403 cases that we analysed within the period August 2002 to August 2016 we observed 139 rejected or closed cases (35 per cent), 191 concluded or withdrawn cases (47 per cent), 15 blocked cases (4 per cent), and 58 cases with suspended or pending decisions or in which there was no information and no details of the case (14 per cent).

From the data, and the reporting outcomes, the Guidelines procedure appears, on the face of things, to do its job. At first glance, there are 47 per cent of cases that appear resolved, and a number that are in the process of resolution. Yet a deeper analysis of those cases reveals a very different story about how the procedure is resolved.

A secondary analysis of the 191 cases concluded or withdrawn by the complainant is highly revealing. Within this category, only 49 cases (or 27 per cent) yielded a 'positive' and mutually agreed outcome. This amounts to approximately three to four cases on average per year (or about one in eight of our total number of 403 cases set out in Figure 4.1 above). In other words, only one in eight cases or 12 per cent initiated using the Guidelines are resolved with some kind of mutually agreed outcome.

Within this group of 191 concluded or withdrawn cases, 13 cases were *resolved via a separate process* outside of the NCP (7 per cent), and in five cases, 3 per cent, *external factors* in the dispute between the parties changed the material outcome (e.g., corporate takeovers, corporations going in to bankruptcy or corporations ceasing operations in that country).

There were, in contrast, 102 *unresolved* cases, in which one or more parties had not reached agreement about the outcome (57 per cent) and ten cases that remained only *partially resolved* and therefore remained partially *un*resolved (6 per cent). In other words, a total of 112 (63 per cent) of the *concluded and withdrawn* cases were not fully resolved.

It is to the analysis of the 112 'unresolved' and 'partially resolved' cases that the chapter now turns. It is by doing this analysis – by reading and categorising the unsuccessful cases – that we can identify some of the issues or blockages to resolution that arise in the procedure. Thus, in the analysis that follows, we identify four separate types of 'system blockages' that prevented those cases from reaching a successful outcome.

SYSTEM BLOCKAGES[1]

1.   A Lack of Co-operation

Of the cases that are included in our *Unresolved* category noted above, just under half remained unresolved because the corporation demonstrated a lack of co-operation in the process. A lack of co-operation was visible across a range of different cases (e.g., *Sherpa et al. v First Quantum Minerals and Glencore International AG*; *MiningWatch Canada et al. v Barrick Gold Corporation*; *Amnesty International and FoE v Shell*; *ECCHR, Sherpa & UGF v ICT Cotton*; *Sherpa et al v Financière du Champ de Mars, Bolloré and SOCFINAL*; *ForUM and FoE Norway v Cermag ASA*; *Survival International v Vendanta Resources plc*; *Global Witness v Afrimex*; *Nepenthes v Dalhoff, Larsen & Hornemann (DLH)*; *GermanWatch v Bayer*; *CCC v Adidas*). In a further set of cases, the companies simply refused any involvement with the process (e.g., *CIPCE v Skanska*; *CGTP et al. v Grupo Altas Cumbres*; *Thai and Filipino Labour Unions v Triumph International*; *FREDEMI coalition v Goldcorp*; and *CEDHA v Xstrata Copper*), obstructed the process, (e.g., *Fenceline Community and FoE Netherlands v Royal Dutch Shell*); and/or refused NCP mediation (e.g., *Cornerhouse v Rolls Royce, BAE Systems, and Airbus*).

In *Norwegian Support Committee for Western Sahara v Sjøvik*, the parties agreed upon recommendations to the Norwegian government and to the steps the company would take to comply with the OECD Guidelines due diligence provisions. However, *Sjøvik* later refused to disclose anything about what and how it was respecting and/or implementing the agreed pro-

---

[1]   All case citations can be found in 'Cases Cited' at the end of the chapter.

visions; the complainant was meant to simply have faith that the corporation was honouring the agreement.

In a small, but significant number of cases, developments in other legal proceedings relating to the same case preclude an NCP decision, which has sometimes led to corporations unilaterally withdrawing from the NCP case. In *CLEC & ERI v Florida Crystals Corporation, American Sugar Refining Incorporated, Sugar Cane Growers Cooperative of Florida, Fanjul Corporation*, the companies initially agreed to mediation, but later withdrew when parallel civil proceedings were initiated by the victims; although parallel proceedings do not present any obstacle to establishing mediation.

2.   A Lack of Political Will

Several cases demonstrate that NCPs are often reluctant to force an outcome with punitive conditions on the involved corporations, indicating as some observers have commented, that often corporations are given preferential treatment in the process. Černič (2010, p. 82) has noted, for example, that '[i]n many OECD countries major concerns have been expressed about the way NCPs arrive at the statement agreed by the company, the complainant and the NCP by first contacting the company not the complainant'. For him, this is perhaps unsurprising given that NCPs are attached to government bodies that do a great deal of diplomatic work on behalf of their corporations operating abroad:

> … since most of the NCPs are located within business or industry departments of governments, it appears that they are more inclined to support business activities. For example, the UK NCP until recently discussed the initial assessment of a complaint with the companies first and only later with the complainant. There is no simultaneous discussion and companies have been given higher degree of access to the NCP. (Černič, 2008, p. 94)

This observation is entirely consistent with the regulatory consensus approach adopted by the OECD and its member states (set out earlier in this chapter) and appears to indicate a lack of political will on the part of NCPs to intervene in ways that challenge corporations. Indeed, some officially '*Withdrawn*' cases were blocked from going forward by the NCP (e.g., *RAID v Ridgepoint, Tremalt, and Alex Stewart (Assayers) Ltd*). In other cases, the complainant considered the NCP incapable of contributing to a meaningful resolution to the dispute (e.g., *Amnesty International and FoE v Shell*); or the NCP simply ignored complainants' grievances concerning the process (e.g., *CCC & ICN v G-Star*). These cases were thus '*Withdrawn*' following extreme dissatisfaction with the NCP process on the part of complainants. Ultimately none were resolved, apart from the latter through an external process involving the Dutch Minister of Economic Affairs. The Dutch NCP responsible for the case *CCC & ICN v G-Star* declared it was made redundant when the Dutch Minister took over the mediation process, and ultimately ignored the complainants' reservations about the NCP's withdrawal from the process.

Some NCPs demonstrated a lack of commitment to their own process, simply closing cases unilaterally after limited attempts at mediation, stating no consensual agreement was possible (e.g., *Global Sports Technology (Beteiligungsgesellschaft) v Austrian Trade Unions*); without having met with the unions or making a public statement (e.g., *Nestlé v Korean Confederation of Trade Unions (KCTU), International Union of Food Workers, and the International Federation of Chemical, Energy, Mine and General Workers' Union (ICEM)*); based on the company's affirmation of its intention to abide by a court order to reinstate the dismissed workers although it had in fact already convened early retirement and severance schemes with many of them (e.g., *Honda v International Metalworkers' Federation (IMF)*); or claimed that they simply could not offer any useful intervention (e.g., *Eiffage Energie v Fédération Nationale des Salariés de la Construction et du Bois de la CGT, la Fédération Nationale Construction Bois de la CFDT and CFE CGC BTP*). In the case *Novartis v Austrian Union of Salaried Private Sector Employees*, the NCP released a watered-down version of its final statement that glorified the company for its corporate social responsibility efforts, including a social plan for dismissed employees. But the NCP failed to acknowledge the role of the trade union in obtaining the social plan (namely through a parallel legal complaints procedure which had forced Novartis to negotiate the plan).

In other cases, the NCPs simply excluded complainants from negotiations (e.g., *CBE v National Grid Transco* and *RAID v Avient*) or proved incapable of dealing with complaints (e.g., *CEDHA v Xstrata Copper*). In such cases, the NCPs seem to go to great lengths to avoid engaging with the complaints in any serious manner. In another set of cases (*Pobal Chill Chomain Community et al. v Marathon Oil, Statoil, and Shell*), the NCP denied the admissibility of the case, ostensibly because the companies claimed they were in compliance with an existing 'legal' contract with the government, even though the complainant formally disputed the compliance of those contracts with the OECD Guidelines.

In the case *Reprieve v British Telecommunications*, the complainants asserted a clear bias in favour of companies. The NGO complained that throughout the process the NCP accepted the company's assertions without any substantiating evidence, and that the NGO had a greater onus to substantiate the complaint. In the cases analysed by Amnesty International, it concluded that the UK NCP was both woefully under-resourced and clearly exhibiting bias towards corporations. OECDWatch also criticised NCPs for their uneven expectations of standards of compliance with the Guidelines and noted the recent expectation of an 'unreasonably high burden of proof' on complainants (OECDWatch, 2014, p. 18).

3. A Lack of Enforcement Powers

The ineffectiveness of the NCPs highlights a major weakness of the system: that NCPs have no clear mechanism of enforcement and very often simply fail to obtain mediation through 'goodwill' (evident in e.g., *RAID v Ridgepoint, Tremalt, and Alex Stewart (Assayers) Ltd*; *Parmalat v CUT-Brazil*). A key feature that is always latent in the NCP process is an awareness of all parties that the NCPs are toothless: they cannot oblige companies to engage in the complaints process, they can simply recommend the withdrawal of some government services. Even when the complaint may appear to have serious cause, ultimately, the NCPs are dependent upon the co-operation of the companies. The tolerance of a system of regulation without enforcement (Tombs, 2016) may be a factor in the weakening of political will outlined in the previous section.

In the *Fenceline Community* case, for example, complainants noted an unreasonably high confidentiality requirement during the procedure, but also specifically highlighted the NCPs lack of authority vis-à-vis the company. The Guidelines' voluntary nature and the lack of an enforceable supervisory capacity for the NCPs was cited as a major problem in the Specific Instance Mechanism. Whilst in several cases NCPs went ahead with their review despite the company's lack of co-operation – and some NCPs found the companies in breach of the Guidelines (e.g., *Lawyers for Palestinian Human Rights v G4S*; *RAID v ENRC*; *Privacy*

International et al. v Gamma International) – they could only make recommendations with no possibility of enforcement.

The exception to this dependency on corporate 'goodwill' can be seen in *Canada Tibet Committee v China Gold International Resources*. In this case, the Canadian NCP imposed sanctions on the company in response to its refusal to engage. The penalties included withdrawing Trade Commissioner Services and other Canadian advocacy support abroad. The Canadian government supported the NCP to act upon its decision, although this outcome remains exceptional.

Even in cases where the NCPs have demanded action, the corporations involved have sometimes simply ignored them. For example, in *Corner House et al. v BP; CRBM v ENI; ForUM and FoE Norway v Cermaq ASA;* and *Survival International v Vedanta Resources* the corporation simply disregarded the NCP's requests. Lack of enforcement is thus a major weakness of the NCP process that has been recognised by others (see e.g., Ruggie and Nelson, 2015) since governments do not generally provide any reinforcement or support for the NCPs when and if they find companies in breach of the Guidelines.

4.　A Lack of Accountability

In a number of cases, unsatisfied complainants have sought remedy higher up the Specific Instance Mechanism.[2] However, only a small minority of countries have established complaints processes against NCPs directly; and where these systems exist there is no consistency in their structures. This inconsistency is characteristic of the NCPs since countries have substantial flexibility in determining the structure and make-up of their NCPs (Genovese, 2016). In some contexts, complainants can request NCP oversight through ombudspersons, for example, Belgium and Finland, or in other contexts via appointed boards, as is the case in the UK. Complaints are filed after the final assessment is made by the NCP in cases where the applicant(s) consider(s) the NCP not to have acted in accordance with its procedure, including for concerns of bias, negligence, and similar wrongdoings. Ombudspeople are usually part of government and deal with complaints from several government sectors, as is the case in Belgium and Finland where complaints are made to Belgian Federal Ombudsman[3] or the Finnish Parliamentary Ombudsman.[4] However, the UK has set up a Steering Board specifi-

---

[2]　There have also been some instances of complaints against NCPs filed directly with the OECD Investment Committee; e.g., in 2021 OECDWatch, supported by MiningWatch, filed a complaint to the OECD against the Canadian NCP for what they allege was an unpredictable, inequitable, untransparent, unaccountable and biased process. The case was brought by Swiss NGO Bruno Manser Fonds against an Ottawa-based real-estate corporation that was accused of pressuring the Canadian NCP.

[3]　In the Belgian system, federal ombudspersons can examine the action and decisions of the administrative authorities on the basis of complaints directly received from the public or at the request of the Chamber of Representatives. On its website, the ombudsman [sic] describes itself as an independent body that carries out '… independent investigations into the functioning of the federal administrative authorities and see to it that citizens' rights are respected' (https://www.federaalombudsman.be/en/about-us/what-we-do accessed 7 May 2023).

[4]　According to its website, the Finnish Parliamentary Ombudsman [sic] "The Ombudsman oversees the legality of actions taken by the authorities, primarily by investigating complaints received". The ombudsperson has the mandate to investigate any alleged illegality or wrongdoing that comes to their attention. The ombudsperson also conducts on-site investigations in public offices and institutions. The website states that the ombudsperson further concentrates on promoting fundamental and

cally for its NCP. In the UK, either party of the NCP's mediation can ask for a review by the Steering Board if it feels the case has not been treated fairly or been given due consideration.

In *Proyecto Gato v Tractebel*, several NGOs sent a letter to the OECD requesting clarification on the interpretation of the Guidelines, arguing that the Belgian NCP had failed to treat the complaint in accordance with OECD rules. The NGO took their complaint further, and subsequently filed with the Belgian Ombudsperson against the NCP. Proyecto Gato's complaint was upheld, although this is rare. And, in several cases brought by NGOs, the NCPs blatantly refused transparent, non-confidential dialogue consistent with the Procedural Guidance of the Guidelines (e.g., *CCFD et al. v Michelin*; *DECOIN et al. v Ascendant Copper Corporation*). In *DECOIN et al. v Ascendant Copper Corporation*, the complainants 'withdrew' because of the unilateral decision of the NCP to a closed-door mediation; the company later used the withdrawal to claim that the case had been resolved.

In *IAC & WDM v GCM Resources plc*, the complainants were so outraged by the NCP that they filed a complaint with the UK's OECD Steering Board. In this case, the NCP exhibited a bias towards the company when it refused to consider potential human rights impacts and focused instead upon less controversial issues such as the alleged failure by the company to follow its own self-regulatory standards. The NCP's bias was hard to deny given that seven UN Special Rapporteurs had issued a joint UN press release, calling for an immediate halt to the company's proposed project because it was a threat to fundamental human rights, including food, water, adequate housing, freedom from extreme poverty and the rights of indigenous people. The Steering Board found the NCP committed errors and recommended that the complaint be re-examined, but the NCP ignored the Board. It insisted in its final statement that the company was only in breach of its obligations to develop trusted self-regulatory practices and management systems. In its follow-up statement a year later, however, the NCP noted that no significant development had been made by the company, and thus neither in the conditions that led to the complaint. The entire complaint in this case was a series of frustrations for the complainants that ultimately had no impact on the human rights obligations of the company involved.

In its in-depth analysis of the UK NCP, Amnesty International (2016) found a lack of predictability or consistency in applying the Guidelines that often comes down to a discretionary misinterpretation. Moreover, it argued, there is little accountability of NCPs when this does happen. Amnesty International found that inappropriately high evidential thresholds were being expected of complainants, often making 'arbitrary judgements at the initial assessment stage without proper examination' (Ibid., p. 6). At the same time, 'the expectations of the NCP towards companies to provide evidence of responsible business practice are not as stringent' (Ibid., p. 60).

CONCLUSION

The four aspects identified in this analysis have something in common. They all point to serious weaknesses in the NCP process that make it difficult to claim that the OECD Guidelines are by any measure an effective instrument with which to address corporate viola-

---

human rights (https://www.oikeusasiamies.fi/en/the-work-of-the-ombudsman accessed 7 May 2023; see OECDWatch, 2007).

tions of human rights. Our analysis indicates that the pursuit of a consensus approach to resolving such disputes has proven impossible to achieve in all but a handful of cases. Moreover, the analysis of this data demonstrates that the lack of regulatory force has effectively neutered the process. The Specific Instance Mechanism relies on the participation of business in a system of self-regulation, together with a faith in consensus forms of policy-making that is palpably incapable of offering any true remedy to the victims.

Our analysis in this chapter points to four major weaknesses with the OECD Guidelines that are rooted in its 'consensus' approach. First, companies continue to refuse to engage with the NCPs. Second, NCPs display a lack of political will to intervene in ways that challenge corporations. Third, even if there was a clearer political will, because compliance with the Guidelines is effectively voluntary, there is no way for NCPs to oblige or coerce companies to participate in the process. Finally, given the lack of accountability for decisions made by NCPs, there is no adequate redress for complainants. All of this points to a fundamental asymmetry of power in which complaints remain structurally weak when they seek to invoke the Specific Instance Mechanism.

To recap, we found that around one in eight cases or 12 per cent were resolved to the mutual satisfaction of both parties. On average this adds up to *between three and four cases every year* that are resolved with mutual agreement, anywhere in the world. We are therefore dealing with a few cases that can, in global terms, barely be described as token. Indeed, recent research by OECDWatch (2018) albeit based on a much smaller sample of 18 NGO-led cases, found that in almost three-quarters of cases 'no remedy-related outcome whatsoever was achieved for the victims of corporate misconduct' (Ibid., p. 2). This report drew a number of conclusions that we also draw: namely that '[t]he NCP system is currently an unpredictable patchwork of methods and structures' that often lacks adequate resourcing or political will (Ibid., p. 15).

Our analysis of these cases suggests that rather than providing a mechanism that encourages consensual decision-making, NCPs have a different role: they 'manage' rather than resolve complaints. And those cases are managed in ways that do not alter the power imbalances between businesses and complainants, or indeed interrupt business in any meaningful way, even in the face of flagrant human rights violations.

ACKNOWLEDGEMENT

This research was funded by British Academy 'Developing Corporate Liability for Human Rights Violations' (BARDA 53262), the Arts and Humanities Research Council (AH/J011657/1), and the Leverhulme Trust (SAF/8/2001/0014).

REFERENCES

Amnesty International (2016) 'Obstacle Course: How the UK's National Contact Point handles human rights complaints under the OECD Guidelines for Multinational Enterprises.' [online] Available at: https://www.amnesty.org.uk/files/uk_ncp_complaints_handling_full_report_lores_0.pdf (accessed 6 June 2022).

BIAC (2015) 'Responsible Business Conduct: The OECD Guidelines for Multinational Enterprises' [online] available at https://biac.org/wp-content/uploads/2015/06/FIN-15-06-GUIDELINES-BROCHURE.pdf (accessed 5 June 2022).

Bonucci, Nicola and Kessedjian, Catherine. (2018) *40 ans des lignes directrices de l'OCDE pour les entreprises multinationals/40 years of the OCDE Guidelines for Multinational Enterprises* (Paris: OECD).

Černič, Jernej Letnar. (2008) 'Corporate Responsibility for Human Rights: A Critical Analysis of the OECD Guidelines for Multinational enterprises.' *Hanse Law Review*, 4, 71–101.

Černič, Jernej Letnars. (2010) *Human Rights Law and Business: corporate responsibility for fundamental human rights* (Groningen: Europa Law Publishing).

Genovese, Kristen. (2016) 'Access To Remedy: Non-judicial Grievance Mechanisms.' In *Business and Human Rights: From Principles to Practice*, Dorothée Baumann-Pauly and Justine Nolan (eds.) (Abingdon: Routledge), 266–75.

Khoury, Stefanie and Whyte, David (2019) 'Sidelining Corporate Human Rights Violations: The Failure of the OECD's Regulatory Consensus.' *Journal of Human Rights*, 18(4), 363–81.

Khoury, Stefanie and Whyte, David (2017) *Corporate Human Rights Violations: Global Prospects for Legal Action* (London: Routledge).

Murray, Jill. (2001) 'A New Phase in the Regulation of Multinational Enterprises: The Role of the OECD.' *Industrial Law Journal*, 30(3), 255–70.

OECD (1976) Declaration on International Investment and Multinational Enterprises. [online] OECD Publishing. Available at: https://www.oecd.org/corporate/mne/50024800.pdf (accessed 6 June 2022).

OECD (2011) OECD Guidelines for Multinational Enterprises. [pdf] OECD Publishing. Available at: http://www.oecd.org/daf/inv/mne/48004323.pdf (accessed 6 June 2022).

OECD (2016) Implementing the OECD Guidelines for Multinational Enterprises: The National Contact Points from 2000 to 2015. [pdf] Available at: https://www.gov.uk/government/uploads/system/uploads/attachment_data/file/270577/bis-14-518-procedural-guidance.pdf (accessed 6 June 2022).

OECDWatch (2007) Finnish Parliamentary Ombudsperson Receives Complaint in Botnia (Amsterdam: OECDWatch).

OECDWatch (2014) Assessment of NCP Performance in the 2013-2014 Implementation Cycle. OECD Watch Submission to the 2014 Annual Meeting of the National Contact Points (Amsterdam: OECDWatch).

OECDWatch (2018). *The State of Remedy under the OECD Guidelines: Understanding NCP cases concluded in 2017 through the lens of remedy*, OECD Watch Briefing Paper, June 2018 (Amsterdam: OECD Watch).

Pearce, Frank, and Tombs, Steve. (1990) 'Ideology, Hegemony and Empiricism.' *British Journal of Criminology*, 30(4), 423–43.

Ruggie, John, and Nelson, Tamaryn. (2015) 'Human Rights and the OECD Guidelines for Multinational Enterprises: Normative Innovations and Implementation Challenges.' Corporate Social Responsibility Initiative Working Paper No. 66. John F. Kennedy School of Government (Cambridge: Harvard University).

Tombs, Steve, and Whyte, David. (2010) 'A Deadly Consensus: Worker Safety and Regulatory Degradation Under New Labour.' *British Journal of Criminology*, 50(1), 46–65.

Tombs, Steve, and Whyte, David. (2013) 'Transcending the Deregulation Debate? Regulation, Risk and the Enforcement of Health and Safety Law in the UK', *Regulation and Governance*, 7(1).

Tombs, Steve, and Whyte, David. (2015) *The Corporate Criminal* (Routledge: Abingdon).

Tombs, Steve. (2016) *Social Protection After the Crisis: Regulation Without Enforcement* (Bristol: Policy Press).

UK NCP (n.d.) UK National Contact Point for the Organisation for Economic Cooperation and Development guidelines. [online] (London: UK NCP). Available at: https://www.gov.uk/government/groups/uk-national-contact-point-for-the-organisation-for-economic-co-operation-and-development-guidelines (accessed 6 June 2022).

Cases Cited

All links accessed 17 April 2023.
Amnesty International and FoE v Shell (25 January 2011) https://www.oecdwatch.org/cases/Case_197.

Amnesty International and FoE v Shell (30 December 2011) https://www.oecdwatch.org/cases/Case _244.

Canada Tibet Committee v China Gold International Resources (29 January 2014) https://www .oecdwatch.org/cases/Case_324.

CBE v National Grid Transco (25 July 2003) https://www.oecdwatch.org/cases/Case_34.

CCC v Adidas (5 September 2002) https://www.oecdwatch.org/cases/Case_27.

CCC & ICN v G-Star (13 October 2006) https://www.oecdwatch.org/complaint/ccc-icn-vs-g-star/.

CCFD et al. v Michelin (10 July 2012) https://www.oecdwatch.org/cases/Case_254.

CEDHA v Xstrata Copper (1 June 2011) https://www.oecdwatch.org/complaint/cedha-vs-xstrata-copp er/.

CGTP et al. v Grupo Altas Cumbres (25 April 2007) https://www.oecdwatch.org/complaint/cgtp-et-al -vs-grupo-altas-cumbres/.

CLEC & ERI v Florida Crystals Corporation, American Sugar Refining Incorporated, Sugar Cane Growers Cooperative of Florida, Fanjul Corporation (31 October 2012) https://www.oecdwatch.org/ cases/Case_277; https://www.oecdwatch.org/cases/Case_276; https://www.oecdwatch.org/cases/ Case_278; https://www.oecdwatch.org/cases/Case_279.

CIPCE v Skanska (20 May 2009) https://www.oecdwatch.org/cases/Case_169?searchterm=CIPCE.

Corner House et al. v BP (29 April 2003) https://www.oecdwatch.org/cases/Case_31.

Cornerhouse v Rolls Royce, BAE Systems and Airbus (1 April 2005) https://www.oecdwatch.org/cases/ Case_77?searchterm=rolls+royce; https://www.oecdwatch.org/cases/Case_75?searchterm=corner+ house; https://www.oecdwatch.org/cases/Case_76.

CRBM v ENI (29 April 2003) https://www.oecdwatch.org/cases/Case_161.

DECOIN et al. v Ascendant Copper Corporation (16 May 2005) https://www.oecdwatch.org/cases/Case _71.

ECCHR, Sherpa & UGF v ICT Cotton (12 December 2010) https://www.oecdwatch.org/cases/Case _196.

Eiffage Energie v Fédération Nationale des Salariés de la Construction et du Bois de la CGT, la Fédération Nationale Construction Bois de la CFDT, and CFE CGC BTP (1 October 2013) https://www.tresor .economie.gouv.fr/Institutionnel/Niveau3/Pages/23df6117-8c29-4c56-8204-d84ee8b81b6c/files/ f772c625-2f45-42aa-b35d-2328e2ba630b.

Fenceline Community and FoE Netherlands v Royal Dutch Shell (15 May 2006) https://www.oecdwatch .org/cases/Case_93.

FREDEMI coalition v Goldcorp (9 December 2009) https://www.oecdwatch.org/cases/Case_172.

ForUM and FoE Norway v Cermaq ASA (19 May 2009) https://www.oecdwatch.org/cases/Case_166.

GermanWatch v Bayer (11 October 2004) https://www.oecdwatch.org/cases/Case_50.

Global Sports Technology (Beteiligungsgesellschaft) v Austrian Trade Unions (01 March 2006) http:// members.tuac.org/fr/public/e-docs/00/00/09/6F/telecharger.phtml?cle_doc_attach=3132 (pp. 86–87).

Global Witness v Afrimex (20 February 2007) https://www.oecdwatch.org/cases/Case_114.

Honda v International Metalworkers' Federation (IMF) (1 February 2003) http://www.tuacoecdmne guidelines.org/CaseDescription.asp?id=97.

IAC & WDM v GCM Resources PLC (19 December 2012) https://www.oecdwatch.org/cases/Case_285.

Lawyers for Palestinian Human Rights v G4S (27 November 2013) https://www.oecdwatch.org/cases/ Case_327.

Lok Shakti Abhiyan et al. v Government Pension Fund – Global (9 October 2012) https://www .oecdwatch.org/complaint/lok-shakti-abhiyan-et-al-vs-government-pension-fund-global/.

MiningWatch Canada et al. v Barrick Gold Corporation (1 March 2011) https://www.oecdwatch.org/ cases/Case_210.

Nepenthes v Dalhoff, Larsen & Honremann (DLH) (10 March 2006) https://www.oecdwatch.org/cases/ Case_112.

Nestlé v Korean Confederation of Trade Unions (KCTU), International Union of Food Workers and the International Federation of Chemical, Energy, Mine and General Workers' Union (ICEM) (26 September 2003) http://members.tuac.org/fr/public/e-docs/00/00/09/6F/telecharger.phtml?cle_doc _attach=3132, pp.130–131.

Norwegian Support Committee for Western Sahara v Sjøvik (5 December 2011) https://www.oecdwatch .org/cases/Case_247.

Novartis v Austrian Union of Salaried Private Sector Employees (5 February 2008) http://members.tuac
.org/fr/public/e-docs/00/00/09/6F/telecharger.phtml?cle_doc_attach=3132, pp. 43–44.

Parmalat v CUT-Brazil (26 September 2002) http://members.tuac.org/fr/public/e-docs/00/00/09/6F/
telecharger.phtml?cle_doc_attach=3132, pp. 150–151.

Pobal Chill Chomain Community et al. v Marathon Oil, Statoil and Shell (22 August 2008) https://
www.oecdwatch.org/cases/Case_151; https://www.oecdwatch.org/cases/Case_150; https://www
.oecdwatch.org/cases/Case_146.

Privacy International et al. v Gamma International (1 February 2013) https://www.oecdwatch.org/cases/
Case_286.

Proyecto Gato v Tractebel (15 April 2004) https://www.oecdwatch.org/cases/Case_35.

RAID v Avient (28 June 2004) https://www.oecdwatch.org/cases/Case_40.

RAID v ENRC (13 May 2013) https://www.oecdwatch.org/wp-content/uploads/sites/8/2013/11/OECD
-Watch-Quarterly-Case-Update-November-2013.pdf, pp. 3–4.

RAID v Ridgepoint, Tremalt and Alex Stewart (Assayers) Ltd. (28 June 2004) https://www.oecdwatch
.org/cases/Case_44-en; https://www.oecdwatch.org/cases/Case_42; https://www.oecdwatch.org/
cases/Case_43.

Reprieve v British Telecommunications PLC (15 July 2013) https://www.oecdwatch.org/cases/Case
_325.

Ripley Corp. S.A. v UNI Global Union and UNI Americas (3 June 2014) https://mneguidelines.oecd.org/
database/instances/cl0009.htm.

Sherpa et al. v First Quantum Minerals and Glencore International AG(12 April 2011) https://www
.oecdwatch.org/cases/Case_209; https://www.oecdwatch.org/cases/Case_208?searchterm=sherpa+
glencore.

Sherpa et al. v Financière du Champ de Mars, Bolloré and SOCFINAL (7 December 2010) https://www
.oecdwatch.org/complaint/sherpa-et-al-vs-bollore/.

Survival International v Vedanta Resources PLC (19 December 2008) https://www.oecdwatch.org/
complaint/survival-international-vs-vedanta-resources-plc/.

Thai and Filipino labour unions v Triumph International (3 December 2009) https://www.oecdwatch
.org/cases/Case_171.

5. The politics of the OECD

Magdaléna Hadjiisky

INTRODUCTION

The Organisation for Economic Co-Operation and Development (OECD) owes its existence to an eminently geopolitical context. Yet it presents itself as an actor that remains free from political and ideological controversies.

Historically, for a long time the OECD was seen as 'a Cold War institution' (Leimgruber and Schmelzer, 2017, p.1). The successor to the OECE (Organisation for European Economic Co-Operation), which had been created in 1948 to administer the Marshall Plan, was nicknamed an 'economic NATO' (ibid), primarily serving US interests and the geo-economic domination of the 'Western camp' (see Chapter 3 for a detailed historical analysis).

The OECD official presentation, which is consistent with its public image, chiefly emphasises the rigour and objectivity of its data and analyses. To describe how it operates, scholars frequently use analogies such as 'think tank' or 'consulting office' acting 'for a group of States' (Boquet, 2012, p.14). This echoes the dominant public representation of the OECD in the media as neutral source. Because it does not have at its disposal the same kind of binding instruments as, for example, the EU (supranational legal tools) or the World Bank (WB) (conditionality of the loans), the OECD may look like an expert organisation, whose reach depends not on power relations but on the credit given to its analytical output.

Yet, the question of the margin of intervention of economic international organisation (IOs) in sovereign state policies has to be raised, including outside developing countries, which since the 1980s have been used to the conditionality policies of the WB and the International Monetary Fund (IMF). Regarding the OECD, Morten Ougaard has noted that since the 1970s:

> There has (also) been a significant broadening of the scope of cooperation across issue areas, and instruments now concern a fair number of what traditionally are considered 'beyond the border issues', i.e. issues that traditionally were seen as entirely in the realm of domestic politics. (Ougaard, 2004, p.83)

How can we analyse politics in an organisation that does its best to stay away from politics? Could the OECD have succeeded where most national bureaucracies have failed, i.e., serve in a policy advisory capacity without getting mixed up in politics? Does the centrality of expertise in its activities and legitimisation mean that the OECD has no means of exercising political authority over its members?

To answer these questions, this chapter adopts a relational definition to politics and politicisation and draws on sociological institutionalist (Barnett and Finnemore, 2004; Mahon, McBride, 2008) and political sociology (Neveu and Surdez, 2020; Dolowitz, Hadjiisky, Normand, 2020) lenses of analysis. Instead of *a priori* determination of what should be the nature of an IO political power (here the OECD), this approach is mindful of interactions that are pertinent to the actors, sometimes regardless of official frames and organisational rules.

Methodologically, it demands an empirical attention to the organisation's day-to-day activities, to the Secretariat's respective divisions and to the partners[1] that they consider to be strategic and that they include in their practices. Fortunately, a sizeable body of literature has demonstrated the benefits of approaching mezzo-level processes and actor' configurations when studying international activities (Barnett and Finnemore, 1999, 2004; Broome and Seabrooke, 2012; Gayon, 2009; Hadjiisky, Pal, Walker, 2017; Mahon and McBride, 2009; Nay, 2012; Pal, 2012; Radaelli, 2020; Reinalda, Verbeek, 2004; Trondal et al, 2010). Likewise, this chapter shows the interest of considering the OECD as a complex political space in its own right, as a collective constructs, involving various categories of actors (bureaucratic segments of the Secretariat, national delegates, ambassadors, academics, think tanks, NGOs, lobbies) whose conceptions and interests vary.

The chapter proceeds in four steps. First, it addresses the question of the place of politics in intergovernmental organisations like the OECD. It secondly explores the place and definition given to politics inside and by the OECD itself. In line with the organisation' self-presentation, the third section explores whether and to what extent the centrality of expertise makes the OECD an apolitical organisation; more precisely, the question becomes: where and how can an organisation claiming an advisory and expert position exercise political power? Finally, the fourth step reintroduces the margins of power possessed by the governments of the member states (MS), not in order to propose a classic neo-realist conception of power relations, but to account for the part played by multi-actor negotiation in the concrete power exercised by the OECD.

WHERE DO POLITICS LIE IN AN INTERGOVERNMENTAL ORGANISATION LIKE THE OECD?

In most IOs' corridors, the word 'politics' can refer to at least three different and not mutually exclusive meanings. First, it can refer to (and criticise) the ideological foundations of its activities and positions. Second, it can refer to the pressures exerted by governments to orient the IO's activities toward specific interests rather than toward the common multilateral good. And third, it can refer to the ability of the Secretariat to influence the domestic political orientations of its member states (MS) – in this last case, this influence is generally described as deriving from the MS governments' will or from the autonomous legitimacy acquired by the organisation in itself.

The two first meanings (ideological stance and governmental pressure) are the ones, which are generally implied in the frequent assertion, that 'IOs don't do politics'. And indeed, in order to balance and coordinate the interests of the MS, IOs are conceived as (and supposed to be) distant from ideological cleavages and political calculations. That is why the label 'political' is generally disqualifying in international arenas. The UN Assembly has been, for example, often blamed for its 'politicisation' when, after the decolonisations, it became an arena for the Non-Aligned Movement. Subsequently, the alleged 'politicisation' of UNESCO

---

[1]   A terminological note is here needed: this chapter will use the generic term of 'partners' to refer to the various categories of actors that are strategic for the OECD activities. These exceed the sole member states' governments, as they can be bureaucratic segments of other IOs' secretariats, consultancy firms, INGOs, and academic networks.

justified the American suspension of its contribution to this organisation in 2011, in protest against the recognition of Palestine as a member of UNESCO (Serhan, 2017).

An Impartial and Competent Adviser?

From this point of view, the OECD presents the particularity of being a selective (non-universal) organisation that has historically brought together MS sharing a common set of values and objectives, which has earned it the characterisation of a 'club'. The OECD may be less affected than other IOs by ideological controversies because MS have agreed on a common basis set out in the Convention. Signed in December 1960, the OECD Convention positions the organisation's objectives within the liberal economic and political doctrine.[2] Unlike UN organisations, the OECD has from the outset been anchored in the Western camp and has not had to handle the co-existence of states claiming to represent opposite geopolitical camps or interests (East-West during the Cold War or North-South since the 1990s).

Rarely targeted as 'political' by MS officials, the OECD could have been characterised as such by non-state actors and alter-globalist social movements (on these, see Held and McGrew, 2007). One example is the mobilisation against the negotiation on the Multilateral Agreement on Investment (MAI) in 1995–1997 (Mabey, 1999). In this case, the critical charge is linked to the unveiling of the ideological basis of the economic expertise developed by the OECD and on the priority given to the development of international trade over all other considerations (on the testing of chemicals, see e.g., Martin, 2020). Yet, the political exposure of the OECD remains limited, which sets it apart from organisations such as the WB or the IMF: the OECD has rarely elicited public protests targeting its legitimacy or its mode of action and the MAI episode appears to be the exception rather than the rule.

Do its Western economist roots make the OECD the equivalent of an international academic institution partly influenced by the intellectual controversies of its time, or is the OECD similar to a think tank with a strong political orientation?

From Intergovernmental to Global Legitimacy

From a strictly institutional point of view, IOs cannot be defined as apolitical organisations. They are political in the sense that their members are governments and that their mandate leads them to take an interest in the public policies of their MS. Let us remind that the Convention explicitly requires the OECD to 'promote policies' designed to achieve its objectives. Many analyses have therefore focused on the power exercised (or not) by IOs. They have done so in particular in relation to their constituents (the member states), orienting research towards the issue of implementation (its successes, difficulties, means, etc., e.g., Joachim et al., 2008), and the relative autonomy of national secretariats in relation to the MS (or conversely the room for manoeuvre of even weak governments in relation to international conditionality, e.g., Woods, 2006, 4). From 'politics' in the sense of ideologically oriented, analyses have moved on to 'politics' in the sense of governing power, i.e., the recognised capacity to say, regulate and

---

[2]   The Convention insists on the importance of 'economic strength and prosperity' to preserve 'individual liberty and the increase of general well-being', favours the 'further expansion of world trade' and considers as one of the three objectives of the organisation 'to contribute to the expansion of world trade on a multilateral, non-discriminatory basis'. OECD, Convention, Paris, 14 December.

decide what is right (and must be applied) for and within a given community, regardless of the ideological assumptions.

From this point of view, the power of IOs has been interpreted from two different perspectives, intergovernmental and global: power through the diplomatic mandate and power through a general authority that is often referred to as 'global'. In the first case, the political power of the IOs depends directly upon the mandate delegated to them by the MS; in the second case, the IOs are credited with an autonomy that allows them to create standards and rules beyond the mere conciliation of the MS' national interests.

The first pole draws on the institutional character of most IOs (including the OECD) as traditional treaty based 'formal intergovernmental organisations', as coined by Diane Stone in her chapter in this volume. According to its statutes, the OECD is granted power to act within the framework of missions that are set out in the Convention on the OECD signed by MS.[3] The IO's legitimacy to intervene on 'political' subjects (meaning, those that are up to sovereign governments to settle) depends on a delegated, and therefore heteronomous mandating relationship. IOs are not credited of political power in their own right, as their margin of influence depends on the quality of cooperation between their MS (which may or may not agree on a resolution) and on the degree of confidence these states entrust to the Secretariat.

What do IOs do with the agency that has been initially passed on to them (and is constantly renegotiated) by MS (Barnett and Finnemore, 1999, p.5)? Do they turn it into a 'political' power? The second pole considers that the IO's power is political if it entails a recognised authority to elaborate rules that are not only technical or bound to an inter-state negotiation, but that are general and universal. In this second sense, an IO's political power depends on its capacity to develop standards, norms, and values, whose scope extends *beyond* the juxtaposition of national interests and contributions and that apply to all stakeholders (MS and beyond). In these cases, the organisation is recognised as having an intrinsic authority to act in political domains and to define public issues as 'global' and accordingly falling within its purview (Neveu and Surdez, 2020). From this point of view, the question is whether and to what extent the OECD can be considered as an agent of the globalisation of policy models, although it has only limited binding levers of power?

The following sections propose to apply to the OECD the axis of interpretation here identified: is the political power of the OECD of a global type and linked to the nature of the expertise it produces and disseminates (section 2)?; is the OECD political power reliant on the control that the governments of its most powerful MS exercise (or think they exercise) on its activities and how does this (relative) dependence affect the power it tries to build on and with MS (section 3)? Along the way, this chapter will highlight the existence of a third, more discreet but very much adjusted to the OECD lever of power, which will be called method-driven power or governmentality (Foucault, 2009).

---

[3]   Convention on the OECD, 14 December 1960.

AN EXPERT ORGANISATION IN THE SERVICE OF 'BETTER POLICIES'

In its official presentation, the OECD acknowledges the political nature of its executive level, but claims to provide impartial expertise based on specialised skills, not political preferences or ideological affinities.

The OECD According to the OECD

The OECD's statutes classically define the institution's policy reach as the power of control and initiative shared by national representatives at the meetings of its executive body, the Council, established by the signatories to the Convention on the OECD on 14 December 1960. Here, political power derives from the state (governmental) mandate.

The Council is tasked with setting the organisation's agenda and budget. It operates on the classical basis of equality of MS' votes. However, it favours 'mutual agreement' between Members (Article 6); 'consensus' is also a recurring term in the OECD's presentation. Instances of direct confrontation of interests (and formal votes) are therefore kept to a minimum.

Logically, diplomatic alliances are most visible (and acceptable) when it comes to the Council's activities. This happens first at times when a new Secretary-General (SG) is due to be elected as the head of the organisation. As this happens fairly rarely (these five-year mandates are generally renewed), chancelleries are well aware of the strategic implications of these periods, which effectively spark an unusual governmental investment in the life of the organisation.

The Councils 'at Ministerial level', held roughly once a year, are other times of relatively visible and predictable governmental activity at the OECD. In these meetings, the Ministers for the Economy, Finance and/or Foreign Affairs decide the overall strategic and most importantly budgetary orientations of the OECD for the upcoming year.

Concerning its routine organisation, the OECD states, that:

> The secretariat collects and analyses data, the committees examine the progress made in specific areas of public policy, the Council makes the decisions and the governments implement the recommendations (…) Peer review, multilateral surveillance and peer pressure are key to the OECD's effectiveness.[4]

This presentation is telling in itself. The OECD emphasises the participation of governments, highlights the objective of the 'implementation of recommendations' and asserts an equally rational and collegial mode of content validation. Indeed, when it describes its routine practice, the organisation presents its output as rational and specialised, free of diplomatic constraints and of the (electoral) political temporalities of MS.

Additionally, the organisation presents itself as a partner that is capable of rising above the fray and propose general solutions to all of its members. Its ambition draws on the quality and scope of its productions and publications.

---

[4]   Translated from the French version of a previous iteration of the 'How we work' page (2011–2021): http://www.oecd.org/fr/apropos/modesdaction/, last accessed 22 February 2019.

The organisation's publications are therefore particularly highlighted, both in terms of quantity and quality:

> OECD Publishing is one of the world's largest publishers of books in the fields of economics and public affairs. It publishes more than 250 new books, 40 updated statistical databases, and thousands of new statistical tables, working papers, and journal articles each year.[5]

The place granted to publications in the OECD's institutional communication supports the image of transparency and openness to the public that the organisation is striving to convey; second, it attests to the importance of argumentative rationality in the IO's legitimisation of its own activities.

In the sense used internally by the OECD, explicitly political moments (related to party or government politics) are few and far between. The 'real work' seems to be done according to a collegial, rational and argumentative process. Even when it is involved in large-scale international negotiations that are subject to extensive media coverage, the OECD highlights its role as an objective and informed adviser. Since 2008 its privileged participation to the G20, particularly in the negotiation over a mechanism to combat tax havens (see Chapter 16 in this volume), is justified on the OECD's official website in these terms: 'OECD's expertise continues to be increasingly recognised and relied upon for identifying the world's most pressing policy challenges and finding ways to address them.' Aligning with this institutional presentation, many analysts have described the OECD as an expert organisation that manages to stay away from politics.

Within the OECD, this legitimisation through expertise means that 'politics' is often discredited. In the Chateau offices and meetings, the term refers to the geopolitical strategies of the great powers and to struggles over governmental power, in a limited and outdated vision of the collective. Admittedly, 'democratic values' are sometimes invoked as a reference shared by MS. Still, democracy as a political regime is not mentioned in the Convention on the OECD or in the conditions of accession to the organisation. Democracy was brought up at the GOV Directorate when citizens began being considered in public governance, but the extension of the 'citizens and governance' theme to the question of citizens' trust in institutions and governing parties, which was for some time envisioned in 2015, was quickly left out. It should be noted that this reluctance is the result not only of caution on the part of international OECD officials, but also of the refusal of many national delegations to have the organisation intervene in domestic policies (parties, elections, etc.).

Domestic politics is thus swept aside to make way for the construction of a global legitimacy that is supposed to be more noble and selfless than national politics. As Franck Petiteville puts it: 'by asserting an apoliticism based on humanist and universalist values at odds with State realpolitik, these organisations reintroduce "another politics", a "top-down, quasi aristocratic politicisation"' (Petiteville, 2017, p.18).

An Image of Neutrality that is Echoed in Academic Spaces

Some scholars consider this purported political neutrality as an asset (Martens and Jacobi, 2010, Chapter 1). They argue that this muting politics allows the OECD to conduct long-term

---

[5]   https://www.oecd.org/about/publishing/, last accessed 6 February 2022.

work that follows a 'technical temporality' that differs from the political temporality (Boquet, 2012, p. 44). This allowed the OECD to have its work on the fight against tax havens endorsed at the G20 meetings of 2008 (ibid., p.14) even though initially the Chinese delegation had chosen not to acknowledge the legitimacy of the expertise of an organisation of which the country is not a member (ibid., p.45).

These analyses draw on factual elements that make the OECD stand out from other IOs. Let me give two illustrations of this here. First, the OECD's hiring policy suggests that professional skills come first. The SG is granted a margin for manoeuvre, which allows for instance the OECD to operate without the national quotas rule used in other IOs. Obviously, balance is pursued, to avoid an excessively visible over-representation of this or that country in a given area, but this is not a formalised obligation.

Second, the way the organisation operates with committees and specialised working groups is frequently cited as the sign that it manages to remain as far removed as possible from ideological or party pressure in its efforts to promote 'better policies'. The quality and rigour of its data and analyses are singled out as the 'means of persuasion of an organisation without power' (Martens and Jacobi, 2010, p.27); so is the equally professional and informal nature of its collaboration with national delegations.

Certain working and collaboration methods have in time become the organisation's trademarks: the exchange of good practices, peer reviewing, evidence-based policy, and policy benchmarking. Work in small committees is conducive to a mode of collaboration that is based on mutual trust rather than diplomatic negotiation. As the OECD's outputs are often non-binding, national chancelleries also tend to lower their diplomatic guard (Hadjiisky, 2016, 2017).

These distinguishing features are the reason why the OECD has been instrumental to the work of IR scholars with an interest in non-coercive modalities of international influence; it has inspired studies that more specifically emphasise the effects of a collaborative working method and its associated management practices and tools (amongst a rich bibliography, see Lehtonen, 2009; Marcussen, 2004; Mahon and McBride, 2008).

While the OECD draws on the quality of its output to legitimise its authority, the fact remains that, institutionally, it is not a research centre, but indeed an IO. This is why its emphasis on specialised knowledge has also elicited divergent interpretations in the literature.

Is OECD Expertise Politically Neutral?

Informed by the sociology of science and technology, a number of scholars have criticised the interpretations portraying the OECD as an 'expert' organisation.

More precisely, they have called into question the politically neutral stance generally associated with expertise' production. The quality of its scientific evidence cannot possibly be the only reason explaining one IO's performance among its partners. As stated by Littoz-Monnet, the 'expertization of knowledge is itself political': 'what constitutes expert knowledge is itself the object of negotiation amongst relevant stakeholders in a given issue domain.' (Littoz-Monnet, 2017: p.2; see also Stone, 2003; Broome and Seabrooke, 2012; Vadrot, 2014; Dolowitz et al., 2020). Technicisation often results in hiding the political dimensions of a given policy model or instrument. About the regulatory reform, De Francesco and Guaschino show how the OECD 'selected regulatory impact analysis (RIA) as the policy innovation for simplifying the policy discourse on regulatory Reform'; it 'translated, reframed and packaged

[it] as an international best practice'; at the same time, 'the administrative preconditions for and the political ideologies of RIA were omitted' (2020, p.123).

In other words, an IO's claim to a non-political character should itself be a subject of analysis. Indeed, depoliticisation can be a strategy devised to position in political power games (Fawcett, Flinders, Hay and Wood, 2017; Lagroye, 2003). Many IO scholars have noted that the international secretariats' emphasis on knowledge is a way to construct an ethics of knowledge that gives them a leeway of functional autonomy from their MS. Barnett and Finnemore write for instance, 'IOs use their knowledge to help create social reality. (…) IO are often the actors empowered to decide if there is a problem at all' (2004, p.7). They consider that IOs exercise power by classifying and fixing the meaning of the social world, as well as by spreading new norms and principles (Barnett and Finnemore, 1999; see also Addey, 2021; Louis and Maertens, 2021).

Indeed, the OECD can help governments discover what their needs are, whenever 'problems' have not been clearly identified. An illustration is provided by the case of Central and Eastern European states, which in the early 2000s literally 'discovered' regulatory policy either through the interventions of SIGMA (Support for Improvement of Governance and Management, a programme funded by the European Union, see also Chapter 25) or during one of the OECD's first reviews of their country in that area.[6]

In the process, the OECD builds what Pierre Bourdieu calls 'symbolic power' (Bourdieu, 1979), a recognised authority to name and categorise reality. This characteristic highlights the strategic importance, for the OECD, to create indicators, provide international comparisons, build benchmarks – all tools of the policy naming, framing and modelling. The mastery of certain expertise techniques constitutes a strategic comparative advantage for the OECD. For example, the creation, from 1988 onwards, of a method for the statistical processing of measurement of learning outcomes has enabled the OECD to compete with, and even outperform, UNESCO as a reference agency in the field of education (Heyneman, 2012; Addey, 2018). Far from being neutral, indicators and rankings are part of the geopolitical bargaining at the international level.

To be effective, symbolic power needs to be 'misrecognised' as a power and to be exerted not as overt physical force, but as knowledge (Bourdieu, 2002). In other words, its alleged ideological neutrality is strategic for the OECD to build its global framing power.

Economist Framing of Reality

Due to its economic mandate, the OECD' symbolic power tends to frame reality through an economist lens. In the process, it participates in a trend towards 'economism' in public policy, which may be defined as the application of principles and instruments from the economics to validate policy options in domains that are not traditionally based on profit-oriented rationales.[7] Dolowitz, Hadjiisky and Normand argue that the 'legitimization of the economic

---

[6]   Sources: author's interview with an OECD official, formally a civil servant in one of the new MS of 2004, conducted in December 2015); Czech government archives, 1999–2001. See (Hadjiisky, 2017).

[7]   I draw on Tero Erkkila and Ossi Piironen, who state: 'By economism we do not refer to the science of economics but to all definitions that primarily and fundamentally focus on economic aspects of governance – often at the cost of alternative values (e.g. democracy, environment, social cohesion).' (2014, p.349).

IO's expertise into new (non-economic) policy domains favours the adoption of economised frames to interpret the 'problems' and the 'solutions' in the diverse policy domains concerned' (2020, 13, see also Erkkilä and Piironen, 2014; Djelic and Sahlin-Andersson, 2006). This line of research has explored the effects of the expansion of OECD expertise on fields, such as education (Grek, 2009, Araujo et al., 2017, see also Chapter 13 in this volume), health (Martens, 2007) or public governance, where the PUMA committee played an important role in legitimising and disseminating the ideas of New Public Management in the 1980s (Sahlin-Andersson, 2000; Pal, 2012; Hadjiisky, 2017, see also Chapter 24 in this volume).

This strand of research unveils the ideological dimension of the OECD's recommendations and links it to the prominence of economics within the organisation. Porter and Webb (2008, p.45) write, for example:

> The OECD Secretariat is heavily populated by professional economists, because western societies accord such a high value to this kind of expertise and because economic liberalization is central to the OECD's mission. The professional orientation of the Secretariat in turn shapes the policy analysis it produces and the guidance it provides to meetings of national officials. Thus, the OECD advice often takes the form of applying liberal economic theory to policy problems.

Because 'economics' is far from being disconnected from political doctrines, the OECD can be analysed as having evolved in line with the changing global ideational context in economist circles. This approach to economics has been expanded upon extensively in the literature, particularly about two sets of OECD publications: the McCracken Report of 1977, and the Jobs Study and Jobs Strategy exercises of the 1990s and early 2000s (Keohane, 1978; Noaksson and Jacobsson, 2003; Dostal, 2004; Gayon, 2012, 2020; Beroud, 2017). This focus reflects the legitimacy attributed to the Economics committee and in particular to its Working Party 3, both internally among OECD staff and among the national delegates in various committees. In this sense, the OECD can be described as an organisation, which strongly defended the Keynesian economic principles in the 1960s and early 1970s, which endorsed the neoclassical synthesis in the 1980s and early 1990s, which integrated institutional economics and behaviour management during the 2000s, and which, after the 2008 financial crisis, turned to look for 'a new economic approach' integrating also social and environmental considerations of the time (OECD, 2017, 2018, 2019b).

Without denying the possible ideological foundations of number of OECD's prescriptions, other scholars criticise the tendency to overestimate the intellectual nature of OECD activities, and bring back into the analysis the political pressures exerted over the organisation by powerful interests.

A TRANSNATIONAL, ELITE POLITICAL SPACE

The OECD is not an academic institute, but an intergovernmental organisation and, as such, a political organisation. Politics is involved in multiple ways at various stages, even routine ones, of the functioning of the organisation, whose intergovernmental character should be recalled here.

The Strategic Importance of Government Power Games

First, unlike its presentation suggests,[8] the elaboration of OECD expertise gives a clear advantage to national executives: governments, civil servants, senior officials and government-mandated experts. Members of parliament, who were included in the process only in 2020, have had virtually no influence at this point. Civil society groups have been stakeholders since the early 2000s, but primarily in a consulting capacity, in the exploratory and promotional phases of the OECD' initiatives. The OECD 'Forums', which regularly bring together actors in a given policy area, do not have the decision-making prerogatives of the Committees, in which national delegates sit.

The production process of OECD expertise, from agenda-setting to data collection, the choice of the method used to analyse them and the presentation of statistics in reports, depends on multiple negotiations that involve agents, especially at the middle levels, of Secretariat, and delegations made up chiefly of national senior civil servants.

Here state interests and powers come into play again, as has been pointed out by such authors as Matthieu Leimgruber and Matthias Schmelzer (2017), who evidence the prominent role played by the US in the OECD's history and evolutions. Their geopolitical analysis of politics within the OECD logically emphasises the importance of budgetary resources and the fact that the OECD receives 20 per cent of its funding from the US. Some national delegates acquire more influence than others, especially when their government accounts for a significant part of the OECD's budget or makes voluntary contributions. It is worth noting here that this question has acquired strategic significance since mi-1990, as the OECD activities depends, to greater extent, upon the MS' voluntary contributions (voluntary contributions represent around half of the overall budget of the OECD (OECD, 2019a)).

Despite the image of independence associated with OECD expertise, it is often national governments that prompt the organisation to address new topics and produce new statistics. It was after the US withdrew from UNESCO in 1984 – they re-joined in 2002 and left again in December 2019 – that the OECD and the WB more actively developed their own expertise in the field of education – for the former, at the express request of Washington (Martens 2007). Likewise, when the US suspended their contribution to the WHO (1986), the OECD and the WB reinforced their own expert capacity in the field of health. More recently, the publication of a global ranking of healthcare systems in which they fared poorly (WHO, *World Health Report*, 2000) led the US, Australia and Japan to make voluntary contributions that allowed the OECD's Health Division to make a fresh start (Brissaud 2019, esp. 201 ff., Addey, 2021).

These interventions sometimes relate to governments' expectations of what the OECD's output should be. This leads national delegations to interfere into the core of Secretariat's work: data collection, comparative methods and modes of statistical analyses. Kerstin Martens has for instance shown that the reintroduction of statistical research on education and learning in the 1980s was motivated by requests from the US and France, against the initial opinion of the OECD Education's Centre for Educational Research and Innovation (CERI), which contended that quantification was subject to caution in educational matters (Martens, 2007,

---

[8]   The official OECD website's 'How we work. How we engage with…' sections puts 'governments', 'parliaments' and 'civil society' on equal footing. https://www.oecd.org/about/how-we-work/, last accessed 31 January 2022.

pp.45–48). In the same vein, Addey (2021, p.4; see also Addey, 2018, Heyneman, 2012, Ydesen and Grek, 2019) writes:

> Following the Sputnik launch, the publication of *Nation at a Risk* in 1983, and the comparatively bad results of the U.S. in the Second International Mathematics Study, comparative educational indicators suddenly became the priority for the U.S. (…) In response, the OECD modified its approach to education indicators (…) with an increasing focus on educational outputs and performance measurement.

These interferences raise questions about the impartiality and rigour of the expertise produced at the OECD.

Does the fact that OECD expertise is not totally free from political pressure mean that the Secretariat has no margin of manoeuvre and is first and foremost the expert arm of its most powerful MS governments, namely the US? The answer to this question must be nuanced and take into account the effects inherent in the organisation's working method.

A Complex Political Space Unified by a Method-driven Power

The MS' interventions often also *differ* from government' expectations. To continue with the education example, Martens claims that the OECD 'gradually took over the task and developed comparable, easily digestible international statistics and indicators on the basis of its own perception, which today are seen as international standards' (2007, p.49). One must also have in mind the diversity of the agents involved. OECD policy is not always Atlanticist, even if it rarely neglects the position of the US' delegation. Indeed, the somewhat significant presence of European countries among the MS, reinforced by the EU's institutional membership, complexifies strategic anticipations and diversifies the range of public policy models that are cited as examples of good practices (see Mahon, 2010). Depending on the subject, diverse initiatives may be made and varied alliances may be formed. It would for instance be interesting to analyse the influence of the propositions of Scandinavian countries within OCDE-GOV, particularly regarding the ethics of public officers and the importance of citizen participation. It seems thus essential not to 'overestimate the coherence of the interests, actors, and social forces that use the OECD' or 'to underestimate the independent social effects of the knowledge-producing processes at the OECD itself' (Porter and Webb, 2008, p.47).

To make sense of this apparent ambivalence, it is necessary to take into account, not only the official statements and initiatives of the Secretary General' Office, but also the recommendations, analyses and activities developed by the 17 Directories and Centres in close cooperation with the 31 committees of the organisation.[9]

From this point of view, a distinction needs to be made, which helps to grasp the nature of the participation of MS in the OECD's work. It differentiates two types of national delegates which can be named the 'diplomats' and the 'specialists'. The ambassadors and permanent representatives to the OECD are diplomats who make 'political multilateralism' work. The members of the national delegations sent from the capitals contribute to the work of the committees and working groups. Often senior practitioners in the domain in question, they need a diplomatic accreditation but may still assert their own thematic legitimacy as 'specialists'.

---

[9]   Source: On-Line Guide to OECD Intergovernmental Activity, https:// oecdgroups .oecd .org/ Bodies/ListByNameView.aspx, accessed on 10 Sept. 2022.

They are those who are committed to what might be called the 'sectoral multilateralism' of the OECD's 250 committees and working groups. In that space, political neutrality extends to the national delegates. To be effective (meaning socially pertinent), their arguments must be of a rational and specialised nature. These peers are expected to behave more as professionals/experts in a given policy area than as representatives of a country in the diplomatic sense. This emphasis on expertise over diplomacy favours delegates who are actively involved in the day-to-day activities of the committee – not just the representatives of the most powerful states. Geopolitical and budgetary resources play a role, but they are not the only factors in play. Investments in time and skills can also make a difference. The forms of power that are associated with the OECD's working methods allow some delegations to influence the course of negotiations regardless of their country's geo-economic power.

In this sense, detailed analysis of the operation of the committees and working groups suggests the existence of what could be called a method-driven power in the OECD. This authority is constructed through processes of collaboration that in the long run create an effect of persuasion and identification among the participants (see, about the 'regulatory policy' case, Hadjiisky, 2016). It is indeed a method, and thus an openly formulated, instrumentally rational way of doing things (and of having people do things), and not simply the unintended effect of organisational routines. The importance of this 'managerial approach' (Joachim et al., 2008, p.10; for a discussion Hadjiisky, 2021) leads the OECD toward 'governmentality'-type of power (Foucault, 2009), where politics is present through the ability to influence the scope of what is conceivable through ways of doing things and of having others do things.

Alongside power as a diplomatic mandate and power as global authority (identified in the first section of this chapter), these intermediate-level routine activities highlight the effectiveness of a third lever of influence. Without being exclusive of the other two, this third pole draws attention to the multiple moments when IOs use persuasion methods and incentive instruments rather than direct binding power methods and pressures. Many OECD activities have something to do with learning and what Broome and Seabrooke name 'a particular type of socialization by experience' (2015, p.959).

This governmentality involves transactions whose principle could be encapsulated by the phrase 'performance through peer emulation'. The nature of performance depends partly on what peers decide to present and emphasise within the OECD, as well as on the frames of emulation set by the OECD's Secretariat. The OECD's working method explains the identity-defining and reputational dynamic pointed out by a number of scholars who have sought to explain the organisation's attraction for governments. As Porter and Webb (2008, p.46) have put it: 'The OECD can be seen as a paradigmatic example of an identity-defining international organization. (…) It defines standards of appropriate behaviour for states that seek to identify themselves as modern, liberal, market-friendly, and efficient (March and Olsen, 1998, p.961)'. There is still a sense among the OECD's members that they belong to an inner circle of experts, despite the geographical and numerical expansion experienced by the organisation since the 1990s and the 40 000 annual visitors to the OECD's headquarters before the COVID-19 pandemic.

Transnationalised Intergovernmental Negotiations

Authors such as Vincent Gayon (2020) and Sotiria Grek (2014, 2020) have rightly stressed that the authority of OECD expertise comes largely from its negotiated character, but one of the effects of this complex negotiation process is precisely that its political dimensions are concealed. Through a fine-grained sociology of the routine internal functioning in two areas (economic affairs and education respectively), each of them has shown that the social effectiveness of the OECD's global standards depends on multiple approaches made locally by OECD agents in close collaboration with national delegations and administrations. While some issues are 'depoliticised' and framed as technical issues or unavoidable global constraints, it is with the tacit agreement of governments, which in doing so take politically challenging or divisive problems off their hands and contribute to removing them from public and democratic discussion.

This approach suggests a different outlook on the authority of the OECD's economic expertise, interpreted here in a manner that is more relational than hegemonic. It is doubtful that a science or an academic network, regardless of their theoretical power or of the excellence of the pedigrees and training of its members, may in themselves constitute an effective hegemonic reference in an intergovernmental organisation such as the OECD. If the OECD's recommendations in some areas have supported and legitimated neo-liberal principles without eliciting the withdrawal of socio-democrat governments, it is thanks to the negotiated and sectoral character of their elaboration. De Francesco and Guaschino write for example that 'the OECD's discourses are forged out of MS' knowledge and experiences and negotiated and vetted by the same members (Theodore & Peck, 2012). As a consequence, OECD knowledge discourses aim to catalyse consensus over policy innovations', [which] 'are packaged and framed in common-sense governance standards to facilitate rapid emulation'. (De Francesco and Guaschino, 2020, p.123).

Scholars who have analysed the OECD's economic and social policies have pointed to the power asymmetry in the organisation (regarding the roles assigned in collective work, the status given to proposals and objections depending on their sources, etc.) between the delegates of the Ministries of Finance and their colleagues in Social Affairs. The imbalance in favour of economicist arguments within the OECD appears similar to that observed in favour of the economic and financial branches of the MS. This is not due to an ideological preference of the Secretariat, but to the effects of structural homology with the governments of the MS (see in particular Gayon, 2020).

For the actors involved in the OECD's work, it is essential both that national delegates participate, but also that their participation is then concealed (Gayon, 2020). For MS, one of the key functions of the apparent neutrality of the OECD's output resides in the possibility of using it for political purposes, especially at the domestic level (in the media and among voters). In MS' view, one of the functions of the OECD's expertise is undoubtedly to neutralise potentially politicised proposals and translate them into consensual terms, and in so doing, to facilitate their domestic implementation.

To identify the form of political power exerted in an arena like the OECD, a mezzo-sociological approach is worth implementing; one that pays attention to the work of mid-level agents, national delegates, mandated experts, and that retraces the logics at work within the spaces outlined by their interrelations. This approach has the benefit of shedding light on many of the characteristics identified by alternative interpretations (focusing on expertise and on the global level) by closely studying the routine of the organisation. In the process, this approach evidences the emergence of a form of political power that is partially emancipated from MS control, without overstating the autonomy of the OECD Secretariat.

CONCLUSION

Like other international arenas with which it maintains relations of consolidating competition (e.g., the WB), the OECD exercises a political power whose objective is to make the regulation and 'moderation' of liberalised markets conceivable; this objective is legitimated by an (ideologically founded) belief in the benefits of liberalisation in all policy areas.

Yet, a nuanced and realistic picture of the political power of the OECD needs to integrate its inner complexity and to welcome its possible ambiguity. This is not a hegemonic sort of power; it is negotiated and partially heteronomous, as it depends to some extent on the effectivity (and the acceptation by its strategic partners) of the type of governmentality by peer emulation it implements.

The kind of political power exercised by the OECD must be considered within the two spaces of interdependence in which it is constructed. To ensure the social effectiveness of their initiatives, Secretariat agents must build their contextual validity. They take into account the stances and investments of MS and remain aware of global trends in international politics, in the sense of relationships between powers (e.g., by investing in the G20) and of the global geo-economic context (i.e., the evolution post-2008 or post-pandemic crisis). This constitutes the first space of interdependence, of a geopolitical and geo-economic nature, in which the groups contributing to the OECD's activities act jointly.

On the other hand, when they tackle an issue, the OECD's national delegates and agents consider the organisation's previous productions: flagship reports, key data, instruments, analyses, recommendations, etc. and its methods of action: exchanges between specialists, peer reviews, data collection – constraints that are valuable as they are identified as ensuring the institution's 'quality' and 'credibility'. This is the second space of interdependence, and it contributes to defining the range of what can (and cannot) be said and conceived within the OECD.

Instead of responding to a binary alternative between power as diplomatic mandate and power as global framing, our analysis indicates that the OECD builds its legitimacy thanks to a method-driven governmentality, which requires the continuous co-optation of elite segments of national executives. In other words, the OECD appears as a weakly politicised organisation, not only thanks to the expert excellence of its outputs, but also because the latter are elaborated in a constant process of negotiation with their recipients – in a word, because of the very method of elaboration of this shared expertise. The OECD's power is political because, through a method that closely involves national executives, it acquires power over the way in which public problems are framed, solutions to these problems are found, and certain policy practices are preferred.

ACKNOWLEDGEMENT

This chapter was translated from French by Jean-Yves Bart, with support from the Maison Interuniversitaire des Sciences de l'Homme d'Alsace (MISHA) and the Excellence Initiative of the University of Strasbourg.

REFERENCES

Addey, C. (2018). 'The Assessment Culture of International Organizations: From Philosophical Doubt to Statistical Certainty through the Appearance and Growth of International Education Assessments.' In C. Alarcón and M. Lawn (eds), *Assessment Cultures – Historical Perspectives* (pp.379–408), Peter Lang.

Addey, C. (2021). 'Passports to the Global South, UN Flags, Favourite Experts: Understanding the Interplay between UNESCO and the OECD Within the SDG4 Context.' *Globalisation, Societies and Education, 19(5)*, 593–604. DOI: 10.1080/14767724.2020.1862643.

Araujo, L., A. Saltelli and S.V. Schnepf (2017). 'Do PISA Data Justify PISA-based Education Policy?' *International Journal of Comparative Education and Development, 19(1)*, 20–34.

Barnett, M. and M. Finnemore (1999). 'The Politics, Power, and Pathologies of International Organizations.' *International Organization, 53(4)*, 699–732.

Barnett, M.N. and M. Finnemore (2004). *Rules of the World: International Organizations in Global Politics*, Cornell University Press.

Beroud, S. (2017). '"Positive Adjustments": The Emergence of Supply-Side Economics in the OECD and G7, 1970–1984.' In M. Leimgruber and Schmelzer (eds), *The OECD and the International Political Economy Since 1948*, Palgrave Macmillan, Cham.

Boquet, D. (2012). *Pour une mondialisation raisonnée. Les révolutions discrètes de l'OCDE.* La documentation française.

Bourdieu, P. (1979). 'Symbolic Power.' *Critique of Anthropology, 4(13–14)*, transl. Sur le pouvoir symbolique, *Annales ESC* (1977).

Bourdieu, P. (2002). 'Dévoiler les ressorts du pouvoir.' In P. Bourdieu, *Interventions—Science sociale et action politique* (pp.173–176), Agone.

Brissaud, C. (2019). *La production internationale d'un sens commun réformateur: concurrences expertes et arguments statistiques de la 'crise' des dépenses de santé à l'OCDE (1972–2018).* Thèse de doctorat de science politique soutenue à l'Université de Strasbourg, France. https://www.theses.fr/2019STRAG042 accessed 23 May 2023.

Broome, A. and L. Seabrooke (2015). 'Shaping Policy Curves: Cognitive Authority in Transnational Capacity Building.' *Public Administration, 93(4)*, 956–972.

Broome, A. and L. Seabrooke (2012). 'Seeing like an International Organisation.' *New Political Economy, 17(1)*, 1–16.

De Francesco, F. and E. Guaschino (2020). 'Reframing Knowledge: A Comparison of OECD and World Bank Discourse on Public Governance Reform.' *Policy and Society, 39(1)*, 113–128.

Djelic, M.-L. and K. Sahlin-Andersson (eds) (2006). *Transnational Governance: Institutional Dyamics of Regulation*, Cambridge University Press.

Dolowitz, D., M. Hadjiisky and R. Normand (eds) (2020). 'Introduction.' In D. Dolowitz, M. Hadjiisky and R. Normand (eds), *Shaping Policy Agendas: The Micro-Politics of Economic International Organizations* (pp.1–14), Edward Elgar Publishing.

Dostal, J.M. (2004). 'Campaigning on Expertise: How the OECD Framed EU Welfare and Labour Market Policies – and why Success could Trigger Failure.' *Journal of European Public Policy, 11(3)*, 440–460.

Erkkilä, T. and O. Piironen (2014). '(De)politicizing Good Governance: The World Bank Institute, the OECD and the Politics of Governance Indicators.' *Innovation: The European Journal of Social Science Research, 27(4)*, 344–360.

Fawcett, P., M. Flinders, C. Hay and M. Wood (eds) (2017). *Anti-Politics, Depoliticization, and Governance*, Oxford University Press.

Foucault, M. (2009). *Power/Knowledge: Selected Interviews and Writings, 1972–1977*, Pantheon Books.

Gayon, V. (2009). 'Le crédit vacillant de l'expert: L'OCDE face au chômage dans les années 1990 et 2000.' *Cultures & Conflicts, 75*, 53–73.

Gayon, V. (2009). 'Un atelier d'écriture internationale: l'OCDE au travail. Éléments de sociologie de la forme "rapport".' *Sociologie du travail, 51(3)*, 324–342.

Gayon, V. (2020). 'Neoliberalism and the "think-tank image" Fallacy: A Sociological Exploration of Homologies of Structuration Inside the OECD, EU, and Governments.' In D. Dolowitz, M. Hadjiisky and R. Normand (eds), *Shaping Policy Agendas: The Micro-Politics of Economic International Organizations* (pp. 36–56), Edward Elgar Publishing.

Grek, S. (2009). 'Governing by Numbers: The PISA "effect" in Europe.' *Journal of Education Policy*, *24(1)*, 23–37.

Grek, S. (2014). 'OECD as a Site of Coproduction: European Education Governance and the New Politics of "policy mobilization".' *Critical Policy Studies*, *8(3)*, 266–281.

Grek, S. (2020). 'Beyond the Standardisation vs. Contextualisation Debate: The Role of the OECD in European Education Governance.' In D. Dolowitz, M. Hadjiisky and R. Normand (eds), *Shaping Policy Agendas: The Micro-Politics of Economic International Organizations* (pp.56–75), Edward Elgar Publishing.

Hadjiisky, M. (2016). 'Policy Tranfers in Europe. The European Union and Beyond.' In R. Normand and J.L. Derouet (eds), *European Politics of Education? Perspectives from Sociology, Policy Studies and Politics* (pp.31–51), Routledge.

Hadjiisky, M. (2017). 'SIGMA: un programme international de renforcement des capacités administratives en terres européennes (1992–2012).' *Revue française d'administration publique*, *161(1)*, 73–88.

Hadjiisky, M. (2021). 'International Organizations as Complex Agents in Policy Transfer Processes.' In O. Porto de Oliveira (ed), *Handbook of Policy Transfer, Diffusion and Circulation* (pp.121–154), Edward Elgar Publishing.

Hadjiisky, M., L.A. Pal and C. Walker (eds) (2017). *Public Policy Transfer: Micro-Dynamics and Macro-Effects*, Edward Elgar Publishing.

Held, D. and A. McGrew (2007). *Globalization, Anti-Globalization, Beyond the Great Divide*, second edn, Polity Press.

Heyneman, S. (2012). 'The Struggle to Improve Education Statistics in UNESCO: 1980–2000.' Paper presented at the World Bank, May 21, 2012.

Keohane, R. (1978). 'Economics, Inflation, and the Role of the State: Political Implications of the McCracken Report.' *World Politics*, *31(1)*, 108–128.

Joachim, J., B. Reinalda and B. Verbeek (2008). *International Organizations and Implementation. Enforcers, Managers, Authorities?* Routledge/ECPR Studies in European Political Science.

Lagroye, J. (ed.) (2003). *La politisation*, Belin.

Lehtonen, M. (2009). 'OECD Organisational Discourse, Peer Reviews and Sustainable Development: An Ecological-Institutionalist Perspective.' *Ecological Economics*, *69(2)*, 389–397.

Leimgruber, M. and M. Schmelzer (2017). 'Introduction: Writing Histories of the OECD.' In M. Leimgruber and M. Schmelzer (eds), *The OECD and the International Political Economy Since 1948* (pp.1–22), Palgrave Macmillan.

Littoz-Monet, A. (ed.) (2017). *The Politics of Expertise in International Organizations: How International Bureaucracies Produce and Mobilize Knowledge*, Abingdon, Routledge.

Louis, M. and L. Maertens (2021). *Why International Organizations Hate Politics: Depoliticizing the World*, Abingdon, Oxon, New York, Routledge.

Mabey, N. (1999). 'Defending the Legacy of Rio: The Civil Society Campaign against the MAI.' In S. Picciotto and R. Mayne (eds), *Regulating International Business* (pp.60–81), Palgrave Macmillan.

Mahon, R. (2010). 'After Neo-Liberalism? The OECD, the World Bank and the Child.' *Global Social Policy*, *10(2)*, 172–192.

Mahon, R. and S. McBride (eds) (2008). *The OECD and Transnational Governance*, University of British Columbia Press.

Mahon, R. and S. McBride (2009). 'Standardizing and Disseminating Knowledge: The Role of the OECD in Global Governance.' *European Political Science Review*, *1(1)*, 83–101.

March, J.G. and J.P. Olsen (1998). 'The Institutional Dynamics of International Political Orders.' *International Organization*, *52(4)*, 943–969.

Marcussen, M. (2004), 'The Organization for Economic Cooperation and Development as Ideational Artist and Arbitrator: Reality or Dream?' In B. Reinalda and B. Verbeek (eds), *Decision Making within International Organizations* (pp.90–105), London and NY: Routledge.

Martens, K. and A. Jakobi (2010). *Mechanisms of OECD Governance: International Incentives for National Policy Making*, Oxford University Press.

Martens, K. (2007). 'How to Become an Influential Actor – The "Comparative Turn" in OECD Education Policy.' In K. Martens et al. (eds), *New Arenas of Education Governance* (pp.40–56), Palgrave Macmillan.

Martin, A. (2020). 'The OECD's Rules and Standards for the Testing and Sssessment of Chemicals.' In D. Dolowitz, M. Hadjiisky and R. Normand (eds), *Shaping Policy Agendas: The Micro-Politics of Economic International Organizations* (pp.116–136), Edward Elgar Publishing.

Nay, O. (2012). 'How do Policy Ideas Spread Among International Administrations? Policy Entrepreneurs and Bureaucratic Influence in the UN Response to AIDS.' *Journal of Public Policy, 32(1)*, 53–76.

Neveu, E. and M. Surdez (eds) (2020). *Globalizing Issues. How Claims, Frames, and Problems Cross Borders*, Palgrave Macmillan.

Noaksson, N. and K. Jacobsson (2003). 'The Production of Ideas and Expert Knowledge in OECD: The OECD Jobs Strategy in contrast with the EU employment strategy.' Working Paper, Stockholm, SCORE (Stockholm centre for organizational research).

OECD (1960). *Convention relative à l'OCDE*, Paris, OCDE, 14 décembre 1960.

OECD, Nos modes d'action, version 2011–2021. Retrieved February 22, 2019 from: http://www.oecd .org/fr/apropos/modesdaction/.

OECD (2017). *New Approaches to Economic Challenges: Towards a New Narrative*, OECD Publishing.

OECD (2018). *Elements of a New Growth Narrative. Draft Report* (SG/NAEC(2018)1).

OECD (2019a). Financing the OECD. In *Secretary-General's Report to Ministers 2019*, OECD Publishing.

OECD (2019b). Beyond growth: towards a new economic approach. Report of the Secretary General's Advisory Groupe on a New Growth Narrative, 17–18 September 2019 (SG/NAEC(2019)3).

OECD, How we work. Retrieved January 31, 2022 from https://www.oecd.org/about/how-we-work/.

OECD, *OECD Publishing*. Retrieved February 6, 2022 from https://www.oecd.org/about/publishing/.

Ougaard, M. (2004). *Political Globalization: State, Power, and Social Forces*. Palgrave.

Pal, L.A. (2012). *Frontiers of Governance: The OECD and Global Public Management Reform*, Palgrave Macmillan.

Petiteville, F. (2017). 'La politisation résiliente des organisations internationals.' *Critique internationale, 3(76)*, 9–19.

Porter, T. and M. Webb (2008). 'Role of the OECD in the Orchestration of Global Knowledge Networks.' In R. Mahon and S. McBride (eds), *The OECD and Transnational Governance* (pp.43–59), UBCPress.

Radaelli, C.M. (2020). 'Regulatory Indicators in the European Union and the Organization for Economic Cooperation and Development: Performance Assessment, Organizational Processes, and Learning, *Public Policy and Administration, 35(3)*, 227–246.

Reinalda, B. and B. Verbeek (2004). *Decision Making Within International Organisations*, London, Routledge.

Sahlin-Andersson, K. (2000). 'Arenas as Standardizers.' In N. Brunsson and B. Jacobsson (eds), *A World of Standards* (pp. 100–114), Oxford University Press.

Serhan, Y. (October 12, 2017), How Did UNESCO Get So Politicized? *The Atlantic*. Retrieved July 26, 2022 from https://www.theatlantic.com/international/archive/2017/10/how-did-unesco-get-so -politicized/542733/.

Stone, D. (2003). 'The "Knowledge Bank" and the Global Development Network.' *Governance, 9(1)*, 43–61.

Theodore, N. and J. Peck (2012). 'Framing Neoliberal Urbanism: Translating "commonsense" Urban Policy across the OECD Zone.' *European Urban and Regional Studies, 19(1)*, 20–41.

Trondal, J., M. Marcussen, T. Larsson and F. Veggeland (2010). *Unpacking International Organizations: The Dynamics of Compound Bureaucracies*, Manchester University Press.

Vadrot, A.B.M. (2014). 'The Epistemic and Strategic Dimension of the Establishment of the IPBES: "Epistemic Selectivities" at Work.' *Innovation: The European Journal of Social Science Research, 27(4)*, 361–378.

WHO (2000). *The World Health Report 2000, Health Systems: Improving Performance*, World Health Organization.

Woods, N. (2006). *The Globalizers: The IMF, the World Bank, and their Borrowers*, Cornell University Press.

Ydesen, C. and S. Grek (2019). 'Securing Organisational Survival: A Historical Inquiry into the OECD's Work in Education during the 1960s.' *Paedagogica Historica, 56*, 412–427.

6. Public management

Denita Cepiku and Marco Amici

INTRODUCTION

International institutions, although later and to a minor extent compared to national public administrations, have been part of the public management reforms implemented worldwide such as the New Public Management and Public Governance. In particular, managerial reforms have been an answer to their legitimacy crisis. Forms of globalization as migration, financial stability and crime, influence people's life simultaneously and call for a broader role of international organizations. In this scenario, they were found constrained between high expectations to solve complex transnational problems and the continuous lament of poor performance.

In the debate over the legitimacy of international organizations, less attention has been devoted to the concept of the output legitimacy, which focuses on the positive results that any state or administrative entity can bring about (Schimmelfennig 1996). The legitimacy of a political system depends on its capacity to achieve general interest goals and solve public problems effectively and efficiently. Thus, the extent to which the actions taken by the international organizations are legitimized depends on the results of such actions. Therefore, legitimacy is invariably linked to performance, and improvements in performance lead to an increased legitimacy of the organization as such (Mehde 2007). If this is true, then performance becomes a crucial aspect, especially for the more influential international organizations (Zürn 2004). From a management perspective, performance depends on how inputs are organized and managed to deliver outputs, and how outputs impact on the environment and collective needs producing outcomes. Thus, performance improvements are linked to the modernization of the management structures dealing with inputs, outputs, and outcomes (Pollitt and Bouckaert 2004; Amici and Cepiku 2020).

International organizations are, similarly to other public, non-profit, and private entities, considered organizations created to achieve specific objectives, laid down in their founding treaties (Cepiku 2021). Reforming international organizations should be a primary concern, considering their spectacular growth in terms of number, size, and competences, as well as their chronic management problems that quickly turn into pathologies unless correctly addressed (Dijkzeul and Beigbeder 2003). By contrast, the management reforms of international organizations have attracted minimal attention and have hardly been subject to comprehensive investigations (Balint and Knill 2007). This dimension of international organizations has been 'consistently neglected in the analytical framework of global governance and its alleged democratic deficit' (Mehde 2007: 168).

Therefore, each organization requires the following two elements for monitoring and improving performance. First, a constant commitment to modernize their management structures to increase the work efficiency and effectiveness of the different organizational units/functions responsible for services and product delivery. Second, the set-up of a performance management system able to measure the results achieved vis-à-vis the ex-ante objectives and to support the organization in using performance information (Pollitt and Bouckaert 2017).

Evidence shows that many international organizations started modernizing their internal management structures in an attempt to be more effective and more efficient (Amici and Cepiku 2020). Some embarked on lengthy reform programmes with very ambitious aims. For instance, the United Nations committed to 'adapt the internal structure, the operational processes and the culture of the United Nations to the expectation of greater efficiency, effectiveness, openness, and problem-solving readiness of the constituency' (United Nations 1997: 2). Similarly, the European Commission management reform aimed to equip the Commission to fulfil its role in addressing the challenges facing Europe with maximum effectiveness, as well as making sure that every action taken delivers maximum performance and value-added (European Commission 2014: 3). On the same line, the World Bank's reform aimed at making the Bank more effective in delivering its regional programme and in achieving its basic mission of reducing poverty (World Bank 1997).

Few studies have been carried out on the OECD management reforms and even fewer with a comparative approach (Carroll and Kellow 2011; Bourgon 2009; Woodward 2009; Wolfe 2008; Mahon and McBride 2009; Pal 2012). The most important in this respect is the comparative analysis of Balint and Knill (2007) on the reform of the human resource management in the OECD. Much is left unknown about how the OECD collects and analyses information and data, how it produces policy concepts and principles, and whether these products or services make any difference in national or international settings (Clifton and Díaz-Fuentes 2011).

The aim of the chapter is to contribute to the understanding of the internal functioning of the OECD, and specifically its administrative body, following thorough management reforms focused on performance and budgetary planning and control, taking place since the mid-1990s. It will highlight how the peculiarities of an international organization – vis-à-vis national public administrations – have affected the management reform processes and the characteristics of its management systems. More specifically, we focus on how issues of low measurability of results are overcome and on other adaptations to the traditional performance managerial planning and control system.

ORGANIZATION AND FUNCTIONING OF THE OECD

The organizational design of the OECD is rather basic and comprises the council, the committees, and the secretariat. The council, the highest body of the OECD and ultimate responsible for decision-making, is made up of member state representatives and chaired by the Secretary-General. It oversees the OECD's work and broad agenda. Through the yearly ministerial meeting, it sets the broad direction for the future of the organization. It has three plenary standing committees such as the budget, the executive and the external relations committees. In particular, the budget committee assists the council in preparing the budget priorities and the biennial Programme of Work and Budget. It monitors the implementation of the agreed budget and assists the council on the Integrated Management Cycle. Although in council decisions by mutual agreement are the rule, since 2006 there have been several exceptions involving majority voting.

A hierarchical system of specialized committees – populated by senior officials from national administrations – oversees advancing ideas and reviewing progress in specific policy areas. Through its committee structure, the OECD's substantive policy agenda and outputs respond directly to the needs of, and are closely monitored by, senior policy officials from capitals in a way that is unique among international organizations. It is these committees that produce the outputs of the OECD, the policy advice, guidelines, principles ('soft law') and best practices. The working methods of the committees are one of the institution's hallmarks, the source of its added value and the support it enjoys in capitals.

The OECD secretariat, in charge of administrative and management duties, supports both the council and the committees. It consists of the Secretary-General and some 2500 permanent staff, the core of whom are policy experts in the diverse fields within which the OECD is involved. Thus, the OECD is half diplomatic and half think-tank (Pal 2012). The secretariat collects and analyses data, after which committees discuss policy regarding this information, the council makes decisions, and then governments implement recommendations. The final outputs are generated by its committees, which function through some 228 working groups and subgroups, task groups (some of them ad hoc). Every year the OECD publishes more than 500 major reports and country surveys and over 5 billion data points. It is widely seen as an authoritative source of independent data (Salzman 1999; Woodward 2007), also essential to the work of other international bodies (Woodward 2006).

Information sharing and data collection

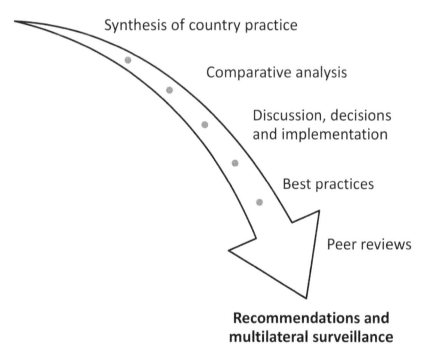

Synthesis of country practice

Comparative analysis

Discussion, decisions and implementation

Best practices

Peer reviews

Recommendations and multilateral surveillance

Source: Adapted from https://www.oecd.org/about/how-we-work/ accessed 18 April 2023.

Figure 6.1   *OECD's way of working*

The range of methods and instruments that the OECD has developed during its half century of existence are not based on the threat of sanctions, but rather on voluntary compliance with agreements, cooperation, persuasion, proposal of alternative views and the systematic comparison of strengths and weaknesses (Figure 6.1 above; AIV 2007).

One of the tools worth mentioning is peer review: mutual examination by governments, multilateral surveillance, and a process through which the performance of individual countries is monitored by their peers, all carried out at committee-level, are at the heart of its effectiveness (see Chapter 9 in this volume).

Discussions at OECD committee-level sometimes evolve into negotiations where OECD countries agree on rules of the game for international cooperation. Ougaard (2010: 29) shows a rapid increase in the number of formal instruments in force by the OECD such as *decisions* that are binding on countries approving them; *recommendations* with which countries can voluntarily comply or not regardless of if they voted or not; and *agreements* that are legally binding on all members (Hunter 2013).

The OECD budget consists of two parts. Part I includes member country contributions calculated according to a formula consisting of a portion related to relative size of the national economy and a portion shared equally. Part II is dedicated to special purpose bodies and specific projects and is also funded by members' contributions. Both Part I (representing around two-thirds of Part I expenditure) and Part II budgets can contain voluntary contributions for specific projects. These are frequently solicited at the director or departmental level within a directorate and contribute to the further decentralization of the OECD as an organization (Pal 2012).

REFORM DRIVERS

Four main forces – two external and two internal – could be identified as the drivers of OECD reforms. First, the end of the Cold War brought the risk of losing the central political imperative of the OECD members at the global level, given their declining economic weight and, consequently, *weakened the OECD's representativeness and influence* (Bourgon 2009; Woodward 2011). To address this external challenge the Organization effectively engaged in a cooperation and accession process some Central and Eastern European countries. However, China, India, Brazil, and other developing countries grew and became more integrated into the global economy, making this driver persistent. Policy decisions of the emerging economic players were having a greater impact on member countries, most notably in the areas of investment, intellectual property, energy, environment, and development assistance, threatening the Organization's ability to set international norms and guidelines (Bourgon 2009).

The second external driver for reform was the *intensified institutional competition* and overlap, especially with the European Union, leading to declining interest by some of its larger members and most important financial contributors (Woodward 2007; OECD 1997; 2003a). When asked what the major challenge the OECD was facing, Gurría responded: 'Relevance, relevance, relevance' (Pal 2012).

The *identity crisis* that followed was a third driver and was addressed through an increase in the number of topics and membership enlargement rather than strategic prioritizing. However, this strategy worsened the identity crisis and intensified financial constraints. According to

Carroll and Kellow (2011), the expenditure cuts were imposed also because the OECD lacked a sense of strategic priorities and was wasting resources.

Finally, the expenditure cuts gave way to *high financial pressures* that started in the mid-90s and were enduring. The 1995 Ministerial Meeting asked the OECD to 'accelerate the process of change with a view to further enhancing the relevance, efficiency and effectiveness of the Organisation' (OECD 1995). The newly appointed secretary general at the time, Donald Johnston, was asked to reduce expenditures by 10 per cent over three years. These financial pressures, initially urged by the US, UK and Australia, continued for a decade (Bourgon 2009). As a result, between 1996 and 1999, the OECD budget was reduced by approximately 18 per cent. Successively, Part I contributions came under severe strain in the early 2000s relative to the overall budget, and so the OECD and its committees began to search more assiduously for voluntary contributions. The budget was stretched to bursting point, with the OECD itself conceding that it 'has come to rely heavily on voluntary contributions to accomplish its work programme' (OECD 2003b: 7). In 2007, the ministers agreed 'to provide a strong and sustainable financial foundation for the Organization, both now and in the long term, that will allow it to maintain at least the quality and volume of outputs […] and the real level of part I budget resources taking into account the rate of inflation' (OECD 2008).

This financial commitment was subject to several conditions, the three main ones being: (i) strict prioritization; (ii) budget transparency; (iii) efficiency savings. Regarding the latter, the Secretary-General made an attempt of planning productivity gains, which attainment is however difficult to assess given the lack of genuine cost accounting (OECD 2008).

Later, Johnston noted: 'Members did not deliver the budget stability they promised would follow the reductions. Instead, the staff have had to deal with further cuts and repeated job uncertainty at the end of each year, in addition to the upheaval of the move and adapting to new ways of working' (Pal 2012).

In 2010–2011, the distinction between permanent and project staff eroded almost completely – partly since more and more staff with longer tenure spend a significant portion of their time working on projects (Pal 2012). The OECD's PWB for 2011–12, which encompassed the celebrations for the 50th anniversary of the Organization, was based on zero real growth, with nominal increases of 0.7 per cent in 2011 and 1.5 per cent in 2012, following a decision of OECD ministers in 2008. The Secretary-General noted that, within this constrained budget, significant reallocations were made to adjust to new priorities.

These external and internal reform drivers did not act in isolation but rather combined, increasing the pressure to change. Moreover, reforms had mixed financial repercussions: efforts to improve relevance through membership enlargement increased the financial burden putting further stress on an already tight budgetary situation (Woodward 2007), while management for results reforms attempted to improve efficiency.

The great increase in the number of topics covered by the Organization, the membership enlargement, and its limited funding, pointed to the need to adopt managerial instruments to review and plan its goals and activities. Before reforming its management systems, the OECD lacked effective means to set priorities and evaluate the work of the secretariat (Bourgon 2009). Managerial reform resulted also in changing the structure of the OECD committees.

REFORM CONTENTS

The OECD reacted to the drivers by implementing several reforms for increasing its global relevance and effectiveness, as well as efficiency and accountability.

The reforms, implemented since the mid-90s, had an initial internal focus followed by a second cycle addressing the need to open the Organization. These could be grouped under four categories (Woodward 2007; 2011; Bourgon 2009; Pal 2012):

- *Structural reforms (1996–1997)*: these included consolidating organizational structures, reviewing committees, introducing clusters for addressing cross-cutting interdisciplinary issues, the creation of key central committees. All support services were regrouped under a new Executive Directorate to improve services and reduce costs. The Centre for Co-operation with non-members was created to improve coherence and coordination of rapidly expanding outreach relations. The Directorate for Public Affairs and Communications was established to raise the OECD's visibility and enhance its engagement with civil societies.
- *Management reforms*: human resources management reforms (in 1995 and 2008), strategic prioritizing through the Strategic Management Framework, and results-based budgeting and control through the Integrated Management Cycle (2002). This group of reforms is addressed in this chapter.
- *Financial reforms*: financial management reforms (2001), introduction of across-the-board cuts through the Priorities and Resource Allocation System (PRAS; 2001–2002), zero based budgeting and budget reform through the Budget and Financial Management Programme (BFMP; 2008), reallocation of the burden among member countries.
- *Governance reforms*: revised decision-making mode (shifting from consensus to qualified majority voting) and membership enlargement and enhancement of outreach activities, aimed at making the Organization more transparent, inclusive and influential.

These reforms were carried out under the leadership of the secretary-general Donald J. Johnston (1996–2006), and continued by his successor Angel Gurrìa, who refined and accelerated the process of change (Woodward 2011). Reform directions came from the annual ministerial meetings (especially in 1995 and in 2007), the Vinde exercise, reviews undertaken by special advisors such as Nicholson (2003), Julin (2003) and Noburn (2004) and by the Heads of Delegations. All proposed greater reliance on evaluation (such as for instance selective evaluation of activities, rolling reviews of committees and their mandates).[1]

The Programme of Work and Budget for 2001 included a mechanism – the priorities and resource allocation system (PRAS) – inviting the secretariat to identify what activities would be dropped or reduced with 3 per cent fewer resources and what additional work would be done if resources were to be increased by 3 per cent. The PRAS was retained for 2002, with the plus/minus provision raised to 5 per cent. It was then abandoned for imposing potential reductions across the board and hence being not strategic; however, it did create widespread

---

[1]   Past attempts to evaluation – such as the Vinde reviews – have failed due to the lack of a corporate framework, a focus on processes rather than outputs, no clear planning, limited involvement of senior officials in capitals and other stakeholders, unclear accountability arrangements, a 'one-off process' approach.

uncertainty for a lengthy period throughout the Programme of Work and Budget preparations. Most of all, it did not in the end deliver significant reallocations (OECD 2009a). At the same time, a financial reform was implemented including the introduction of an accrual accounting system and the adoption of a biannual budget process starting 2003/2004.

An external consultant (Peter Nicholson) was hired in 2002 to consider ways in which to enhance the influence of the OECD on policy outcomes by investment. Part of his mandate covered a thorough review of committees, as well as a survey conducted in late 2002 of members' medium-term priorities.

These piecemeal reforms preceded a report by a Heads of Delegations working group in 2002 that recommended to adopt 'a comprehensive, integrated programme of reform to improve decision-making on the OECD's priorities and Programme of Work and Budget and to implement results-based budgeting and management' in order to 'shift the culture of the Organisation away from a focus on activities, processes and budgeting by institutions to one focused on strategic objectives and outcomes, performance indicators and achieving value for money'.

The implementation of the Integrated Management Cycle, described in the next section, started immediately after. The first step in implementing the Integrated Management Cycle was the adoption of a Programme of Work and Budget for 2003–2004 partially using outputs rather than activities. This reform was fully implemented for the 2005–2006 budget. The budget reforms of 2008 and the implementation of the Budget and Financial Management Programme mean that from 2009 financial management was to be based on outputs and their cost rather than inputs. The application of staff performance objectives and assessments linked to the results-based framework began across the Organization in 2008.

OECD reforms ranked high also in the '21 for 21' agenda of Angel Gurría: the eighth and last goal refers to 'ensuring effective and efficient financial, administrative, communications and management practices within the Organization' (OECD 2017). In the words of the Secretary-General: 'Unlike other institutions which have embarked in long and protracted internal reform processes, I believe the OECD requires "evolution" rather than "revolution"' (Gurría 2015).

Mathias Cormann's strategic orientations for 2023–2024 mention future reform areas including: human resources management, with a focus on diversity in merit-based selection processes, staff professionalism and integrity, and the long-term financial stability of the Organization.

PERFORMANCE MANAGEMENT REFORMS: THE INTEGRATED MANAGEMENT FRAMEWORK

The Integrated Management Framework (Figure 6.2 below) is the sequence of planning, budgeting, and monitoring/reporting aimed at underpinning effective performance. Planning is focused on the Medium-Term Orientation Survey; budgeting on the Programme of Work and Budget; and monitoring/reporting on the Programme Implementation Reporting and the In-Depth Evaluation. It is aimed at introducing a coherent set of strategic planning and priority-setting; at establishing a work programme and the related allocation of resources; and at introducing standardized monitoring and evaluation (OECD, 2009a).

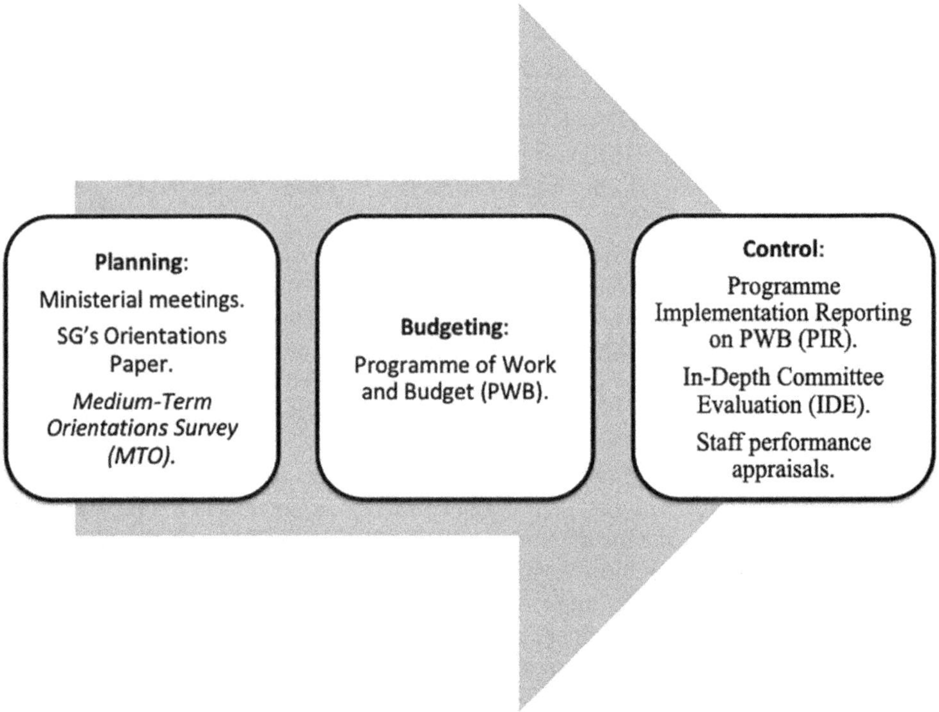

| Planning:
Ministerial meetings.
SG's Orientations Paper.
Medium-Term Orientations Survey (MTO). | **Budgeting:**
Programme of Work and Budget (PWB). | Control:
Programme Implementation Reporting on PWB (PIR).
In-Depth Committee Evaluation (IDE).
Staff performance appraisals. |

Source: The authors.

Figure 6.2   *The Integrated Management Cycle at the OECD*

The Integrated Management Cycle is intended to provide a systematic linkage between:

- Strategic planning or medium-term priority setting at the council level providing a medium-term planning focus (three–six years);
- Biennial committee planning and prioritization;
- Biennial resource reallocation decisions by council;
- Programme of work and budget;
- Annual performance reporting (Programme Implementation Reporting); and
- In-depth, rolling evaluations within a medium-term cycle.

The implementation of the Integrated Management Cycle started with a survey of members' medium-term priorities conducted, in late 2002, in the framework of the Nicholson review. This review served as a prototype for the subsequent Medium-Term Orientation Survey. The second step was the Programme of Work and Budget, which evolved over time.

Planning

Since 2002, the OECD has had in place a Strategic Management Framework based on strategic objectives (or clusters) that reflect the OECD Convention. These strategic objectives cascade down to output groups and, at a lower level, to output areas. The Strategic Management Framework provides the basis for council decisions on resource allocations, and for committee planning, budgeting and reporting. Since 2007–2008, this framework has encompassed Part II programmes.

The Medium-Term Orientation Survey is an exercise aimed at gaining input from capital-based delegates to ensure that the committees' policy objectives are well aligned with the needs of policy makers. As such, it addresses the aim of strengthening the Organization's relevance. The aims of the Medium-Term Orientation are to: (i) influence the strategic directions and resource allocations for the next Programme of Work and Budget and possibly subsequent biennia; (ii) better integrate medium-term policy and resource planning frameworks and decisions; and (iii) have a medium-term strategic view as part of the budget planning and resource reallocation framework. Responses need to assume zero real resource growth. In the words of the Secretary-General: 'the identification of what to stop doing has always been the Achilles' heel' of such exercises.[2]

The first round of the Medium-Term Orientation Survey had several significant limitations and provided only indicative guidance on desired shifts in priorities and budgets for 2005–2006. The main limitations were a partial coverage of activities; a disequilibrium between the proposals to increase priorities and to decrease priorities, as some of the areas identified for cuts involved relatively small budgets; some members, including one major budget contributor did not respond to the questionnaire; some responses focused on committees and their subsidiaries rather than output areas. Some member countries suggested that the exercise was akin to the unsuccessful former Priorities and Resource Allocation System exercises and questioned the merit of the approach. Also, some delegations expressed reservations about using such data in making judgements on priorities and the Programme of Work and Budget.

Budgeting

The Programme of Work and Budget was the first element of the Integrated Management Cycle linking planning, prioritization, budgeting, reporting and evaluation to be implemented. It is the expression of the OECD's priorities and the result of a mixed top-down and bottom-up process, formal and informal, involving members and the Secretary-General.

Top-down priority-setting consists in members influencing priorities when they discuss issues in council, in the executive committee in special session, as well as in sectoral ministerial and other high-level meetings. A major opportunity for members to establish and comment on priorities is the annual ministerial council meetings, which are preceded by preparation by the Secretary-General of a strategic orientations paper.

Bottom-up priority-setting refers to the prioritization of all OECD outputs and resources, mainly carried out at the committee level, engaging all members. Output results are reviewed, prioritized, adjusted or terminated in the early part of the Programme of Work and Budget preparations. This process considers expected resources: each output result is costed on the basis of these likely resources.

The programme of work sets out the strategic objectives, output groups, output areas and output results. Within output areas, the OECD output results are organized and through them

---

[2]   Letter of the Secretary-General, accompanying the MTO survey, to all Permanent Representatives. 2 August 2005.

accountabilities are attributed. In institutional terms, output groups in most cases correspond to directorates.

The OECD delivers eight types of output results: data/models/indicators, statistical reports; analytical/outlook reports; good practice reports; peer reviews or surveys; policy recommendations; soft law, guidelines, and declarations; hard law: conventions and legal agreements; evaluations. The output area costs refer to total resources (Part I or Part II budget allocations and voluntary contributions) to be used to produce the output results in each output area. The first round of Programme of Work and Budget for 2003–2004 saw an unprecedented shift of resources towards high priority areas (OECD 2003b: 2). Since the Programme of Work and Budget for 2005–2006, committees have had the opportunity to be engaged from the outset, to articulate the expected outcomes they wanted to achieve, and to specify the output results they assessed would be most likely to have the desired policy impacts in member and non-member economies over the biennium. The improved outcome and output specification in the 2005–2006 Programme of Work and Budget included three levels of impact identified for expected outcomes; the introduction of output result categories in the Programme of Work and Budget to facilitate benchmarking and comparative evaluations of outputs; and the phasing-in of council and committee templates.

In the OECD glossary, outcomes are impacts on end-users deriving from applying the output results. Outcomes describe what the OECD member governments want to achieve in funding OECD output results and explain why those output results are undertaken. Outcomes help define committee mandates and are essential for subsequent evaluation of impacts. The OECD identifies three broad levels of outcomes: (i) increased awareness/understanding of OECD output results; (ii) actual application of output results by members (e.g., a policy change); (iii) the effects of the use of output results and their contribution to achieving the strategic objectives. The higher the level of outcome, the more difficult it is to measure and, usually, the longer the timeframe for it becomes evident. The review the Programme of Work and Budget process and the effectiveness of the priority-setting mechanism in 2003 concluded that 'the new system worked better than its predecessors, resulting in a record shift in corporate priorities across the organisation and a more strategic, coherent budget planning and communications tool' (OECD 2003a).

Performance Controls

Since 2002, the progressive introduction of results-based planning and budgeting has enabled the implementation of control and evaluation mechanisms such as the Programme Implementation Report (PIR) and the In-Depth Evaluation (IDE). The PIR is undertaken shortly after the end of a biennium – to get feedback from members while the completed output results are relatively new (and familiar) – and covers that period. In the IDE process, each committee is reviewed on a six-yearly cycle.

The PIR responds to members and management need to know whether the approved Programme of Work and Budget was delivered and how well this was done; the IDE to the need to know how well individual committees are planning, organizing, and delivering their work, and the extent to which it is being used and having an impact over a longer timeframe. Moreover, the IDE fulfils the need to understand why a committee is performing well or otherwise and what actions can be taken to improve its performance when this is shown to be necessary.

Five indicators of performance are applied in the framework of the PIR at the corporate level: *quantity*, *timeliness* and *cost* for the monitoring of performance; *quality* and *impact/ potential impact* for the evaluation of performance. IDE focuses on assessing committees with regard to the evaluation criteria of *relevance*, *efficiency* and *effectiveness*. The results of successive PIR exercises provide an important input into IDE.

The IDE are primarily retrospective in nature, using both quantitative and qualitative data as basis for assessing the: (i) relevance of a committee's work programme and mandate objectives; (ii) extent to which it is effective in achieving impacts that are in line with its objectives; (iii) efficiency with which it functions. The process involves a considerable effort of data collection through the conducting of surveys and interviews (OECD 2009b). Evaluation results are used to reinforce transparency and accountability, to inform council decisions on mandate renewals, and to help improve future committee performance.

DISCUSSION AND CONCLUDING REMARKS

OECD reform results can be assessed against the main objectives: first, enhanced accountability towards member countries in terms of efficiency and effectiveness and, second, relevance of outputs compared to the most important policy concerns of governments and impact on policy making in capitals. A third aim was to assist the OECD council in identifying priorities and allocating resources. There has been no formal evaluation of the reform results although the Integrated Management Cycle tools have been periodically reviewed and some elements are to be found in Bourgon (2009).

The most important result is the performance orientation that has been gradually adopted in managing resources. The OECD is the most advanced among international institutions in this regard. According to the Secretary-General, a culture of value for money has been established that is now delivering results (Gurría 2015).

The planning, budgeting and control of outcomes is not an easy task and several difficulties were encountered in addressing the trade-off between high relevance and low measurability. From this experience, both international institutions and national public administrations have much to learn.

Reforms led member states to be more involved in setting priorities and allocating resources. However, external transparency and accountability have not much improved. For example, the PIR and IDE exercises are based on surveys in capitals that engage civil servants and politicians already involved in OECD activities, rather than external stakeholders.

Another key issue is the relationship between strategy and structure: it can be said that the organizational structure drives planning as outputs correspond to directorates. Such an approach is known in literature to pose a risk especially in terms of neglecting topics that are cross-directorate. The creation of clusters did not noticeably improve the ability to address cross-cutting issues (Bourgon 2009).

By 2003, operating costs were reduced by 20 per cent through internal management and administrative simplification, efficiency gains in support services and through outsourcing (OECD, 2003b). Such savings were more a result of budget cuts than efficiency gains. The main result of structural reforms was to build momentum towards successive reforms. Also, the committee review was the most costly and least successful reform.

In conclusion, the case study analysis of OECD's management reform offers several insights for other international institutions struggling to address legitimacy and financial issues. Among the strengths, the following can be listed: a strong and committed leadership from the Secretary-General and a clear and urgent need to change. Weaknesses include the absence of a clearly defined strategy on how the performance management system would develop. Finally, the criterion of leaning on trustworthy and available data was difficult to meet due to the very specificities of the OECD as a coping organization (i.e., an organization characterized by outputs and outcomes that are not observable typical of diplomacy, research and intelligence organizations; Wilson 1989). A major effort was made to adopt meaningful performance indicators, although this meant, in some instances, that the measurement was qualitative and highly subjective.

The development of a performance management system at the OECD has yet to encompass the incorporation and to boost the use of performance information. The latter is used in a soft way mainly to learn and to prioritize activities and budget. External control, accountability and communication are less explored paths, although the main drivers to change were external.

REFERENCES

AIV – Advisory Council on International Affairs (2007). The OECD of the future. Report No. 54.
Amici, M., and Cepiku, D. (2020). *Performance Management in International Organizations*. Palgrave - Springer Nature.
Balint, T., and Knill, C. (2007). *The Limits of Legitimacy Pressure as a Source of Organizational Change: The Reform of Human Resource Management in the OECD*.
Bauer, M.W. (2007). 'Introduction: Management Reform in International Organizations.' In *Management Reforms in International Organizations*, (eds) Bauer M. and Knill C., Nomos.
Bourgon, J. (2009). *Reform and Modernization of the OECD*. Centre for International Governance Innovation.
Carroll, P., and Kellow, A. (2011). *The OECD: A Study of Organisational Adaptation*. Edward Elgar Publishing.
Cepiku, D. (2021), 'Performance Management in a Networked Organization: The OECD', *International Journal of Public Sector Management*, 34(3), 292–311.
Clifton, J., and Díaz-Fuentes, D. (2011). 'The OECD and Phases in the International Political Economy, 1961–2011'. *Review of International Political Economy*, 18(5), 552–569.
Dijkzeul, D., and Beigbeder, Y. (2003). 'Introduction'. In *Rethinking International Organizations* DennisDijkzeul and Yves Beigbeder, 1–26, Berghahn Books.
European Commission (2014). Communication from the President Mission letter to Commissioner to Competition.
Gurría A. (2015) '21 for 21'. A Proposal for Consolidation and Further Transformation of the OECD. Available on: https://www.oecd.org/about/secretary-general/21-for-21-A-Proposal-for-Consolidation-and-Further-Transformation-of-the-OECD.pdf accessed 18 April 2023.
Hunter, C. P. (2013). The Organization for Economic Cooperation and Development's changing (?) discourse on higher education (Doctoral dissertation, University of British Columbia).
Mahon, R., and McBride, S. (2009). 'Standardizing and Disseminating Knowledge: The Role of the OECD in Global Governance.' *European Political Science Review*, 1(1), 83–101.
Mehde, V. (2007) 'Creating a Missing Link? Administrative Reforms as a Means of Improving the Legitimacy of International Organizations.' In *Management Reforms in International Organizations*, pp. 163–175. Nomos Verlagsgesellschaft mbH & Co. KG.
OECD (1995). The Future of the Organization. Paris: Organization for Economic Co-operation and Development.
OECD, (1997). The Future of the Organization. Paris: Organization for Economic Co-operation. The OECD: Challenges and Strategic Objectives 1997. Note by the Secretary-General.

OECD (2003a). Report by the Chair of the Budget Committee on the new system for developing the OECD's Programme of Work and Budget (PWB).

OECD (2003b). Reform and Modernisation of the OECD. HOD (2003)3.

OECD (2008). Financial Regulations of the Organization.

OECD (2009a). The Integrated Management Cycle, priority-setting, resource reallocations and performance evaluation at the OECD. General Secretariat. Council. Working Party on Priorities.

OECD (2009b). Implementing In-depth Evaluation of OECD Committees. Evaluation Sub-Group.

OECD (2017). Budget Committee Financial Statements of the Organisation for Economic Co-operation and Development.

Ougaard, M. (2010). 'The OEC's Global Role: Agenda-setting and Policy Diffusion.' In *Mechanisms of OECD Governance: International Incentives for National Policymaking?* pp. 26–49, Oxford University Press.

Pal, L. (2012). *Frontiers of Governance: The OECD and Global Public Management Reform.* Springer.

Pollitt, C., and Bouckaert G. (2004). *Public Management Reform: A Comparative Analysis.* Oxford University Press, USA, 2004

Pollitt, C., and Bouckaert, G. (2017). *Public Management Reform: A Comparative Analysis – into the Age of Austerity.* Oxford University Press.

Salzman, J. (1999). 'Labour Rights, Globalization, and Institutions: The Role and Influence of the Organization and Development.' *Mich. J. Int'l L.,* 21, 769.

Schimmelfennig, F. (1996.) 'Legitimate rule in the European Union.' Center for German and European Studies – University of California at Berkeley.

United Nations (1997). Renewing the UN: A Program for Reform.

Wilson, J. Q. (1989). *Bureaucracy: What Government Agencies Do and Why They Do It.* New York: Basic Books.

Wolfe, R. (2008). *From Reconstructing Europe to Constructing Globalization: the OECD in Historical Perspective.* The OECD and Transnational Governance, 25–42.

Woodward, R. (2006). 'Offshore Strategies in Global Political Economy: Small Islands and the Case of the EU and OECD Harmful Tax Competition Initiatives.' *Cambridge Review of International Affairs,* 19(4), 685–699.

Woodward, R. (2007). 'Global governance and the Organization for Economic Cooperation and Development.' In *Global Governance and Japan,* pp. 83–99. Routledge.

Woodward, R. (2009). *The Organisation for Economic Co-operation and Development (OECD).* Routledge.

Woodward, R. (2011). 'Fifty More Years?: Reform and Modernisation of the OECD.' *Political Insight,* 2(2).

World Bank (1997). The World Bank Annual Report 1997.

Zürn, M. (2004). 'Global Governance and Legitimacy Problems.' *Government and Opposition* 39(2) 260–287.

PART II

MECHANISMS AND TOOLS OF GOVERNANCE

7. The OECD as an international bureaucracy

Martin Marcussen and Jarle Trondal

INTRODUCTION

International bureaucracies constitute distinct and important features of both global governance studies and public administration scholarship. This chapter empirically illustrates the
development of the OECD secretariat. It shows how an established international bureaucracy
still is in the making. To understand what the empirics mean conceptually, we will guide the
readers through three bodies of literature before moving to the subject matter of the OECD.

One fundamental question throughout the chapter is the autonomy of the OECD. On a daily
basis, modern governments formulate and execute policies with significant consequences for
society (Hupe and Edwards, 2012). With the growing role of international bureaucracies, one
unresolved question is to what extent and under what conditions such institutions may formulate their own policies – pursuing a *de facto* autonomous regulatory agenda – and thereby
transcend a mere secretarial role. The influence of international organizations (IOs) to a large
extent rests on the autonomy of its bureaucratic arm, that is, the ability of international bureaucracies to act relatively independently of member governments (Barnett and Finnemore, 2004;
Biermann and Siebenhüner, 2009, 2013; Cox and Jacobson, 1973; Reinalda, 2013; Trondal,
2013). Scholars of various disciplines have explored the conditions under which international
bureaucracies may be 'truly' independent of member-state governments, yet the findings
remain inconclusive (e.g., Beyers, 2010; Checkel, 2007; Moravcsik, 1999). International
bureaucracies are rifted between member-state dominance, the concern for the collective
good, administrative 'siloization' and portfolio concerns, as well as transnational regulatory
institutions driven by epistemic communities of experts (Trondal et al., 2015). Consequently,
academics, politicians and international civil servants present different views on the independent role of international bureaucracies. This chapter shows how the OECD secretariat is
rifted between integration and fragmentation, autonomy and dependency, and between classic
macroeconomics and "neo-economics".

KEY QUESTIONS OF THE FIELD

To begin with, we speak to three distinct political science literatures that provide the conceptual framework where we situated the empirical analysis of the OECD. They are the public
administration literature (with its concept of bureaucratic autonomy), the literature on the
autonomy of international bureaucracies, and finally the organization sciences that deal with
organizational fragmentation and integration. We review these literatures in three steps.

First, the public administration literature has focused on the conditions under which bureaucracy is independent from politics. We saw already how bureaucratic autonomy may be forged
endogenously within bureaucratic organizations. This literature has been interested in explaining and measuring autonomy. *Auto nomos* refers to the Ancient Greek city-state – implying

forms of self-governing (Olsen, 2009: 441). '[A]utonomy is about discretion, or the extent to which [an organization] can decide itself about matters that it considers important' (Verhoest et al., 2010: 18–19). Contemporary understanding of this concept, however, varies and has been hotly debated. The way organizational structure shapes interaction, loyalty, cooperation, and information-processing are particularly recognized in the organization theory literature but much less in most other social science literatures – for example the IO literature (e.g., Cox and Jacobsen, 1973), governance literature (e.g., Levi-Faur, 2012) and broader political science literatures (Olsen, 2006).

A Weberian bureaucracy model assumes that bureaucracies possess endogenous capacities to shape staff through mechanisms such as socialization (behavioural internalization through established bureaucratic cultures), discipline (behavioural adaptation through incentive systems) and control (behavioural adaptation through hierarchical control and supervision) (Page, 1992; Weber, 1983; Yi-Chong and Weller, 2004, 2008). These mechanisms ensure that bureaucracies perform their tasks relatively independently from societal influence, but within boundaries set by the legal authority and (political) leadership of which they serve (Weber, 1924). Causal emphasis is thus put on the internal organizational structures of the bureaucracy. The Weberian bureaucracy model provides a picture of bureaucratic organizations as creator of 'organizational man' (Simon, 1965) and as a stabilizing element in politics more broadly (Olsen, 2010). According to this model, bureaucracies develop their own nuts and bolts quite independently of society. The model implies that civil servants may act upon roles that are shaped by the organization in which they are embedded. The organizational structure of international bureaucracies consists of the bureaucratic structure, as well as how this structure is embedded in the wider IO structure. Organizational dynamics and decision-making behaviour are thus framed by 'in-house' organizational structures (Ellis, 2011; Radin, 2012: 17). Organizations create elements of robustness to policy processes of bureaucracies (Olsen, 2010). Organizational literature therefore suggests that the supply of organizational capacities have implications for how international bureaucracies are likely to act. This approach departs from the assumption that organizational structures mobilize biases in public policy because organizations supply cognitive and normative shortcuts and categories that simplify and guide decision-makers' search for problems, solutions and consequences (Schattschneider, 1975; Simon, 1965). Lipsky (1980: 19) claimed that bureaucratic autonomy is driven by actors' conspicuous desire for maximizing their own autonomy. By contrast, the organizational literature argues that bureaucratic autonomy is organizationally contingent. It is thus the formal rules established within a bureaucracy that regulate, constitute and bias the decision-making behaviour and role perceptions evoked by civil servants, ultimately advancing bureaucratic autonomy (Barnett and Finnemore, 2004: 3).

Second, the literature on international bureaucracies has focused on their daily role in formulating and executing global policies. With the gradual increased role of international bureaucracies one unresolved question is to what extent and under what conditions such institutions may indeed express own policies and thus transcend a mere intergovernmental role. The autonomous role of international bureaucracies is contested in many literatures. The classical study of IOs did not permit an independent role for international bureaucracies (Knill and Bauer, 2016). International-relations approaches viewed IOs as epiphenomena to inter-state relations. Regime literature similarly downplayed the organizational dimension of IOs, and they are largely seen as regime facilitators (Gehring, 2003: 11). The seminal work of Cox and Jacobson (1973: 428) reflects this view by concluding that 'international organizations facilitate the orderly management of intergovernmental relations without significantly changing the structure of power that governs these relations'. The 1960s and 1970s thus saw several studies of IOs that treated them as hubs of international networks and regimes rather than as organizations and institutions in their own right (e.g., Nye, 1975). The epistemic community literature similarly focused on IOs as facilitators of transnational epistemic communities (E. Haas, 1990; P. Haas, 1992). This literature made 'experts' and their 'ways of doing things' ever more paramount (Barnett and Finnemore, 2004; Joerges, 1999; Joerges et al., 1997: 7).

Contemporary studies of international bureaucracies have established that the craft of IOs to a large extent is *supplied* by the autonomy of its bureaucratic arm, that is, by the ability of international bureaucracies – and their staff – to act relatively independently of mandates and decision premises from member-state governments (Barnett and Finnemore, 2004; Biermann and Siebenhuner, 2009, 2013; Trondal, 2013). Studying three international bureaucracies in three IOs (the OECD, the WTO and the EU), Trondal et al. (2010) demonstrated that the autonomy of international bureaucracy is largely explained by organizational capacities and in-house socialization processes within these administrations. This study shows that similar actor-level behavioural patterns are present among civil servants in three different international bureaucracies. Interestingly, the European Commission is *not* substantially different in this regard from the two other international bureaucracies (the OECD and the WTO secretariats). One theoretical implication is that international bureaucracies may possess considerable capacity to shape autonomous behaviour of their staff through the two causal mechanisms: (i) behavioural and role *adaptation* to organizational rule-following, and (ii) behavioural and role *internalization* of 'in-house' socialization processes.

Third, the organization sciences are particularly helpful in dealing with organizational fragmentation and integration. International bureaucracies vary on the extent of organizational fragmentation, as is empirically demonstrated in the sections below. Over time, organizations tend to accumulate multiple and often conflicting organizational properties through organizational growth and subsequent horizontal and vertical specialization of the organization (Olsen, 2005). They are thus likely to become multi-organizations. As a consequence, variation in administrative styles within international bureaucracies have been shown to vary systematically between organizational sub-units, reflecting the departmentalization of international bureaucracies (Knill et al., 2016). When specializing bureaucratic organizations horizontally, one (among several) generic principle has been suggested by Luther Gulick (1937): organization by major *purpose* served – such as research, health, and food safety. This principle of organization is shown to activate patterns of cooperation and conflicts among incumbents along *sectoral* cleavages (Egeberg, 2006). Coordination and contact patterns tend to be channelled within sectoral portfolios rather than between them, leading to bureaucratic fragmentation. Arguably, organization by major purpose served is likely to bias decision-making dynamics *inwards* towards bureaucratic sub-units where preferences, contact patterns, roles and loyalties are directed towards sectoral portfolios, divisions and units more than towards the organization as a whole. This mode of horizontal specialization results in less than adequate horizontal coordination *across* departmental units and better co-ordination *within* them (Ansell, 2004: 237). This principle of specialization is prevalent in most international bureaucracies. The OECD Secretariat is a horizontally specialized administration consisting of divisions and directorates responsible for a variety of policy domains areas such as macroeconomics, agriculture, environment, development, statistics, etc. As illustrated below, such horizontal specialization of the OECD secretariat is conducive to autonomization of the behavioural patterns among staff and fragmentation of the secretariat.

The following section discusses how the development of the OECD and its secretariat reflect patterns of bureaucratic autonomy, the autonomy of international bureaucracies, organizational structuring, and bureaucratic coordination and fragmentation. The discussion concludes that challenge number one for the OECD is keeping the organization all together.

THE OECD AT A TURNING POINT

Some 20 years ago, we concluded that it was 'Game Over' for the OECD (Marcussen, 2002a).[1] The organization found itself at a crossroads, and important and transformative decisions had to be made. Moreover, the argument draws a direct line back to the original philosophical basis of the organization. Back in 1961, the new OECD was essentially a 'think tank', whose finest function was to challenge the member states and their conventional routines and ideas. The OECD was created to 'think the unthinkable' – to provide an alternative and science-based perspective on primarily economic policy. It was in that spirit that the OECD, during the 1980s and 1990s, stood up as a powerful international voice for structural reforms of national labour markets and the so-called stability-oriented economy which focused on low inflation, low debt and balanced public budgets. It also promoted reforms of public administration along the lines of New Public Management, and it was a vigorous proponent of globalization in all its guises. 'Globalize or fossilize', as one of the previous Secretary-Generals, Donald Johnston, argued (Johnston, 1999: 3; see also Chapter 3 for the historical evolution of the OECD).

Over many years, the OECD attracted the very best economists and civil servants from the member states who very much perceived of themselves as the finest representatives of a positivist science. In short, it was an epistemic logic that reigned high in the OECD's international secretariat during the years (Marcussen and Trondal, 2011). By 2000, the epistemic logic was challenged by a much more functionalist logic with an emphasis on keeping the organization alive. The mood around the OECD – particularly in the largest member state, the USA – had changed profoundly. The prominent idea that came to dominate most internal transactions seemed to be that the organization should not challenge and 'irritate' the member states, but rather service them in ways that facilitated the national reform processes that were already unleashed and underway. In other words, the job of the OECD was not to trigger reforms, but rather to provide a so-called scientific basis for the established practices in the member states (Marcussen, 2004b).

Several interlinked reasons can be mentioned for this radical shift in self-understanding and organizational logic inside the OECD. First, it became clear that the OECD's decade-long quasi-monopoly of producing authoritative data and science-based analysis was ultimately broken. Think tanks, university research centres, ministries and not least several other international organizations (see also Chapter 8 on the OECD dialogue with other IOs and international NGOs) had – with the help of new technology – gradually been able to establish their own highly qualified analytical capacity. They were now able to provide the same, and

---

[1]   The authors conducted background interviews with three levels of OECD management as well as OECD ambassadors in November and December 2021. References to some of these interviews are made in the text, but the interview persons remain anonymous.

sometimes even better, data and analysis than the OECD. For instance, by 2000, all central banks with a degree of self-respect had established a research capacity that in many ways outcompeted the OECD (Mudge and Vauchez, 2017). Therefore, there was a serious risk 20 years ago, that the OECD would soon become superfluous.

To make things worse, the so-called 'OECD-method' of countries' peer review (see Chapter 9) and benchmarking (see Chapter 10) had become so successful and taken for granted that everyone forgot the OECD originally invented it (Marcussen, 2004a). To establish a set of explicit criteria for measurement, and then to rank member states according to the success with which they fulfilled these criteria became a method that was soon overtaken by the European Union (EU), and any other organization, department or centre that aspired to make comparative analysis. Even the more or less open sessions where member states could be shamed, blamed or famed for their relative performance, became widely adopted. OECD distinctiveness in this regard thus seemed to disappear.

Secondly, and connected with the previous point, member states became increasingly hesitant to paying their membership fees – at least not without conditions. Budget restrictions became preoccupation number one for any Secretary-General heading the OECD. Between 1996 and 1999, the OECD budget was cut by around 18 per cent in real terms, administrative costs reduced by up to 23 per cent and staff numbers cut by 15 per cent (see Figure 7.1 below). Under these conditions, the Secretary-General had, in all imaginable ways, to sweet talk the members. Thus, the days when the Secretary-General stood up and talked truth to power had long gone (Marcussen, 2004c). Instead, the Secretary General encouraged the rest of the organization to produce almost whatever the member states would be willing and able to pay for. A still larger amount of the operational budget was defined by so-called voluntary contributions. In short, the OECD had taken a large step toward becoming an international consultancy.

Thirdly, in line with the general performance measurement revolution in public administrations among the OECD member states (Neely, 1999), the OECD itself was obliged to constantly document its *raison d'être*. Preferably a documentation that in quantitative ways would indicate that performance, from one year to the next, had improved (see Chapter 6). In that spirit, the OECD speeded up the printing machine. The number of publications produced by the OECD just continued to increase. It increased to such an extent, that the most important publications – the flagship reports, such as the economic surveys – seemed to drown in the overwhelming number of papers. However, to the surprise of the organization itself the OECD became less and less – and not more and more – visible in the national media. Whereas the OECD could easily take any front page in the national media ten years earlier, the OECD now had a hard time positioning itself in the national reform debates. Did anyone any longer pay attention to the OECD (Marcussen, 2002a)? The quantification of performance also manifested itself in other unintended ways. For instance, the OECD started to count the number of meetings that were organized at all levels of the organization, as if meeting activity – and not so much what was discussed on those meetings – was an appropriate indicator of high performance. In those years it apparently underpinned the relevance of the organization that the Secretary-General was seen shaking hands with one political protagonist after the other.

Fourthly, it made a difference for the profile of the organization that the number of member states continued to increase. At some point, it was clear to everyone that one could hardly refer to the OECD as being a club of the wealthiest countries in the world any longer. This was simply no longer true. For better or for worse, the OECD was no longer the exclusive club that it once was, as a result of which the OECD became less and less attractive as a playground for the very large global players. For these, and for other reasons, the OECD, by 2000, stood at a turning point (Marcussen and Trondal, 2011). In principle, two separate routes could be taken: either the OECD took a turn backwards with a view to going back to basics, or the organization could make the decision to go all the way to transform itself to become a global multi-organization.

There were indeed arguments favouring the 'back to basics' strategy. One argument was that the OECD – and other organizations which are endowed with a capacity enabling them to develop critical new knowledge that can be applied to underpin evidence-based decision-making – even had a democratic obligation to engage in active and open knowledge development and diffusion (Marcussen, 2002b; Lacey, 2016). If not, taxpayer-financed organizations should be obliged to assist in improving collective problem-solving by producing independent knowledge, who would then 'think the unthinkable' (Cockett, 1994)? Another argument was that a 'a back to basics' scenario would probably have been facilitated by an ever-increasing tendency towards scientization of political issues (Marcussen, 2010). In the early 2000s, there was a tendency towards leaving critical political issues to autonomous and semi-autonomies agencies, central banks and IOs, thereby de-politicizing policy issues and preventing broader public and political debates (Hay, 2007; Trondal, 2014; Verhoest et al., 2012). In such a context, an autonomous knowledge producer such as the OECD could have gained considerable leverage in global governance. The back-to-basics option would ideally have given a much-needed input to global discussions about some of the largest challenges that society, as a global collective, are confronting such as climate change, health crises, hybrid security challenges, and social cohesion. However, that option was not chosen.

Rather, it was the global multi-organization that was in the making. Some of the developments that had brought the organization into its deepest crisis so far were not brought to an end, but rather reinforced. With the dictum, 'making a virtue out of necessity', it was more of the same, much more of the same, rather than a new vision that came to characterize the organizational development of the OECD since the 2000s to this day.

DEFINING FEATURES OF A GLOBAL MULTI-ORGANIZATION

To enhance the relevance and legitimacy of the OECD – and to engage in a transformation from a 'think tank' to a 'do tank' – the Secretary General Angel Gurría (2006–2021) literally looked beyond the OECD box and decided for expansion in all respects of the organization. Firstly, the organization needed, according to his analysis, to reach out to the world. The days were gone, where the OECD should be seen as an exclusive rich country club. Secondly, the organization needed to expand the number of issue areas dealt with. In addition, the days were gone, where all complex problems should be studied through the narrow lens of classical economics.

More Members and More Outreach

In contrast to many other international organizations, the operational budget of the OECD has expanded since 2005. The organization has grown in terms of members and in terms of portfolio, and so has the secretariat of the OECD (Figure 7.1). This growth in personnel can, for instance, be seen in the Global Relations secretariat in the Secretary-General's office.

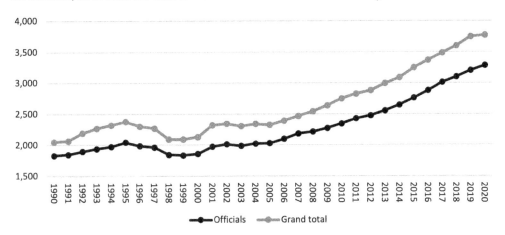

Note: The staff category 'Officials' includes both permanent and temporary staff employed on specific and time limited projects. The 'Grand total' furthermore includes staff on loan and trainees.
Source: OECD (2001: 3; 2011: 8; 2021: 7).

Figure 7.1   *Evolution of OECD staff, 1990–2020*

Today, it is difficult to claim that the OECD is a club of likeminded countries. On the one hand, entry requirements have indeed been established with a view to ensuring a certain degree of conformity in the group of OECD members, and membership in itself can be argued to have an isomorphic impact on member states (as well as non-member states, see Chapter 20 and 21 on OECD impact on Brazil and Kazakhstan); yet, it is also clear that the objective of continuous membership enlargement is no longer primarily about fostering a very special and close community of countries sharing perspectives, philosophies and ideals. Membership enlargement is equally, and increasingly so, about strategic considerations related to geographical representativeness. The ambition of becoming a veritable global organization is about including a critical mass of countries from all continents as distinct members, and then, in addition, concluding various sort of cooperation and partnership agreements with the rest. Already today, the OECD member states, and its key partners represent 80 per cent of world trade and investment.

The immediate payoff from a strategy of continuous geographical expansion and strengthened representation is that the OECD can speak with a larger voice on other international arenas. Thus, the OECD has positioned itself to become a 'secretariat' for the G20, a group of 19 countries and the EU accounting for some 90 per cent of gross world product, 75 per cent of international trade, two-thirds of the global population, and about half the world's land area. Clearly, since a good portion of the G20 countries are members or partners of the OECD, the organization would be able to play a prominent role in the G20.

However, geographical expansion is also about contributing to reinvigorating multilateralism as an international mechanism of governance. The idea, also employed by the EU, albeit to a less successful extent, concerns 'enhanced cooperation' and differentiated integration

(Leruth et al., 2022). As a group, the OECD members – or considerable parts of the members – can conclude agreements, which eventually, *de facto* or *de jure*, become agreements for others to follow. The lesson from failed governance in the UN, WTO, UNESCO and other international organizations is that important decisions are not being made when many veto points are present. However, important decisions can be made if a critical mass of countries, i.e., the OECD countries, take the lead. Then the rest are likely to eventually follow.

The costs associated with expansion, however, is considerable on other accounts. Over the last decade, the OECD has opened up to eight new members – Chile, Colombia, Costa Rica, Estonia, Israel, Latvia, Lithuania and Slovenia – and has received membership requests from six other countries – Argentina, Brazil, Bulgaria, Croatia, Peru and Romania. Most members of the OECD ambassador group think that these further enlargements will indeed take place within a quite short time span. Seen from the point of view of the OECD secretariat, to keep things together – logistically, culturally and procedurally – requires a formidable effort, pressing the entire organization to its limits.

More Services and Less Economic Science

Another expansion has to do with the kind of services provided by the OECD. 'We are not doing religion and war', one member of the leadership group explained to us, 'but we are doing virtually everything else.' On one hand, the OECD has expanded its field of interests to new areas in order to stay relevant for the member countries. This happens at the initiative of the various OECD directorates, but also because member states, partner states and not least the EU to an increasing extent demands specific services of the OECD secretariat. Primarily financed by way of voluntary contributions, the portfolio expansion clearly contributes to the growth of the consolidated budget of the OECD (Figure 7.2) below. Roughly speaking, 50 per cent of the entire operational budget is constituted by voluntary contributions of which the EU is by far the largest contributor.

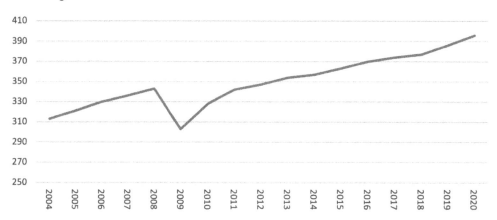

Note: The consolidated budget illustrated does not constitute the entire operational budget of the OECD. Until 2016, the voluntary contributions amounted to at least a third extra income. From 2017 onwards, the so-called voluntary contributions add 50 per cent to the consolidated budget.
Source: OECD Annual Reports 2004–2009; Secretary-General's Report to Ministers 2010–2021.

Figure 7.2   Consolidated budget of the OECD, million euros

The annual reports (until 2009) and the Secretary-General's reports to ministers (from 2010 onwards) provide very scarce information about the entire operational budget of the OECD. Indeed, some reports refrain from mentioning the size of the consolidated budget all together, and all reports do not mention the exact size of the voluntary contributions paid by member states and, to a very considerable extent, the EU. This is in itself a quite interested feature of an organization that prides itself for advising member and partner countries on organizational transparency and good governance. However, the consolidated budget indicated in Figure 7.2 above is supplemented by a considerable number of voluntary contributions amounting until 2016 to approximately one-third extra income to the organization, and from 2017 onwards 50 per cent extra.

In addition to expanding the scope of activities and the number of publications, the basic analytical philosophy of the organization has changed. In the larger public perception, the OECD is probably best known as a distinct 'economic' organization that do macroeconomics at a global scale. This has earned the organization its reputation over the years, and in some periods even played a trend- and agenda-setting role among the OECD member states. Gradually, the classical macroeconomic take on society has been supplemented and even replaced by a much broader, cross-disciplinary approach. Over recent years, green growth, inclusive growth, justice, equality, gender, sustainability and happiness have been common focus points for analysis. For the old macroeconomic guard remaining in the organization, this development is observed with increasing degrees of frustration. 'I still can't figure out what "green growth" is', one senior economist told us when preparing this chapter. 'We run the risk of watering down our organizational reputation if we give in to meaningless, but very fashionable ideas that cannot be substantiated in analysis', he reports. He continues by arguing that:

> another risk is that accepted criteria for sound and solid knowledge is increasingly being disregarded when recruiting people for the top positions in the directorates. In earlier times, the head of directorate would typically be an outstanding and reputed economist. An intellectual leader for all of us. Today, employment does not seem to be based on scientific merits.

Not all employees are equally frustrated as the senior economist cited here, though. However, the frustration illustrates that the OECD Secretariat today is far from united in its move towards holistic analysis and 'neo-economics'. The OECD leadership team seem to be well aware of the challenge emanating from academic turf-wars and is now claiming to take action to 'protecting the core'. The OECD should, according to a member of the leadership team, remain a world-class leader in economic analysis.

Clearly, a risk for any organization that attempts to cover too much at the same time is its organizational overstretch. It may lack the capacity to do it all, and do it well. Doing too much could mean not doing anything at all or, even worse, getting it entirely wrong because the organization does not possess sufficient analytical capabilities in all areas (Trondal et al., 2005). On the other hand, an advantage of looking at complex societal phenomena with an eclectic and cross-disciplinary approach seem to be obvious. 'Everything is connected to everything else when we study society', a member of the leadership team explained to us. 'We would be laughing stuff if we turned up with a one-dimensional and very narrow-minded neo-classical analysis each time we were asked for advice.' The point here is that for some problems and for some analyses, the traditional pillar-structure of the OECD seems to be entirely out of sync with the type of collective societal challenges that call for nuanced comprehension. A major objective of breaking up the old silo thinking is to enhance the relevance of the organization in the eyes of the world.

CHALLENGE NUMBER ONE: KEEPING THE ORGANIZATION ALL TOGETHER

The organizational challenge with which the OECD is now confronted very much resembles the challenges that many OECD member states have struggled with for years. One of the results of the predominant move towards New Public Management has been an increased level of organizational fragmentation – horizontally and well as vertically. An answer to this fragmentation has been to increase coordination and inclusion in all sorts of ways, variably referred to as whole-of-society, whole-of-government and, which is most relevant in this regard, whole-of-organization (Christensen and Lægreid, 2007, 2011). A whole-of-OECD approach would ideally deal with both competing civil servant role conceptions as well as organizational cohesion.

So far, three moves have been made in this regard. Firstly, the previous Secretary-General, Angel Gurría, has mobilized a considerable organizational capacity around his office. This is particularly the case, but not only, in the area of global relations. One answer to fragmentation, therefore, is bureaucratic centralization inside the OECD secretariat. Similar observations have been made elsewhere, for example, on presidentialization of the European Commission by making the Secretariat General into a service unit for the Commission president (Kassim et al., 2016). Clearly, centralization and top-down control has its own challenges, but in some regards it helps keeping things together in a large and complex organization. The new Secretary-General, Mathias Cormann, has so far not done much to alter the established organizational structures. Yet, he has mobilized his deputy-secretaries-generals to delegate organizational responsibilities, thus allowing the entire leadership team to engage more actively with the secretariat as a whole.

A second move has been to nurture organizational structures that are 'born' horizontal. The Centre for Entrepreneurship, SMEs, Regions and Cities as well as the Centre on Well-being, Inclusion, Sustainability and Equal Opportunity (WISE) are just some examples of horizontal organizational units geared towards including and integrating expertise and organizational capacity from various directorates of the OECD secretariat. The idea being that by working together on complex, cross-disciplinary challenges the secretariat learns to integrate different sorts of expertise in their work.

A third move, which was in the pipeline when this chapter was written, is to address the organizational culture of the entire OECD. 'As a first step, we will have to work harder to make the directors understand that they work for the OECD, and not only for their own directorate', a member of the leadership team explains. 'We are very competitive when it comes to attracting highly skilled people and extremely competent leaders, and we will do more to recruit people who understand their whole-of-OECD responsibility.' Clearly, silo thinking can be seen as an organizational characteristic engrained in cultural practices (Trondal et al., 2010). It is also clear, that cultural transformation is difficult and does not easily or quickly happen overnight (Egeberg and Trondal, 2018).

CONCLUSION

It seems clear that the OECD – just as was the case 20 years ago – is an organization in the making. It is continuously struggling to establish its *raison d'être* among the member states, but also for the rest of the world. In that sense, the OECD is a dynamic organization that is sensitive to its varied external contexts. It does not hesitate to take on new challenges and expand its portfolio. At the same time, it is also clear that the organization seems to be less sensitive to its internal context. As the OECD has been transformed into a global multi-organization there is a danger of overstretching and fragmentation (Trondal et al., 2010). The leadership is actively engaged in keeping the bits and pieces together within the OECD secretariat. We should not expect, however, that the current attempts of increasing cohesion and coordination within the organization will manifest itself any time soon. Rather, we would expect that the OECD, as it always has been, will continue to be an organization in search of an adequate organizational model.

Compared to 20 years ago when we first analysed the OECD, the context of knowledge production seems to be markedly different. Rather than discussing scientization and de-politization, today we more often speak about politicization, polarization, securitization and all kinds of political framing that strategically promote a particular problem definition, causal interpretation, moral evaluation and treatment recommendations (Voltolini et al., 2020). This trend may moreover undermine public trust and confidence in the value of science and knowledge in policymaking (Feine and Jakubovics, 2021; Kabat, 2017). In such a context, it may not be viable for the OECD to turn to a back-to-basics scenario in which the *raison d'être* for the organization is to produce independent knowledge. Another scenario, therefore, might be to locate this global multi-organization in a scenario in which its mission number one becomes to serve as an enthusiastic secretariat for the G20 and as a willing supplier of analysis to whomever is willing to pay. In such a scenario the organization has taken the final step away from the dreams and ambitions of its first Secretary-General, Thorkil Kristensen (1961–1969) (Kristensen, 1989), whom – to the surprise of many observers at the time – used the momentum of the foundational period to build an independent transnational research institution (Sjöstedt, 1973: 200–201).

REFERENCES

Ansell, Christopher (2004), 'Territoriality, authority, and democracy', in Christopher Ansell and Giuseppe Di Palma (eds) *Restructuring Territoriality*, Cambridge: Cambridge University Press.

Barnett, Michael and Martha Finnemore (2004), *Rules for The World,* Ithaca: Cornell University Press.

Beyers, Jan (2010), 'Conceptual and methodological challenges in the study of European socialization', *Journal of European Public Policy* 17(6): 909–20.

Biermann, Frank and Bernd Siebenhuner (2009), *Managers of Global Change*, Cambridge, Mass.: The MIT Press.

Biermann, Frank and Bernd Siebenhuner (2013), 'Problem solving by international bureaucracies: the influence of international secretariats on world politics', in Bob Reinalda (ed) *Routledge Handbook of International Organization*, London and New York: Routledge.

Checkel, Jeffrey T. (2007), 'International institutions and socialization in Europe: Introduction and framework', in Jeffrey T. Checkel (ed) *International Institutions and Socialization in Europe*, Cambridge: Cambridge University Press.

Christensen, Tom and Per Lægreid (eds) (2007), *Transcending New Public Management*, Aldershot: Ashgate.

Christensen, Tom and Per Lægreid (eds) (2011), *The Ashgate Research Companion to New Public Management*, Aldershot: Ashgate.

Cockett, Richard (1994), *Thinking the Unthinkable: Think-Tanks and the Economic Counter-Revolution, 1931–1983*, London: Harper Collins.

Cox, Robert W. and Harold K. Jacobson (1973), *The Anatomy of Influence*, New Haven: Yale University Press.

Egeberg, Morten (ed) (2006), *Multilevel Union Administration*, London: Palgrave Macmillan.

Egeberg, Morten and Jarle Trondal (2018), *An Organizational Approach to Public Governance*, Oxford: Oxford University Press.

Ellis, David C. (2011), 'The organizational turn in international organization theory', *Theorizing International Organizations* http://journal-iostudies.org/sites/default/files/2020-01/JIOS1012.pdf accessed 18 April 2023.

Feine, Jocelyn and Nicholas Jakubovics (2021), 'Science in the spotlight: A crisis of confidence'? *JDR Clinical & Translational Research*, 6(1): 4–7.

Gehring, Thomas (2003), 'International institutions as decision-making systems. Lessons from the European Union', paper presented at the 8th Biennial International Conference of the European Studies Association, Nashville, TN.

Gulick, Luther (1937), 'Notes on the theory of organizations. With special references to government in the United States', in Luther Gulick and L. Urwick (eds) *Papers on the Science of Administration*, New York: Institute of Public Administration, Columbia University.

Hay, Colin (2007), *Why We Hate Politics*, London: Polity Press.

Hupe, Peter and Arthur Edwards (2012), 'The accountability of power: Democracy and governance in modern times', *European Political Science Review* 4(2): 177–94.

Haas, Ernst (1990), *When Knowledge Is Power. Three Models of Change in International Organizations*, Berkeley: University of California Press.

Haas, Peter (1992), 'Epistemic communities and international policy coordination', *International Organization* 46(1): 1–35.

Joerges, Christian (1999), 'Bureaucratic nightmare, technocratic regime and the dream of good transnational governance', in Christian Joerges and Ellen Vos (eds), *EU Committees: Social Regulation, Law and Politics*, Oxford: Hart Publishing.

Joerges, Christian, Karl-Heiz Ladeur and E. Vos (eds) (1997), *Integrating Scientific Expertise into Regulatory Decision-Making*, Baden-Baden: Nomos.

Johnston, Donald (1999), 'Globalize or fossilise', *OECD-Observer*, no. 2019, December.

Kabat, Geoffrey C. (2017), 'Taking distrust of science seriously: to overcome public distrust in science, scientists need to stop pretending that there is a scientific consensus on controversial issues when there is not', EMBO Report, 18(7): 1052–5.

Kassim, Hussein, Sara Connolly, Renaud Dehousse, Oliver Rozenberg and Selma Bendjaballah (2016), 'Managing the house: the Presidency, agenda control and policy activism in the European Commission', *Journal of European Public Policy* 24(5): 654–74.

Knill, Christoph and Michael W. Bauer (2016), 'Policy-making by international public administrations: concepts, causes and consequences', *Journal of European Public Policy* 23(7): 949–59.

Knill, Christoph, Steffen Eckhard and Stephen Gros (2016), 'Administrative styles in the European Commission and the OSCE secretariat: striking similarities despite different organizational settings', *Journal of European Public Policy* 23(7): 1057–76.

Kristensen, Thorkil (1989), *Erindringer*, Odense: Odense Universitetsforlag.

Lacey, Hugh (2016), 'Science, respect for nature, and human well-being: democratic values and the responsibilities of scientists today', *Foundations of Science* (21)1: 51–67.

Leruth, Benjamin, Stefan Gänzle and Jarle Trondal (eds) (2022), *The Routledge Handbook of Differentiation in the European Union*, London: Routledge.

Levi-Faur, David (ed) (2012), *The Oxford Handbook of Governance*, Oxford: Oxford University Press.

Lipsky, Michael (1980), *Street-Level Bureaucracy*, New York: Russel Sage Foundation.

Marcussen, Martin (2002a), *OECD og idéspillet: Game Over?* Copenhagen: Hans Reitzels Forlag

Marcussen, Martin (2002b), 'OECD's demokratiske forpligtelse', *Udenrigs* 57(2): 33–8.

Marcussen, Martin (2004a), 'Multilateral surveillance and the OECD: Playing the idea-game', in Klaus Armingeon and Michelle Beyeler (eds), *The OECD and European Welfare States*, Cheltenham, UK: Edward Elgar Publishing, pp. 13–31.

Marcussen, Martin (2004b), 'The OECD as ideational artist and arbitrator: Reality or dream?', in Bob Reinalda and Bertjan Verbeek (eds), *Decision Making Within International Organizations*, London: Routledge, pp. 90–106.

Marcussen, Martin (2004c), 'OECD governance through soft law', in Ulrika Mörth (ed), *Soft Law in Governance and Regulation: An Interdisciplinary Analysis*, Cheltenham, UK: Edward Elgar Publishing, pp. 103–28.

Marcussen, Martin (2010), 'Scientization', in Tom Christensen and Per Lægreid (eds), *Ashgate Research Companion to New Public Management*, Aldershot: Ashgate, pp. 321–33.

Marcussen, Martin and Jarle Trondal (2011), 'The OECD civil servant: Caught between Scylla and Charybdis, *Review of International Political Economy* 18(5): 592–621.

Moravcsik, Andrew (1999), 'A new statecraft? Supranational entrepreneurs and international coopera-tion', *International Organization* 53(2): 267–306.

Mudge, Stephanie L. and Antoine Vauchez (2017), 'Fielding supranationalism: The European Central Bank as a field effect', *The Sociology Review* 64(2): 146–69.

Neely, Andy (1999), 'The performance measurement revolution: Why now and what next?', *International Journal of Operations & Production Management* 19(2): 205–28.

Nye, Robert O. (1975), 'International organization and the crisis of interdependence', *International Organization* 29(2): 357–65.

OECD (2001), 'Staff Profile Statistics 2000', C(2001)129, Paris: OECD.

OECD (2011), 'Staff Profile Statistics 2010', C(2011)39, Paris: OECD.

OECD (2021), 'Staff Profile Statistics 2020', C(2021)54, Paris: OECD.

Olsen, Johan P. (2005), 'Unity and diversity – European style', ARENA working paper 24.

Olsen, Johan P. (2006), 'Maybe it is time to rediscover bureaucracy', *Journal of Public Administration Research and Theory* 16(1): 1–24.

Olsen, Johan P. (2009), 'Democratic government, institutional autonomy and the dynamics of change', *West European Politics* 32(3): 439–65.

Olsen, Johan P. (2010), *Governing Through Institutional Building*, Oxford: Oxford University Press.

Page, Edward C. (1992), *Political Authority and Bureaucratic Power*, New York: Harvester Wheatsheaf.

Radin, Beryl A. (2012), *Federal Management Reform*, Washington DC: Georgetown University Press.

Reinalda, Bob (2013), 'International organization as a field of research since 1910', in Bob Reinalda (ed), *Routledge Handbook of International Organization*, London and New York: Routledge.

Schattschneider, E.E. (1975), *The Semisovereign People*, Fort Worth: Harcourt Brace Jovanovich College Publishers.

Simon, Herbert A. (1965), *Administrative Behavior,* New York: The Free Press.

Sjöstedt, Gunnar (1973), *OECD-samarbetet: funktioner och* effekter, SU, Statsvetenskapliga Inst., Stockholm Political Studies 3, Stockholm.

Trondal, Jarle (2013), 'International bureaucracy: organizational structure and behavioural implications', in Bob Reinalda (ed), *Routledge Handbook of International Organization*, London and New York: Routledge.

Trondal, Jarle (2014), 'Agencification', *Public Administration Review* 74(4): 545–49.

Trondal, Jarle, Martin Marcussen and Frode Veggeland (2005), 'Re-Discovering International Executive Institutions', *Comparative European Politics* 3(2): 232–58.

Trondal, Jarle, Martin Marcussen, Torbjörn Larsson and Frode Veggeland (2010), *Unpacking International Organisations. Dynamics of Compound Bureaucracies*, Manchester: Manchester University Press.

Trondal, Jarle, Zuzana Murdoch and Benny Geys (2015), 'Representative bureaucracy and the role of expertise in politics', *Politics and Governance* 3(1): 26–36.

Verhoest, Koen, Paul G. Roness, Bram Verschuere, Kristin Rubecksen and Muiris MacCarthaigh (2010), *Autonomy and Control of State Agencies*, Houndmills: Palgrave Macmillan.

Verhoest, Koen, Sandra Van Thiel, Geert Bouckaert and Per Lægreid (2012), *Government Agencies*, Houndmills: Palgrave Macmillan.

Voltolini, Benedetta, Michal Natorski and Colin Hay (2020), 'Introduction: The politicisation of permanent crisis in Europe', *Journal of European Integration*, 42(5): 609–24.

Weber, Max (1924), 'Legitimate Authority and Bureaucracy', in Derek S. Pugh (ed), *Organization Theory. Selected Readings*, London: Penguin Books.

Weber, Max (1983), *On Capitalism, Bureaucracy and Religion*, Glasgow: Harper Collins Publishers.

Yi-Chong, Xu and Patrick Weller (2004), *The Governance of World Trade. International Civil Servants and the GATT/WTO*, Cheltenham: Edward Elgar.

Yi-Chong, Xu and Patrick Weller (2008), 'To be, but not to be seen: Exploring the impact of civil servants', *Public Administration* 86(1): 35–51.

8. The OECD in the ecosystem of international organization

Diane Stone

INTRODUCTION

The OECD is an inter-governmental organization made up of member states. Generally, discussion of this organization has focused on its interactions and initiatives with other states. However, the OECD also interacts extensively with other international organizations (IOs), and these IOs are both formal and informal in design and constitution. Over the past 30 years the ecosystem of IOs has diversified and grown and the OECD has adapted with these changes in its organizational environment.

As discussed in Chapter 9, the OECD has pioneered peer-to-peer review: That is, diffusing policy tools and transferring governance knowledge through international teams of experts and experienced bureaucrats who examine and assess the public performance of another state with the ultimate goal of helping the reviewed state improve its policy making, adopt best practices, and comply with established standards and principles (see also Pal, 2019). By contrast, this chapter will examine why and how an international organization like the OECD builds its authority beyond international *policy coordination* among nation-states to expand and bolster international *rule-making* in conjunction with other international organizations. Through their partnerships, joint-funding or collective action with other international bodies like the World Bank and United Nations (UN) agencies or bodies like the World Meterological Organization, the OECD's inter-relationships with other IOs helps create the rules and standards that feed into wider processes of global and regional governance.

A note on terminology is needed here on three counts. First, rather than the phrase 'global governance', the cognate phrase 'transnational governance' is used in this chapter. The latter puts greater emphasis on the governing roles of non-state actors. This perspective becomes relevant in the last third of the chapter. Both 'global governance' and 'transnational governance' are broader conceptual categories and sets of practices than the OECD's preference for the term 'international rule making' (IRM).

Second, IRM can be thought as a sub-set of global governance and regional regulatory processes as it is focused upon agreements between states. That is, IRM is primarily 'transgovernmental' in character. This accords with the focus of the OECD as an entity primarily concerned with 'modernising the state' (De Francesco and Guaschino, 2020: 122).

Third, 'formal international organization' is a traditional treaty based intergovernmental organization (FIGO). By contrast, 'informal international organization' (IIGO) are said to fall between norms and FIGOs on the spectrum of IOs with looser more flexible organizational formats and legal status. 'IIGOs are based on *recurrent meetings among high-level state representatives* but are *not legalized through a treaty* and have *no permanent secretariat*' (Vabulas and Snidal, 2021: 859). In its publications and deliberations, the OECD uses the term 'international organization' to refer to both FIGO and IIGO. Nevertheless, it is important to maintain the distinctions of these terms as power and authority are wielded in quite different ways in each.

The role of IOs in what the OECD refers to as 'international rule making' has been a key concern of the Organization. In 2014, it launched a voluntary partnership convening some 50 secretariats of IOs to promote and debate the requirements for greater quality, effectiveness and impact of international rules, irrespective of their substantive scope. Known as the IO Partnership, the data and documentation presented by this initiative demonstrates the vast arsenal of policy tools and instruments used both individually and collectively by IOs. However, this initiative also serves to highlight the OECD's key convening role among other IO Secretariats to facilitate the exchange of information and peer learning in 'international rule making'.

The chapter proceeds in two steps. First, in the bulk of the discussion, the chapter addresses the concept of transgovernmentalism. This dynamic has three interconnected dimensions; (i) horizontal relations of government actors between states, (ii) vertical transgovernmentalism when an IO, like the OECD, act as interlocutors between states, and (iii) the less frequently analysed set of direct horizontal relationships of IO to IO in policy coordination.

Second, the chapter distinguishes between traditional intergovernmental international organization, of which the OECD is an exemplar, to look at the way in which the Organization interacts, or does not interact, with the burgeoning growth of *informal* international organizations like the Group of Twenty (G20) and the BRICs. Here the chapter moves towards a more expansive understanding of 'international organization' to address the ways in which the OECD intersects with or becomes involved in multi-stakeholder partnerships and other forms of policy cooperation and joint initiative with transnational private actors. The OECD's preference for IRM is symptomatic of it being 'country driven' (Zapp, 2021).

THE OECD'S TRANSGOVERNMENTAL RELATIONS WITH IOs

For decades, the OECD has been working with many other IOs. For instance, various units of the OECD work with the International Monetary Fund (IMF) on national growth strategies, with the International Labour Office (ILO) on matters of youth employment, with the World Bank (WB) and United Nations Development Programme (UNDP) as well as other international organizations in the field of development, with the International Energy Agency (IEA) on fossil fuels, and with the World Trade Organization (WTO) monitoring investment and trade, or yet again the Bank of International Settlements (BIS) on external debt of countries.[1] These forms of interaction are to be expected. The world of IOs is a relatively small one, collaboration is a necessity. Even so, the examples mentioned above are some large, well-known multi-purpose IOs – the tip of the iceberg of the IO ecosystem – whereas the majority of IOs are much smaller entities usually with a highly specialized policy focus and mission or operating in specific regions and localities.

Accordingly, the nature of interaction also varies in line with the different types of IO as well as their different missions. There are various forms of cooperation such as engineered through 'Letters of Intent', 'Memorandum of Understandings', or 'Statements of Cooperation'

---

[1]   https://www.oecd.org/g20/about/ accessed 19 April 2023.

that outline the guiding principles of partnership and collaboration. These frameworks have enabled the OECD to be involved in joint projects (of both short term or permanent character). For instance, the knowledge partnership such as the 'The Joint BIS-IMF-OECD-World Bank statistics on external debt', to disseminate data on the external debt of developed, developing and transition countries as well as statistics on selected foreign assets. Another tactic is to attain Observer Status within the ambit of other IOs. These horizontal IO initiatives of policy collaboration or coordination between IOs (of either the FIGO or IIGO variety) are best explained by the concept of transgovernmentalism, a concept that the OECD utilizes in its own discourse.

Transgovernmentalism is a contemporary reconfiguration of sovereignty and extension of state power. The concept resists notions that the state is under duress in an era of globalization, and that sovereignty is being shorn. Instead, attention is drawn to forms of official cooperation across borders. For example, networks of judges adjudicating on international tax issues or legislators harmonizing legal standards and regulation on policy issues like insurance, consumer protection and competition law, or procedures for confronting intractable problems like cross-border criminal activity.

In transgovernmental practice, it is important to note that the state remains core as a sovereign actor. Transgovernmental action is delivered by official power holders and government rule makers who derive their authority from their formal posts within the public bureaucracies of their nation-state. The agents in this form of policy coordination are on the one hand, government bureaucrats, judges and state regulators and on the other, international civil servants. These 'trans-governmental interactions are distinct activities' from other forms of global governance 'insofar as they operate exclusive of non-(state) policy officials, are separate from foreign/diplomacy institutions, and deploy collectively their separate domestic formal authorities and resources to achieve common outcomes' (my inclusion, Legrand, 2019: 204). Transgovernmentalism is part of the 'Westphalian imaginary' of the sovereign nation state (Stone, 2019). Classic examples of transgovernmentalism include the Basel Committee on Banking Supervision and the International Organization of Securities Commissions (IOSCO) as well as the OECDs peer review processes.

Often transgovernmental strategies take a network form of organization. Indeed, the OECD describes transgovernmental networks as 'cooperation based on loosely-structured, peer-to-peer ties developed *through frequent interaction* rather than formal negotiation, involving specialized domestic officials (typically regulators) directly interacting with each other' (my italics, OECD, 2019). For example, the European Public Administration Network (EUPAN) composed of the Directors General responsible for Public Administration in the Member States of the EU. It exists as an informal network without a secretariat or its own budget but has a 30-year history with its bi-annual meeting institutionalizing in step with the rotation of the Presidency of the Council of the European Communities (see Demmke, 2017). EUPAN creation and consolidation has lead to some blurring of boundaries of this network with that of the OECD-Public Employment and Management (PEM) committee. The PEM Working Group is also transgovernmental. It is a collaborative forum for those engaged with civil service management responsibility in public sector entities to address PEM and human resource management issues.

While these network relations are managed between government agencies, the degree of informality and the socialization function that comes from 'frequent interactions' – not only via newsletters and professional websites, in conferences and training activities but also in weekly or monthly (zoom) meetings and email traffic – of everyday work practices, is not to be underestimated. It is in this lengthy quote that the value of professional networking of civil servants is captured:

> In contrast to the political élite and diplomats, civil servants represent the part of the public sector with which citizens have contact and thus help shape citizens' perceptions as to how a political system functions ... It is often up to civil servants to decide 'how policy should be constructed and how public goods and services should be delivered' ... They directly influence the operation of a system and are crucial actors for both the stabilization of a regime and the consolidation of institutions ... In such a way, regular and sustained sharing of best practices within networks might directly impact civil servants' practices, and, therefore, be reflected in states' performance in the corresponding field. After all, it is not states or regimes as unitary entities that interpret and implement legislation on an everyday basis, but individual public servants. (Shyrokykh, 2019: 154)

The most common form of transgovernmentalism is this horizontal mode of policy coordination *between states*. Examples can be found in Chapters 9 and 11 of this Companion.

Vertical transgovernmentalism involves policy coordination between states and IOs. (It can also involve IOs interacting with subnational units such as cities, regions or federal units – a topic this chapter cannot address.) This has also been called 'up-loading' and 'down-loading'. However, vertical and horizontal modes of transgovernmentalism are not easily separable. Instead, they form the warp and weft of international policy coordination.

Another form of transgovernmentalism that has so far received little academic attention are the policy coordination initiatives jointly instigated by IOs. The OECD transgovernmental policy innovations include initiatives like Tax Inspectors Without Borders (TIWB). This was a horizontal FIGO to FIGO initiative launched in mid 2015 by the OECD in conjunction with UNDP to strengthen developing countries' auditing capacity as well as multinational compliance on tax matters. Through TIWB platform, audit norms, principles for criminal tax investigations, and effective practices for the 'effective use of automatically exchanged information' are downloaded to developing countries via tax experts who work on real time audits employing a 'learning by doing' approach. This is OECD (and UNDP) promotion of policy transfer which is done transgovernmentally. When non-state actors become involved (as they often do), the policy transfer becomes transnational in character. Some have suggested, however, that OECD's extensive involvement in international tax issues has meant that incrementally over time the Organization 'is in the gradual process of transformation into an international tax organization' (Tychmanska, 2021).

A second case of a formal FIGO-to-FIGO relationship is that of SIGMA.[2] Better known by its acronym, *Support for Improvement in Governance and Management* is a joint initiative of the OECD and the European Union that was initially directed towards post-Soviet transition countries (Hadjiisky, 2017). SIGMA's website indicates it was designed to spread best practices in public administration in order 'to build the capacities of the public sector, enhancing horizontal governance and improving the design and implementation of public administration reforms, including proper prioritisation, sequencing and budgeting'. For instance, it has played a critical role in the spread and development of procurement policies (Ladi and Tsarouhas, 2017). Today, the programme continues to work with EU candidate countries providing the expertise and recommendations, training and workshops, legal frameworks and methodologies

---

[2]   SIGMA: http://www.sigmaweb.org/about/ acccessed 19 April 2023.

'to partner administrations in transition to help them create a stable democracy and access the benefits of a free market economy'. Three decades following SIGMA's work, the traction of its advice and recommendation has come under serious question given the back sliding and resistance if not outright rejection of some EU accession requirements by illiberal governments such as Hungary and Poland.

The OECDs engagement with the EU through SIGMA, is symptomatic of other regional networks, in different guises, which have now consolidated over the decades. For instance, the OECD Southeast Asia Regional Programme or the MENA-OECD Initiative on Governance and Competitiveness for Development. Known collectively as the Comprehensive Regional Programmes, these are designed to 'strengthen the relevance and the impact of OECD activities at a global level'. Again, it is a case of the OECD working 'with governments ... through regional initiatives and activities ... in order to facilitate policy benchmarking and the exchange of good practices within and across regions'.[3]

A third case of what appears to be an increasingly important focus of activity for OECD, is the OECD acting as the convenor of the 'IO Partnership'. This is a clear-cut example of horizontal transgovernmentalism operating primarily between IOs (rather than between states). Not dissimilar to peer review approaches downloaded to the national level, the IO Partnership is an information gathering instrument for the purpose of collective action among IOs to to improve transparency, inclusiveness, impact and coherence of international rule making practices. Towards this end, the Partnership created in 2021 a *Compendium of IO Practices for Effective International Rulemaking* which aims to provide a practical tool and guidance to support IO secretariats in ensuring the transparency, quality and impact of their international instruments, and thus help build confidence of national policymakers in the international instruments they adopt.[4]

The value of IO to IO communication and cooperation is multi-faceted, according to the organizations associated with this initiative. The IO Partnership represents an opportunity to 'cooperate on a larger scale' compared to bilateral agreements between states. IO transgovernmental cooperation offers 'platforms for continuous dialogue on and anticipation of new issues, help establish a common language; facilitate the comparability of approaches and practices; develop international legal and policy instruments; and offer resolution mechanisms in case of disputes' (OECD, 2019: 1). This initiative is also indicative of the OECD reinventing itself as a 'scientific knowledge hub' in its ongoing quest for status and legitimacy in the IO ecosystem (Zapp, 2021).

In this convening activity, the term 'international rule making' is predominant. This is defined as 'encompassing the entire rulemaking cycle from the design and development of international instruments to their implementation and enforcement' (OECD, 2019: 1). The phrase 'global governance' is scarcely seen. Instead, there tends only to be reference to a 'globalised economy'. The idea of transnationalism is nowhere to be found in OECD documents despite the Organization's proclamation to be a 'global policy forum'.

Arising from this focus upon 'international instruments' and supporting 'international regulatory cooperation' among member states, the IO Partnership is less observant of the

---

    3   https://www.oecd.org/global-relations/keypartners/#d.en.194387 accessed 1 August 2021.
    4   From the Summary notes of the September 2020 meeting of the IO Partnership: https://www
.oecd.org/gov/regulatory-policy/7th-annual-meeting-of-international-organisations-list-of-participants
-executive-summary.pdf accesssed 19 April 2023.

roles and responsibilities of non-state actors in transnational governance, perhaps to a greater extent than some other IOs. For example, the WB and UN agencies are heavily reliant on their partners in the business sector or in civil society for the implementation of their programs. By contrast, the OECD has a stronger normative and standard setting role with fewer resources and financial instruments at its disposal to undertake operational objectives in-country. The OECD persuades and promotes ideas rather than imposing pressure for policy reforms. Accordingly, broadcasting its terminology underscores the persuasive power of the ideas and values attached to those terms.

INFORMAL INTERNATIONAL ORGANIZATION AND MULTI-STAKEHOLDER INITIATIVES

The individuals and organizations associated with the IO Partnership are among the first to recognize and agree that the term 'international organization' is rife with different meanings. Discussion of the meaning and types of international organization is as much a policy driven debate (OECD, 2019) as it is a scholarly one (inter alia, Vabulas and Snidal, 2021). With the OECD as the main driver behind this partnership, the objectives and operations of the IO Partnership provides good insight into how the OECD views its own relations with other IOs. OECD is one of the lead organizations, heading one of the five focal points of actions: Enhancing understanding of the variety of international instruments.

In its 2014–15 survey of 50 IOs, the Partnership developed four categories of international organization:

- 32 IGOs – inter-governmental organizations. IGOs are created by a treaty or another kind of legal instrument that is government by international law and which gives the IO its own legal personality. IGO members are primarily states but can include other IGOs and very occasionally non-state actors. This type of IO developed rapidly in the 1950s and 1960s.
- nine transgovernmental networks. TGNs are more recent organizations that differ from IGOs in terms of their membership, legal basis nature of their decisions. That is, non legally binding decisions that generally rely on member agencies to implement within their jurisdiction. Typically, network members are specialised units of regulatory agencies or government ministries. TGNs are established through voluntary agreements and function through regularised, albeit loosely structured, peer-to-peer connections.
- five private standard setting organizations. These are generally created under domestic law and composed of non-governmental actors as well as of governmental agencies.
- four secretariats of international conventions.

Notwithstanding the above categorization, the partners are not wedded to it. There is an understanding within the IO Partnership that there are ongoing innovations in international organization formats. There are IOs with some non-state members, this is particularly the case with IIGOs. The categories are not watertight nor are they meant to be. Instead, the phrase 'ecosystem' is often seen among IO Partnership documents to emphasize the dynamic characteristics of IOs and their evolution. In this ecosystem, the OECD is a classic FIGO.

The international organizations who participated in the 2015 Survey have produced a total of some 70 000 legal and policy instruments (OECD, 2019, 9). However, the effectiveness of these instruments, and the quality and consistency of cooperation among IOs to ensure compliance and/or implementation of international rule making is matter of concern for the IO Partnership and regarded as a field where there is considerable potential for improvement. In this regard, the OECD's position has been to point to the ongoing and essential relevance of IO member states. The quality of international instruments is ultimately a shared responsibility between the international and the national levels. IO rules are given effect through national implementation and impacts materialise to a large extent locally and co-ordination among IOs is often a function of alignment across policy communities at national level (OECD, 2019: 9).

However, the 'OECD Monitoring of Country Practices to Account for International Considerations in National Rulemaking' that took place in conjunction with the 2018 *OECD Regulatory Policy Outlook*, exhorted: 'Greater transfer of expertise and of evidence between the national and the international levels would support a better understanding of the impacts of international instruments and build a better evidence base across countries and IOs' (OECD, 2019: 10). In other words, the OECDs approach to partnerships of IOs, improved cooperation and enhanced coordination has been mostly transgovernmental.

The OECDs standard operating procedures have very much characterized the form of operation of the IO Partnership. For instance, the analytical work of the IO Partnership follows 'OECD's long-standing method of peer exchange and evidence based analysis' (OECD, 2019: 19). The other two pillars of the IO Partnership's 'Structured Framework' of activities – peer learning and exchange alongside identification of good practices – are also templated on OECD standard operating procedures of technical expertise and advice (De Francesco and Guaschino, 2020). This might be thought of as another form of policy transfer of operational procedures and practices into the new partnership entity. Additionally, this transfer process for interoperability between IOs might possibly be a reason why it is less evident how and when the OECD interacts with – or rather less inclined to interact with – the new species of international organization that take a more informal structure than the classic style treaty-based IO or FIGO.

The new breed of informal international organization tend to be smaller and leaner IOs. Although there are exceptions, informal IOs are not treaty based and generally do not operate with a permanent secretariat. Prominent examples include global entities like The Group of 20 (G20) and the BRICS but there are also more regionally discrete and issue specific bodies like the Visegrad Four in Central and Eastern Europe as well as the Human Security Network promoting the abolishment of antipersonnel mines or the Montreux Document Forum articulating good practices for private security companies during armed conflict (Vabulas and Snidal, 2021).

In the case of the G20, for example, which emerged in the wake of the global financial crisis of 2008, the OECD is a 'strategic partner of the G20' participating in G20 meetings not only at the highest political level (Leaders, Ministers, Sherpas, Finance Deputies) but also at the technical level (Working Groups and notably the WG on Bribery) with data, analytical reports, policy recommendations and standards on matters such as women and youth unemployment, on social protection, in harnessing the opportunities afforded by digitalization as well as on the trade, taxation and investment agendas. For instance, the OECD Secretary-General participates in the G20 Summits while the OECD Chief Economist represents the OECD at Finance Deputies meetings.[5] A prominent example of cooperation are the 'G20/OECD Principles of

---

[5]   https://www.oecd.org/g20/ accessed 19 April 2023.

Corporate Governance' designed to help policy makers evaluate and improve the legal, regulatory, and institutional framework for corporate governance.

The OECD has an extensive interest in, and engagement with, the G20. However, the same cannot be said of its relations with BRICS as an association. Instead, Brazil, China, India, Indonesia, and South Africa have been designated as the OECD's 'Key Partners'. That is, the OECD interacts with them at the nation-state level, or through various regional programmes rather than through an IIGO like BRICS.

This is not to say that OECD is averse to informality as an organizing principle. The OECD is responsible for creating informal bodies and networks. For example, a case of an OECD FIGO to IIGO relationship, is the Sahel and West Africa Club (SWAC).[6] The Secretariat of SWAC is hosted by the OECD. SWAC is an independent, international platform to improve the regional governance of food and nutrition security as well as to promote understanding of transformations in the region and their policy implications through regional, spatial and forward-looking analyses.

There are also 15 'Global Forums created and convened by the OECD.[7] A Global Forum is a framework for policy dialogues with various communities of stakeholders that are not necessarily member country governmental dialogues. For example, the Global Forum on Nuclear Education, Science, Technology and Policy is the most recently created in 2021 and it brings in the 'non-state' stakeholder group of academia. These Global Forums enable the OECD to enhance the relevance and expand the reach of its standards. That is, help foster convergence of views by a broad range of relevant players. The OECD Global Forum on the Future of Education and Skills 2030 is an international multi-stakeholder platform for educational policy communities active in the area of curriculum design and implementation. It brings together policy makers, curriculum implementers (teachers, teacher educators), students, thought leaders and social partners to foster regular sharing of experiences and good practice, as well as mutual learning and convergence of views on the future of education and skills.

In other words, the OECD's approach to informal action is one that is managed through its existing institutional structures and initiated from within the OECD house. As a traditional intergovernmental treaty-based organization, the OECD is necessarily focused upon member states and international rule making. By contrast, the concept of transnational governance affords greater scope for private actors playing roles in the design, delivery or evaluation of not only the 'international rules' developed by governments and international organizations but also becoming part of the logic and practice of policy making in nascent domains of transnational administration.

This category of international organization is known by a number of different labels – reflecting both the diversity of these organizations but also different disciplinary perspectives from academia. Multi-stakeholder initiatives is common parlance in the UN system but they are also referred to as 'global and regional programs' in the World Bank, or 'global public policy networks' and 'transnational public private partnerships' in the academic literature (Stone, 2019). The point of commonality among these labels for what are a diverse range of organizations is that they incorporate private sector, civil society actors and other relevant non-state actors in governance design and implementation. They are yet another type of IO in

---

[6]   https://www.oecd.org/swac/aboutus/ accessed 19 April 2023.
[7]   https://www.oecd.org/global-relations/globalforums/ accessed 19 April 2023.

the ecosystem. Importantly, they are not only a smaller and more issue specific type of organization but also a faster growing form of IO than FIGO.

The OECD's Development Assistance Committee (DAC) is the key unit for engagement with developing countries, bilateral providers of development cooperation and international organizations but also civil society, the private sector, trade unions and private philanthropy. Its 'Global Strategy' (OECD, 2018: 11) outlines the important fora for policy dialogue for DAC to interact with development stakeholders in the United Nations system and the Global Partnership for Effective Development Co-operation (GPEDC) and its various voluntary initiatives, the International Dialogue on Peacebuilding and Statebuilding and the Effective Institutions Platform. One of the main vehicles for OECD engagement is Partnership for Policy Coherence and Sustainable Development which is linked to Principle 17 of the Sustainable Development Goals (SDGs). It brings together governments and IOs with civil society, think tanks, private sector actors and other stakeholders.[8]

In another unit (with a similar name to DAC), the OECD Development Centre hosts, netFWD. The Network of Foundations Working for Development is a venue for philanthropic foundations to meet policy makers as well as partners in multilateral organizations. It is a much looser network structure than an IIGO but is indicative of many of the networks the OECD cultivates and in the case of netFWD, hosts. Likewise, the Multilateral Organisation Performance Assessment Network (MOPAN) is hosted by the OECD's Development Co-operation Directorate but it was originally established as an informal entity aiming to exchange information. A permanent secretariat was created in 2013 through a formal Hosting Arrangement with the OECD. Such evolutions in the life of individual IOs signal the diversity of the ecosystem.

CONCLUSION

The OECD is an IO found within a diverse ecosystem of international organizations that range from formal/public/official forms of international organization at one end of an organizational spectrum towards mixed/hybrid/partially private IOs such as multi-stakeholder initiatives at the other end. Understanding and mapping the range of roles and responsibilities of the OECD in conjunction with other international organizations hinges on the definition of international organization adopted. Accordingly, this chapter has sought to unpack the idea of IO to show that the OECD's language of, and interest in, 'international rule making' very much accords with an older understanding or classic definition of IO that focuses on FIGO.

This chapter has focused primarily upon the transgovernmental relations of the OECD with both member states and with other IOs. This accords with the Organization's legal personality as well as its international perspective and transgovernmental mode of operation. The OECD does not have the power or resources, nor perhaps the desire, to act as a transnational institution with interoperability protocols with governance actors from global civil society. While those in the OECD are cognizant of their operating environment and recognize that 'IO' is a rapidly evolving category of organization, nevertheless, the primary type of IO that OECD engages with are the classic treaty-based bodies. Rather than being a 'global actor' in the sense that the EU (Ladi and Tsarouhas, 2017) or the World Bank are often tagged, the OECD works

---

[8]   https://community.oecd.org/community/pcsdpartnership accessed 19 April 2023.

primarily with 'member countries' and is best thought of as a traditional 'international actor' in the ecosystem of international organizations rather than a transnational policy player.

BIBLIOGRAPHY

Demmke, C. (2017). 'The European Public Administration Network (EUPAN): which contribution to the informal civil service cooperation in the EU?' *Revue française d'administration publique, 161*, 31–44. https://doi.org/10.3917/rfap.161.0031 accessed 19 April 2023.

De Francesco, F. and Guaschino, E. (2020). 'Reframing knowledge: A comparison of OECD and World Bank discourse on public governance reform'. *Policy and Society, 39*(1), 113–128.

Hadjiisky, M. (2017). 'SIGMA: An international program of administrative capacity building in European lands (1992–2012)'. *Revue française dadministration publique*, (1), 73–88.

Haines, A. (2020). James Karanja reflects on five years of Tax Inspectors Without Borders. *International Tax Review.*

Ladi, S. and Tsarouhas, D. (2017). 'International diffusion of regulatory governance: EU actorness in public procurement'. *Regulation & Governance, 11*(4), 388–403.

Legrand, T. (2019). 'Sovereignty renewed: transgovernmental policy networks and the global-local dilemma', in Stone, D., and Moloney, K. (eds) *The Oxford Handbook of Global Policy and Transnational Administration*. Oxford: Oxford University Press.

OECD (2018). Revison of the DAC Global Relations Strategy, item 5 of the Draft Annotated Agenda for the DAC meeting of 6 June 2018 [DCD/DAC/A(2018)8]. https://one.oecd.org/document/DCD/DAC(2018)21/En/pdf accessed 4 May 2023.

OECD (2019). The contribution of international organizations to a rules based international system: Key results from the partnership of international organisations for effective rulemaking, April https://www.oecd.org/gov/regulatory-policy/IO-Rule-Based%20System.pdf accessed 19 April 2023.

Pal, Leslie (2019). 'Standard setting and international peer review: The OECD as a Transnational policy actor', in Diane Stone and Kim Moloney (eds) *The Oxford Handbook of Global Policy and Transnational Administration*, OUP.

Shyrokykh, Karina (2019). 'Policy-specific effects of transgovernmental cooperation: a statistical assessment across the EU's post-Soviet neighbours', I, *26*(1): 149–168.

Stone, D. (2019). *Global Policy Making*, Cambridge University Press.

Tychmanska, A. (2021). 'The OECD as the future international tax organization: An inevitable course of events?'. *Intertax, 49*(8/9).

Vabulas, F. and Snidal, D. (2021). 'Cooperation under autonomy: Building and analyzing the Informal Intergovernmental Organizations 2.0 dataset.' *Journal of Peace Research 58*(4): 859–869.

Zapp, M. (2021). 'The authority of science and the legitimacy of international organisations: OECD, UNESCO and World Bank in global education governance.' *Compare: A Journal of Comparative and International Education 51*(7): 1022–1041.

9. Peer reviews

Thomas Conzelmann

INTRODUCTION

The OECD utilizes peer reviews in most of the policy domains where it has competences. Building on the idea of peer learning, mutual transparency and the search for best practices, peer reviews aim at the alignment of member state policies with international standards. The present chapter discusses how peer reviews may create effects at the domestic level and probes into three examples of peer review in the OECD, covering the fields of economic, development, and anti-corruption policies. The comparison between these different peer reviews shows the versatility of the instrument and the different compliance logics that it can employ. Critics of peer reviews refer to limited effectiveness in triggering policy alignment. This may overlook the important indirect effects of peer reviews. Challenges for peer reviews in the OECD are high administrative workload and the organization's growing and increasingly diverse membership. The comparison with peer reviews outside the OECD shows that the relatively small and homogeneous membership of the OECD and the limited value conflicts between its members allow peer reviews to function well in the Château de la Muette.

THE PEER REVIEW APPROACH

Peer reviews among states are procedures through which information on country performance with respect to certain international standards or rules is evaluated by peer states, with the goal of aligning member state policies with these standards (Pagani, 2002, p. 15). Peer reviews are characterized by a 'soft tripartism' (Dimitropoulos, 2016, p. 292), involving the reviewed state, the 'peers' (i.e., representatives of other states), and the secretariat of the international organization (IO) hosting the peer review. The secretariat draws up reports on member state policies; the 'peers' evaluate and provide recommendations; and the reviewed state is expected to heed the advice. Two further defining principles of peer reviews are reciprocity and recurrence. Reciprocity means that member states alternate in their roles of reviewee and 'peer' reviewer of others, creating a structure of equals. The recurrence of reviews refers to their periodical nature. Reviewed states have to expect a next round in which progress since the last review and compliance with peer recommendations will be in the focus. Both principles imply that a quasi-permanent policy dialogue among the peers is initiated. This sets peer reviews apart from contingent (case-driven) monitoring techniques, such as inspection, verification, or adjudication measures (Pagani and Wellen, 2008, p. 262).

Peer reviews are not formally linked to incentives or sanctions. Rather, they seek to establish 'peer accountability' (Grant and Keohane, 2005) between states that are economically or politically interdependent. Reviewed countries have to explain and justify their policies to the peers, who have the right to help or sometimes pressure the reviewed state to align its policies (also see Gray, 2017; Thygesen, 2008, pp. 137–138). More specifically, peer reviews may generate effects through two distinct mechanisms. The first mechanism concerns learning processes in domestic administrations about international 'best practices' (Bernstein and van der Ven, 2017). Peer reviews involve officials from different departments of the domestic executive, both during the review of one's own country and in the preparation for the review of other countries. Scholars have identified such situations of repeated interactions and dialogue as an important conduit for policy learning and the questioning of domestic policies (Dunlop and Radaelli, 2018; Milewicz and Goodin, 2018). Critical assessments by peers may unsettle established policies and inject new knowledge into the domestic debate; a mechanism that has been called 'democratizing destabilization' by Sabel and Zeitlin (2008).

A second mechanism relates to the social expectation of norm compliance, which may materialize in *'peer pressure'* on the reviewed state to change course. A possible strength of peer reviews is that states may feel a greater obligation to comply with recommendations or demands made by their peers; compared to reviews by external experts or the bureaucracy of an IO.[1] If there is sufficient publicity around the review, parliaments, civil society organizations, and the media may amplify this effect by exerting *public pressure* on recalcitrant states (Carraro, Conzelmann, and Jongen, 2019; Pagani and Wellen, 2008, p. 263). The process may also work in the opposite direction, if peer recommendations empower reform-minded actors in domestic policy struggles, or if reviewed governments utilize peer recommendations to legitimize policy changes that are controversial domestically (Gray, 2017, p. 220; Jongen, 2021, p. 348).

THE OECD AS A PROGENITOR OF PEER REVIEW

An important element that the OECD took over from its predecessor organization was the multilateral surveillance of member state policies (see Chapter 2, this volume). The OEEC had required its member states to report on economic developments and trade liberalization measures, and used the instrument of sending expert teams to countries in economic turmoil, as during the 1950/51 balance of payments crisis in Germany. This approach continued, albeit in a changed form, in the OECD 'peer reviews' of member state economic policies. The work of the OECD Economic and Development Review Committee (EDRC), whose remit was closest to the traditional mandate of the organization, forms the earliest example of modern peer review in the OECD (Gray, 2017; Thygesen, 2008, p. 137). Another early example is the peer review organized by the OECD Development Assistance Committee (DAC) since 1962 (see Chapter 12, this volume). Other peer reviews added later are the Environmental Performance Reviews (Lehtonen, 2007, 2020, see also Chapter 14, this volume), and the peer reviews of the OECD Working Group on Bribery (WGB) (Jongen, 2021). The OECD also hosts a number of special bodies that conduct peer reviews, such as the International Energy Agency (van de Graaf and Lesage, 2009; Lehtonen, 2020) and the Financial Action Task Force (Dimitropoulos, 2016; Nance, 2018).[2] In the vast majority of cases, the standards around

---

[1]   Examples of expert reviews are the monitoring procedures in most UN human rights Treaty Bodies (Carraro 2017) and the PISA reviews of national education policies by the OECD (Chapter 13, this volume).

[2]   This discussion is far from complete. Annexes A and B in Pagani (2002) give an impression of the various forms of peer review and other monitoring and surveillance activities conducted by the OECD.

which peer reviews are organized are non-binding: 'peer review is essentially a compliance instrument used to put soft law into effect' (Paulo and Reisen, 2010, p. 543).

The practical operation of peer reviews can be analysed along the stages that a peer review typically goes through, namely (1) collection of information, (2) evaluation and assessment, and (3) follow-up and dissemination.[3] As shown below for three specific OECD peer reviews, considerable variation can exist concerning both the relative weight of the individual phases and how each phase is organized.

Economics

Over its 60 years of existence, the review of member states' economic policies has been a key task of the OECD (Chapter 17, this volume). The OECD Economics Department and the EDRC both play a key role in the production of the *Economic Surveys*. The reviews focus on adherence to 'broad economic policy principles and best practices that have been developed over the years' (Pagani and Wellen, 2008, p. 266); alongside some more specific standards such as the OECD Jobs Strategy. Each member state is reviewed every 18–24 months.[4] Reviews are conducted by the Economic Counsellors working in the Permanent Representations of member states, while observers from relevant IOs such as the WTO and the World Bank may attend the review meetings of the EDRC.

Collection of information

The review starts with answers by the reviewed state to an extensive questionnaire, which covers a broad range of economic policies and specifically two thematic areas that are of specific interest to the reviewed member and the EDRC membership at large. In addition to the questionnaire, the Economics Department, acting as the 'Secretariat' of the review, conducts its own analyses, usually with the help of other branches of the OECD bureaucracy. To collect further perspectives, the Secretariat organizes a week-long 'structural mission' to the capital, during which government officials, central bank representatives, research institutes and non-state actors are consulted. Based on these various sources of information, the Secretariat prepares a first draft report. After further consultations and factual checks during a second country visit (the 'policy mission'), the draft Economic Survey is produced and distributed to the EDRC members.

Evaluation and assessment

The draft report by the Secretariat not only contains a description of facts, it also identifies weaknesses and potential problems in its so-called 'Assessment and Recommendations' (A&R) section. As stated in the Agreed Principles and Practices of the EDRC, these recommendations 'should be sharply focused, clearly articulated and constructive and should address the key challenges to economic policy'. Moreover, '[i]f in the Secretariat's view, economic trouble may be looming, the Committee expects the Secretariat to be vocal in iden-

---

[3]   This differentiation diverges from the one proposed by Pagani (2002); and Pagani and Wellen (2008, pp. 269–270), who distinguish 'preparatory', 'consultation' and 'assessment' phases.

[4]   https://www.oecd.org/economy/surveys/, accessed 19 April 2023.

tifying prospective problems'.[5] Specifically, the Economic Surveys contain an annex devoted to compliance with the recommendations from the previous review round, to emphasize the importance of implementation of the recommendations.[6]

The draft report and the A&R section are discussed in a day-long plenary review meeting of the EDRC. The session starts with a statement of the reviewed country and comments on the report by two lead reviewers from other member states, followed by observations and questions for clarification by the membership. Observers note that the plenary discussions are relatively frank,[7] and that 'participants do not shy away from voicing concerns and critique' (Schäfer, 2006, p. 74). After the member state interventions, the Secretariat and the reviewed state provide answers to points raised on the floor. The objective of the discussion is to arrive at a consensus view of the quality of the reviewee's economic policies and joint recommendations. At the end of the day, the EDRC chairperson wraps up, including suggested changes to the A&R section, and 'issues on which consensus has not been reached'.[8] These concluding comments form an important element for the subsequent finalization of the report.[9]

While until this stage the review process is largely beyond the control of the reviewed member state, the *published* versions of the Economic Surveys are prepared in bilateral consultations between the secretariat and the reviewed member. These consultations are held for another full day after the EDRC meeting. It is in this stage that 'messages in OECD Economic Surveys may ... be diluted and some issues fudged because of the need to bring also the authorities of the examined country on board' (Thygesen, 2008, p. 144). Such influence by the reviewee is intended to secure 'government "buy-in" to the ... advice offered and hence a common ownership of the product'.[10] The revision of the report can also help to enhance messages that the government wants to convey in the domestic debate. However, the published version of the Survey has to be adopted by the entire EDRC,[11] so that the reviewee cannot simply rewrite the report to its liking. The objective thus is to create a report which is acceptable to both the reviewed country and the EDRC membership, and which at the same time 'contributes to the OECD's ongoing work of defining principles and best practices for economic policy' (Lindstrøm, 2018, p. 23).

Dissemination and follow-up

Final versions of the Economic Surveys are published on the OECD webpage, including the recommendations. The existence of clear recommendations allows both public pressure on the reviewed state, and peer pressure when the Secretariat and the peers review the implementa-

---

[5]   Economic And Development Review Committee, Agreed Principles and Practices, Document ECO/EDR/DIV(2015)1 of 8 June 2015, paras 3.14 and 4.3.

[6]   Para 3.15, Agreed Principles and Practices.

[7]   Own observation of one review session, July 2016. Also see Schäfer (2006), Thygesen (2008), and Lehtonen (2020).

[8]   Para 4.23, Agreed Principles and Practices.

[9]   Paras 4.23 and 5.1, Agreed Principles and Practices. Also see the detailed account by Lindstrøm (2018, pp. 20–22) on the procedure of redrafting the report.

[10]   https://www.oecd.org/economy/role-of-the-economic-and-develoment-review-committee-edrc .htm, accessed 19 April 2023.

[11]   This is done by a 'silent procedure', in which the edited report is opened for discussion and approval in the EDRC's 'Electronic Discussion Group'. If any disagreements cannot be resolved there, personal meetings are possible, or, in protracted cases, a formal plenary discussion during one of the next committee meetings.

tion of recommendations during the next review cycle. In terms of public pressure, Economic Surveys are formally launched in the reviewed country through a high-level press conference and receive a relatively high degree of media attention. Favourable or unfavourable results sometimes make the headlines of the business and financial press. In addition, country desk officers of the OECD keep contact with governments, the national media and civil society, so as to perpetuate the discussion on the merits of national policies (Marcussen, 2004, p. 118).

Development Policy

Like the EDRC, the DAC is one of the oldest OECD formations. Peer reviews are conducted since 1962 (Carey, 2021, pp. 18–20) in the 'committee meetings' of the DAC, which bring together member state counsellors and observers from major development IOs; notably the World Bank Group and the UNDP. The DAC aims at around five peer reviews per annum, which implies that each of the currently 30 DAC members[12] is reviewed every five to six years. Other than in the EDRC, the review centres on clearly defined guidelines and standards adopted in the 'high level' or 'senior level meetings' of the DAC, such as the DAC Principles for Effective Aid, or the DAC Recommendations on Untying ODA (see Chapter 12, this volume). Other international commitments, like the UN Sustainable Development Goals or the concept of Policy Coherence for Development likewise play a role (Ashoff, 2013; Lim, 2014, p. 865).

Collection of information

The DAC reviews show a number of differences to the practice developed in the EDRC. First, the DAC seeks more forcefully than the EDRC to 'hold members to account for the commitments they have made', to 'monitor implementation of recommendations from previous reviews, [and] track adherence to OECD and DAC Recommendations and instruments'.[13] The focus on monitoring compliance with specific standards is in contrast to the approach of the EDRC, which centres on broader policy principles and best practices (see above). Second, DAC peer reviews allow greater room for the reviewee to influence and steer the focus of the discussion. Apart from the use of self-reporting by the reviewed state, there is the possibility for this member to 'identify… its strengths and areas of good and innovative practice, and … areas where it faces challenges and wants to improve'.[14] Third, the element of a *peer* review is enhanced, as the preparation of the country report is in the hands of a 'review team' consisting of senior officials from two other DAC members in addition to staff of the OECD Development Cooperation Directorate (DCD). Representatives from developing countries or civil society organizations can also be admitted as observers.[15] Like in the EDRC, country visits provide further information and opportunities for the review team to consult stakeholders. Importantly, and differently to the EDRC, this also includes visits to developing countries, with a focus on the implementation of a reviewee's aid policies.

---

[12]   Membership in the DAC is voluntary, so that not all OECD member states are also members of the DAC.
[13]   Development Cooperation Directorate and Development Assistance Committee, DAC Peer Review Methodology, Updated 2021; Document DCD/DAC(2020)69/FINAL, 17 February 2021; para 5.
[14]   Ibid., para 9.1.; also see paras 20–22.
[15]   Ibid., paras 12 and 13.

Evaluation and assessment

The DAC plenary review meeting broadly follows the EDRC model discussed above. The focus is again on agreeing a consensus view on the merits of the reviewed country's policies and joint recommendations. Similar to the EDRC, observers report that the meetings experience 'significant areas of contestation [as] a normal feature' (Carey, 2021, p. 22). A redrafting session between the Secretariat and the reviewed member takes place after the review meeting, and any changes to the report or the recommendations have to be agreed by the entire committee. A similar silent procedure as in the EDRC is applied (footnote 11). One difference to the EDRC is that the plenary meeting only lasts a half day, thus leaving less time for discussion and questioning of the reviewed member. Another difference is that the college of peers consists mostly of officials from domestic ministries and aid agencies, while only some member states have a dedicated counsellor for development policy in their permanent representations.

Dissemination and follow-up

A notable feature of the DAC peer review is its strong emphasis on the follow-up to the review session. After the report has been published on the OECD website and launched in the member state's capital, the reviewed member can agree to provide a 'management response' to the peer review. This response lays out plans for the implementation of peer recommendations, but also provides room for disagreeing with recommendations and explaining why no action on a specific recommendation may be planned.[16] Another original instrument is the possibility for the reviewed member to undergo a 'mid-term review' by the Secretariat three years after the review session. While both elements are voluntary, especially the mid-term review has become standard practice for the reviewed members and can serve to enhance the continuous process of policy dialogue between the reviewed country and the DAC Secretariat.[17]

Money Laundering and Corruption Control

The use of peer reviews in the area of money laundering and corruption control is a relatively recent addition to the OECD toolbox. The WGB as the principal review body was established in 1994 and conducts peer reviews since 1999. While the WGB could build on the OECD's decades-long experience in peer review, it entered new territory by assessing compliance with one of the few binding international treaties under the roof of the OECD, the 1997 Convention on Combating Bribery of Foreign Public Officials in International Business Transactions (frequently referred to as the 'Anti-Bribery Convention'). The WGB, under the mandate provided by Article 12 of the Convention, monitors implementation of the Convention and several other instruments developed by the WGB. In this respect, the OECD uses strong language about 'enforcing' the Convention.[18] Further significant deviations from the practice of the EDRC and

---

[16]   Ibid., para 36 and Annex D.

[17]   Ibid., para 37.

[18]   See https:// www .oecd .org/ corruption/ anti -bribery/ anti -briberyconvention/ oecda ntibribery convention .htm accessed 19 April 2023 for an overview. Also see the High-level Statement on the occasion of the launch of the '2021 Recommendation for Further Combating Bribery of Public Officials in International Business Transactions', during which the importance of the existing peer review for 'vigorously implementing the OECD Anti-Bribery Convention' and 'robustly enforcing' the Convention was reiterated https://www.oecd.org/investment/anti-bribery/high-level-statement-on-the-2021-anti-bribery -recommendation.htm accessed 19 April 2023.

the DAC are the use of domestic anti-corruption experts as reviewers (instead of diplomats from the permanent representations of the member states) and the enhanced possibilities to put pressure on non-implementing countries (Jongen, 2019, p. 915). A final important difference is that the monitoring process is arranged in different 'phases', which become increasingly demanding. While Phase 1 focuses on the adequacy of national legislation, Phase 2 and the subsequent phases deal with the actual implementation of the Convention and specific policies. Countries are expected to successfully pass the peer review of their policies in a specific phase. Outstanding recommendations for a specific country are carried over to the next review phase.[19]

Collection of information, evaluation and assessment

As in the EDRC, the WGB relies on a combination of self-reporting based on a standardized questionnaire and a secretariat report. The composition of the review team follows the DAC model (two senior experts from the member states acting as lead examiners, supported by secretariat staff). From the Phase 2 reviews upwards, country visits of about one week are held to allow consultations with governmental agencies, parliamentarians, the judiciary, legal and accounting professionals, business actors, civil society experts, and the media. The draft report as created by the review team is discussed in a plenary meeting of the WGB, during which an open discussion is held and peer pressure can be exerted (Jongen, 2019, p. 915).

A key difference to the other two reviews is that the report and recommendations are adopted at the end of the plenary meeting, without a further editing round between Secretariat and reviewed country. This happens through a consensus minus one procedure, excluding the reviewed state from voting on its recommendations. This element is marked by some as a 'strength' of the WGB (Jongen, 2021, p. 341), but also implies a more adversarial model of review, with less emphasis on the 'ownership' of recommendations by the reviewed country. Jongen reports that participants in the meetings describe the atmosphere as 'tense', had experienced 'emotion in the room', or even talked about 'quite a lot of aggression', while acknowledging that the ensuing dynamics 'worked' to create results (ibid., pp. 343–344).

Dissemination and follow-up

The agreed reports and peer recommendations are published on the OECD webpage, similarly to the other reviews. The WGB is unique though in applying a graduated model of peer and public pressure on states whose implementation of the Convention or peer recommendations was considered unsatisfactory. There are various and increasingly harsh mechanisms: first, the WGB can step up its monitoring efforts, for instance by expediting reporting requirements, organizing further review missions to the country, requiring an 'action plan', or by sending a letter of concern to the country. Second, states can be forced to undergo a second or even a third review of their implementation efforts within the same 'phase' of review ('*bis*' and '*ter*' evaluations), effectively delaying completion of the respective phase and causing negative publicity and additional workload. Another wounding sanction is the publication of a notice of 'high-priority unimplemented recommendations' on the OECD webpage. Such public exposure can be consequential for the reviewed country, considering the attention that cor-

---

[19] https://www.oecd.org/daf/anti-bribery/Fighting-the-crime-of-foreign-bribery.pdf, accessed 19 April 2023. Also see Jongen (2021, pp. 340–341).

ruption perception ratings play in investor decisions.[20] In consequence, the WGB is perceived among participants as exerting high degrees of peer and public pressure on reviewed countries (Carraro et al., 2019; Jongen, 2019).

CONCLUSION

The comparison of three peer reviews in the OECD shows a number of differences, which materialize along two dimensions: first, the shape of the 'tripartism' in the review, i.e., the balance between the secretariat, the member states and the peers during the review process. Second, the balance between the different compliance logics reviewed above, which build either on peer and public pressure or on benchmarking and learning.

Among the three reviews, the OECD Economic Surveys give the biggest influence to the secretariat and the college of peers. While the OECD Economics Department consults widely in the reviewed country, there is no input by officials from other member states during the writing of the report. Moreover, participants in the EDRC review sessions are mostly the Economic Counsellors from the Paris-based member state delegations, rather than ministry officials or other functionaries flown in from the capitals. This element enhances collegiality and trust among the peers, an effect that is also fostered by the comparatively high frequency of EDRC reviews. In contrast, both the WGB and the DAC involve 'peers' from other OECD members during the writing of the reports. The WGB review session are held between experts and officials from the member states, while the DAC brings together administrators and officials from domestic ministries and aid agencies and only some counsellors from the permanent delegations of larger member states. Both elements enhance the member-driven nature of the WGB and the DAC. The DAC also allows the reviewed member state to put forward specific thematic focal points. While such specific areas of attention also exist in the EDRC, they are agreed by the entire membership in consultation with the reviewed member. In sum, the EDRC builds on collegiality and expertise among a close-knit circle of Paris-based diplomats, while the other two reviews put more emphasis on input from the capitals and the peer states during both the preparation and the review of the reports.[21]

The three review formats also differ in how they combine 'soft' compliance logics, which focus on policy learning and best practice exchange, and 'harder' logics that apply peer pressure and public shaming. The EDRC most clearly focuses on policy learning and best practice exchange, fostered by frank but collegial discussions behind closed doors and the attention paid to the reviewee's 'ownership' of the process and the recommendations. Participants in the EDRC assess the extent to which it exerts peer and public pressure as moderate to low, especially when compared with the WGB (Carraro et al., 2019). In contrast, the WGB achieves high degrees of peer and public pressure by the graduation logic discussed above. Reviewed

---

[20]   https://www.oecd.org/daf/anti-bribery/countrymonitoringoftheoecdanti-briberyconvention.htm accessed 19 April 2023, provides an overview and further explanation of the various measures that the WGB can adopt in this respect. See Jongen (2021, pp. 347–348) on how these have been experienced as unpleasant and hurting by reviewed states.

[21]   As discussed above, the EDRC however enhances member state input and 'ownership' after the review session, when the secretariat and the reviewee edit the public version of the report and recommendations.

countries have to demonstrate compliance with specific requirements before their peers consider them ripe to finish a specific phase of the review. The system identifies 'laggards' and generates strong pressure on them through various and sometimes hurting measures. This adversarial logic is further enhanced through the adoption of recommendations through a consensus-minus-one approach. The DAC likewise defines its mandate as checking compliance with agreed standards and holding members accountable, however borrows from the EDRC's collegial approach by giving reviewees a voice in the formulation of recommendations. The DAC approach is also less adversarial than the WGB because of the more flexible nature of the review standards, the lower review frequency, and the member-state driven character of the follow-up monitoring.

Despite the various ways in which peer reviews can exert influence, most observers agree that their effectiveness in directly triggering policy change is limited. Pressure on delegates in the review meetings may not necessarily transpire in domestic administrations, and the echo of critical reviews in the public discussion is not guaranteed. Similarly, domestic resource constraints and competing political priorities may prevent domestic uptake (Armingeon and Beyeler, 2004; Carraro, 2019; Jongen, 2021). Declaring peer reviews as inconsequential on such grounds however fails to recognize indirect ways in which peer reviews can engender change. The dialogical consolidation and specification of norms, injection of new ideas and 'best practice' in national policy discourses, and the emergence of transnational bureaucratic learning networks are all important in this respect. These processes may have less direct, but nonetheless relevant effects on domestic policies (Sabel and Zeitlin, 2008; also see Carraro, 2019; Lehtonen, 2020; Jongen, 2021, p. 351).

Regardless of whether the focus is on direct or indirect effects, institutional design matters. Comparative research shows that participants experience some peer reviews to hold greater authority and function more satisfactorily than others. This applies to reviews that combine an extensive collection of information with frank discussions in the plenary, clear recommendations, and stringent monitoring of the domestic follow-up to recommendations. Often these reviews show an enhanced role of the secretariat (Carraro et al., 2019; Carraro and Jongen, 2020). In contrast, reviews that have a more cautious diplomatic nature score lower (Conzelmann, 2014; Jongen, 2019; Karlas and Parízek, 2019).

A number of challenges exist for peer reviews. First, the instrument can be extremely demanding on member states. The preparation and follow-up to the review of one's own country and the review of other states binds considerable administrative and financial resources. The problem is enhanced if peer reviews of different IOs on the same topic overlap, or if peer reviews are held in parallel to other monitoring formats. Examples exist in the fields of corruption and human rights, leading to reports about 'review fatigue'. High workload from peer reviews and limited capacities are also experienced by the OECD secretariat. The increasing complexity of peer reviews and the growing OECD membership have created calls for lighter reviews and an extension of review cycles. Second, the increasing diversity of the OECD membership may jeopardize the trust and value-sharing on which successful peer reviewing rests (Thygesen, 2008, p. 145). Until now, key advantages of the OECD in the conduct of peer reviews are its relatively small and homogeneous membership, the comparatively small value conflicts, and its largely technical and depoliticized nature. This opens avenues for peer learning and dialogical exchange; in contrast to the sometimes more strongly politicized and value-laden procedures in the WTO or the UN (Carraro et al., 2019). While OECD peer reviews are not held in highly controversial and politicized policy fields such as human rights (Carraro, 2017) or the rule of law (Conzelmann, 2022), these fields demonstrate the difficulties that polarization and fragmentation can create for peer reviews.

REFERENCES

Armingeon, Klaus, and Beyeler, Michelle (Eds.) (2004). *The OECD and European Welfare States*. Cheltenham: Edward Elgar.

Ashoff, Guido (2013). *50 Years Of Peer Reviews by the OECD's Development Assistance Committee: An Instrument of Quality Assurance and Mutual Learning*. DIE Briefing Paper 12/2013. Bonn: Deutsches Institut für Entwicklungspolitik.

Bernstein, Steven, and van der Ven, Hamish (2017). ‚Best practices in global governance.' *Review of International Studies, 43*(3), 534–556.

Carey, Richard (2021). 'Development, development cooperation, and the DAC: Epistemologies and ambiguities.' In G. Bracho, R. Carey, W. Hynes, S. Klingebiel, and A. Trzeciak-Duval (eds), *Origins, Evolution and Future of Global Development Cooperation. DIE/GDI Studies 104*. Bonn: Deutsches Institut für Entwicklungspolitik 11–72.

Carraro, Valentina (2017). 'The United Nations treaty bodies and Universal Periodic Review: Advancing human rights by preventing politicization?' *Human Rights Quarterly, 39*(4), 943–970.

Carraro, Valentina (2019). 'Promoting compliance with human rights: The performance of the United Nations' Universal Periodic Review and treaty bodies.' *International Studies Quarterly, 63*(4), 1079–1093.

Carraro, Valentina, Conzelmann, Thomas, and Jongen, Hortense (2019). 'Fears of peers?: Explaining peer and public shaming in global governance.' *Cooperation and Conflict, 54*(3), 335–355.

Carraro, Valentina, and Jongen, Hortense (2020). *Peer Review in Financial Integrity Matters*. FACTI Panel Background Paper 8. New York: United Nations.

Conzelmann, Thomas (2014). 'The politics of peer reviewing: comparing the OECD and the EU.' In T. Blom and S. Vanhoonacker (eds), *The Politics of Information. The Case of the European Union*. Basingstoke: Palgrave Macmillan 49–62.

Conzelmann, Thomas (2022). 'Peer-reviewing the rule of law?: A new mechanism to safeguard EU values.' *European Papers. A Journal on Law and Integration, 7*(2), 671–695.

Dimitropoulos, Georgios (2016). 'Compliance through collegiality: Peer review in international law.' *Loyola of Los Angeles International and Comparative Law Review, 37*(3), 275–340.

Dunlop, Claire A., and Radaelli, Claudio M. (2018). 'The lessons of policy learning: Types, triggers, hindrances and pathologies.' *Policy & Politics, 46*(2), 255–272.

Grant, Ruth W., and Keohane, Robert O. (2005). 'Accountability and abuses of power in world politics.' *American Political Science Review, 99*(1), 29–43.

Gray, William G. (2017). 'Peer pressure in Paris: Country reviews at the OECD in the 1960s and 1970s.' In M. Leimgruber and M. Schmelzer (eds), *The OECD and the International Political Economy Since 1948*. Basingstoke, Hampshire: Palgrave Macmillan 209–231.

Jongen, Hortense (2019). 'The authority of peer reviews among states in the global governance of corruption.' *Review of International Political Economy, 25*(6), 909–935.

Jongen, Hortense (2021). 'Peer review and compliance with international anti-corruption norms: Insights from the OECD working group on bribery.' *Review of International Studies, 47*(3), 331–352.

Karlas, Jan, and Parízek, Michal (2019). 'The process performance of the WTO Trade Policy Review Mechanism: Peer-reviewing reconsidered.' *Global Policy, 10*(3), 376–384.

Lehtonen, Markku (2007). 'Environmental policy integration through OECD peer reviews: Integrating the economy with the environment or the environment with the economy?' *Environmental Politics, 16*(1), 15–35.

Lehtonen, Markku (2020). 'Harder governance built on soft foundations: Experience from OECD peer reviews.' *Journal of Environmental Policy & Planning, 22*(6), 814–829.

Lim, Sojin (2014). 'Compliance with international norms: Implementing OECD DAC principles in South Korea.' *Globalizations, 11*(6), 859–874.

Lindstrøm, Maria D. (2018). 'The dual messages of OECD Economic Surveys: Observations from the OECD's Economics Department.' *Economic Sociology, 19*(2), 19–24.

Marcussen, Martin (2004). 'OECD governance through soft law.' In U. Mörth (ed), *Soft Law in Governance and Regulation*. Cheltenham: Edward Elgar 103–126.

Milewicz, Karolina M., and Goodin, Robert E. (2018). 'Deliberative capacity building through international organizations: The case of the Universal Periodic Review of human rights.' *British Journal of Political Science, 48*(2), 513–533.

Nance, Mark T. (2018). 'Re-thinking FATF: An experimentalist interpretation of the Financial Action Task Force.' *Crime, Law and Social Change, 69*(2), 131–152.

Pagani, Fabrizio (2002). *Peer Review: A Tool for Co-operation and Change: An Analysis of an OECD Working Method*. SG/LEG(2002)-1. Paris: OECD.

Pagani, Fabrizio, and Wellen, Ursula (2008). 'The OECD peer review mechanism: Concept and function.' In K. Tanaka (ed), *Shaping Policy Reform and Peer Review in Southeast Asia. Integrating Economies amid Diversity*. Paris: OECD 261–277.

Paulo, Sebastian, and Reisen, Helmut (2010). 'Eastern donors and western soft law: Towards a DAC donor peer review of China and India?' *Development Policy Review, 28*(5), 535–552.

Sabel, Charles F., and Zeitlin, Jonathan (2008). 'Learning from difference: The new architecture of experimentalist governance in the EU.' *European Law Journal, 14*(3), 271–327.

Schäfer, Armin (2006). 'A new form of governance?: Comparing the Open Method of Coordination to multilateral surveillance by the IMF and the OECD.' *Journal of European Public Policy, 13*(1), 70–88.

Thygesen, Niels (2008). 'Comparative aspects of peer review: OECD, IMF, and the European Union.' In K. Tanaka (ed), *Shaping Policy Reform and Peer Review in Southeast Asia. Integrating Economies Amid Diversity*. Paris: OECD 135–148.

van de Graaf, Thijs, and Lesage, Dries (2009). 'The International Energy Agency after 35 years: Reform needs and institutional adaptability.' *The Review of International Organizations, 4*(3), 293–317.

10. Indicators and benchmarking
Matthias Kranke[1]

INTRODUCTION

The Organisation for Co-operation and Development (OECD) is known for 'soft' governance. This label generally refers to the absence or a shortage of 'hard control' (Abbott, Genschel, Snidal, and Zangl, 2015: 4), which derives, for instance, from loan conditionality or even legislative powers. Not equipped with such 'hard governance' tools, the OECD resorts mostly to its epistemic authority on transnational social, economic and environmental challenges (Mahon and McBride, 2009; Niemann and Martens, 2018), through which it has shaped the trajectory of the global political economy to a remarkable degree (Clifton and Díaz-Fuentes, 2011). Its influence in this respect is significant as even non-members may adopt OECD standards or be held to them by third parties (Jarvis, 2017).

However, in this chapter I draw on the concept of 'harder soft governance' (Knodt and Schoenefeld, 2020) to suggest that the OECD's approach may be less soft than is commonly assumed. While Markku Lehtonen (2020) makes this point about the OECD peer review process (see also Chapter 9), I characterize its quantitative indicators, ratings and rankings for benchmarking state performance as tools of harder soft governance. The sheer number of such instruments renders the OECD's traditionally soft governance approach harder. International organizations (IOs) differ in the extent to which they create and disseminate metrics to govern the conduct of states. Public and scholarly debate has centred on a few highly prominent and highly contentious benchmarks crafted by the World Bank (Arndt, 2008; Schueth, 2011). Despite occasional coverage of OECD benchmarks (e.g., Erkkilä and Piironen, 2014; Radaelli, 2020), many others have flown under the radar. This relative lack of attention is surprising given the organization's widely acknowledged role as a transnational knowledge hub, which makes it occupy a central position among IOs (see Chapter 8). As I show in this chapter, the OECD is an avid benchmarker – or what I call a 'benchmarking machine' – especially when compared with other IOs.

Against this background, the chapter proceeds as follows. I begin by reviewing two largely separate bodies of scholarship that would benefit from greater mutual engagement: work on the OECD's role in global governance on the one hand and on global benchmarks on the other. Then, I present a list of 25 current OECD benchmarks, which were gleaned from various sources. Finally, I explain how these benchmarks harden the OECD's governance approach. In the conclusion, I summarize the argument and reflect on avenues for future research.

[1]   I wish to thank the volume editors, Fabrizio De Francesco and Claudio Radaelli, for their overall support and helpful comments on earlier drafts. The chapter also benefited from insightful suggestions by John Berten, Tero Erkkilä, Susan Robertson and Diane Stone. Ana G. Sousa Bleser and Lena Surmann provided expert research assistance.

OECD GOVERNANCE AND GLOBAL BENCHMARKS

Analysts of the OECD typically highlight epistemic authority as its main source of influence. Rianne Mahon and Stephen McBride (2009: 84), for example, call the organization 'an important site for the construction and dissemination of transnational research and policy ideas embracing a wide range of contemporary issues'. For Judith Clifton and Daniel Díaz-Fuentes (2011: 553), it is similarly 'one of the world's pre-eminent forums where officials from member and non-member countries meet to deliberate on a wide range of economic, social, technical, environmental and political issues'. In domains as diverse as corporate governance (Baker, 2012), education (Niemann and Martens, 2018), finance (Abdelal, 2006), foreign aid (Eyben, 2013), public governance (De Francesco and Guaschino, 2020) and taxation (Sharman, 2009), the OECD has defined widely respected policy norms. Together with other inter- and supranational organizations, it has reinforced the transnational traction of these norms (Dostal, 2004; Grek, 2010), sometimes by co-producing such formative concepts as 'economic growth' (Schmelzer, 2016) or 'state fragility' (Nay, 2014). Thus, a key lever of influence for the OECD is the supply of comparative policy knowledge that gets adopted and diffused by member and non-member states, as well as other IOs.

Scholarship on global benchmarks similarly foregrounds the provision of comparative policy knowledge about states. A sizeable literature now exists to demonstrate that quantified performance measures influence political processes in profound ways indirectly or 'at a distance' (Broome, Homolar, and Kranke, 2018; Broome and Quirk, 2015; Hansen and Mühlen-Schulte, 2012; Uribe, 2015). Benchmarks can sway specific decisions and reorient overarching discourses (Davis et al., 2015: 21). Many benchmarks, especially when they take the form of rankings (see esp. Espeland and Sauder, 2007), are designed to induce behavioral change through reputational incentives and disincentives (Kelley and Simmons, 2019). Concerned about their public standing, states tend to see high ranks as external validations and low ones as calls for action (Cooley, 2015: 13–14; Grek, 2009: 28–30; Kelley and Simmons, 2015). In addition, widely accepted benchmarks can reconfigure the political landscape beyond mechanistic responses to performance assessment results. Such more diffuse effects often stem from the redefinition of collective meanings associated with concepts such as 'corruption' (Bukovansky, 2015) or 'security' (Homolar, 2015).

These two basic channels of predominantly indirect influence mirror the distinction between power and authority. To exert power, benchmarkers must possess enough capacity to push others into action (potentially against their will) or offer sufficiently attractive incentives for a particular type of behavior; and they possess authority only if others ascribe legitimacy to them in their governance role. Whether an actor enjoys power and/or authority in deploying a benchmark is an empirical question. Researchers cannot answer it through an analysis of a benchmark as such without considering the environment in which it is produced, used or not used, legitimated or not legitimated. That is, the relational dynamics unfolding between benchmarkers, the benchmarking targets and key audiences are pivotal for the take-up of indicators, ratings and rankings. It is nonetheless heuristically helpful to distinguish these two modes of influence in the production, diffusion and application of benchmarks.

Benchmarkers exercise power when either the threat of a negative or the prospect of a positive assessment leads others to take action even when these others do *not* (yet) subscribe to the underlying values of a particular benchmark. This dynamic plays out most clearly in rankings, which – as 'a zero-sum technology' (Sauder and Espeland, 2009: 73) – constantly stoke competition between states over relative achievements (Towns and Rumelili, 2017: 758). A study on the World Bank's (now abolished) EDB Index shows, using a survey experiment, that 'investors' expressed intent to recommend investment' strengthens dramatically for higher-ranked countries (Doshi, Kelley, and Simmons, 2019: 631). Related research highlights that countries had perverse incentives to 'game' their EDB scores and reap the tangible rewards of an enhanced reputation through strategic reforms (Broome, 2022; Schueth, 2011; also Doshi et al., 2019: 623). Another prominent example is the US State Department's Trafficking in Persons Report, which has been found to enact anti-trafficking laws in other countries (Kelley and Simmons, 2015). In such instances, the power of benchmarkers lies in their ability to push other actors to do things that they would not do otherwise, such as crafting shallow reforms to climb the rankings.

However, benchmarkers have epistemic authority – rather than or in addition to wielding benchmarking power – when their policy knowledge is accepted as credible by policymakers and, potentially, even the wider public. The mechanism of change here is not the hasty response to a negative assessment but rather the sustained internalization of goals embodied in the benchmark of a respected actor. These effects are more diffuse because benchmarking authority does not immediately alter government objectives but instead gradually molds the mindsets of politicians and citizens alike about what is considered 'good' policy on certain issues (Kelley and Simmons, 2021: 173). These changes may surface in political processes at a much later point in time. Given such lags, casual attribution of concrete changes to benchmarking authority becomes challenging. Nevertheless, benchmarkers can succeed in discursively defining a range of legitimate state policies, which can ultimately lead to the universalization of particularistic visions of what a 'normal' state ought to look and act like (Broome et al., 2018; Fougner, 2008; Kuzemko, 2015).

Not only is it difficult to pinpoint the degree of power or authority exerted through a given benchmark, the distinction is also fluid as its practical effects cannot always be neatly attributed. For instance, benchmarks that once worked primarily through the pressure of evaluation when they were seen as externally imposed may over time become more accepted through internalization (Sauder and Espeland, 2009). A specific factor to consider here is that all OECD member states are advanced economies with comparatively high levels of state capacity, which mitigates the pressure from a negative assessment, such as a drop in a ranking. Vis-à-vis such countries, OECD benchmarks tend to be more consequential as an authoritative source of policy knowledge than as a powerful instrument for punishing 'deviant' behavior. Curiously, poorer low-capacity states that are not members of the OECD are more exposed to the power of its benchmarks. In the following section, I present an inventory of current OECD benchmarks while also briefly considering how they the organization exercise power and authority over their targets.

MAPPING OECD BENCHMARKS

This section takes stock of the OECD's benchmarking toolbox. I have compiled a list of a total of 25 active benchmarks (including indicator sets) through desk-based research that triangulates three principal types of data sources. First, the starting point for the stock-take was the Global Benchmarking Database[2] (2014), the latest version of which encompasses over 300 global benchmarks. I surveyed the database for benchmarks produced or co-produced by the OECD. Second, I identified additional benchmarks with the search function on the organization's website. As this exploratory strategy proved successful, I subsequently had a student assistant run a more systematic search, using the keywords 'benchmarks', 'index', 'indicators' and 'rankings', and then perusing the first ten pages of results for each. These comprehensive searches on the OECD website were performed in January and February 2022. Third, I added further benchmarks based on either incidental identification or suggestions from other scholars with proven expertise on the OECD and/or global benchmarks. All OECD benchmarks included in the list meet the criterion of having had some visible activities – that is, data releases or related reports according to information from the OECD itself – since 2017.

Although even this rather long list is far from exhaustive, it offers a representative overview of the indicators, ratings and rankings deployed by the OECD to benchmark the performance of its members and non-members. Proceeding in chronological order, Table 10.1 below presents the benchmarks that were identified through the procedures described above. The list also features information on issue areas, which was assigned based on benchmark names and, where necessary, additional information derived from summaries on the OECD website.

Table 10.1 reveals several trends and patterns. First and foremost, the OECD is an avid benchmarker. It is noteworthy that the organization has often developed indicators from long-established comparative assessments (Godin, 2006: 22–23). Yet it has added many new benchmarks to its toolbox over time, and it continues to do so without necessarily abandoning others. The oldest metrics in the list are from the late 1990s whereas the most recent one was launched in 2021. If anything, the list underestimates the scope of the organization's portfolio of benchmarks because the search is likely to have captured relatively prominent benchmarks. It further excludes not only conventional databases but also benchmark 'spin-offs' and other closely related tools. To give but one example, the high-profile Programme for International Student Assessment (PISA) has inspired the PISA for Development programme, and the International Early Learning and Child Well-being Study (IELS); the OECD has also combined data from the 2018 Teaching and Learning International Survey (TALIS) with PISA data to create 'the TALIS-PISA link' (OECD, n.d.).[3]

Moreover, the OECD applies indicators, ratings and rankings to various domains, which reflects its broad mandate as a multi-issue IO. While some issue areas, especially 'economy' and 'public governance', dominate the list, the scope of quantification across the organization's mandate is considerable. The OECD is thus a benchmarking machine not only for its number of quantitative instruments but also for the breadth of their coverage. In this capacity, it directs attention to its numerous benchmarking exercises by providing detailed public information on its website, which underlines its ambition to shape domestic policymaking through comparative assessments. I elaborate on this point in the remainder of this section.

The OECD can leverage its many benchmarks to push countries toward immediate policy responses and reshape their long-term political priorities. In line with the previous section, pushing can be seen as the exercise of power and reshaping as the exercise of authority through

---

[2]   Available at https://warwick.ac.uk/fac/soc/pais/research/csgr/benchmarking/database, accessed 19 April 2023.
[3]   I thank Susan Robertson for drawing my attention to these kinds of tools.

Table 10.1   OECD benchmarks

Year	Name	Area
1997	Country Risk Classifications	Economy
1997	Main Science and Technology Indicators	Science and technology
1998	Education at a Glance	Education
1999	Indicators of Employment Protection Legislation	Labor
1999	Main Economic Indicators	Economy
2000	Programme for International Student Assessment	Education
2001	Health at a Glance	Health
2001	Society at a Glance	Social
2003	FDI Regulatory Restrictiveness Index	Economy
2005	Environment at a Glance	Environment
2005	Pensions at a Glance	Social
2006	SME Policy Index	Economy
2009	Government at a Glance	Public governance
2009	Social Institutions and Gender Index	Social
2011	Better Life Index	Well-being
2011	Green Growth Indicators	Economy
2012	Indicators of Immigrant Integration	Migration
2014	Services Trade Restrictiveness Index	Economy
2015	Indicators of Regulatory Policy and Governance	Public governance
2015	Open, Useful and Re-usable data (OURdata) Index	Public governance
2016	Measuring Distance to the SDG Targets	Development
2019	Digital Government Index	Public governance
2019	OECD Indicators of Talent Attractiveness	Labor/Migration
2020	OECD Consumer Barometer	Economy
2021	OECD Public Integrity Indicators	Public governance

Note: 'Year' refers to the launch – that is, first official use – of a benchmark.
Source: Author, based on information from the OECD website (https://www.oecd.org/), especially the OECD iLibrary (https://www.oecd-ilibrary.org/), accessed 19 April 2023.

benchmarks. Two brief examples illustrate how OECD benchmarking power and authority can spur policy change.

1. *Programme for International Student Assessment.* PISA is a comprehensive benchmark that rates and ranks countries' educational levels in three-year intervals. The OECD is very explicit about its desire to 'help shape education reform', as it declares in a promotional video on its website. The video speaks of Germany's 'PISA shock' on reading proficiency in the inaugural assessment in 2000 as an experience that triggered substantive changes to its educational policies. In the second half, a similar argument is made about Brazil's poor performance on mathematics proficiency three years later.[4] By ranking countries against each other, the OECD creates pressure to enact policies that improve scores in the next assessment. Beyond this immediate pressure, the OECD can mobilize its epistemic authority to promote the revamping of educational systems when countries do not simply 'teach

----

[4]   'How does PISA help education reform? The cases of Germany & Brazil' (2:45), 6 December 2016, available at https://www.oecd.org/pisa/aboutpisa/ (also at https://www.youtube.com/watch?v=-xpOn0OzXEw), accessed 19 April 2023.

to the test' but begin to endorse the PISA standards (Grek, 2009; Niemann and Martens, 2018: 271–278).

2. *FDI Regulatory Restrictiveness Index.* The annual FDI Regulatory Restrictiveness Index operates in a similar fashion. Even without officially ranking countries, the benchmark uses sector-specific ordinal scores for openness to foreign direct investment (FDI) that can be compared across time and space. Countries generally want to avoid a worsening score, which might compromise their ability to attract FDI. Especially as some emerging countries with relatively many restrictions have continued to successfully court FDI, the benchmark's power potential may be limited. Yet it still authoritatively contributes to normalizing the contestable position that the 'ideal' economy imposes minimal restrictions on the activities of transnational investors (Broome et al., 2018: 525–529).

GOVERNING 'SOFTLY'? THE OECD AS A BENCHMARKING MACHINE

So far, I have suggested that the OECD routinely produces a vast array of quantitative governance instruments and, thus, can be considered a benchmarking machine. But how does this finding fit with the standard portrayal of the organization as a 'soft' governor? As Michèle Knodt and Jonas J. Schoenefeld (2020) argue, soft governance can be rendered harder in various ways. In light of the number and breadth of benchmarks deployed by the OECD, I contend that the quantification of its governance tools across issue areas constitutes an instance of 'harder soft governance'. In this section, I briefly outline notable 'hardening elements' (Knodt and Schoenefeld, 2020: 764). From the list provided by Knodt and Schoenefeld (2020: 765), I identify three as particularly relevant to the hardening of the OECD's soft governance approach: (1) precision, (2) blaming and shaming, and (3) justification. I discuss each hardening element in turn.

First, the OECD's benchmarks insert greater *precision* into the political objectives that the organization wants its members to pursue. Concrete goals harden governance tools (Knodt and Schoenefeld, 2020: 765) because the underlying norm is 'worked out in detail' (Terpan, 2015: 73). Typically, the producers of contemporary metrics spell out precisely what gets counted, and how. They provide detailed information on their methodologies, including how they classify data, construct indicators, assign weights, produce ratings and assemble rankings. By relying on numerous indicators and rankings to govern state conduct across a range of issue areas, the OECD specifies what its goals are and how states can meet them. The availability of benchmarks, especially those that come in the form of rankings rather than just ratings, makes it easy to track the extent to which a particular state complies with these expectations. The 'distance' from the ideal becomes immediately visible in ways that would not be possible in text-based reports alone.

Second, OECD benchmarks intensify *blaming and shaming*, partly as a result of greater goal precision. Harder soft governance facilitates the blaming and shaming of non-compliant actors, often via closer monitoring and reporting mechanisms (Knodt and Schoenefeld, 2020: 765). Through extensive coverage of both topics and countries, the organization routinely blames and shames countries (Niemann and Martens, 2018: 274). It blames them by locating the factors relevant to a rating or ranking (primarily) within the country, which is typical for benchmarks (Broome and Quirk, 2015: 831). It shames them by regularly publicizing the results of its evaluations in accessible formats, especially on its website; again, this effect is normally stronger for rankings and, generally, for all forms of benchmarks that intensify competition rather than fostering learning (De Francesco, 2016). Compared to non-numerical forms of assessment, the shaming potential is magnified by the wide dissemination of easy-to-digest league tables and data visualizations (Bandola-Gill, Grek, and Ronzani, 2021). Those interested in the results do not need to dissect long texts but can find relevant information with just a few clicks.

Third, the large number of OECD benchmarks places a higher demand for *justification* on states. As Knodt and Schoenefeld (2020: 765) explain: 'The more states have to explain in detail why and how they do (not) react to a recommendation, the harder the governance becomes.' Although not all benchmarks come with explicit recommendations attached, many quantitative evaluations of state performance can be interpreted in this manner. Rankings create a particularly strong need for justification. Countries that fall in a ranking are not merely recommended but incentivized to reorient their behavior along the standards prescribed by the benchmarker. Like a law school dean who tries to make sense of a disappointing result and to take remedial action (Espeland, 2015: 67–68), states are under immense public pressure to justify their decisions and craft policies conforming with the objectives promulgated through a benchmark. This pressure increases further when there is a variety of metrics out there according to which both OECD members and non-members get assessed.

In combination, these three elements carry the potential for the hardening of the OECD's soft governance through quantification. While from the OECD's perspective harder soft governance promises greater traction of its governance initiatives and control over countries' policies, a large body of work warns of the dangers of quantifying what are effectively incommensurable units. This warning rings as much true for university rankings (Sauder and Espeland, 2009) as for state rankings (Høyland, Moene, and Willumsen, 2012). Pointing to 'the avalanche of printed numbers' (Hacking, 1982) and the relentless search for 'good enough data' (Rocha de Siqueira, 2017), observers have repeatedly noted that much of the spectacular growth in metrics is self-referential. The widespread use of benchmarks thus guarantees only a higher degree of comparability among states, not better global governance *per se*. In sum, the hardening of soft governance at the OECD risks reducing complex political dynamics to simplistic checklists of measures to be taken, rather than enabling deeper reflection about the underlying norms and principal objectives of global governance.

CONCLUSION

This chapter has provided an overview of the OECD's benchmarking activities. Among contemporary IOs, the OECD stands out for its routine production and use of quantitative indicators, ratings and rankings for assessing the performances of member and non-member states alike across a wide spectrum of issue areas. This reliance hardens what has conventionally been dubbed a 'soft' governance approach as the OECD's many benchmarks sharpen goal precision, reinforce blaming and shaming, and heighten the need for justification. As a benchmarking machine, the OECD engages in more-than-soft governance in global politics.

Although the literature on global benchmarks has grown significantly since the 2010s, this chapter has pointed to a relative blind spot: the variable propensity of IOs to utilize benchmarks. Why do some IOs embrace benchmarking while others do not? With its many benchmarks, the OECD represents an outlier. Other IOs have been less eager in this regard. Future research should thus conduct in-depth case and comparative studies about the mechanisms that shape IOs' production and take-up of benchmarks. In search for general patterns, one might surmise that organizational culture, institutional design, mandate scope and stakeholder preferences are important factors. IOs are widely recognized as central players in contemporary global governance, but previous research has not systematically explored the differences and similarities in their approaches to quantification. This lack of comparative knowledge should guide empirical inquiry into when, how and why IOs quantify – or do not quantify – what they seek to govern.

REFERENCES

Abbott, K.W., Genschel, P., Snidal, D., and Zangl, B. (2015). 'Orchestration: Global governance through intermediaries.' In K.W. Abbott, P. Genschel, D. Snidal, and B. Zangl (eds), *International Organizations as Orchestrators* (pp. 3–36). Cambridge: Cambridge University Press.

Abdelal, R. (2006). 'Writing the rules of global finance: France, Europe, and capital liberalization.' *Review of International Political Economy, 13*(1), 1–27.

Arndt, C. (2008). 'The politics of governance ratings.' *International Public Management Journal, 11*(3), 275–297.

Baker, A. (2012). 'The "public interest" agency of international organizations? The case of the OECD Principles of Corporate Governance.' *Review of International Political Economy, 19*(3), 389–414.

Bandola-Gill, J., Grek, S. and Ronzani, M. (2021). 'Beyond winners and losers: Ranking visualizations as alignment devices in global public policy.' In L. Ringel, W. Espeland, M. Sauder, and T. Werron (eds), *Worlds of Rankings* (pp. 27–52). Bingley: Emerald Publishing.

Broome, A. (2022). 'Gaming country rankings: Consultancies as knowledge brokers for global benchmarks.' *Public Administration, 100*(3), 554–570.

Broome, A., Homolar, A. and Kranke, M. (2018). 'Bad science: International organizations and the indirect power of global benchmarking.' *European Journal of International Relations, 24*(3), 514–539.

Broome, A. and Quirk, J. (2015). 'Governing the world at a distance: The practice of global benchmarking.' *Review of International Studies, 41*(5), 819–841.

Bukovansky, M. (2015). 'Corruption rankings: Constructing and contesting the global anti-corruption agenda.' In A. Cooley and J. Snyder (eds), *Ranking the World: Grading States as a Tool of Global Governance* (pp. 60–84). Cambridge: Cambridge University Press.

Clifton, J. and Díaz-Fuentes, D. (2011). 'The OECD and phases in the international political economy, 1961–2011.' *Review of International Political Economy, 18*(5), 552–569.

Cooley, A. (2015). 'The emerging politics of international rankings and ratings: A framework for analysis.' In A. Cooley and J. Snyder (eds), *Ranking the World: Grading States as a Tool of Global Governance* (pp. 1–38). Cambridge: Cambridge University Press.

Davis, K.E., Kingsbury, B. and Merry, S.E. (2015). 'Introduction: The local-global life of indicators: Law, power, and resistance.' In S.E. Merry, K.E. Davis, and B. Kingsbury (eds), *The Quiet Power of Indicators: Measuring Governance, Corruption, and Rule of Law* (pp. 1–24). New York, NY: Cambridge University Press.

De Francesco, F. (2016). 'Transfer agents, knowledge authority, and indices of regulatory quality: A comparative analysis of the World Bank and the Organisation for Economic Co-operation and Development.' *Journal of Comparative Policy Analysis: Research and Practice, 18*(4), 350–365.

De Francesco, F. and Guaschino, E. (2020). 'Reframing knowledge: A comparison of OECD and World Bank discourse on public governance reform.' *Policy and Society, 39*(1), 113–128.

Doshi, R., Kelley, J.G. and Simmons, B.A. (2019). 'The power of ranking: The Ease of Doing Business indicator and global regulatory behavior.' *International Organization, 73*(3), 611–643.

Dostal, J.M. (2004). 'Campaigning on expertise: How the OECD framed EU welfare and labour market policies – and why success could trigger failure.' *Journal of European Public Policy, 11*(3), 440–460.

Erkkilä, T. and Piironen, O. (2014). '(De)politicizing good governance: The World Bank Institute, the OECD and the politics of governance indicators.' *Innovation: The European Journal of Social Science Research, 27*(4), 344–360.

Espeland, W. (2015). 'Narrating numbers.' In R. Rottenburg, S.E. Merry, S.-J. Park, and J. Mugler (eds), *The World of Indicators: The Making of Governmental Knowledge through Quantification* (pp. 56–75). Cambridge: Cambridge University Press.

Espeland, W.N. and Sauder, M. (2007). 'Rankings and reactivity: How public measures recreate social worlds.' *American Journal of Sociology, 113*(1), 1–40.

Eyben, R. (2013). 'Struggles in Paris: The DAC and the purposes of development aid.' *European Journal of Development Research, 25*(1), 78–91.

Fougner, T. (2008). 'Neoliberal governance of states: The role of competitiveness indexing and country benchmarking.' *Millennium: Journal of International Studies, 37*(2), 303–326.

Global Benchmarking Database. (2014, 15 June 2021). *v2.0.* Retrieved from www.warwick.ac.uk/globalbenchmarking/database, accessed 19 April 2023.

Godin, B. (2006). 'The knowledge-based economy: Conceptual framework or buzzword?' *The Journal of Technology Transfer, 31*(1), 17–30.

Grek, S. (2009). 'Governing by numbers: the PISA "effect" in Europe.' *Journal of Education Policy, 24*(1), 23–37.

Grek, S. (2010). 'International organisations and the shared construction of policy "problems": Problematisation and change in education governance in Europe.' *European Educational Research Journal, 9*(3), 396–406.

Hacking, I. (1982). 'Biopower and the avalanche of printed numbers.' *Humanities in Society, 5*(3–4), 279–295.

Hansen, H.K. and Mühlen-Schulte, A. (2012). 'The power of numbers in global governance.' *Journal of International Relations and Development, 15*(4), 455–465.

Homolar, A. (2015). 'Human security benchmarks: Governing human wellbeing at a distance.' *Review of International Studies, 41*(5), 843–863.

Høyland, B., Moene, K., and Willumsen, F. (2012). 'The tyranny of international index rankings.' *Journal of Development Economics, 97*(1), 1–14.

Jarvis, D.S.L. (2017). 'The OECD and the reconfiguration of the state in emerging economies: Manufacturing "regulatory capacity".' *Development and Change, 48*(6), 1386–1416.

Kelley, J.G. and Simmons, B.A. (2015). 'Politics by number: Indicators as social pressure in International Relations.' *American Journal of Political Science, 59*(1), 55–70.

Kelley, J.G. and Simmons, B.A. (2019). 'Introduction: The power of global performance indicators.' *International Organization, 73*(3), 491–510.

Kelley, J.G. and Simmons, B.A. (2021). 'Governance by other means: Rankings as regulatory systems.' *International Theory, 13*(1), 169–178.

Knodt, M. and Schoenefeld, J.J. (2020). 'Harder soft governance in European climate and energy policy: Exploring a new trend in public policy.' *Journal of Environmental Policy and Planning, 22*(6), 761–773.

Kuzemko, C. (2015). 'Climate change benchmarking: Constructing a sustainable future?' *Review of International Studies, 41*(5), 969–992.

Lehtonen, M. (2020). 'Harder governance built on soft foundations: Experience from OECD peer reviews.' *Journal of Environmental Policy and Planning, 22*(6), 814–829.

Mahon, R. and McBride, S. (2009). 'Standardizing and disseminating knowledge: The role of the OECD in global governance.' *European Political Science Review, 1*(1), 83–101.

Nay, O. (2014). 'International organisations and the production of hegemonic knowledge: How the World Bank and the OECD helped invent the Fragile State Concept.' *Third World Quarterly, 35*(2), 210–231.

Niemann, D. and Martens, K. (2018). 'Soft governance by hard fact? The OECD as a knowledge broker in education policy.' *Global Social Policy, 18*(3), 267–283.

OECD. (n.d.). TALIS FAQ. Retrieved from https://www.oecd.org/education/talis/talisfaq/, accessed 7 July 2023.

Radaelli, C.M. (2020). 'Regulatory indicators in the European Union and the Organization for Economic Cooperation and Development: Performance assessment, organizational processes, and learning.' *Public Policy and Administration, 35*(3), 227–246.

Rocha de Siqueira, I. (2017). 'Development by trial and error: The authority of good enough numbers.' *International Political Sociology, 11*(2), 166–184.

Sauder, M. and Espeland, W.N. (2009). 'The discipline of rankings: Tight coupling and organizational change.' *American Sociological Review, 74*(1), 63–82.

Schmelzer, M. (2016). *The Hegemony of Growth: The OECD and the Making of the Economic Growth Paradigm*. Cambridge: Cambridge University Press.

Schueth, S. (2011). 'Assembling international competitiveness: The Republic of Georgia, USAID, and the *Doing Business* Project.' *Economic Geography, 87*(1), 51–77.

Sharman, J.C. (2009). 'The bark *is* the bite: International organizations and blacklisting.' *Review of International Political Economy, 16*(4), 573–596.

Terpan, F. (2015). 'Soft law in the European Union—The changing nature of EU law.' *European Law Journal, 21*(1), 68–96.

Towns, A.E., and Rumelili, B. (2017). 'Taking the pressure: Unpacking the relation between norms, social hierarchies, and social pressures on states.' *European Journal of International Relations, 23*(4), 756–779.

Uribe, M.A.P. (2015). 'The quest for measuring development: The role of the indicator bank.' In S.E. Merry, K.E. Davis, and B. Kingsbury (eds), *The Quiet Power of Indicators: Measuring Governance, Corruption, and Rule of Law* (pp. 133–155). New York, NY: Cambridge University Press.

11. The network of economic regulators

Francesca Pia Vantaggiato

INTRODUCTION

The OECD Network of Economic Regulators (NER) is a transnational network of national regulatory agencies of infrastructure industries, or utilities: energy, telecommunications, water, and railway. Created in 2013, the network has grown from a dozen to over 80 member agencies today, from a total of 37 between OECD and non-OECD countries. Thus, the NER is perhaps the most policy-relevant network orchestrated by the OECD (Abbott and Snidal, 2010). The purpose of the NER is to support 'a global dialogue on the application of effective regulatory governance among economic regulators' via 'building and enriching comparative data, disseminating lessons'. The NER is a subsidiary body of the OECD Regulatory Policy Committee (RPC), established to strengthen its action and support the implementation of its work programme. The RPC was established in 2009 as forum for policy dialogue between senior regulatory officials to 'assist Members and non-Members in building and strengthening capacity for regulatory quality and regulatory reform'. Studying the NER is important for our understanding of the OECD and how it operates, and contributes to ongoing conversations in the literature on regulatory networks concerning their rationale and added value.

This chapter will argue that: (1) the rationale of the NER is similar to that of other transnational regulatory networks, which means that the literature can learn from this case; (2) the NER provides some unique added value to its members, which explains their sustained engagement in the network; and (3) the NER might become more influential in the future, provided closer working relationships with the RPC are established.

The stated rationale of transnational regulatory networks (TRNs) typically is to close the gap between the national and the international governance levels by exchanging information and best practices and fostering some degree of regulatory harmonisation between the jurisdictions involved. The NER is no different. As this chapter will show, the NER was established to fill the gap between 'regulatory design' – the set of tools and institutions that governments use to design high-quality regulation – and what the OECD calls 'regulatory delivery', i.e., regulatory implementation or 'the enforcement side of regulation' (Russell and Hodges, 2019). While the RPC oversees the implementation of regulatory reforms and the Better Regulation agenda of the OECD (see also Chapter 15), it does not deal with enforcement. The OECD identified the gap between design and delivery upon realising that many countries achieved suboptimal regulatory outcomes even though they had adopted the OECD recommended best practice of regulatory design and regulatory reform still achieved suboptimal outcomes. This realisation prompted a renewed focus on identifying the obstacles to implementation and developing solutions to address them. This is the purpose of the NER.

Similarly to other regulatory networks studied in the literature, the NER fosters learning among its members (Vantaggiato, 2019b; Vestlund, 2015). Soon after its establishment, the NER addressed the topic of regulatory independence upfront (OECD, 2016) with the stated aim of creating a common 'regulatory culture'. Moreover, the NER offers some unique benefits to its members. These include exposure to regulatory practice from different regions of the world, interaction with senior regulatory officials, dedicated secretariat support and cross-fertilisation from other areas of work of the OECD e.g., big data and artificial intelligence. However, the NER has yet to fulfil its stated aim of closing the gap between regulatory design and regulatory delivery. This chapter offers some suggestions as to how to enhance its effectiveness.

The arguments in this chapter are based on both primary and secondary data. Primary data consists of two interviews I carried out with informants who are very familiar with the workings of the NER to understand how the network operates. The two interviews took place via MS Teams in early 2022 and lasted around one hour. Secondary data consists of analysis of policy reports and desk-based research on the NER and regulatory networks. In addition, I rely on my own observation of the events surrounding the origins of the NER in 2014, when I started my doctoral research on networks of European energy regulators, and met regulators who were involved in the set-up of NER.

The chapter will proceed as follows: the next section will outline the key findings of existing literature on regulatory networks and explain how they help understand the NER; the third section will focus on the NER itself: its origins, functioning, and activities; the fourth section will outline the ways in which the NER is both a 'typical' regulatory network as well as a unique one, and its elements of uniqueness; the fifth section will conclude with some policy implications and suggestions for further research.

REGULATORY NETWORKS: FILLING THE GAP BETWEEN GOVERNANCE LEVELS

Transnational regulatory networks (TRNs) are well-studied (Bach and Newman, 2014; Bruszt and McDermott, 2014; Djelic and Sahlin-Andersson, 2006; Raustiala, 2002; Slaughter, 2004; Verdier, 2009). In the early 1990s, TRNs were described as a path-breaking phenomenon establishing a new 'world order' of transnational regulation (Slaughter, 1997). By now, regulatory networks are considered part and parcel of the institutional architecture of transnational policy-making. Typically, they are wholly informal associations of national regulatory agencies for a specific sector of regulation, where regulators exchange information and best practices, supported by a small secretariat in charge of coordination (Saz-Carranza et al., 2016).

The literature has concluded that regulatory networks typically emerge (whether spontaneously or as mandated networks, see (Saz-Carranza et al., 2016)) to fill a gap between levels of governance by fostering regulatory harmonisation, i.e., a commonality of practices and approaches to similar regulatory problems (Slaughter, 2004). In some sectors of regulation, TRNs have had success in creating shared rules (Raustiala, 2002); examples of particularly effective TRNs include the International Competition Network (Townley et al., 2022) or networks of financial and banking regulators (Bach and Newman, 2010), which have developed rules and practices that have diffused around the world. In utility sectors, however, harmonisation has been limited.

Networks of utility regulators typically have regional scope (i.e., they comprise regulators from a specific world region, e.g., Latin-America, the European Union (EU), different regions of Africa, Asia-Pacific etc) (Bianculli, 2021). This is partly because, unlike financial or banking activities, utility sectors have a physical infrastructure component that limits the geographical scope of transnational interactions and transactions. The stated purpose of these regional regulatory networks (Fernández-i-Marín and Jordana, 2015) is, however, similarly oriented to bridge across the national and the international level of governance to promote sharing of information and best practices in hopes of creating harmonised rules (Jordana, 2017). Their success has been, however, limited, for reasons of political interference with regulatory decision-making as well as differences in national political economies which prevent the development of common approaches (Guardiancich and Guidi, 2016; Jordana and Levi-Faur, 2014).

The concept of regulatory harmonisation is intended as either the development of common standards and rules and/or as the development of common enforcement practices of supranational law. In the multilevel regulatory governance system of the EU, these combined goals were pursued via European Regulatory Networks (ERNs) (Coen and Thatcher, 2008; Iborra et al., 2017), created in the early 2000s as advisory bodies to the European Commission (the EU's policy-making expert body). While some studies document the successful adoption and diffusion of standards by ERNs (Maggetti and Gilardi, 2014), overall the goal of harmonisation has proven elusive, particularly in sectors of utility regulation. This is part of the reasons why ERNs were transformed into European Agencies with limited, but binding decision-making powers on issues of European scope (Busuioc, 2009). As concerns implementation and enforcement, ERNs report a similarly mixed record. The European Competition Network – the enforcement network *par excellence* – created a common competition culture among national competition authorities in the EU (Cengiz, 2010) and empowered them to set agendas (Vantaggiato et al., 2020), but struggled to engage in actual joint enforcement (Cseres and Outhuijse, 2017).

Despite their relative failure to bring about harmonisation, many regulatory networks display remarkable longevity and sustained participation from member regulators. Yet, participation in regulatory networks is self-financed (regulators typically cover the costs of their membership via voluntary annual contributions that fund the network secretariat and all network activities) and not linked to explicit rewards: participation in TRNs does not result in bigger budgets or more resources being allocated to the regulatory authority (Maggetti, 2013).

If networks are costly to attend and only partially successful in achieving their goals, why do regulators stick with them? The literature has identified two sets of reasons: functional and political. Functional reasons refer to the role of learning: by having access to more expert and resourceful peers, regulators learn and even compensate for their lacking resources (Vantaggiato, 2019a). Moreover, regulators use networks as platforms to voice issues of concern and be helped identify solutions (Vantaggiato et al., 2020). Political reasons include enhancing regulators' (domestic) independence from politicians (Yesilkagit, 2011), responding to pressure from regulated entities (Bach and Newman, 2014) and influencing the policy agenda via leveraging their collective expertise (Vantaggiato, 2020). Namely, in the European context the literature has found that regulatory networks help regulators strengthen their autonomy vis-à-vis national executives (Bach and Ruffing, 2013). Research has also shown that European regulators have used networks to bypass domestic opposition to their policy proposals by raising those proposals at supranational level, increasing the chances they will become Europeanised and therefore mandatory across the Member States (Newman, 2008; Ruffing, 2015).

Functional and political reasons of network participation often intersect and build upon each other. In some cases, the functional demands of regulatory harmonisation have ended up empowering regulatory networks with agenda setting capabilities (Mathieu, 2020; Vantaggiato, 2020). More generally, regulators play an intermediary role between national executives and the international arena; this gatekeeping role affords them great influence on domestic and international policy-making (Jordana, 2017; Ruffing, 2015). Enforcement, however, remains a gap in both regulatory practice and the study of regulatory networks (Mastenbroek and Martinsen, 2018).

The next section will unpack the origins, structure and functioning of the NER. In turn, the fourth section will point to the core similarities and the differences between the NER and other well-studied regulatory networks. The similarities will help understanding what the NER could learn from the experience of similar networks; the differences will highlight the unique features of the NER. The section will also offer recommendations to increase the policy impact of the NER.

THE OECD NER: ORIGINS, STRUCTURE, AND FUNCTIONING

Origins

The origins of the NER date back to a series of informal conversations (interview 2), in the early 2010s, between OECD staff working in regulatory policy and regulators in various OECD member countries, e.g., Australia and the UK. Those conversations identified an important gap in the impact of the work of the OECD regulatory policy division: implementation. OECD staff could observe that even where countries adopted their recommended best practice of regulatory design, regulatory outcomes were often suboptimal. Thus, the NER was born out of a concern with what the OECD began calling the 'delivery space' of regulation – in other words, enforcement and implementation.

In the OECD structure, regulatory design is the realm of the Regulatory Policy Committee (RPC). The committee comprises ministerial representatives in charge of regulatory policy from several OECD countries. To address the challenges of regulatory delivery, OECD staff proposed involving national regulatory agencies – as the agencies in charge of enforcement and implementation – into the conversation on Better Regulation alongside those who set the policy agenda and direction (the RPC). Indeed, the OECD document establishing the NER states:

> The NER shall provide a unique forum for regulators from different sectors and industries for policy dialogue, cooperation and exchange among those responsible for the delivery of economic regulation. Under its current structure, this dialogue is not available within the RPC which is primarily comprised of officials responsible for the quality of the design of regulation. The NER shall provide direct access to officials with first hand responsibility for its effective implementation. (OECD, 2013)

At the time, the idea to create a regulatory network embedded within the OECD resonated with several RPC members who were familiar with the workings of European Regulatory Networks and had observed their relative success in setting the European regulatory policy agenda in their respective sectors (own observation). The setting-up of the NER was supported by the RPC in November 2011 and included in its Programme of Work and Budget for 2013-14. During 2012, NER meetings were held on an informal basis, back-to-back with the RPC meetings in at OECD Headquarters in Paris (OECD, 2013). Only 12 regulators attended the very first meeting (interview 2). They started working on what became an important NER publication: the Governance of Regulators (OECD, 2014), focused on independence and autonomy in the day-to-day operation of regulatory agencies. This focus on regulators' *de facto* independence – as opposed to their *de jure* independence i.e., independence enshrined in statutory documents – 'woke a lot of people up to realise that having a piece of paper that says they're independent is not enough' (interview 2). That publication garnered the interest of more regulators, expanding the scope of the network. The first formal meeting of the NER – formally established as a subsidiary body of the RPC, coordinated via the OECD secretariat and financed via small budgetary allocations from the OECD and voluntary contributions from members – took place in Paris in November 2013.

Structure

The structure of the NER is not complex. The NER has a chair, who sits in a Bureau comprising seven members. The Bureau sets the strategic direction of the NER. The chair rotates annually. Bureau members are nominated annually and serve for two–three years. Other network members are referred to as 'delegates'. The NER gathers over 80 regulatory agencies from 37 countries. Most of the countries are OECD members although the NER also comprises regulators from some non-OECD countries which are either strategic partners or appear on the list of 'approved' countries to work with redacted by the RPC within framework of their Global Engagement Strategy.

The NER also comprises two task forces. One task force focuses on developing the governance indicators; it only operates when the OECD revises them every five years. The second task force, which is joint between RPC and NER, was established two years ago and focuses on the interaction between new and emerging technologies and regulation.

Functioning

The NER meets twice a year for a full day. In addition, the secretariat typically organises two–three webinars a year on specific topics decided by the Bureau and the chair in coordination with the secretariat.

The interviews carried out for this research report that participation in the NER is sustained. Members regularly attend NER meetings, reply to the surveys submitted to them by the secretariat, and engage in discussion constructively. Importantly, and unlike many other regulatory networks, NER meetings are typically attended by high-level regulatory officials, e.g., board members / commissioners, who are the decision-makers within regulatory agencies. This is because of the specific focus of the work of the NER:

> We don't look at the content of the regulation in any given country, transposition of the objectives etc. We look at cross cutting issues and put a lot of emphasis on performance. In our assessment, we find that across countries and sectors the issues that come up are always the same so here's another reason why NER is useful: members can talk about issues that affect them all. It's also useful because it takes a step back from the nuts and bolts of regulation to consider broader questions of political economy, internal culture, drivers of performance etc. (interview 1)

The secretariat fulfils a pivotal function within the NER. It organises the meetings, coordinates with the NER Bureau, facilitates discussions in the network, collects data on new tools, trends and challenges, and disseminates data to its members. Upon invitation, the secretariat also carries out in-depth performance reviews, called Performance Assessment Framework for Economic Regulation or PAFER. The Secretariat has carried out 12 PAFERs so far. The regulatory agencies involved take the recommendations very seriously, 'as a to-do list' (interview 2). PAFERs typically also include recommendations that require action from other stakeholders, indirectly addressing government and regulated entities as well as the targeted regulatory agencies. The secretariat also provides comparative analyses of governance arrangements to its members and coordinates the release of NER publications, which are publicly available on the NER webpages.

While the secretariat is clearly important, the work of the NER is peer driven. The NER chair and Bureau have the main say in setting the overall strategies and deliverables of the network for the current year. The PAFER reviews involve two–three regulators from other countries and sectors, who contribute to the review.

In its ninth year of operation, the NER is successful in catalysing sustained engagement by members. But is the NER able to fulfil the goal it set itself, i.e., filling the gap between regulatory design and regulatory delivery?

> We understand the gap, but I am not sure we know how to bridge it yet. We now understand better where the pinch points are… the risk arises in the regulators having difficulty discharging their mandates. We developed guidance papers and performance reviews. Now we are working on performance criteria and measurement. Sometimes what regulators measure and what they want to achieve are widely different things. Lately we have worked on how regulators can modernise and use data much more actively in the delivery of regulations, for enforcement and for evaluation. Ideally, we'd like to move from ex-ante to real time almost. We'd like to understand where lack of compliance by regulated firms comes from and how to address it.' (interview 2)

TYPICAL, BUT DIFFERENT: THE LIMITS AND THE ADDED VALUE OF THE NER

As outlined above, a common finding of the vast literature on regulatory networks, whether European or transnational, is that they often fall short of expectations (Bach et al., 2016; Cengiz, 2010; Coen and Thatcher, 2008; Cseres and Outhuijse, 2017; Fernández-i-Marín and Jordana, 2015; Verdier, 2009). The case of European regulation is perhaps closest to the challenges faced by the NER because although the NER does not comprise regulators from a single polity, it is embedded in an international organisation whose remit is formulating regulatory policy and encouraging regulatory reform in its member countries. Therefore, some of the lessons learnt from the European experience may prove useful to the NER as it evolves.

To explain the relative ineffectiveness of European networks, scholars often point to differences in the institutional setup of regulatory agencies as well as differences in the political economy of various countries, including different degrees of political influence of the regulated entities and different levels of government interference with regulatory decision-making (Guardiancich and Guidi, 2016). These differences militate against achieving compromise between regulators. Even when compromise could be achieved, differences in powers and competences severely limit the room for manoeuvre of some regulators, rendering the credible commitment that must underpin harmonised implementation (Gilardi, 2007) impossible. This is why regulatory networks have typically been more successful at influencing policy *formulation* rather than at achieving harmonised policy *implementation*. As a matter of fact, regulators have used the influence of their expert consensus at the policy formulation stage to achieve harmonised (or homogenised) regulatory provisions (including statutory requirements of independence) across the whole EU (Vantaggiato, 2020).

The main difference between European regulatory networks and the NER is that the former emerged as the European regulatory policy framework was being developed. That was a moment of considerable policy uncertainty, which afforded European regulators relatively ample influence on policy formulation: the institutions of the EU needed national agencies' knowledge of national markets and their sectoral expertise to formulate supranational regulatory policy (Vantaggiato, 2020). In contrast, the OECD Better Regulation Agenda already exists, as does the Committee in charge of it; the NER set itself the task of identifying and addressing obstacles to its implementation. The fact that the policy framework is already in place does not offer as ample a room for expert influence as European regulators had in their time. However, other features of the NER render it a suitable platform for coordination on regulatory policy.

The same section above also mentioned that, despite their relative ineffectiveness, regulators cherish their networks and maintain sustained engagement in them. The OECD NER is also highly participated and cherished by its members, even though their regulatory agencies are typically already members of several other regulatory networks. This suggests that the NER provides them with added value. For one, the NER has proven very effective at one of the goals it set itself: increasing regulatory capacity. Regulators benefit from the learning opportunities offered by the NER; PAFER coordinated by the secretariat come with recommendations (normative guidance) that regulators can use to argue for domestic reform or more fulfilled independence and autonomy. This is an important source of potential leverage in attaining the network goals: regulatory independence and autonomy are difficult concepts to operationalise, particularly across different jurisdictions – thus far, the NER has invested a lot of effort in achieving a comprehensive definition and operationalisation of *de facto* independence, capable of being applicable across jurisdictions. Contributions like these have the potential to, in time, make a practical difference to regulatory practice that would strengthen the collaboration even further.

Moreover, the NER covers multiple sectors of utility regulation. This means that, within the NER, regulators are exposed to practice and solutions from a variety of regulated sectors. Other regulatory networks are usually focused on a single sector of regulation. Relatedly, most other networks of utility regulators have regional geographic scope. The broad geographical scope of the NER membership provides regulators with the opportunity to exchange views and learn from regulators that they would not otherwise have much opportunity to meet. In the NER, regulators 'get interaction with peers who are not the usual suspects' (interview 1). Finally, the NER is focused on regulatory policy more than regulatory provisions. Most other regulatory networks are technical, focused on the nuts and bolts of regulation. The NER, with its policy focus, attracts high-level regulatory officials, who appreciate a platform where they can interact with high-level peers from all over the world. Moreover, the NER maintains informal relationships with many other sectoral regulatory networks. Sometimes, NER representatives or the secretariat have presented the work and analyses produced by the network at meetings of other regulatory networks e.g., the Council of European Energy Regulators (CEER), the Latin American Association of Energy Regulators (ARIAE), the Latin American

Association of Telecommunications Regulators (REGULATEL), the Network of European Water Regulators (WAREG).

With its broad membership of high-level regulatory officials, its unique institutional context and its focus on regulatory policy, the NER is well-positioned to have tangible impact on regulatory implementation in the utility sectors around the world. The experience of European regulatory networks suggests that close cooperation between policy-makers and policy implementers is more effective in achieving harmonised implementation than coordination between implementers on its own. Translated to the case of the NER, their experience suggests that closer coordination between the RPC and the NER would enhance the effectiveness of the work of the OECD regulatory policy division.

CONCLUSIONS: THE ROLE OF NER IN THE BETTER REGULATION AGENDA

This chapter outlined the main features of the OECD Network of Economic Regulators (NER). The NER was established to bridge the gap, ever more apparent, between regulatory design and regulatory implementation (or, in OECD lingo, 'regulatory delivery') in fields of economic regulation of infrastructure, ranging from energy to telecommunications to water. The NER has a specific focus on the day-to-day practice of regulation and the difficulties that regulators face in discharging their mandate for effective delivery of regulatory policy. Unlike other networks of utility regulators, the NER is multi-sectoral, has broad geographic scope and a policy focus which attracts high-level regulatory officials, e.g., Commissioners or Board Members to its membership.

This chapter has briefly outlined what is known about regulatory networks concerning the reasons of their establishment, the conditions under which they are or are not successful in fulfilling their goals, and the regulators' motivations to take part in them. This knowledge has been deployed as a roadmap to understand the NER and its potential contribution to the Better Regulation agenda of the OECD. The chapter argues that the NER has much in common with other networks of economic regulators, particularly European ones, in that the NER was also set up to close a governance gap between regulatory policy design and enforcement and faces similar challenges to achieving that goal. Recent research shows that the task of joint enforcement has proven challenging to accomplish even for networks with some actual powers and ample autonomy, like the European Competition Network (Cseres and Outhuijse, 2017). This chapter proposes that one way to increase the effectiveness of the NER is via closer collaboration with the RPC in future refinements of the Better Regulation Agenda to consider the challenges of implementation and enforcement across different countries.

There are many open questions in the study of enforcement networks (Mastenbroek and Martinsen, 2018): these include understanding the limits that differences in institutional features of regulatory agencies pose on their ability to discharge their mandate and the contribution that transnational coordination can have on different aspects of regulatory implementation. The experience of the NER can contribute to answering some of those questions and therefore deserves closer scholarly attention in the future.

REFERENCES

Abbott, K.W. and D. Snidal (2010). 'International regulation without international government: Improving IO performance through orchestration.' *The Review of International Organizations*, *5*(3), 315–344. https://doi.org/10.1007/s11558-010-9092-3 accessed 20 April 2023.

Bach, D. and A. Newman (2014). 'Domestic drivers of transgovernmental regulatory cooperation.' *Regulation & Governance*, *8*(4), 395–417. https://doi.org/10.1111/rego.12047 accessed 20 April 2023.

Bach, D. and A. Newman (2010). 'Transgovernmental networks and domestic policy convergence: evidence from insider trading regulation.' *International Organization*, *64*(03), 505–528. https://doi.org/10.1017/S0020818310000135 accessed 20 April 2023.

Bach, T., F. De Francesco, M. Maggetti and E. Ruffing (2016). 'Transnational bureaucratic politics: An institutional rivalry perspective on EU network governance.' *Public Administration*, *94*(1), 9–24. https://doi.org/10.1111/padm.12252 accessed 20 April 2023.

Bach, T. and E. Ruffing (2013). 'Networking for autonomy? National agencies in European networks.' *Public Administration*, *91*(3), 712–726. https://doi.org/10.1111/j.1467-9299.2012.02093.x accessed 20 April 2023.

Bianculli, A. C. (2021). 'Regulatory cooperation and international relations.' In *Oxford Research Encyclopedia of International Studies*. Oxford University Press. https://doi.org/10.1093/acrefore/9780190846626.013.658 accessed 20 April 2023.

Bruszt, L. and G.A. McDermott (2014). *Leveling the Playing Field: Transnational Regulatory Integration and Development*. OUP Oxford. https://books.google.co.uk/books?id=DgwbBAAAQBAJ accessed 20 April 2023.

Busuioc, M. (2009). 'Accountability, control and independence: The case of European agencies. *European Law Journal*, *15*(5), 599–615. https://doi.org/10.1111/j.1468-0386.2009.00480.x accessed 20 April 2023.

Cengiz, F. (2010). 'Multi-level governance in competition policy: The European Competition Network.' *European Law Review*, *35*(5), 660–677.

Coen, D. and M.Thatcher (2008). 'Network governance and multi-level delegation: European Networks of Regulatory Agencies.' *Journal of Public Policy*, *28*(01), 49–71. https://doi.org/10.1017/S0143814X08000779 accessed 20 April 2023.

Cseres, K. and Outhuijse, A. (2017). 'Parallel enforcement and accountability: The case of EU competition law.' *Law Enforcement by EU Authorities*. https://www.elgaronline.com/view/edcoll/9781786434623/9781786434623.00010.xml accessed 20 April 2023.

Djelic, M.L. and K. Sahlin-Andersson (2006). *Transnational Governance: Institutional Dynamics of Regulation*. Cambridge University Press. http://books.google.co.uk/books?id=0-9_LF9yT4gC accessed 20 April 2023.

Fernández-i-Marín, X. and J. Jordana (2015). 'The emergence of regulatory regionalism: Transnational networks and the diffusion of regulatory agencies within regions.' *Contemporary Politics*, *21*(4), 417–434. https://doi.org/10.1080/13569775.2015.1010776 accessed 20 April 2023.

Gilardi, F. (2007). 'The same, but different: Central banks, regulatory agencies, and the politics of delegation to independent authorities.' *Comparative European Politics*, *5*(3), 303–327.

Guardiancich, I. and M. Guidi (2016). 'Formal independence of regulatory agencies and varieties of capitalism: A case of institutional complementarity?' *Regulation & Governance*, *10*(3), 211–229. https://doi.org/10.1111/rego.12080 accessed 20 April 2023.

Iborra, S.S., A. Saz-Carranza, X. Fernández-i-Marín and A. Albareda (2017). 'The governance of goal-directed networks and network tasks: An empirical analysis of European Regulatory Networks.' *Journal of Public Administration Research and Theory*, mux037–mux037. https://doi.org/10.1093/jopart/mux037 accessed 20 April 2023.

Jordana, J. (2017). 'Transgovernmental networks as regulatory intermediaries.' *The ANNALS of the American Academy of Political and Social Science*, *670*(1), 245–262. https://doi.org/10.1177/0002716217694591 accessed 20 April 2023.

Jordana, J. and D. Levi-Faur (2014). 'Regional integration and transnational regulatory regimes: The polycentric architecture of governance in Latin American telecommunications.' In L. Brusztand

and G.A. McDermott (eds), *Leveling the Playing Field. Transnational Regulatory Integration and Development*. Oxford University Press.

Maggetti, M. (2013). 'The rewards of cooperation: The effects of membership in European regulatory networks.' *European Journal of Political Research*, *53*(3), 480–499. https://doi.org/10.1111/1475-6765.12042 accessed 20 April 2023.

Maggetti, M.and F. Gilardi, (2014). 'Network governance and the domestic adoption of soft rules.' *Journal of European Public Policy*, *21*(9), 1293–1310. https://doi.org/10.1080/13501763.2014.923018 accessed 20 April 2023.

Mastenbroek, E. and D.S. Martinsen (2018). 'Filling the gap in the European administrative space: The role of administrative networks in EU implementation and enforcement.' *Journal of European Public Policy*, *25*(3), 422–435. https://doi.org/10.1080/13501763.2017.1298147 accessed 20 April 2023.

Mathieu, E. (2020). 'Functional stakes and EU regulatory governance: Temporal patterns of regulatory integration in energy and telecommunications.' *West European Politics*, *43*(4), 991–1010. Taylor and Francis+NEJM. https://doi.org/10.1080/01402382.2019.1622353 accessed 20 April 2023.

Newman, A.L. (2008). Building transnational civil liberties: Transgovernmental entrepreneurs and the European Data Privacy Directive.' *International Organization*, *62*(01), 103–130. https://doi.org/10.1017/S0020818308080041 accessed 20 April 2023.

OECD. (2013). *Establishment of the Network Of Economic Regulators (NER) as subsidiary body of the REGUlatory Policy Committee. Mandate of the Network of Economic Regulators*. GOV/RPC/NER(2013)4.

OECD. (2014). *The Governance of Regulators, OECD Best Practice Principles for Regulatory Policy*. OECD Publishing.

OECD. (2016). *Being an independent regulator.* [The Governance of Regulators]. OECD Publishing.

Raustiala, K. (2002). 'Architecture of international cooperation: Transgovernmental networks and the future of international law, The. *Virginia Journal of International Law*, *43*(1), 1–92.

Ruffing, E. (2015). 'Agencies between two worlds: Information asymmetry in multilevel policy-making.' *Journal of European Public Policy*, *22*(8), 1109–1126. https://doi.org/10.1080/13501763.2015.1011198 accessed 20 April 2023.

Russell, G. and C. Hodges (2019). *Regulatory Delivery*. Bloomsbury Publishing.

Saz-Carranza, A., S. Salvador Iborra and A. Albareda (2016). 'The power dynamics of mandated network administrative organizations.' *Public Administration Review*, *76*(3), 449–462. https://doi.org/10.1111/puar.12445 accessed 20 April 2023.

Slaughter, A.-M. (1997). 'The real new world order.' *Foreign Affairs*, 183–197.

Slaughter, A.-M. (2004). *A New World Order*. Princeton University Press.

Townley, C., M. Guidi and M. Tavares (2022). *The Law and Politics of Global Competition: Influence and Legitimacy in the International Competition Network*. Oxford University Press.

Vantaggiato, F.P. (2019a). 'Networking for resources: How regulators use networks to compensate for lower staff levels.' *Journal of European Public Policy*, *26*(10), 1540–1559. https://doi.org/10.1080/13501763.2018.1535611 accessed 20 April 2023.

Vantaggiato, F.P. (2019b). 'The drivers of regulatory networking: Policy learning between homophily and convergence.' *Journal of Public Policy*, *39*(3), 443–464. Cambridge Core. https://doi.org/10.1017/S0143814X18000156 accessed 20 April 2023.

Vantaggiato, F.P. (2020). 'Regulatory relationships across levels of multilevel governance systems: From collaboration to competition.' *Governance*, *33*(1), 173–189. https://doi.org/10.1111/gove.12409 accessed 20 April 2023.

Vantaggiato, F.P., H. Kassim and K. Wright (2020). 'Internal network structures as opportunity structures: Control and effectiveness in the European competition network.' *Journal of European Public Policy*, 1–20. https://doi.org/10.1080/13501763.2020.1737183 accessed 20 April 2023.

Verdier, P.-H. (2009). 'Transnational regulatory networks and their limits.' *Yale Journal of International Law*, *34*(1), 113–172.

Vestlund, N.M. (2015). 'Pooling administrative resources through EU regulatory networks.' *Journal of European Public Policy*, *24*(1), 61–80. https://doi.org/10.1080/13501763.2015.1118147 accessed 20 April 2023.

Yesilkagit, K. (2011). 'Institutional compliance, European networks of regulation and the bureaucratic autonomy of national regulatory authorities.' *Journal of European Public Policy*, *18*(7), 962–979. https://doi.org/10.1080/13501763.2011.599965 accessed 20 April 2023.

PART III

POLICY SECTORS

12. Development assistance and cooperation

Joren Verschaeve

INTRODUCTION

From its inception in 1961, the Development Assistance Committee (DAC) of the OECD has figured for most of its existence as one of the leading international venues for the so-called 'developed countries' to discuss aid efforts (see Chapter 2 for the historical context of DAC). In doing so, it played a key role in the shaping of the global aid architecture both the post WWII and Cold War period (Bracho et al., 2021; Ydesen and Verschaeve, 2019). More recently, however, the DAC's role in international cooperation is becoming less clear, if any left. For more than a decade, now, the DAC has been confronted with an unprecedented number of challenges. While initially, questions arose on how to engage with a growing number of new public as well as private development actors, more recent challenges run deeper and link with new paradigms on international cooperation and development, which emerged both from within as well as outside the traditional aid architecture. Most notably is climate change, which fundamentally challenges dominant thinking on international cooperation and the promotion of economic development which has been at the heart of the DAC's mission for the past 60 years.

In line with the aims and scope of this edited volume, this chapter seeks to address questions on the role of the DAC in future transnational policy making. Building upon the existing streams of literature on the DAC and OECD, as well as international cooperation, we aim to offer a toolbox for researchers to study the place of the DAC in the world. In doing so, we will first provide an overview of the history of the DAC, paying particular attention to its functioning, membership and peculiar relationship with the OECD. In the subsequent sections, we delve deeper into the different strands within the literature that have come to assess the different aspects of the DAC's role in transnational policy making. The chapter concludes with a number of more general reflections on the OECD-DAC at large, and its ramifications on the literature on the committee in particular.

ON THE ORIGINS OF THE DAC

The origins of the DAC lay in the late 1950s. Few people know, however, that the DAC and the OECD were established as two separate international organizations, with the latter integrating the former once becoming fully operational. All of this happened in a timespan of two years. More specifically, the DAC was formally established as Development Assistance Group (DAG) in January 1960 (Führer, 1996; Verschaeve and Takács, 2013). Being a child of its time, this happened largely at the initiative of the United States (US). Confronted with new waves of decolonization, a growing economic involvement of the Soviet Union in the global South and socialist/communist forces on the rise in various countries, the US wanted to safeguard and strengthen the Western position in the world. In line with their strong (financial) involvement in the restoration of Europe after WWII, they wanted to achieve this by boosting Western aid budgets towards what was then coined the 'developing world'. Aside from geopolitical reasoning, also humanitarian aspirations pushed Western countries to do more at that time (Rostow, 1985; Esman and Cheever, 1967).

Interestingly, though, the US itself was unable to further step up its aid budgets. This had everything to do with the fact that the Eisenhower administration was confronted with the US first balance of payment deficits since the ending of WWII. Given that other Western countries were economically flourishing at that time, the idea arose in Washington to have a better sharing of efforts among Western countries in terms of providing development aid to the rest of the world. This was formalized in 1958 by the Eisenhower administration in a proposal for a 'Common Aid Effort', with the underlying ambition to significantly increase both the overall volume and effectiveness of Western development aid (Bracho et al., 2021; Esman and Cheever, 1967). Western allies quickly responded positively to the US proposal, and by the end of 1958 diplomats started to discuss the implementation of the Common Aid Efforts. One of the biggest issues to tackle, was the level of institutionalization of this new partnership. While virtually all countries were in favour of a strong, permanent institutional set-up which could become operational very quickly, a majority opposed the idea of establishing yet another international organization (IO). Hence, the formula that was agreed upon was the following: the establishment of IO on the short term – called the Development Assistant Group – which then afterwards would be absorbed by another organization. The choice ultimately fell on the OECD, which at that point still needed be established. Furthermore, in the absence of a DAG secretariat, the group came to rely on the then still existing Organisation for European Economic Cooperation (OEEC) for these services (Carroll and Kellow, 2011; Esman and Cheever, 1967; Verschaeve and Orbie, 2016b).

By the time that the OECD was fully operational, however, the DAG had already established itself as an effective institution, successfully hosting a series of meetings in Washington, Bonn, London and Tokyo. As a result, its members did not want to jeopardize its functioning when taking office in the OECD buildings in Paris in late 1961. Therefore, apart from a change in name, the DAC largely maintained an autonomous status within the OECD, as is reflected for example, by the fact that the Committee today has its own membership criteria which can – but not necessarily do – overlap with those of the OECD, its own – independent – permanent chair, representing the Committee vis-à-vis the OECD and the wider international community, a partly independent budget. Furthermore, and arguably most important, the DAC upholds a much higher working pace than most other OECD committees, stemming from the fact that the so-called DAC delegates – referring to the representatives of the different members of the Committee – reside in Paris on a permanent basis, allowing the DAC to schedule meetings at the level of the committee (and underlying working groups) throughout the year. As a result, the DAC is often coined as an 'OECD within the OECD', with a status somewhere between that of other OECD Committees and that of the International Energy Agency (IEA) (Verschaeve and Orbie, 2016b; Woodward, 2009).

While this institutional set-up might seem trivial for some, it is highly relevant for fully grasping the functioning of the DAC and its current and future role in transnational policy making. Amongst others, it implies that scientific insights on the OECD cannot simply be extrapolated to the DAC (and vice versa). While this might be the case for some research, for example, on the impact soft law governance through peer reviewing (see Chapter 9), comparing the OECD and the DAC is much trickier when addressing other research questions.

Therefore, existing scholarship on the DAC as well as the OECD which embark in more depth on the institutional set-up and/or organizational culture of both institutions is indispensable when studying the Committee.

UNDERSTUDIED EQUALS UNIMPORTANT?

The objective of the DAC has always been to contribute to increasing both the volume and effectiveness of development finance. To achieve these goals, the Committee's activities can – at the risk of oversimplification – be divided into three interlinked workflows. First, the DAC has always played a central role in defining what counts as aid, as well as monitoring how much aid flows from its members to partner countries. To do so, it established in 1969 the concept of official development assistance (ODA). Ever since, ODA has served as the international 'gold standard' of foreign aid. It is the DAC that governs the definition of ODA. Being a member of the Committee entails a yearly reporting of a countries ODA flows, allowing the DAC to publicly rank and evaluate the efforts of its membership (Bracho et al., 2021; Hynes and Scott, 2013). Second, the DAC serves as a forum for its members to coordinate their aid efforts as well as establish new development concepts. Indeed, apart from serving as a forum that counts ODA, the DAC has always played a normative role in defining how countries should come to think and shape their development programmes. In doing so, it played a pivotal role in launching or refining development concepts such as (un)tied aid, policy coherence for (sustainable) development, aid effectiveness and even the Millennium Development Goals (Eyben, 2013; Keijzer and Verschaeve, 2018). Third and final, and similar to most other OECD committees, the DAC also plays an important role as policy evaluator for its members, both quantitatively (cf. the annual ODA reporting), but also qualitatively. Most notably in this regard are the periodic peer reviews of the development programs of all DAC members which are conducted, allowing to identify best practices as well as areas where improvements can be made (Ashoff, 2013; Ydesen and Verschaeve, 2019).

While the above overview, rightfully, looks impressive, the scholarly community thus far has largely overlooked the DAC. This is odd, given that for most of its existence there was a widespread consensus among scholars, policy makers and NGOs about the Committee's central and influential role in the aid architecture. Nonetheless, until very recently, studies on the DAC's role in transnational policy making were scarce, especially in comparison to the multitude of scholarship on development institutions such as the World Bank, International Monetary Fund or the United Nations and its many affiliated organizations. Furthermore, among those who actually did study the DAC, there has always been a strong overrepresentation of (former) Committee officials and delegates. Most notably in this regard are the excellent pieces of scholarship of for example, Helmut Führer (1996), Xu and Carey (2015), Gerardo Bracho (2018) or William Hynes and Simon Scott (2013). While in itself, there is nothing wrong with such endeavours, it reflects once more the general appetite among development and international relations scholars for studying the DAC (Verschaeve, 2015).

This changed more recently, with a slight but steady uptake of studies devoted to the DAC from 2015 onwards. This can be attributed to two larger evolutions. First, since the late 2010s, there has developed a growing body of literature on the OECD, largely inspired by the latter's 50th anniversary. Given that both institutions history is strongly intertwined (see *supra*), as well as due to the fact that the DAC constitutes one of the leading committees of the OECD, various OECD scholars devoted special attention to the DAC in their work, as such doing the groundwork for others (Carroll and Kellow, 2011; Woodward, 2009). Second, the period 2005–15 marked an important era in development thinking. In an unprecedented striving towards eradicating global poverty, the international community adopted in the Millennium Development Goals (MDGs) in the early 2000s, as well as embarked on a journey towards improving aid effectiveness through a series of so-called high-level fora. Importantly, the DAC had played a pivotal role in both agendas, as such raising scholarly interests as to how the Committee had been so successful in drafting the global development agenda, as well as whether or not such role is desirable from a legitimacy point of view (e.g., Bracho et al., 2021; Eyben, 2013; Verschaeve and Orbie, 2016a; Kragelund, 2019). The result of both evolutions was a growing scholarly interest in the DAC, which we will discuss in more detail in the subsequent section. In doing so, we will both elaborate on the current state of play in the literature, as well as important research questions that are not yet or insufficiently addressed.

INWARD LOOKING: THE DAC THROUGH AN INSTITUTIONAL LENS

A first stream of literature on the DAC is constituted by a body of literature which looks at the Committee from the outside in. Indeed, studies within this tradition seek to unravel the DAC from an institutional point of view, wondering about the Committee's history, institutional set-up and decision-making processes. This stream of literature emerged largely in parallel with the literature on the OECD. One of the pioneers in this field was Helmut Führer, head of the DAC secretariat between 1975 and 1993, who compiled the first comprehensive overview of the DAC, offering an extensive annual overview of the Committee's work going back all the way to its inception in 1961. Building upon this empirical treasure of Führer, as well as other sources, various other scholars made important contributions to the scholarship on the DAC. Most notably in this regard has been a series of studies on the OECD, in which specific attention has been devoted to the DAC, typically at a descriptive level. Amongst others, these studies shed a light on important institutional aspects of the Committee's functioning or its position within the OECD (e.g., Carroll and Kellow, 2011; Mahon and McBride, 2008; Marcussen, 2003; Woodward, 2009). More recently, and also largely falling within this institutional tradition, a number of scholars started to focus on some elements of the DAC's functioning and/or history that had not yet been explored in greater depth. Most notably in this regard are a series of studies in which particular attention has been paid to for example, the DAC's relationship with individual members – for example, how it is that the EU has always been a full member of the DAC, whereas a full observer of the OECD – (Verschaeve and Takács, 2013), or key areas of work of the committee such as its peer review process (e.g., Manning 2008).

Of particular relevance for this stream of literature on the DAC, however, has been the recent publication of the first full-blown edited volume on the Committee, including several in-depth chapters on the Committee's history and institutional design (Bracho et al., 2021). In doing so, it is highly symbolic for the current state of the literature on the DAC, given that the various accounts that exist at present – and have been touched upon in the previous paragraph – jointly offer a comprehensive picture of the Committee's institutional set-up for the first time in history. As a result, it comes as no surprise that a growing number of studies have come to move beyond the above set of descriptive studies – with the utmost respect – as such offering valuable insights on how the institutional rules and set-up play out. For example, various case studies, for example, on Official Development Assistance reporting, Policy Coherence for Development, have come to show the important interplay between the EU – referring to both the EU institutions and its members – and the DAC in understanding policy outcomes (Manning, 2016; Verschaeve and Keijzer, 2018; Verschaeve and Orbie, 2018; Verschaeve, Delputte and Orbie, 2016). In a similar vein, various other in-depth case studies on the DAC's work in coining key development norms such as the ones on (un)tied aid, gender equality or fragile states, provide a detailed overview of the – often informal – dynamics at play within the DAC, both between the different members as well as with the Committee's secretariat (DCD), typically pointing out how the Committee served very often as an influential 'epistemic community' for the creation and/or mainstreaming of new development concepts and norms (e.g., Eyben, 2013; Grimm, Lemay and Nay, 2014; Bracho et al., 2021).

In sum, it can thus be concluded that whereas the DAC has been a black box for most of its existence, recent years have witnessed a growing scholarly interest for the Committee's institutional set-up and functioning, as such unravelling the mystery of the Committee. Building upon a first wave of descriptive institutional accounts, scholars have now come to explore the decision-making processes of the DAC in greater depth. Nonetheless, a number of important questions still need to be addressed. In depth accounts of the impact of the DAC on its members – for example, in terms of aid allocations or policy learning – are still rather limited. In a similar vein, few scholars thus far studied in greater depth the extent to which findings on the DAC decision-making or impact can be extrapolated to other OECD committees (and vice versa). Addressing such questions will offer important insights in further improving our understanding of the DAC's current and future role. This leads us to the second strand of research on DAC.

OUTWARD LOOKING – THE POSITION AND LEGITIMACY OF THE DAC IN INTERNATIONAL COOPERATION

A second stream of literature is constituted by studies which take the DAC as a 'starting point' and rather than unravelling its internal functioning, wonder about its role in international policy making. Amongst other, scholars within this tradition study the interaction between the DAC and other international (development) institutions, its impact on shaping international norms and policies, as well as raise questions as to what extent the DAC's role in international relations is a legitimate one. Importantly, studies within this tradition only started to emergence from the 2000s onwards. This was triggered by the widespread observation amongst policy makers, scholars and NGOs that the DAC had played a key role in shaping the international development thinking in the post-Cold War period. Especially its role in the design of the MDGs, which heavily drew upon the DAC's 1996 report 'Shaping the 21st Century', drew a lot of scholarly attention on to the Committee. This resulted in a series of studies, typically revolving around a particular development concept, in which a detailed account was provided of the role played by the DAC in its creation and/or mainstreaming of specific policy norms. This latter strand of literature overlaps to some extent with certain more institutional studies (cf. *supra*), albeit the main distinction with these studies links to both (i) the degree to which intra-DAC processes have been untangled, as well as (ii) the audience to whom these studies are addressed – i.e., typically more IR than development studies. Albeit, it had to be pointed out that the distinction between both is not always that clear-cut (Masujima, 2004; Ruckert, 2008; Verschaeve, Delputte and Orbie, 2016).

The vast majority of scholars, however, focused on the DAC's work on aid effectiveness. Governed by a series of so-called high-level fora (HLF), these were prepared by the DAC's working party on aid effectiveness (WP-EFF) and brought together the wider development community and. These HLF took place in Rome (2003), Paris (2005), Accra (2008) and Busan (2011) and served as venues for both defining the international agenda on aid effectiveness, as well as monitoring whether or not progress had been achieved thus far. As a consequence of the international political importance of these HLF, various scholars subsequently came to study the role of the DAC on aid effectiveness in greater depth (e.g., Brown and Morton, 2008; Eyben, 2013; Eyben and Savage, 2012; Hammad and Morton, 2009). In doing so, scholars not only raised question about the impact of the DAC in transnational policy making or its success (or failure) in including all relevant actors in the process, more fundamental – and critical – questions were addressed as well, for example, as to what extent the DAC – being considered a Western dominated institution – had a legitimate role to play in this area at all (e.g., Ruckert, 2008).

In parallel, and partly linked to questions on the DAC's legitimacy, the late 2000s also witnessed the proliferation of a wide range of new as well as re-emerging public and private development actors, ranging from philanthropic foundations (e.g., the Bill and Melinda Gates Foundation) to BRIC countries and others. Moreover, and inspired by these dynamics, the international community also saw the birth of a number of new international development institutions, with the explicit ambition to take on and over (certain) areas of work of the DAC. Most illustrative in this regard was the creation of the UN Development Cooperation Forum (UN-DCF) which aspired itself a prominent place in the thinking on aid – and later on development – effectiveness. As a consequence, various scholars subsequently have come to study questions as to what extent (and how successful) the DAC has been in expanding its membership and/or integrating relevant third actors into its work (e.g., Bracho et al., 2021; Bräutigam, 2011; Kragelund, 2019; Swiss, 2021; Zimmermann and Smith, 2011). Others have come to compare the DAC with other international institutions, addressing questions related to the Committee's legitimacy vis-à-vis other international development fora (Verschaeve and Orbie, 2016a). The main findings of this literature are that while the DAC does suffer on various fronts from a lack of legitimacy – largely linked to its exclusive membership – it also derives a great deal of legitimacy from its effectiveness in comparison to other development institutions. Whether this is sufficient is, however, yet to be seen.

In recent years, however, the scholarly debates on the DAC's role in transnational development policy making has steadily declined. Notwithstanding valuable contributions and insights (Bracho et al., 2021), it is fair to state that such questions are increasingly becoming irrelevant. This has everything to do with the fact that the international community – at large – has increasingly come to think 'beyond development', structuring most of its thinking and actions through the lens of the sustainable development goals (SDGs). Furthermore, monumental global challenges linked to climate change and biodiversity loss have become – rightly so – the number one priority on the international stage. While obviously international cooperation – and with it the DAC – still has a key role to play in the decade(s) to come, research questions linked to for example, the impact of the DAC in shaping the international agenda – and with it its legitimacy to do so – have become obsolete given that the Committee operates in a very different context today. As a result, scholars should – and increasingly do – start to wonder about what role is (left) for the DAC in this changed international context. In doing so, it will be vital to distinguish between the different areas of work of the Committee, ranging from, for example, the monitoring of aid flows or its peer-reviewing process to its role in the shaping and dissemination of policy norms. While at present there is an emerging consensus that the DAC's areas of work linked to its so-called services towards its members (e.g., peer reviewing) will continue to have an added value in the future, it still remains very unclear as to what extent the Committee will continue to have a role in helping to shape international thinking about cooperation and development. Open questions which remain to be addressed, link, for example, with whether or not the DAC's historical focus on promoting economic growth in order to achieve development, still fit with new thinking on climate change and bio-diversity loss where a growing emphasis is being placed on concepts such as degrowth (e.g., Hickel, 2020; Belmonte-Ureña et al., 2021). Furthermore, a wide range of other institutions – both within and beyond the scope of the OECD – have a much stronger tradition of policy making in these areas, and are increasingly taking up holistic framework on e.g., just transi-tion. Obviously, this calls for new comparative studies of the DAC vis-à-vis those institutions, allowing to gain new insights on the Committee's future in transnational policy making.

CONCLUSION

As outlined in this chapter, the DAC suffered for most of its existence from a lack of scholarly interest. This was rather odd, given that the Committee has always been one of the leading venues for discussing international development cooperation, deriving this status from its particular composition and effectiveness (Bracho et al., 2021; Verschaeve and Orbie, 2016a). However, it was not until the last decade that a growing number of scholars have more system-atically come to study the Committee's particularities, as well as role in international policy making. This cumulated in the emergence of two distinct strands of literatures, respectively, studying the DAC from an institutional point of view, as well as studying the role of the Committee within the larger international constellation of actors and policy norms. As a result, we find ourselves today at a position where the study of the DAC has matured, with most gaps in the literature being finally addressed. This serves as a solid foundation for new, additional – and finer grained – research on the DAC in the years to come.

However, and somewhat ironically perhaps, the question is to what extent it will still make sense to have a somewhat distinct body of literature on the DAC – separate from the larger scholarship on the OECD – in the years to come. This has everything to do with the more fundamental debate which currently takes place on the future of development cooperation. In a context of increased horizontal thinking on international cooperation – as is reflected most prominently in the sustainable development goal framework – as well as more philosophical debates emerging on what is development in the light of climate change and other interna-tional threads, the DAC is seeking its place in the evolving global architecture. Certainly, the Committee will continue to prove itself as a valuable venue for policy learning among its membership, but other aspects of its work linked to international policy norm making might increasingly lose its relevance. The outcome of this search will greatly influence the study of the DAC in the years to come. If the DAC turns into a venue for policy learning only, it no longer makes sense to study the committee separately from the rest of the OECD. On the contrary, when the DAC manages to carve out a unique space in the emerging new international architecture, it will most likely build upon its own particularities and strengths which might be different from those of the OECD. However, if we know one thing for certain, it is that we (finally) have a strong bulk of literature on the DAC, allowing future researchers to make solid claims about the Committee's future.

REFERENCES

Ashoff, Guido (2013). '50 Years of Peer Reviews by the OECD's Development Assistance Committee: an instrument of quality assurance and mutual learning.' DIE Briefing Paper, 2.

Belmonte-Ureña, L. J., J. A. Plaza-Úbeda, D. Vazquez-Brust and N. Yakovleva (2021). 'Circular economy, degrowth and green growth as pathways for research on sustainable development goals: A global analysis and future agenda.' *Ecological Economics*, 185, 107050.

Bracho, G., R. H. Carey, W. Hynes, S. Klingebiel and A. Trzeciak-Duval (2021). 'Origins, evolution and future of global development cooperation: The role of the Development Assistance Committee' (No.104). Studies.

Bracho, Gerardo. (2018). 'Towards a common definition of South-South cooperation: Bringing together the spirit of Bandung and the spirit of Buenos Aires.' *Development Cooperation Review* 6, 9–13.

Bräutigam, Deborah (2011). 'Aid 'With Chinese Characteristics': Chinese foreign aid and development finance meet the OECD-DAC aid regime.' *Journal of International Development*, 23(5), 752–64.

Brown, Stephen and Bill Morton (2008). *Reforming Aid and Development Cooperation: Accra, Doha and Beyond*. Ottawa: North-South Institute.

Carroll, Peter and Aynsley Kellow (2011). *The OECD. A study of organizational adaptation*. Cheltenham: Edward Elgar Publishing.

Esman, Milton and David Cheever (1967). *The Common Aid Effort: the development assistance activities of the Organization for Economic Co-operation and Development*. Ohio: State University Press.

Eyben, Rosalind. (2013). 'Struggles in Paris: The DAC and the purposes of development aid.' *European Journal of Development Research*, 25(1), 78–91.

Eyben, Rosalind and Laura Savage (2012). 'Emerging and submerging powers: Imagined geographies in the new development partnership at the Busan Fourth High Level Forum.' *Journal of Development Studies*, 49(4), 457–69.

Führer, Helmut. (1996). *The Story of Official Development Assistance: A History of the DAC and DCD in dates, names and figures*. Paris: OECD.

Grimm, Sonja, Nicolas Lemay-Hébert and Olivier Nay (2014). 'Fragile states: introducing a political concept.' *Third World Quarterly*, 35(2), 197–209.

Hammad, Lama., and Morton, Bill. (2009). Non-DAC donors and reform of the international aid architecture. The North-South Institute, Issues Brief.

Hickel, J. (2020). *Less is more: How degrowth will save the world*. Random House.

Hynes, William and Simon Scott (2013). 'The evolution of Official Development Assistance: Achievements, Criticisms and a Way Forward.' OECD Development Co-operation Working Papers, 12.

Keijzer, N and J. Verschaeve (2018). 'United in diversity? Analyzing behavior expectations of the European Union as a non-state member of the OECD's development assistance committee.' *Contemporary Politics*, 24(4), 379–97.

Kragelund, P. (2019). *South-south Development*. Routledge.

Mahon, Rian and Stephen. McBride (eds) (2008). *The OECD and Transnational Governance*. Toronto: UBC Press.

Marcussen, Martin. (2003). 'Multilateral surveillance and the OECD: Playing the idea games.' In K. Armingeon and M. Beyeler (eds), *The OECD and European Welfare State*s. Cheltenham: Edward Elgar Publishing.

Masujima, Ken. (2004). Good governance and the DAC: ideas and organizational constraint. In Morton Boas and Desmond McNeill (eds), *Global Institutions and Development: Framing the World?* London: Routledge.

Manning, Richard. (2008). 'The DAC as a Central Actor in Development Policy Issues: Experiences over the Past Four Years.' In DIE (ed), Discussion paper (Vol.7). Bonn.

Manning, R. (2016). 'OECD-DAC and Japan: Its past, present, and future.' In *Japan's Development Assistance* (pp. 276–92). London: Palgrave Macmillan.

Rostow, Walt Withman. (1985). *Eisenhower, Kennedy, and Foreign Aid*. Austin: University of Texas Press.

Ruckert, Arne. (2008). 'Making Neo-Gramscian sense of the DAC.' In Rian Mahon and Stephen McBride (eds), *The OECD and Transnational Governance*. Vancouver: UBC Press.

Swiss, L. (2021). 'The globalization of foreign aid: global influences and the diffusion of aid priorities.' In *The Palgrave Handbook of Development Cooperation for Achieving the 2030 Agenda* (pp. 113–25). Palgrave Macmillan, Cham.

Verschaeve, J and T. Takács (2013). 'The EU's international identity: The curious case of the OECD.' In *The European Union's Emerging International Identity* (pp. 187–209). Brill Nijhoff.

Verschaeve, J. (2015). An eroding relationship: an inductive analysis of the relations between the EU and the DAC of the OECD. PhD Dissertation, Ghent University. Faculty of Political and Social Sciences, Ghent, Belgium.

Verschaeve, J., S. Delputte and J. Orbie (2016). 'The rise of policy coherence for development: a multi-causal approach.' *The European Journal of Development Research*, 28(1), 44–61.

Verschaeve, J. and J. Orbie (2016a). 'The DAC is dead, long live the DCF? A comparative analysis of the OECD DAC and the UN DCF.' *The European Journal of Development Research*, 28(4), 571–87.

Verschaeve, J. and Orbie, J. (2016b). 'Once a member, always a member? Assessing the importance of time in the relationship between the EU and the DAC.' *Cambridge Review of International Affairs*, 29(2), 512–27.

Verschaeve, J and J. Orbie, (2018). 'Ignoring the elephant in the room? Assessing the impact of the EU on the DAC's role in international development.' *Development Policy Review*, 36.

Woodward, Richard (2009). *The Organization for Economic Development and Coordination*. London: Routledge.

Xu, Jiajun and Richard Carey (2015). 'Post-2015 global governance of official development finance: Harnessing the renaissance of public entrepreneurship.' *Journal of International Development* 27, 856–80.

Ydesen, C. and J. Verschaeve, (2019).' The OECD-DAC and peace: Instituting peace by economic means.' In *The Palgrave Handbook of Global Approaches to Peace* (pp. 477–95). Palgrave Macmillan.

Zimmermann, Felix and Kimberly Smith, (2011). 'More actors, more money, more ideas for international development co-operation.' *Journal of International Development*, 23(5), 722–38.

13. Education

Sotiria Grek and Bob Lingard

INTRODUCTION

Although the OECD has been primarily concerned with economic policy, education took on increasing importance in the OECD mandate, due to its relevance to economic competitiveness and growth. Since the early 1990s, the OECD has contributed to the construction and development of a global educational policy field with its production of education indicators and global education performance comparisons (Lingard *et al.* 2005; Grek 2009).

Through its Indicators in Education project (Grek and Ydesen 2021), including World Education Indicators developed in conjunction with UNESCO and the World Bank, the Programme for International Assessment (PISA), as well as through national and thematic policy reviews, the OECD educational agenda has become significant in framing policy options at the national level and in consolidating a global policy space in education (Lingard, Rawolle and Taylor 2005). This chapter will show how a 'policy as numbers' approach (Rose 1999, Ozga and Lingard 2007) has been central to the development and hegemony of the OECD as a global education research and policy actor.

THE OECD'S EDUCATION WORK: HISTORY, STRUCTURE AND CHANGING FUNCTIONS

In his institutional history of the OECD and education, Papadopoulos (1994) states that education has always had an 'inferred role' in respect to its economic significance. Such an inferred role became more explicit in the context of globalization and the associated knowledge economy discourses, which the OECD was also central in disseminating. The end of the Cold War and the apparent triumph of global capitalism placed further pressures on the OECD to focus its work not only on producing education performance metrics (and their accompanying league tables), but also policy recommendations for reform, especially for national education systems appearing as 'failing'.

Unlike other international organizations, the OECD has no prescriptive mandate over its member countries or indeed over many of the non-member countries that participate in its testing programmes. The OECD itself argues that it operates through 'consensus building' and through 'peer pressure': it is proud of the 'traditions of transparency: of providing explanations and justifications for policy, and of engaging in critical self-appraisal' (OECD 1998 p.102). The OECD seeks to exert influence through processes of mutual examination by governments, multilateral surveillance and peer pressure to conform or reform. This is achieved through an elaborate system of directorates, committees and boards, at the apex of which is a Council comprising representatives from each member country, normally at ambassadorial or ministerial levels. In this way, the OECD asserts its agenda in rather informal ways through the processes of opinion formation and coordination, in a manner that is dynamic and constantly shifting. The OECD's ability to create education policy impact within nations might be seen to be an effect of its soft power and its reputation as providing the 'golden standard' of comparative education research (Grek 2014).

Education at the OECD: A Short History

Historically, education-related activities were carried out initially under the rubric of the Office for Scientific and Technical Personnel, which in turn grew out of the former OEEC's pivotal work in mapping the technological gap between Europe and North America in the context of the Cold War (Papadopoulos 1994).

In 1968, the Centre for Research and Innovation (CERI) was established within the OECD, partly as a result of a growing recognition within the Organization of the 'qualitative' aspects of economic growth 'as an instrument for creating better conditions of life' and, along with that, of a more comprehensive view of education's multiple purposes. By the early 1970s, then, the Organization had come to the realization that 'the full range of objectives of education had to be taken into account if the educational activities of the Organization were to make their rightful contribution to economic policy' (Papadopoulos 1994, p.64). According to Papadopoulos (1994, p.122), this marked the triumph of a more comprehensive, less economistic or human capital view of education policy within the OECD, which possibly gave more importance to education's social and cultural purposes. Papadopoulos (1994) also shows that a (European) network of progressive sociologists of education was important to the emergence of this more balanced approach to researching education. This framing was apparent in the educational work the OECD pursued, organized under four programmes: two of them emerging from the Education Committee and the CERI Governing Board, with the other two being the more specialist programmes of Educational Buildings (PEB) and Institutional Management in Higher Education (IMHE). As Rizvi and Lingard (2006, p.250) illustrate, the educational projects sponsored by the OECD during the 1970s and 1980s demonstrated the significance of social justice purposes of education and a complex and mediated relationship between education and economic development.

However, by the mid-1980s, CERI came under pressure – not least from the United States (US) – for a new push to develop international comparative indicators. International comparative studies conducted by the International Association for the Evaluation of Educational Achievement (IEA) had shown the US lagging behind the other participating nations in terms of performance (Morgan 2009). This irked the US Department of Education considerably; consequently, it raised questions about the quality of the indicators hitherto used. The US thus emerged as a powerful actor in the scene of the production of education data. Given that the US was one of the prime funders of the OECD, its influence was particularly important. The US intervention led to the report *A Nation at Risk* (1983), which used a series of so-called risk indicators as a factual representation of US students' poor performance on national and international tests (Morgan 2009), an analysis that was also repeated two years later, in the US Department of Education's 1985 publication 'Indicators of Education – Status and Trends'.

From the US perspective, education in the 1980s had become a precarious business. In 1987, the US proposed an international conference on educational indicators to be held under the auspices of the OECD. In this document, the US authorities described the background for this push as follows:

Over the past three years, the United States has been evolving a set of indicators of education's status and progress in this country. These indicators are intended to describe the "health" of the educational system so that the public and citizens who make decisions about the future of education in this country might be better informed. (US Department of Education 1985, 1)

Thus, the US strongly framed the reasons for the need to produce education indicators. These reasons related closely to economic concerns, though the right to education also appears here as an American value that requires protection. Permeating these reasons is the view that indicators are providers of reliable data that are statistically valid and able to provide benchmarks for measuring progress in respect of the quality of school provision. As mentioned, on the one hand, the production of indicators by the IEA bothered the US; on the other, the proposal for new indicators was strongly embedded in the nation's policies to improve economic prospects. In this vein, negative educational progress, as manifested in the IEA data, was seen to affect economic indicators and growth. As Henry *et al.* (2001) argue, drawing on interview data, the US repeatedly called for work on outcome indicators, particularly in relation to school effectiveness, at one stage even threatening to withdraw its support of CERI if its demands were not met. However, Henry *et al.* also demonstrate that, from a different ideological direction, France – with its bureaucratic interest in statistical data collection – joined the US in pushing the OECD towards developing educational indicators. France did not link education performance to economic growth as the US did; nonetheless, France was always characterized by a strong bureaucratic interest in collecting education data. In Bürgi's (2015) reading of the situation, although the US and France had different interests in pushing for the making of education indicators, in the end they came to have a fairly open, fluid, but shared belief in the need for numbers to serve policy purposes. Actors such as the IEA, the OECD, the US, and France, although setting off from quite divergent interests and values, became key players in the education performance data game. Therefore, because of the considerable groundwork that had already been done, the OECD was 'well placed to respond to the mounting pressure in the late eighties for a new governmental effort to develop such indicators' (Papadopoulos 1994, p.190). It is to the production of these indicators that we will now turn.

EDUCATION AT A GLANCE: THE OECD INES PROJECT

Indeed, since the late1980s, indicators have become a highly significant part of the OECD's work in education (see Chapter 10 on an overall discussion of policy benchmarking and indicators). Its annual publication *Education at a Glance: OECD Indicators* (INES) is disseminated widely not only across the OECD countries, but elsewhere as well, just as participation in PISA now involves a large number of countries in addition to OECD member nations. In addition, since 1996 this publication has been supplemented by an analytical volume which draws on the database to comment in more detail on selected themes deemed to be of key importance to governments, policy makers and the public. The first volume of *Education at a Glance* was published in 1992. Subsequent volumes continued to provide data that reflected both on the resources invested in education as well as on its returns, illuminating 'the relative qualities of education systems' (OECD 1996, p.9). By 1998, six themes emerged: the demographic, economic and social context of education; financial and human resources invested in education; access to education, participation and progression; the transition from school to work; the learning environment and the organisation of schools; and student achievement and the social and labour-market outcomes of education.

The OECD argues that this exercise in international comparison is designed to assist in the processes of policy formation in member countries and to contribute to the public accountability of education systems:

> At a time when education is receiving increased priority but, like other areas of public spending, is facing the prospect of limited public funds, understanding better the internal processes that determine the relationship between educational expenditures and educational outcomes is particularly important. (CERI 1995, p.7)

The INES project also provides a useful illustration of the shift in the OECD's role as a policy instrument and forum (Henry *et al.* (2001) – that is, as a catalyst facilitating policy development in member countries and assisting processes of policy dissemination, adaptation and borrowing – to that of an international mediator of knowledge and global policy actor. These 'faces' of the OECD are not mutually exclusive, of course, because the indicators work at two levels. At one level, indicators may indeed assist member countries to clarify and compare their own policy stances and also, in relation to PISA, allow some focus on matters of equity; simultaneously, though, international indicators draw countries into a single comparative field made commensurate, which pivots around certain norms of provision and performance. This has witnessed the emergence of a global policy field in education.

More recently consideration has been given to linking the indicators used by OECD with outcomes measures of school performance such as those of PISA, which is the focus of the next section.

THE PROGRAMME FOR INTERNATIONAL STUDENT ASSESSMENT (PISA)

The Programme for International Student Assessment (PISA), first administered in 2000, is conducted in three-yearly cycles and examines the knowledge and skills of 15-year-olds in compulsory education. The OECD develops the assessment tasks used in PISA through commissioning agencies to produce the tests. Thus, unlike the Indicators, which are reported in *Education at a Glance* and which utilise data supplied by member nations, PISA works with tests developed by the OECD and those contracted to produce the tests. Although PISA began as a joint survey of the OECD member countries, it has developed its scope to involve non-member countries as well. More than 80 countries participated in the 2022 PISA. The international dimension of the survey, which overrides the boundaries of Europe to compare student performance of countries as diverse as the US, Greece and Indonesia, gives PISA a particularly significant weight in terms of interpreting and analysing the processes of educational policy and governance at a national and an international, even global level.

Indeed, the inclusion of non-member countries in the assessments is indicative of the global influence the PISA results have not only in the developed but also the developing world. They do not only occupy media headlines (see Santos, Carvalho and e Melo 2022, Baroutsis and Lingard 2017), they shape policy and sometimes even lead to urgent reforms:

Such researches produce a set of conclusions, definitions of 'good' or 'bad' educational systems, and required solutions. Moreover, the mass media are keen to diffuse the results of these studies, in such a manner that reinforces a need for urgent decisions, following lines of action that seem undisputed and uncontested, largely due to the fact that they have been internationally asserted (Nóvoa and Yariv-Mashal 2003, p.425).

Since 2000, PISA has been conducted every three years. Its innovative dimension lies in the fact that, rather than examining students' mastery of the school curricula, the focus is on an assessment of young people's ability to practically apply their skills in everyday life situations. PISA measures what the OECD calls reading literacy, numerical literacy and scientific literacy. The emphasis on 'real-life' circumstances, that is the application of knowledge, and on students' capacity to enter the labour market with core skills, such as literacy and numeracy, has taken PISA's focus of interest away from older educational values which arguably cannot be so readily measured (i.e., democratic participation, citizenship development, artistic talents, understanding of politics, history, etc), towards a more pragmatic view of valuing education's worth; according to PISA, it is 'its relevance to lifelong learning' (OECD 2003), that is one of its key features, with lifelong learning being a key policy theme of the OECD. Indeed, PISA has been one of the first international student assessment surveys that, even though it examines pupils who are still at a school level, applies concepts such as 'literacy', previously connected only with adult learners. According to the OECD (2003), PISA has an '…innovative approach to lifelong learning, which does not limit PISA to assessing students' curricular and cross-curricular competencies but also asks them to report on their own motivation to learn, their beliefs about themselves and their learning strategies' (OECD 2003, no page numbers). Finally, and perhaps most significantly, according to the same document, a key feature of PISA is, '…its policy orientation, with design and reporting methods determined by the need of governments to draw policy lessons' (OECD 2003, no page numbers).

The report on the first PISA results *Knowledge and Skills for Life* (OECD, 2001) declared PISA as the most rigorous, 'forward-looking' (OECD 2001, p.4) assessment of student performance; according to the report, even though the programme assesses pupils who are still in school, 'PISA is based on a dynamic model of lifelong learning' (OECD 2001, p.4). In fact, the term 'literacy', usually used in adult and lifelong education, is used by PISA as the new concept that combines not only knowledge of curricula, but most crucially its application in real-world situations. According to the report, literacy should be measured on a continuum that would give an indication of students' ability to continue learning throughout life. Apart from reading literacy, mathematics and science are also assessed, as well as student motivation, attitudes towards learning, familiarity with computers and what was called 'self-regulated' learning, i.e., 'aspects of students' strategies for managing and monitoring their own learning' (OECD 2001, p.19). In addition, data is collected on students' economic and social background, as well as their study habits in school and at home. By examining patterns of student proficiency in different countries alongside information about the characteristics and experiences of students, PISA aims to cast light on the combined factors that promote student and school success, focusing on both quality and equity.

Hence, PISA's design aims to provide policy makers with useful information in regard to what contributes to broader educational success, rather than provide them with results in isolation. The emphasis is thus upon effectiveness. The concepts of comparison and internationalisation give PISA its substance, since it is in the comparisons of school outcomes across the world that policy makers can now find answers for their problems: 'PISA offers a new approach to considering school outcomes, using as its evidence base the experiences of students across the world, rather than in the specific cultural context of a single country. The international context allows policy-makers to question assumptions about the quality of their own country's educational outcomes' (OECD 2001, p.27).

This field of comparison through numbers has become very powerful in relation to the politics of education policy production within member and other participating nations. Finally, in terms of policy making, apart from considerations regarding quality, equity is also in the list of priorities for PISA. It is interesting to examine what issues are regarded as related to equity in education:

> Gender differences in student performance, attitudes and motivation; the needs of both the most vulnerable and the exceptionally well-performing students; the role of engagement and motivation as prerequisites for adequate performance and future destinations; the nature, development and impact of literacy skills; and aspects of learning strategies and self-concept. (OECD 2001, p. 28)

PISA has come a long way in a short period of time and has consolidated the role of OECD and its Education Directorate as preeminent globally as the organization for developing and analysing comparative international educational performance data. This is evident not only through PISA's success, but also through its expansion to a range of new tests (and associated income streams) for the OECD: these include PISA for Development, PISA for Schools, PIAAC (Program for International Assessment of Adult Competencies), and the International Early Learning and Child Well-being Study (IELS) (baby PISA) (see Sellar and Lingard 2014). PISA results now receive a very high profile within national media and as such they are always at the fore in the consciousness of senior policy makers in education in participating nations, as well ministers and other politicians. Media coverage of PISA results is very substantial and perhaps represents another manifestation of the 'mediatization' of education policy processes (Fairclough 2000, Lingard and Rawolle 2004, Baroutsis and Lingard 2017, Santos, Carvalho and e Melo 2022).

CONCLUSION

This chapter focused on the role of the OECD's education work in the creation of the globe as a commensurate space of education measurement via PISA and the OECD's broader indicator and data production regime. If INES transformed the OECD from a minor player among many educational policy actors into a key actor with the sufficient technical know-how to conduct global education performance comparisons, PISA established the OECD as a policy player with the governing capacity to – slowly yet surely – direct and change education governance transnationally.

Of course, this is not to claim that the OECD has been alone in pushing this agenda forward. A number of comparative studies laid the groundwork, as did the efforts of other international organizations – such as the IEA and UNESCO – in the business of collecting educational data. Nonetheless, it is the enmeshing of a technocratic exercise with policy concerns and the influence of policy actors that renders the OECD especially instrumental in its function and effects, working at the boundary between education science and policy.

FUNDING ACKNOWLEDGEMENT

This manuscript is part of a project that has received funding from the European Research Council (ERC) under the European Union's Horizon 2020 research and innovation program, under grant agreement No 715125 METRO (ERC-2016-StG) ('International Organisations and the Rise of a Global Metrological Field', 2017–2022, PI: Sotiria Grek). This manuscript was also supported by an Australian Research Council (ARC) research grant, 'Data infrastructures, mobility and network governance in education' (DP RG151529), CI Bob Lingard. Both authors contributed equally to the writing of this chapter.

REFERENCES

Baroutsis, A. and Lingard, B. (2017) Counting and Comparing School Performance: An Analysis of Media Coverage of PISA in Australia, 2000–2014. *Journal of Education Policy*, 32 (4), 432–449.

Burgi, R. (2015) 'Systemic Management of Schools: the OECD's Professionalisation and Dissemination of Output Governance in the 1960s', *Paedagogica Historica*, 52 (4), 1–15.

CERI (1995) *Education at a Glance. The OECD Indicators* (Paris: OECD).

Fairclough, N. (2000) *New Labour, New Language?* (London: Routledge).

Grek, S. (2009) Governing by Numbers: The PSA 'effect' in Europe. *Journal of Education Policy*, 24 (1), 23–27.

Grek, S. (2014) 'OECD as a Site of Coproduction: European Education Governance and the New Politics of Policy Mobilization', *Critical Policy Studies*, DOI:10.1080/19460171.2013.862503.

Grek, S. and Ydesen, C. (2021) Where Science Met Policy: Governing by Indicators and the OECD's INES Programme. *Globalisation, Societies and Education*, 19 (2), 122–137.

Henry, M., Lingard, B., Rizvi, F. and Taylor, S. (2001) *The OECD, Globalization and Education Policy* (Oxford: Pergamon Press).

Lingard, B. and Rawolle, S. (2004) 'Mediatizing Educational Policy: The Journalistic Field, Science Policy, and Cross-field Effects', *Journal of Education Policy*, 19 (3), 361–380.

Lingard, B., Rawolle, S. and Taylor, S. (2005) 'Globalising Policy Sociology in Education: Working with Bourdieu', *Journal of Education Policy*, 20 (6), 759–777.

Morgan, C. (2009) *The OECD Programme for International Student Assessment: Unraveling a Knowledge Network* (Saarbrucken: VDM Verlag).

Nóvoa, A. and Yariv-Mashal T. (2003) 'Comparative Research in Education: A Mode of Governance or a Historical Journey?', *Comparative Education*, 39 (4), 423–438.

OECD (1996) *Globalisation and Linkages to 2030: Challenges and Opportunities for OECD Countries* (Paris: OECD).

OECD (1998) *Annual Report 1997* (Paris: OECD).

OECD (2001) *Science and Technology Labour Markets* (Paris: OECD).

OECD (2001) *The Wellbeing of Nations* (Paris: OECD).

OECD (2003) *What is PISA?* Online material. URL: http://www.oecd.org/ accessed 16 April 2023.

Ozga, J. and Lingard, B. (2007) 'Globalisation, Education Policy and Politics', in: B. Lingard and J. Ozga (eds) *The RoutledgeFalmer Reader in Education Policy and Politics* (London: RoutledgeFalmer), pp.65–82.

Papadopoulos, G. (1994) *Education 1960–1990: the OECD Perspective* (OECD: Paris).

Rizvi, F. and Lingard, B. (2006) 'Globalisation and the Changing Nature of the OECD's Educational Work', in H. Lauder *et al.* (eds) *Education, Globalisation and Social Change* (Oxford: Oxford University Press).

Rose, N. (1999) *Powers of Freedom Reframing Political Thought* (Cambridge: Cambridge University Press).

Santos, I., Carvalho, L-M and e Melo, B. (2022) The Media's Role in Shaping the Public Opinion on Education: A Thematic and Frame Analysis of Externalisation to World Situations in the Portuguese Media. *Research in Comparative and International Education*, 17 (1), 29–50.

Sellar, S. and Lingard, B. (2014). The OECD and the Expansion of PISA: New Global Modes of Governance in Education. *British Educational Research Journal*, 40 (6), 917–936.

US Department of Education (1985) *Indicators of Education – Status and Trends*, Washington DC.

14. Environment

Markku Lehtonen

INTRODUCTION

The OECD work on the environment was institutionalised with the setting up of the Environment Committee in 1970 and the Environment Directorate a year later. This happened in the context of the emergence of new environmental movements, social upheaval, and the questioning of the post-war economic growth paradigm (Schmelzer 2017). In these early years of its existence, the OECD Environment Committee and Directorate innovated and led international environmental policy, contributing to the establishment of environment ministries and the adoption of key notions such as the polluter pays principle. Ever since these early years, the OECD environment work has been characterised by constant balancing between the radical and moderate versions of environmental thought and governance.

Three areas of OECD contribution merit being highlighted: (1) developing environmental policy instruments, from end-of-the-pipe measures, through economic instruments, towards policy integration and cross-sector collaboration; (2) strengthening the status of environmental administrations in national-level policymaking; and (3) mediating between the competing visions and strands of environmentalism – between the growth-optimists and growth-critics – within and between member countries, and within the OECD secretariat. Often, the OECD has been described as a promoter of 'liberal environmentalism', which postulates the primacy of economic instruments and compatibility between economic growth and environmental protection (Skovgaard 2017, 344). However, the true picture appears to be more complex, as the OECD has played an 'ambivalent role in both promoting and then containing its criticism of mainstream economics' (Borowy 2017, 211), balancing between pro-growth and no-growth narratives and discourses (Urhammer and Røpke 2013), and to some extent between the rival schools of environmental and ecological economics, thus shaping the evolution of academic environmental economics during the first decades of existence of the discipline.

This chapter provides a brief historical overview of the evolution of OECDs environment work, with a focus on the enduring debates concerning the relationships between economy and the environment, between economics and environmentalism, and between growth optimism and Malthusianism. The need for such debate and arbitration is unlikely to diminish, despite the rising geopolitical concerns of the early 2020s, as global environmental challenges grow increasingly acute. Environmental policy work is therefore likely to become increasingly central for the organisation's identity. Despite significant changes in international policy environment, many of the early challenges faced by the OECD in this area remain: seeking reconciliation between economic growth and environmental protection, in a context of enduring growth needs of the Global South, the seemingly ever-greener industrialised world, and the rise of countries such as China and India as major powers and sources of global environmental pressures.

EVOLUTION OF THE OECD'S ENVIRONMENT WORK: BETWEEN GROWTH OPTIMISM AND PESSIMISM

Science and Research Committees as Precursors to Environment Work (1957–1970)

Environment was not part of OEEC work programme. However, as Borowy (2019) observes, problems such as industrial air and water pollution control entered its work programme with the establishment of the Committee for Applied Research in 1957. This work was in 1961 taken up by the Committee for Scientific Research (soon after renamed Committee for Research Cooperation), which pursued work on the scientific and technological aspects related to environmental protection, in cooperation with other OECD Committees and Directorates but also with other international organisations (OECD 2000; Borowy 2017, 215; Meyer 2017, 383). This early environment work emerged in the context of environmental problems associated with the rapid post-War reconstruction and industrialisation, manifested in events such as the smog episodes in Los Angeles and London, and the Minamata mercury pollution catastrophe in Japan. Work on chemical pollution came to be one the oldest and longest-running sub-fields of OECD environment work.

The OECD science and research branch was also the one that first addressed the emerging critique against the prevailing economic growth patterns. It was well-positioned to develop such critique, by virtue of its uniquely interdisciplinary approach, which encompassed not only economics, but also other social sciences, such as sociology, history, and political science. Designed to foster modernisation through economic growth, the OECD transformed in the late 1960s and early 1970s into a major international actor dedicated to addressing the 'problems of modern society' (Schmelzer 2017, 30).

Institutionalisation of the Environment Work: The Creation of the Environment Committee and Directorate

The Environment Committee and Environment Directorate were established, respectively, in 1970 and 1971, in a context of 'the social, intellectual, and economic turmoil of the late 1960s' that prompted questioning even within an organisation created to drive the post-war industrial growth regime (Schmelzer 2017, 29). A note from the Secretary-General Kristensen to the OECD Ministerial Council, 'Problems of a Modern Society', explicitly mentioned the social upheaval and protests as a demonstration of the feeling shared widely among the OECD countries that the rapid economic development had created new problems and required new solutions (Borowy 2017). The principal task of the new Environment Committee 'was to determine who was to pay for pollution reduction and environmental improvement "while retaining the values of the market economy"' (Borowy 2017, 219). Thanks to persistent advocacy by the then Director-General, van Lennep, the Environment Directorate received 19 officials from other directorates and 15 new recruits (ibid.).

The OECD environment work came to internalise an ambiguity inherent in the environmentalism of the time, between moderates advocating environmental policies within the existing economic system, and radicals favouring replacement or at least fundamental transformation of this system (Borowy 2019). Somewhat surprisingly, the OECD became a major player elaborating critique against the quantitative, GDP-focused growth paradigm. It provided a venue for the intellectual debates and controversies that led to the creation of the Club of Rome –

probably the most well-known growth critic of the time, with its Limits to Growth report in 1972 (Schmelzer 2017). However, the OECD shied away from the radical rhetoric and data of Limits to Growth (Borowy 2017, 219). Over the same period, the OECD's general policy doctrine was shifting from predominantly Keynesian to strictly neoliberal policy advocacy (Thiele 2019, 36).

The OECD secretariat operated as an active innovator, spurring new thinking within national governments. The OECD was the first international organisation to set up a permanent committee dedicated to environmental questions (Borowy 2019), aiming to become 'the primary international organization for the rich countries' environmental policies', with the development of 'qualitative indicators for human welfare' as one of its main tasks (Schmelzer 2016, 279). This preceded by two years the first UN environment conference in Stockholm and the establishment of the UN Environment Programme (UNEP), in 1972. It also contributed to the wave of establishment of national environment ministries in the 1970s and early 1980s. The internationalisation of environmental policies benefited from competition in this policy area between OECD and international organisations such as the ECE, the OECD, and NATO (Borowy 2019). The remarkably growth-critical tone of some of the OECD documents at the time had its counterpoint in the scepticism in the Global South, which saw stronger environmental policies as neocolonialistic attempts by the North to maintain its hegemony. Hence, the negotiators at the Stockholm 1972 conference made great efforts to avoid deepening the North-South cleavage and placing any restrictions on economic activities in the developing world.

In the wake of the Stockholm conference, the OECD introduced the polluter pays principle (PPP), still today probably the single most fundamental cornerstone of environmental policies, adopted formally as an OECD Council Recommendation in 1972 (Wingate 2019, 173). The fundamental objective was to avoid new environmental protection measures being financed by governments in the form of subsidies, as differences in subsidies between countries could distort international trade and investment (Ruffing 2010, 204). As a means of reconciling the radical and reformist views on environmental policy, the PPP paved the way for the kind of 'ecological modernisation' discourse that would characterise international environmental and economic policy debates from the late 1970s through to the early 21st century (Wingate 2019).

The Neoliberal Turn: Ecological Modernisation as a Means of Overcoming the Liberalism/Environmentalism Divide

The neoliberal revolution under Thatcherism and Reaganism compelled those working on the environment in the OECD to tone down the critique against economic growth and seek ways of reconciling liberalism with environmental protection. At the same time, with the basic legislative and administrative framework for environmental policy established in many OECD countries, the attention turned away from command-and-control and end-of-pipe measures towards economic instruments. The Environment Directorate was restructured in 1980, with the Environment and Economy Division as one of its four divisions. The Directorate declared economic-environmental management as one of its priority areas of work (Borowy 2017, 223). Wingate (2019, 193) argues that the polluter pays principle allowed the introduction of a distinctly neoliberal mode of governing the environment, thus paving the way for 'ecological modernisation', brought to the academic debate by such pioneers of environmental policy scholarship as Martin Jänicke and Maarten Hajer (for a review, see Mol and Sonnenfeld 2000).

Thiele (2019, 47) characterises ecological modernisation as a political project, in which 'environmental critiques of capitalism have been taken up – and/or deflected – by liberal institutions with the aim of further "modernizing" industrial-capitalist societies towards a reconciliation with environmental stewardship'. As a champion of ecological modernisation, the OECD facilitated the transformation of environmental thought away from the Malthusianism that had prevailed in the late 1960s and early 1970s (Wingate 2019). The OECD picked up sustainable development as a key concept that aligned well with ecological modernisation, and brought onto the international policy agenda in the so-called Brundtland Commission report in 1987 (see also the Chapter 25 on sustainable development in this volume). Where the environment work in the early 1970s had been a means to avoid addressing the possible need for systemic changes in the growth paradigm, selective use of the concept of sustainable development now served a similar purpose, by eschewing the topics of economic limits, redistribution, and profound changes in economic structures (Borowy 2017, 228).

Development of economic policy instruments was a task that aligned readily with the OECD's traditional remit and thus helped the Environment Directorate to survive in an otherwise difficult period of economic liberalism and renewed growth enthusiasm. The OECD environmental economists introduced to the national environmental policy debates key tenets of ecological modernisation. These included the double dividend hypothesis, which underlies the green tax reform, entailing the idea that environmental taxation would allow easing taxation of labour and thus help achieve conventional growth objectives (Barde 2007; Ruffing 2010). OECD economists' attempts in the early 1980s to develop biodiversity valuation and optimal biodiversity protection policies failed to attract much attention among policymakers (Barde 2007). By contrast, inspired by the PPP, the user pays principle made its way to the OECD set of principles in the late 1980s, first in the area of water resource management (Ruffing 2010, 206).

Systematic peer reviews of member countries' environmental policies (see Chapter 9 on a general discussion on the OECD peer review system), initiated in 1992, came to illustrate the balancing between the OECD's dominant liberal-economics doctrine and the more radical yet marginal discourse of environmental protection. Within the peer reviews, the secretariat operated as a mediator, with the task of reconciling the OECD doctrine – ultimately defined by the powerful Economics Department – with the often more radical demands from the country delegates, who most often came from the national environment ministries (Lehtonen 2007).

OECD in Search for its Lost Identity: From Sustainable Development to Green Growth

Towards the late 1990s, in an atmosphere of accelerating globalisation, intensification of international economic collaboration, the end of the Cold War, the OECD faced increasing competition from organisations such as the WTO and the European Union. It had by then lost its privileged position as the leading Western organisation for international economic cooperation. In international environmental governance, the negotiating process established by the UN Conference on Environment and Development in 1992 had reduced the demand for organisations such as the OECD to lead international negotiations (Ruffing 2010, 214).

In search for a new identity, the OECD set up a high-level committee on Sustainable Development. Where the OECD in the early 1970s envisaged its role as the leading international organisation addressing the environmental problems caused by the modern society, the report of the high-level committee now in a similar manner suggested sustainable development as the leading star for the organisation (see Chapter 25 in this volume). This opened a window of opportunity for the Environment Committee and the Environment Directorate, initially charged with the task of coordinating OECD's sustainable development work. However, the work was hampered by many factors: difficulties to agree on a common definition of sustainable development, especially on its social dimension (Caccia 2003); governments' tendency to prioritise activities carried out by a single OECD Committee at the cost of 'whole-of-government' themes; the weak status of environment ministries in national policy-making; and constant resource scarcity (OECD 2003a; 2004; Lehtonen 2005).

Time was now ripe for the work on an economic approach to biodiversity conservation, as testified by landmark publications such as the OECD 'handbook' of biodiversity valuation (OECD 2002), in support of the implementation of the UN Biodiversity Convention (Barde 2007). Biodiversity valuation has continued as one of the most controversial topics in debates and disputes between environmental and ecological economists (see e.g., Spash and Hache 2021). The OECD adopted concepts from the ecological economics discourse, such as the 'safe minimum standard' of natural assets in the spirit of a 'strong sustainability' paradigm, but on the other hand advocated the need for the decisions concerning such standards to be informed by cost-benefit analysis (Barde 2007).

The 2001 OECD Environmental Strategy for the First Decade of the 21st Century, adopted by the OECD Council of Ministers (OECD 2001), could be seen as the Environment Directorate's contribution to the organisation's search for a new identity. Most objectives of the strategy represented continuation from earlier work, such as those relating to pollution control and natural resources management, economic aspects of environmental policies, statistics and indicators, and international environmental governance. True novelties came with the concepts of decoupling and social-environmental interface.

Decoupling of environmental pressures from economic growth combined two major OECD mainstays: concern for economic growth and the production of reliable indicators for cross-country comparison. The OECD had been a leading innovator in the international environmental indicator work since 1989 (OECD 2003b). The so-called Pressures-States-Responses (PSR) framework was a major conceptual innovation. As so often with concepts developed within the OECD, the EU picked up and further developed the PSR framework: the European Environment Agency added Drivers and Impacts into PSR, and the EU adopted the resulting DPISR framework to organise its indicator work. Decoupling indicators built on this foundation, while at the same time linking to scholarly debates in the area. In particular, they helped to test the 'inverted Kuznets Curve hypothesis', which postulates that environmental pressures increase with the rise of GDP per capita, but decline again, once a society reaches a certain level of welfare. Furthermore, the concept of decoupling was accompanied by that of resource efficiency, which sought to combine data on resource consumption, waste, economics, and material flows. These developments, in turn, provided the foundations for contemporary work on circular economy.

Social considerations had remained secondary in the organisation's environment work. In the late 1990s, a handful of member countries, including Canada, Finland, the Netherlands, and Portugal, pushed the Secretariat to work on what was defined as the *social-environmental interface*. The topic made its way to the Environmental Performance Reviews, and into the Directorate's work programme, but failed to generate much enthusiasm among the member countries (Lehtonen 2005, 245). A key reason can be found in institutional inertia and administrative silos: social aspects lacked policy champions within environment ministries, which were structured according to the traditional areas of environmental policy.

During the late 1990s and early 2000s, sustainable development began to lose its appeal as the uniting concept, as alternative concepts such as green growth gained traction, both in the OECD and in international environmental governance. In the midst of the global financial and economic crisis, the OECD adopted green growth as a leading star for its environment-related work. The 2009 Ministerial Council meeting declared that greening and growth could go hand-in-hand, calling on the OECD to develop a Green Growth Strategy that would 'achieve economic recovery and environmentally and socially sustainable economic growth' (OECD 2009). In 2011, the OECD published the Strategy, thereby launching its Green Growth initiative (OECD 2011).

The appeal of the green growth concept was self-evident for an organisation that had since the late 1960s sought to balance between the mainstream and more radical environmental policy approaches. Although the OECD was careful to underline that green growth should not be seen as a substitute or synonym to sustainable development,[1] in practice, the concept did precisely that, i.e., it increasingly crowded out sustainable development from the international and national policy agendas. As Thiele (2019, 37) notes, '[t]he environmental redefinition of growth – along with its inverse, the economically oriented redefinition of environmental protection – was developed by the organization over four decades prior to the study's release.' Thiele (2019, 48) likewise places the concept of decoupling – and its sisters, eco-efficiency and green innovation – within this long OECD tradition that proclaims the compatibility of environmental protection with economic growth, postulating that eco-efficiency and innovation would enable absolute decoupling of economic growth from resource consumption and ecological degradation.

Return of the Growth Critique?

Green growth remained a key element of the OECD Environment Directorate's agenda throughout the 2020s, resulting in a large number of publications. However, the entry of Angel Gurría as the Secretary-General in 2006 transformed also OECD environment work. The social-environmental interface was no longer called as such, but was now addressed under headlines such as inclusiveness, gender, equitable growth, and the UN Sustainable Development Goals. The Secretary-General's report to the OECD Ministerial meeting (OECD 2019a) argued for a paradigm shift, a change of focus from measuring and encouraging traditional economic growth to areas such as 'improving people's well-being and the quality, equity and environmental effects of growth'. Indeed, the first among the five substantive priorities outlined by the Secretary-General for the OECD in 2019 was 'Measuring and promoting well-being, sustainability and inclusiveness' (OECD 2019a, 40–41). In the OECD's constant balancing between growth-optimism and critique, the pendulum may have shifted towards the latter, growth-critical direction. These changes in priorities and orientations have not been to the liking of all. With some regret, an energy economist with a long experience of work in various OECD bodies argued that market liberalism and even the concept market economy had in OECD language being replaced by terms such as inclusion, diversity, and gender equality.[2]

---

[1]   https://www.oecd.org/greengrowth/futurewewant.htm accessed 21 April 2023.
[2]   Interviewed by the author in August 2019.

The concept of natural capital continues to provide the foundations for the green growth agenda, environmental problems being conceptualised as market failures, to be resolved by 'getting the prices right' (Thiele 2019, 46). Meanwhile, greater attention to the role of the state in fostering and steering innovation, for instance in the context of the horizontal New Approaches to Economic Challenges (NAEC) initiative, may signal changes to the liberal-economics doctrine (e.g., OECD 2019a, 77). In a similar manner, the Better Life Initiative[3] has sought to develop new indicators of economic progress. NAEC does not abandon the objective of economic growth but calls for a change in 'the composition and structure of economic activity to achieve the multiple goals of a more rounded vision of economic and social progress' (OECD 2019b, 8). This testifies to the OECD's willingness to discuss and change the way in which it measures progress. Yet, the primacy of economic instruments in the OECD policy portfolio seems to persist, as demonstrated by statements that depict command-and-control measures as 'second-best solutions compared to well-designed pricing instruments' (OECD 2013, 10).

THE ROLE AND INFLUENCE OF THE ENVIRONMENT DIRECTORATE AND ENVIRONMENT COMMITTEE: INNOVATOR, BRIDGE-BUILDER, SHAPER OF FRAMINGS

According to Borowy (2017, 214), the environment is the area of OECD work that has produced 'by far the most legally binding decisions, resulting largely from its studies on chemicals and waste management'. However, just like in its other areas of work, the OECD has exerted its main influence on national and international environmental policies and politics through more indirect pathways, by producing conceptual innovations, mediating and coordinating work across various communities, and by shaping norms, identities, and cognitive frameworks.

Innovator or Follower?

In the early days of its existence, the OECD – through the Environment Directorate as well as the Environmental Policy Committee and its various sub-groups and committees – was vital in bringing about and disseminating innovations in national and international environmental policy. In addition to the landmark polluter pays principle, the innovations included the user pays principle, state of the environment reporting and work on environmental indicators structured around the Pressure-States-Responses model. The OECD pioneered also economic valuation of biodiversity in the early 1980s, although these ideas gained traction only later, in efforts to implement the UN Biodiversity Convention. On other topics, such as sustainable development, green growth, green finance, and inclusiveness, the OECD has been more of a follower, further developing ideas and concepts brought to the agenda of international environmental policy by other actors.

---

[3]   https://www.oecd.org/wise/better-life-initiative.htm accessed 21 April 2023.

Bridge-builder and Mainstreamer of Environmental Issues

Whether as an innovator or as a follower, the OECD has helped to strengthen the position of the environment on domestic and international policy agendas and reinforce the status of environmental administrations in national-level policymaking. In the 1970s and 1980s, the OECD spurred the establishment of environment ministries in its member countries. Bridge-building across sectors and actor groups has been particularly important in a profoundly cross-cutting policy area, given that the arguably most important environment-related decisions are made in sectors such as energy, agriculture, trade, and transport. The country peer reviews represent a typical example of OECD work that combines mainstreaming, coordination, advocacy, and competition, entailing mediation between diverse interests, views, and policy approaches across sectors, both among and within the member countries and within the OECD secretariat (e.g., Lehtonen 2007). The OECD's environment sector has been a leader in involving the civil society in its work, although public and stakeholder participation remains limited in its extent, and mainly designed for the collection of ideas, rather than for collaboration.

Within the secretariat, collaboration with the energy and economics sectors poses particular challenges (e.g., OECD 2000). The Environmental Performance Reviews, for example, face the constant need to balance between the still dominant liberal economics views within the organisation, and the more environmentalist positions of the national delegates to the working group responsible for the reviews (Lehtonen 2007; 2020). The difficulties are compounded in the energy sector, given the importance of economic considerations and the highly diverging energy policy choices of the member countries. Recent years have seen changes in thinking and policy concerning the role of the state in energy policy, towards the idea of an active state facilitating and steering major yet risky low-carbon investments, including those in nuclear energy.

In the formative years of its environment work, in the late 1960s and early 1970s, the OECD collaborated and competed with other international organisations for leadership in international environmental policy. These included the Council of Europe, the European Communities, the UN, and, somewhat surprisingly, NATO. For example, the EC used the prestige of the OECD as a means of pushing for the adoption of the polluter pays principle, while at the same time seeking to show independence in the way it defined PPP in the EC regulatory system (Meyer 2017). More generally, the OECD has decisively shaped international discourses and fostered international cooperation in international environmental governance (e.g., Busch 2009).

Shaper of Ideas: Greening of the Economy or Economising the Environment?

Probably the most powerful type of influence from the OECD environment work has involved socialisation, identity-building, and gradual shaping of cognitive frameworks. The OECD has shaped both written and unwritten norms and principles for adoption by the member countries. It has also contributed to the creation and consolidation of an epistemic community of environmental policy experts and officials across the OECD countries and beyond. The relationships between the economy and the environment – economic and environmentalist thinking – have been central in these processes ever since the late 1960s. Lacking coercive power, the OECD has enjoyed certain freedom to develop and advocate independent views that would be difficult if not impossible to drive through in organisations with clear regulatory functions. Sometimes this fosters adherence to mainstream economics perspectives, while at other times it facilitates the entry of alternative ideas on to the policy agenda. An example of the latter was when the OECD adopted a strict and uncompromising interpretation of the polluter pays principle in favour of the environment, contrasting with the more economically-oriented interpretation of the EC, in its more coercive policy context (Meyer 2017). At other times, the freedom has resulted in more orthodox interpretations of the OECD's economic doctrine and less environment-oriented decisions, such as when the OECD excluded environmental externalities from the scope of energy subsidies (Skovgaard 2017).

Earlier research has amply demonstrated how the OECD's environment work has from the very beginning and throughout the years been marked by a constant search of a balance between what have variously been labelled as pro-growth and no-growth narratives (Urhammer and Røpke 2013), free-market and radical environmentalism (Thiele 2019), ecological modernisation and environmental Malthusianism (Wingate 2019), and between environment- and economics-oriented epistemic communities – both within the OECD secretariat and within the member countries (Lehtonen 2007; 2020). The OECD has thus exploited the unavoidable overlaps and common ground between the seemingly opposing poles of the debate. Areas of agreement include OECD mainstays such as the polluter pays principle, ecological tax-reform, green investments, and redefining the measure of progress (Urhammer and Røpke 2013). However, Borowy (2017, 230) concludes that the OECD arguments in general have ended up integrating the environment into the logic of the economy rather than vice versa. In a similar vein, Thiele (2019, 38) argues that the OECD has adopted a neoliberal interpretation of ecological modernisation, helping this variant to attain a hegemonic status in current environmental policy debates internationally.

If the OECD has shaped environmental policies and administrations in its member countries, it has also had a vital role in the development of environmental economics. The preparatory work to the Stockholm conference, with its landmark publication 'Problems in Environmental Economics' in 1972, was crucial for the new discipline. The OECD has contributed to the consolidation of environmental and resource economics as the dominant mainstream approach for addressing the relationships between economy and the environment, and to the corresponding marginalisation of ecological and institutional economics. Barde (2007) and Ruffing (2010), influential OECD environmental economists, describe the 'political economy of environmental policy' as the core of OECD activity in the environment sector. In this mainstream approach, the OECD has constantly emphasised notions such as monetary valuation of the environment, optimisation and efficiency, cost-benefit analysis, and the primacy of individual preferences. The vigorous efforts by environmental economists such as David Pearce, committed to exercising direct influence on policymaking and policymakers, have been decisive for both the OECD's environmental policy doctrine and for the development of environmental economics as a discipline (Barde 2017).

CONCLUSIONS

The time of writing is one of increasingly apocalyptic future visions and consolidation of persistent and systemic global crises, from the financial and economic crisis of 2007–08, through to the on-going health and geopolitical emergencies triggered by the Covid pandemic and Russia's invasion of Ukraine in February 2022. In this context, the need for venues for mediation and development of new ideas concerning the relationships between economic growth and environmental challenges is as acute as it was when the OECD initiated its environment work in the early 1970s. As Urhammer and Røpke (2013) argued a decade ago, neither the pro-growth nor the no-growth narrative of environmentalism has the power to govern the economy, and hence, strong new narratives are needed to 'change the reproduction of meaning exercised in business as usual'. Cleavages between growth critics and growth advocates persist, also within the OECD secretariat, yet this is precisely why the OECD environment work could provide an arena where such new narratives and policy approaches can be forged. If the OECD Environmental Policy Committee no longer enjoys the prestige it had in the 1970s and 1980s, as 'the place to be' for high-level environmental policy officials in the member countries (OECD 2000, 118), the key OECD strengths remain: the internal organisation of the work, the excellent professional competences of the secretariat staff, and the absence of coercive power, which facilitates frank debates on hot topics.

Further research would be warranted in three areas. The first would explore the dynamics between the rival and partly overlapping epistemic communities – notably those congregated around the environment and economy – whose interaction shapes the policies and debates concerning the economy-environment relationships. Second, the role of the OECD in international environmental governance – its interaction with other international organisations active in the area – remains a little explored topic of research (see Chapter 8 for an initial and general discussion on this topic). Such analysis would usefully explore the inter-organisational dynamics of peer pressure: the role and impact of the OECD peer reviews in fostering learning and accountability can be properly understood only within the complex setting of international environmental governance. Thirdly, the rise of the non-OECD Asian global powers – China at the forefront – has given new twists to the debates. For instance, while China is overtaking the US as the largest polluter, it is also the leader in the development of renewable energy technologies. Comprehensive analysis of the OECD's role in global environmental governance must therefore address the organisation's impact and growing interaction with major non-member countries.

REFERENCES

Barde, Jean-Philippe. (2007). 'Harnessing the political economy of environmental policy: David Pearce's contribution to OECD.' *Environmental & Resource Economics*, *37*(1), 33–42.
Borowy, Iris. (2017). '(Re-)Thinking environment and economy: The Organisation for Economic Co-operation and Development and Sustainable Development.' In: Kaiser, Wolfram and Meyer, Jan-Henrik (eds) *International Organizations and Environmental Protection: Conservation and Globalization in the Twentieth Century*. New York and Oxford: Berghahn Books.
Borowy, Iris. (2019). 'Before UNEP: who was in charge of the global environment? The struggle for institutional responsibility 1968–72.' *Journal of Global History*, *14*(1), 87–106.
Busch, Per-Olof. (2009). 'The OECD Environment Directorate: The art of persuasion and its limitations.' In: Biermann, Frank and Bernd Siebenhüner (eds): *Managers of Global Change: The Influence of International Environmental Bureaucracies*. Cambridge, Mass.: Cambridge University Press, 75-99. DOI:10.7551/mitpress/9780262012744.003.0004
Caccia, Charles. (2003). The OECD and the World Economy. Doc. 9851 prov., 7 July. Provisional Report, to the Committee on Economic Affairs and Development of the Extended Parliamentary Assembly of the Council of Europe. Rapporteur: Mr Caccia, Canada, Liberal Party.
Lehtonen, Markku. (2005). *Environmental Policy Evaluation in the Service of Sustainable Development: Influence of the OECD Environmental Performance Reviews from the Perspective of Institutional Economics*. PhD thesis. Université de Versailles Saint-Quentin-en-Yvelines, France.

Lehtonen, Markku. (2007). 'Environmental Policy Integration through the OECD peer reviews: Integrating economy to the environment or the environment to the economy?' *Environmental Politics, 16*(1), 15–35.

Lehtonen, Markku. (2020). 'Harder governance built on soft foundations: Experience from OECD peer reviews.' *Journal of Environmental Policy and Planning, 22*(6), 814–29.

Meyer, Jan-Henrik. (2017). 'Who should pay for pollution? The OECD, the European Communities and the emergence of environmental policy in the early 1970s.' *European Review of History: Revue européenne d'histoire, 24*(3), 377–98,

Mol, Arthur P. J. and Sonnenfeld, David A. (2000). 'Ecological modernisation around the world: An introduction.' *Environmental Politics, 9*(1), 1–14, DOI: 10.1080/09644010008414510.

OECD. (2000). *International Environmental Issues and the OECD 1950-2000: An Historical Perspective*, by Bill L. Long. Paris: OECD. https://doi.org/10.1787/9789264181113-en accessed 21 April 2023.

OECD. (2001). OECD Environmental Strategy for the First Decade of the 21st Century, Adopted by OECD Environment Ministers, 16 May 2001. Paris: OECD. https://www.oecd.org/environment/indicators-modelling-outlooks/1863539.pdf accessed 21 April 2023.

OECD. (2002). *Handbook of Biodiversity Valuation: A Guide for Policy Makers*. Paris: OECD. https://doi.org/10.1787/9789264175792-en accessed 21 April 2023.

OECD. (2003a). Future Direction of the OECD: Report on OECD's Role in Global Architecture. Report prepared by Ambassador Jorma Julin. HOD(2003)2. 24 March 2003. Paris: OECD.

OECD. (2003b). OECD Environmental Indicators: Development, Measurement and Use. Reference Paper. OECD Environment Directorate. 30 p.

OECD. (2004). Draft Final Report to Ministers: Ad Hoc Group on Sustainable Development. OECD General Secretariat. SG/SD(2004)4/REV1. 8 April. Paris: OECD. 57 p.

OECD. (2009). Declaration on Green Growth, Adopted at the Meeting of the Council at Ministerial Level on 25 June 2009 [C/MIN(2009)5/ADD1/FINAL]. Paris: OECD. https://www.oecd.org/env/44077822.pdf accessed 21 April 2023.

OECD. (2011). Towards Green Growth. Paris: OECD. https://www.oecd.org/greengrowth/towards-green-growth-9789264111318-en.htm accessed 21 April 2023.

OECD. (2013).What have we learned from attempts to introduce green-growth policies? OECD Green Growth Papers, March 2013. Paris: OECD https://doi.org/10.1787/5k486rchlnxx-en accessed 21 April 2023.

OECD. (2019a). Secretary-General's Report to Ministers 2019. Paris: OECD. https://doi.org/10.1787/d4b4a55c-en accessed 21 April 2023.

OECD. (2019b). Beyond Growth: Towards a New Economic Approach. Report of the Secretary General's Advisory Group on a New Growth Narrative. 17-18 September 2019, OECD Conference Centre. SG/NAEC(2019)3. Paris: OECD. https://www.oecd.org/naec/averting-systemic-collapse/SG-NAEC(2019)3_Beyond%20Growth.pdf accessed 21 April 2023.

Ruffing, Kenneth G. (2010). The role of the Organization for Economic Cooperation and Development in environmental policy making.' *Review of Environmental Economics and Policy, 4*(2), 199–220. https://www.journals.uchicago.edu/doi/pdf/10.1093/reep/req007 accessed 21 April 2023.

Schmelzer, Matthias. (2016). *The Hegemony of Growth: The OECD and the Making of the Economic Growth Paradigm*. Cambridge: Cambridge University Press.

Schmelzer, Matthias. (2017). '"Born in the corridors of the OECD": The forgotten origins of the Club of Rome, transnational networks, and the 1970s in global history.' *Journal of Global History, 12*(1), 26–48.

Skovgaard, Jacob. (2017). 'The devil lies in the definition: competing approaches to fossil fuel subsidies at the IMF and the OECD.' *International Environmental Agreements, 17*(3), 341–53.

Spash, Clive L. and Hache, Frédéric. (2021). 'The Dasgupta Review deconstructed: an exposé of biodiversity economics.' *Globalizations, 19*(5), 653–76.

Thiele, Lasse. (2019). The Prospects of 'Green' Capitalism: Systemic Accumulation and Cost Re-Externalizations in the Green Economy. Dissertation zur Erlangung des Grades eines Doktors der Philosophie am Fachbereich Politik- und Sozialwissenschaften der Freien Universität Berlin.

Urhammer, Emil and Røpke, Inge. (2013). 'Macroeconomic narratives in a world of crises: An analysis of stories about solving the system crisis.' *Ecological Economics, 96*(December), 62–70.

Wingate, David. (2019). 'From environmental Malthusianism to ecological modernisation: Toward a genealogy of sustainability.' Submitted in accordance with the requirements for the degree of Doctor of Philosophy. The University of Leeds School of Earth and Environment, School of Sociology and Social Policy, March, 2019.

15. Regulation

Fabrizio De Francesco and Claudio M. Radaelli

INTRODUCTION

What is the role of the OECD in regulation? What has it achieved? What are the new challenges of regulatory governance? We answer these questions by providing an historical account of the emergence of the 'better regulation' agenda, considering the processes that led the organization to become world leader in the production of regulatory indicators, and looking at the debate on regulatory policy 2.0 (OECD 2021a, Chapter 1).

Today, the better regulation language covers a broad range of regulatory reforms, policy instruments, and institutions. More precisely, the better regulation discourse has allowed the OECD to consolidate the role of economics in appraising regulation and the widespread adoption of instruments – such as stakeholders consultation, regulatory impact analysis (RIA), ex post regulatory evaluation, risk regulation, and tools for measuring the cost of administrative obligations arising from regulation. In the name of better regulation many countries in the OECD and beyond have set targets on 'red tape' (Trnka and Thuerer 2019) and re-designed their approach to inspections and enforcement of rules (OECD 2018). As for institutional choice, the OECD has encouraged the adoption of independent regulatory agencies, the emergence of networks of regulators, and the creation of regulatory oversight institutions (OECD 2021a). Finally, the regulatory reform agenda of the OECD contains the goal of promoting international regulatory cooperation, which is seen as essentially to the very mission of the organization to promote growth via deeper economic exchanges among countries.

Broadly speaking, regulatory reform as defined by the OECD is a vision to overcome an asymmetry in contemporary governance. Whilst public expenditure and taxation are based on relatively known economic quantities, and the decisions on how much to spend and tax take place in special fora and institutions (such as the Finance Bill, multi-annual public budget plans, and Parliaments), regulations are not managed the same way. To write a rule affecting production processes, economic activity or personal behaviour (think of a licence or how to register for voting or obtaining a passport), a regulator or a government department do not need to show that money is available. The regulator will have to establish standards and administrative procedures, not to commit public money – apart from the case in which a new inspectorate has to be created, or the case of regulations affecting directly the public sector. The direct cost of complying with the rule falls on the firm or the individual. For this reason, the total regulatory costs of new primary and secondary rules are often not calculated, not debated in Parliaments, not budgeted. Regulatory reform OECD-style is a way to make these costs and of course benefits of regulations (in force and new) visible and therefore managed. We do not have yet a Regulatory Bill counting all the costs and benefits of proposed regulations (Doern 2007), but the tools and institutions (in particular regulatory oversight bodies) promoted by the OECD via better regulation go in this direction.

THE EMERGENCE OF BETTER REGULATION

How did we get there? The early days of OECD engagement with regulation date back to the acknowledgement that public management reforms have profound implications for regulatory quality, and vice versa, regulation is key to the organization and performance of the public sector. In a 1992 report, the OECD Public Management Committee (called PUMA) reported on the member states' concerns about regulation and the negative impact of badly designed and/or wrongly implemented regulations on economic performance. The publication contained the sketch of a vision of good regulation and the need to manage it (OECD Public Management 1992). The report argued for an appraisal of rules grounded in the values of accountability, participation and transparency within the law-making process as well as the extent of effectiveness and economic efficiency of regulatory outcome. The report dealt with management and accountability, efficient allocation of resources, regulatory authorities and processes, and sectoral regulatory reform and deregulation.

The theoretical underpinnings of that report are still key to the OECD programmatic vision for regulatory quality and regulatory oversight institutions:

> Throughout that review there were also clear references to the theory of delegation and the trade-off between bureaucratic discretion and democratic accountability. 'Ongoing central oversights' were deemed to be necessary for improving the information flow from regulators to elected officials by establishing channels for policy direction and, ultimately, balancing competing social goods (OECD Public Management 1992). Feasibility, risk or cost criteria were indicated as the methods with which to limit and justify the use of regulatory authority — criteria that 'define a burden of proof that is expected to be met through analysis before action is taken' (OECD Public Management 1992). (De Francesco 2013, 58)

In the tradition of the OECD publications, the report made reference to international experiences with processes and tools for ensuring regulatory quality. Specifically, Sweden and the United States of America (USA) were mentioned for their experience in measuring regulatory costs; Australia for the sunset clauses (to create an automatic need to update legislation, otherwise they would sunset at a certain date and disappear); and Germany for the overarching Blue Checklist for ensuring regulatory quality through a questionnaire targeting regulators proposing new measures.

In the 1990s the OECD then began to promote a regulatory reform agenda calling member states to consider checklists and methods of ex ante policy appraisal that were already common in countries like Germany, the UK, and in particular the USA, where since Reagan federal executive agencies were required to perform RIA on proposed regulations. In turn, RIAs were (and still are) checked by a regulatory oversight body, the Office for Information and Regulatory Affairs (OIRA). The presence of a director of PUMA with experience with the White House's Office for Management and Budget was an asset in connecting public management reforms with regulatory reform through policy instruments like RIA.

PUMA prepared the intellectual and political ground for the adoption, in 1995, of the Recommendation of the OECD Ministerial Council on Regulatory Reform – effectively the first comprehensive program for better regulation. For the OECD, regulatory reform was necessary because of 'troublesome problems' arising because of the 'maturing and expansion of regulatory systems' (OECD 1995, 8). The three central conceptual elements were: the need to govern and manage systematically rules (because, as we mentioned earlier, their costs and benefits are not assessed via a Finance Bill); standards and benchmarks of high-quality regulation that, because of their adaptability and flexibility to contextual conditions, could be adopted by all OECD countries and beyond; and, finally, the connection between high-quality rules, legitimacy and trust in government.

With generic labels like 'regulatory reform', 'high quality regulation' and 'better regulation' the OECD created a big semantic tent where the clash between explicit de-regulatory agendas and more progressive agendas was reduced. Indeed, the OECD has never endorsed a definition of better regulation based exclusively on cutting red tape and reducing the number and cost of rules, although these strategies could still be pursued by some countries without getting outside the perimeter of the Recommendation. In fact, the Recommendation was not silent on the problem created by increasing regulatory costs and over-regulation.

The OECD Council introduced also a checklist for Regulatory Decision-Making (OECD 1995, 10–14). This checklist was inspired by the cross-country experience with RIA, which from that point onwards became the pivotal policy instrument. The checklist included both economic tests and the consultation of stakeholders at the early stage of proposals for both primary and secondary legislation – hence well before the possibility to comment on legislative drafts when they are examined by Parliament. To provide additional guidance, the OECD published a document on best practice in RIA and thematic studies on regulatory reform (OECD 1997a; 1997b). This intellectual background became the base for carrying out regulatory reviews of individual countries. Over time, the reviews became an influential appraisal of the quality of the regulatory reform efforts and more generally the regulatory environment of a country, from Sweden to China.

The 1995 Recommendation was the origin of a diffusion wave of RIA across the OECD countries. The World Bank facilitated a further spread in developing countries. The European Commission went also along with better regulation since the early 2000s (Radaelli and De Francesco 2007), yet again adopting RIA as the main instrument. On the ground, however, the implementation of RIA has been uneven. The point is that the generic label of RIA allows governments to implement different types of regulatory appraisal. These types differ in breadth and scope of the analysis. In some cases, adoption of the same RIA template is pretty much symbolic. The same can be said of consultation guidelines (Radaelli 2005). This has been a fundamental reason to map out progress with RIA and more generally regulatory reform with indicators. But before we turn to the story of indicators, we need to complete our historical account.

In 2012, the OECD published a second Recommendation (OECD 2012). This time RIA was cast in a wider set of tools, with the overall ambition to manage the whole life cycle of regulations, from the cradle to the grave so to speak, with risk assessment, periodic reviews of legislation, systematic engagement of stakeholders, judicial review, and co-ordination mechanisms between levels of government. The policy instruments suggested by the OECD have a great advantage. They are not sensitive to the specific sector or domain of governmental intervention. They can be used for environmental, social, economic regulations. As standard templates, they can be deployed in a variety of circumstances, allowing for comparison and for cumulative appraisals. To illustrate, one can calculate the total costs and benefits of new regulations introduced in a period by adding up the benefit/cost estimates and ratios in the RIAs supporting these regulations. Going back to what we said at the beginning, this is similar to creating the sketch of a regulatory budget.

On 6 October 2021, the OECD Council adopted a Recommendation on Agile Regulatory Governance to Harness Innovation (OECD 2021b). With this Recommendation, the reach of better regulation extends to innovation. The 2021 Recommendation is anchored to appraisal instruments (including horizon scanning and scenario analysis to enhance the performance of RIA in rapidly changing sectors) and regulatory assessment cycles. The ambition is to produce rules that are 'fit for the future' and 'help innovators navigate the regulatory environment' (OECD 2021b, 4). The presence of disruptive innovations is a component of the challenging scenario in which the OECD regulatory policy needs to be re-launched or re-invented, a point we will go back after we talk about regulatory indicators.

REGULATORY INDICATORS

The OECD has experimented with indicators since the 1990s when 'better regulation' took a proper shape. Various waves of surveys were carried out in 1998, 2005 and 2008/2009. The data was built on self-reported questionnaires. Interestingly, the series 1998 to 2009 do not report information on individual countries, most likely an indication of the resistance of government delegates to explicit comparisons. In the 2010s, however, the OECD was in a different position. First, the Regulatory Policy Committee created in 2009 (RPC, the successor of PUMA, but with a dedicated, specific and exclusive mandate on regulation) was consolidating its role and sense of membership among the delegates in the 2010s (Radaelli 2020). Second, the expertise of the Secretariat of the RPC allowed for more emphasis on examples and fact-checking to support the answers provided by the delegates. This led to the creation of sophisticated composite measures (Arndt et al. 2015). To understand this step-change, we have to trace the process and the fora where the decisions were taken.

The Committee is supported by OECD staff within the Regulatory Policy Division – which in turn belongs to the Public Governance and Territorial Development Directorate. The Division has over the years gained in analytical capacity by hiring staff with skills in governance, public policy and statistics. The Regulatory Policy Division serves as Secretariat of the RPC.

The presence of a new Committee, the RPC, with its own relatively stable membership and an intellectually powerful chair (Gary Banks, at that time Dean of the Australia and New Zealand School of Government) assisted in the generation of a common sense of purpose and trust. It soon became clear that there had to be a change on how the answers were collected, validated and for the first time compared explicitly.

Upon completion of the composite indicators, they are made publicly available with the name iReg.[1] These indicators are supplemented by more qualitative considerations in the Regulatory Policy Outlook of the OECD. In a sense, they are the spine of the Outlook (OECD 2021a). The regulatory indicators cover the dimensions of stakeholders' engagement, RIA, and ex post evaluation (on the latter, see OECD 2014). The consensus inside the RPC (see Radaelli 2020 for this process of consensus building) has led to the identification of four dimensions that combine design and implementation – to correct the discrepancy between on-paper similar

---

[1]   https://www.oecd.org/gov/regulatory-policy/indicators-regulatory-policy-and-governance.htm accessed 22 April 2023.

adoption and very different implementation on the ground. These four dimensions are methodology, transparency, systematic adoption and oversight institutions / quality control.

CHALLENGES

After some 30 years of better regulation, the world appears very different from what it was at the time of the first OECD Recommendation in 1995. One question that the RPC has raised in recent years is what better regulation 2.0 may consist of. The need for a new, adapted or re-invented regulatory reform vision comes from two sources. First, technology and the economy have changed. The presence of disruptive innovations and a digital space for economic and social interactions has posed new issues on the table of those willing to define and implement high-quality regulation. Political-administrative contexts matter. Some administrative procedures have been hard to implement in certain political and administrative settings, so they need structured and rationalized decision-making. But these same procedures may come across as too rigid in settings that are more supple, informal, and trust-driven. The OECD's emphasis on formal administrative procedures – consultation, impact assessment, risk analysis, and evaluation – may not perform well in some contexts.

Second, there have always been limits in how better regulation 1.0 was designed. Its focus on procedural steps is not particular relevant to countries who design high-quality regulation by drawing on informal co-operation rather than rigid procedures. Further, better regulation, as we have seen, is semantically ambiguous. It is a sort of semantic big tent (or coalitional magnet, see Béland and Cox 2016) covering too many things, from the war on red tape to attempts to give a role to values like human dignity in the design of new regulations. New Zealand has experimented with a new language of regulatory stewardship (Van der Heijden 2021) anchored to the core belief that regulations are assets. An asset is expected to generate a flow of benefits. Since regulations are expected to produce net benefits over time, regulatory frameworks covering policy domains (such as climate or pensions) should be conceptually framed and managed as assets. This stands in contrast to regulation as liability, or regulation as red tape, potential obstacle to business activity, and other negative framings of the regulatory enterprise (on the concept of regulation as enterprise see Prosser 2010).

Another point is that the Sustainable Development Goals push towards broader and more inclusive interpretations of whose interests and for what reasons must be included in regulatory analysis and appraisal (Radaelli 2021). This has led some to talk about re-tooling the tools of regulatory reform towards more ambitious and inclusive goals, like the Agenda 2030 of the United Nations (Radaelli et al. 2022). Finally, international regulatory co-operation – a must for the OECD – is questioned at a time of de-globalization where economic and military blocks turn competition into conflict, as shown in the aftermath of the Russian invasion in Ukraine.

A survey of RPC delegates and experts has identified four clusters of beliefs about regulatory policy 2.0 (Radaelli et al. 2022). The clusters point to (1) improving governance processes and fostering innovation; (2) delivering on accountability and enhancing the role of citizens in the regulatory enterprise; (3) becoming more pragmatic and critical in calling for robust reality checks and prudence before embracing grandiose expectations; and (4) re-defining the mission of regulatory policy as an aid to internal government and regulatory processes—or as a tool for 'those inside the decision-making tent', so to speak.

Interestingly, the survey did not find anywhere support for a radical objection to better regulation and its tools – the respondents do not think that RIA or regulatory oversight institutions are obsolete, but they may have different views on whether regulatory oversight should be independent from central government or assist central government from within, so to speak. A call for prudence also emerged about layering regulatory reforms with new additions. Foresight, algorithmic regulation, and technological fixes – the respondents said (Radaelli et al. 2022) – will not deliver unless supported by vision. Thus, at least as far as the RPC is considered, we expect the OECD toolbox to remain anchored to the classic tools, augmented perhaps by foresight and scenario analysis. The European Commission (2021), in its more recent communication, seem to go in the same direction.

CONCLUSIONS

The OECD accomplishment in the field of regulation is remarkable. The organization has promoted a process of diffusion of a regulatory reform agenda under the semantic label of better regulation. At the same time, the role of other organizations like the World Bank and the European Commission should not be under-estimated. But the focus and reach of the OECD are undeniable.

The presence of regulatory indicators allows for systematic comparisons across tools and dimensions of reform, although it is always difficult to establish the final impact of these reforms. Indeed, a crucial question for better regulation is to what extent the adoption and implementation of RIA, risk assessment, regulatory evaluation programs and consultation has an impact on final governance outcomes such as the quality of the business environment or the control of corruption (Jalilian et al. 2007; Dunlop et al. 2020; OECD 2014).

At the same time, the world is rapidly changing, economically, socially and geo-politically. The OECD is engaged in better regulation 2.0, although it is not clear whether this effort will usher is a refinement of the agenda or a radically new approach. Regulation has become more political and more contested, so, independently of the opinions of the RPC delegates, what is 'high quality regulation' and 'for whom' will not depend exclusively on the OECD Recommendation and Guidelines.

REFERENCES

Arndt, C., et al. (2015). '2015 Indicators of regulatory policy and governance: Design, methodology and key results.' OECD Regulatory Policy Working Papers no.1 https://www.oecd.org/gov/regulatory -policy/WP1_Design-Methodology-Key-Results.pdf accessed 10 November 2022.

Béland, Daniel and R.H. Cox (2016). 'Ideas as coalition magnets: coalition building, policy entrepreneurs, and power relations.' *Journal of European Public Policy* 23(3): 428–45.

De Francesco, F. (2013). *Transnational Policy Innovation: The OECD and the Diffusion of Regulatory Impact Analysis*. ECPR Press.

Doern, B. (2007). 'Red Tape-Red Flags: Regulation in the Innovation Age.' Conference Board of Canada CIBC Scholar-in Residence Lecture. Ottawa.

Dunlop, C.A., J.C. Kamkhaji, C.M. Radaelli, G. Taffoni and C. Wagemann (2020). 'Does consultation count for corruption? The causal relations in the EU-28.' *Journal of European Public Policy* 27(11): 1718–741.

European Commission (2021). Better Regulation: Joining Forces to Make Better Laws. Brussels, European Commission https://commission.europa.eu/system/files/2021-04/better_regulation_joining _forces_to_make_better_laws_en_0.pdf accessed 13 May 2023.

Jalilian, H., et al. (2007). 'The impact of regulation on economic growth in developing countries: A cross-country analysis.' *World Development* 35(1): 87–103.

OECD Public Management (1992). 'Regulatory management and reform: Current concerns in OECD countries', working paper OCDE/GD(92)58, Paris: OECD.

OECD (1995). Recommendation of the Council on Improving the Quality of Government Regulation. OECD/LEGAL/0278 Paris: OECD Publications.

OECD (1997a). Regulatory Impact Analysis. Best Practices in OECD Countries. Paris, OECD Publications.

OECD (1997b). Report on Regulatory Reform - Thematic Studies. Paris, OECD Publications.

OECD (2012). Recommendation of the Council on Regulatory Policy and Governance. OECD/LEGAL/0390 Paris: OECD Publications.

OECD (2014). Framework for Regulatory Policy Evaluation. Paris, OECD Publications.

OECD (2018). Regulatory inspections and enforcement toolkit. Paris: OECD Publications.

OECD (2021a). Regulatory Policy Outlook. Paris: OECD Publications.

OECD (2021b). Recommendation of the Council for Agile Regulatory Governance to Harness Innovation. OECD/LEGAL/0464 Paris: OECD Publications.

Prosser, T. (2010). *The Regulatory Enterprise: Government, Regulation, and Legitimacy*. Oxford, Oxford University Press.

Radaelli, C.M. (2005). 'Diffusion without convergence: How political context shapes the adoption of regulatory impact assessment' *Journal of European Public Policy* 12(5): 924–43.

Radaelli, C.M. (2020). 'Regulatory indicators in the European Union and the Organization for Economic Cooperation and Development: Performance assessment, organizational processes, and learning.' *Public Policy & Administration* 35(3): 227–46.

Radaelli, C.M. and F. De Francesco (2007). *Regulatory Quality in Europe: Concepts, Measures, and Policy Processes*. Manchester, Manchester University Press.

Radaelli, C. M. (2021). 'The state of play with the better regulation strategy of the European Commission.' STG Policy Briefs, 2021/06 https://hdl.handle.net/1814/70901 accessed 25 November 2022.

Radaelli, C.M., et al. (2022). Regulatory Policy 2.0 Viewpoints and Beliefs about Better Regulation: A Report from the 'Q Exercise'. Paris, OECD Working Papers Series no.20. https://www.oecd.org/publications/regulatory-policy-2-0-ab640ae8-en.htm accessed 25 November 2022.

Trnka, Daniel, and Yola Thuerer (2019). 'One-in, X-Out: Regulatory Offsetting in Selected Oecd Countries.' Regulatory Policy Working Papers, No. 11, OECD Publishing, Paris.

Van der Heijden, Jeroen (2021). 'Regulatory stewardship: The challenge of joining a virtue and a mechanism'. *Policy Quarterly*, 17(1): 57–63.

16. International taxation

Fayçal Ait Abdellouhab and Claudio M. Radaelli

INTRODUCTION

The Organisation for Economic Co-operation and Development (OECD) plays an important role in the different areas of economic and social lives. Given its official mission to achieve economic growth and social prosperity via 'better policies' (OECD, 2011a), it is not surprising to find tax policy high on the agenda of this international organisation. However, how the OECD has approached international tax policy issues has changed over the decades, from an initial focus on mitigating double international taxation to the fight against harmful tax competition and, today, the emerging issues raised by digital taxation.

Indeed, for quite a long time the OECD activity in this domain has been associated with the efforts to eliminate international double taxation, in the wake of the early efforts to define standards made by the League of Nations.

Since the beginning of its activities, the OECD has made an impact in the international tax world by producing what has effectively become 'the' standard for drafting bilateral tax treaties. The OECD Model Tax Convention on income and capital has now been published in ten editions, the latest in 2017 (OECD, 2017b). Absent a World Trade Organization for Taxation or any other global tax institution, the presence of the OECD in the world of international taxation has been felt via the model tax as well as the production of OECD guidelines for the tax treatment of transfer pricing. In short, the OECD rose as the most important forum in the world for handling issues concerning international double taxation, also with commentaries, studies, statistics and guidelines. As mentioned, in the second part of the 1990s, however, its Committee of Fiscal Affairs (CFA) expanded the mission to issues arising from harmful tax competition and tried to shift gear, from bilateral to multilateral initiatives.

A classic problem in international policy cooperation is how to bring sovereign states to concede some of their national interest (Rixen, 2008) in favour of co-operation. More coherence and stability in the international tax system sounds like a good and desirable goal, but taxation is at the core of state sovereignty, and even in a very integrated organisation like the European Union decisions on direct tax policy require a unanimous vote in the Council of Ministers. The challenge has, if possible, become even more ambitious, with the recent steps to cover both international double taxation and tax competition in a *digital* world and the *politicisation* of tax issues (Hearson, 2020). All this requires epistemic authority, diplomacy, and pragmatism (Christians, 2016) and a global convergence towards principles of fair and efficient taxation.

Today, in the absence of a 'formal' International Tax Organisation (ITO),[1] the OECD is 'the' international actor in the global tax ecosystem. It leads on international efforts to address

---

[1]   In 1999, Vito Tanzi of the International Monetary Fund argued for an ITO to accompany the World Trade Organization, but we have not seen anything like that, Tanzi (1999).

a full range of tax issues that define a good deal of what 'good governance' is or ought to be (Cockfield, 2006). In the last decade, the OECD has recalibrated its position in line with the emergence of global solutions to the financial crisis triggered by Lehman Brothers, often in synch with the G20 efforts. If a global institution like Tanzi's ITO has not seen the light, the G20 has been an effective fellow traveller in the OECD campaigns for a global tax order, with at least some shared fundamental principles. Further, the strategy of the 'Forums' opened to all countries clearly shows the OECD's ambition to continue to lead in the tax policy arena, especially after the emergence of powers calling for a new body with global mandate (see UNECA, 2021).

Our chapter first gives an historical overview of the OECD's actions in the international tax arena, then highlights its resources and *modus operandi*, followed by a discussion on the actual power, reach, autonomy and legitimacy of this organization in setting global tax policies.

HISTORICAL OVERVIEW

Broadly speaking, the OECD tax policy agenda evolved in three phases: the first stage covers the period from the 1960s to the second half of the 1990s, when the Paris-based organisation was primarily concerned with creating convergence in the tax treatment of multinational corporations, orchestrating a level playing field by limiting international double taxation. In this stage, the actors involved were government officers, bureaucrats, companies exposed to international competition. and experts (public economists and tax lawyers), with low politicisation of the issues.

The second stage started in the 1990s and carried on until the global financial crisis: the menu of activities was widened to include international tax erosion and evasion. The conceptual category emerged as 'harmful tax competition', meaning that tax competition across jurisdictions is generally an efficient mechanism, but under certain conditions can become harmful and therefore requires public measures and instrumentations shared at the international level. Lastly, the financial crisis has created a new global dynamic where tax issues are inherently connected with the digital transition and, at the same time, calls for good tax governance – the OECD must orchestrate the work of other international actors and fora like the G20 in a politicised environment.

TACKLING INTERNATIONAL DOUBLE TAXATION

The issue of international double taxation was first brought to attention by the International Chamber of Commerce (ICC) shortly after its creation in 1920. In 1923 the League of Nations published a report on the necessity of an international tax order – to accompany the expansion of international trade after World War I (Picciotto, 1992). The idea was to anchor the international tax order to bilateral tax treaties.

These efforts were continued later by the Organisation for European Economic Co-operation (OEEC) created in 1948. Its Fiscal Committee was asked in the 1950s to draft a model convention on double taxation (Picciotto, 1992; see the tenth edition of the Convention in OECD 2017b). After its establishment in 1961, the OECD issued in 1963 the Draft Double Taxation on Income and Capital and called its member states to conclude or revise the existing bilateral conventions accordingly. The Draft reflected the League of Nations' model with some refinement in favour of residence-based taxation (Picciotto, 1992). In 1971, The Committee of Fiscal Affairs replaced the Fiscal Committee and started the revision of the 1963 Draft Convention leading to the new Model Double Taxation Convention on Income and Capital in 1977. Crucially, although since the early days the OECD political goal was to create a multilateral framework, the divergence of domestic preferences led the OECD to the pragmatic role of orchestrating the growth of a formidable network of some 3,000 bilateral tax treaties, and to facilitate the diffusion of the Convention.

In addition to preventing double taxation, the OECD also engaged in protecting countries' tax bases (OECD, 2022). Indeed the other major product for which the OECD has been historically known is the Transfer Pricing Guidelines (TPGs) (Radaelli, 1998; Schmidtke, 2019: 98), formally adopted by the Council of the OECD in 1995 (OECD, 2022). Since then, the TPGs have continuously been revised and updated to include the newly agreed tax rules. The TPGs have become the main tool to prevent profit shifting. They have been adopted in different jurisdictions, within the OECD member states and beyond (Sharman, 2012: 26).

Harmful Tax Competition

In the second half of the 1990s the Committee for Fiscal Affairs, led by a dynamic director (Jeffrey Owens, see Owens 2011) showed an entrepreneurial attitude. Together with the European Commission and a number of important member states worried about the erosion of their corporate tax base (Radaelli, 1999), the OECD managed to put on the agenda harmful tax competition and to secure its own prominent place in leading towards convergence in this domain. For an organisation dedicated to the promotion of free trade and de-regulation, harmful tax competition was a tricky issue to define. The position of the OECD (on this aligned with the European Commission) was to argue that in general international tax competition is healthy, but there are specific beggar-thy-neighbour policies that are harmful to markets and governance. Incidentally, some have argued that the incoherence in the allocation rules provided by the bilateral model tax treaty and transfer pricing guidelines was not alien to the rise of double non-taxation (Wells and Lowell, 2013; Kleinbard, 2011). But, definitively, those who engaged with international tax avoidance and evasion took advantage of deregulation in financial markets and increased capital mobility (Eccleston, 2013).

What about co-operation among tax administrations? This seems a necessary pre-requisite for engaging with harmful tax competition. But it runs against issues of secrecy and state sovereignty. Well before harmful tax competition became an issue, in 1988, the OECD published, with the Council of Europe, a convention on Mutual Administrative Assistance on Tax Matters – an instrument with good intention, but limited reach. In the 1990s however the language of harmful tax competition emerged clearly, and so did the determination to crack down or at least promote policies on this issue with at least some opening up to co-operation across tax administrations (Radaelli, 1997; Webb, 2004). The OECD report Harmful Tax Competition: An Emerging Global Issue (OECD, 1998) resonated well with the anxieties of OECD revenue authorities and the key player, the US, which was seeking to implement measures against profit-shifting and tax avoidance.

Importantly for the politics of fighting tax evasion and promoting some co-ordination, harmful tax competition did not involve exclusively in exotic or remote jurisdictions somewhere in the world. Indeed, several OECD member states (Belgium, Ireland and the

Netherlands for example, not to mention the Crown Dependencies of the UK) were themselves home to practices that appeared to many observers 'harmful'. So much so that the European Union's initiative for a peer-reviewed based direct tax 'code of conduct' was kicked off in relation to harmful practices in the EU's member states and their dependent territories (Radaelli, 2003; Radaelli and Kraemer, 2008).

For the first time, the OECD went further than facilitating convergence on tax policies via model conventions and guidelines. It was to some extent intervening in the design of domestic tax policies (Webb, 2004; Rixen, 2008). In typical OECD style (see Chapter 9 in this volume), the main practice to address harmful tax competition emerged in the form of peer review, accompanied by a naming and shaming approach in the guise of blacklists to put pressure on commitments to global tax standards (Kudrle and Eden, 2003; Rixen, 2008; Schmidtke, 2019).

In 2000, the peer review conducted by the Forum on Harmful Tax Practices (FHTP) identified 47 potential preferential tax regimes and listed 35 jurisdictions as tax havens (OECD, 2000; Webb, 2004: 806). In addition to the strong objections of both Switzerland and Luxembourg to these measures, the Bush administration, freshly elected, turned against any multilateral agreement on this topic (Rixen, 2008; Eccleston, 2013). Revising its roadmap, the OECD agreed that (1) 'defensive measures' for non-compliant jurisdictions among non-member states would be triggered only after the OECD members met the standards; (2) the trigger of 'substantive economic activity' was abandoned; and (3) the blacklist approach mutated into a less-threatening Collective Memorandum of Understanding (MoU). Tax havens and harmful jurisdictions in general could adhere to the MoU with a public declaration. In a way, dialogue was preferred to confrontation (Sharman, 2006; Rixen, 2008).

The 11 September 2001 attacks exposed the global need for information exchange, including transparency in the tax domain. This was a window of opportunity for those arguing for a more robust international tax order. The US administration revisited its position on the role of the OECD in the fight against harmful tax competition. A Global Forum on Taxation was then established, to achieve higher standards of transparency and exchange of information in an equitable way and fair competition between different jurisdictions (OECD, 2009). The Working Group on Effective Exchange of Information developed the Model Agreement on Exchange of Information on Tax Purposes in 2002, which served as the base for Bilateral Tax Information Exchange Agreements (TIEA) and for the modification of the Article 26 of the OECD Model Tax Convention in 2005 (Eccleston, 2013; OECD, 2002). By 2004, only five jurisdictions were still considered tax havens – an indicator that was read as success in the Paris headquarters (OECD, 2004). A few years later, the themes of transparency and the global tax order re-emerged in a new context of the aftermath of the global financial crisis. In the same period, two domains gain prominence: electronic commerce (with changes in the OECD approach to tax treaties and commentaries) and the international harmonisation of value added taxes / general sales taxes.

Post-financial Crisis: A New Era of Inclusiveness and Openness?

The financial crisis was a push factor for new international tax rules in a globalised and digitalised world (Herzfeld, 2017), although others saw it as logical outcome in a sequence of reforms launched before the crisis appeared (Eccelston, 2013: 81).

The Global Forum on Transparency and Exchange of Information for Tax Purposes

Inside the OECD, the support of the G7 first and then the G20 became an important agenda-setting push factor. In 2008, the G20 had manifested support for enhancing global tax co-operation. The 2009 London Summit reiterated this support, declaring, with grand rhetoric, the end of bank secrecy. The OECD Global Forum for Transparency became the hub for the development of international standards on transparency and exchange of information (OECD, 2011b). The implementation of standards was left to the twin-approach of (a) examination of the legal and regulatory framework and (b) review and assessment of the implementation of the standards. Beyond the member states, OECD officers provided technical assistance to developing economies to help them implementing the standards.

Exchange of information (EOI) changed from on-request (EOIR) only to automatic exchange of information (AEOI). The US enacted new legislation targeting its residents' foreign financial accounts – the Foreign Account Tax Compliance Act (FATCA) of March 2010. The G20 called on the OECD to develop a global standard for the AEOI and to enhance transparency. A new Common Reporting Standard (CRS) was presented and endorsed by the G20 Finance Ministers and Governors meeting in February 2014, followed by a commitment of over 60 jurisdictions to swiftly implement it (OECD, 2014).

Today, the Global Forum includes 163 members working on an equal footing where the decisions are made by consensus. All members are committed to the EOIR and more than 100 countries started the AEOI (OECD, 2021d). The evaluation for both standards is carried out through peer review.

Inclusive framework on base erosion and profit shifting (BEPS)

The agenda for a wider and enhanced international tax cooperation was also bolstered from the OECD presence in the field of electronic commerce and the tax implications of new business models. Base erosion and profit shifting are of course much harder to detect and more harmful in these emerging domains of international economic activity (OECD, 2013). At the same time, international taxation is today a political issue, with the emergence of advocacy organisations and academic work connecting the abuse of the international tax order by cleptocracy, global corruption chains and international inequality (Hearson, 2020: 685; Sharman, 2012). Transnational non-governmental advocacy organisations have indeed taken the role of international enforces of international law, as shown by Eilstrup-Sangiovanni and Sharman (2022).

Once again, the green light came from the G20. In June 2012, G20 Leaders made a request to the OECD to identify the key issues that lead to the base erosion and profit shifting (BEPS) project (OECD, 2017a). The G20 Finance Ministers called on the OECD to include non-G20 countries to work on an equal footing for an efficient international tax co-operation in BEPS. The statement made in their November 2015 *communiqué* was clear and straightforward:

> To reach a globally fair and modern international tax system, we endorse the package of measures developed under the ambitious G20/OECD Base Erosion and Profit Shifting (BEPS) project. Widespread and consistent implementation will be critical in the effectiveness of the project, in particular as regards the exchange of information on cross-border tax rulings. We, therefore, strongly urge the timely implementation of the project and encourage all countries and jurisdictions, including developing ones, to participate. To monitor the implementation of the BEPS project globally, we call on the OECD to develop an inclusive framework by early 2016 with the involvement of interested non-G20 countries and jurisdictions which commit to implement the BEPS project, including developing economies, on an equal footing.

The project was launched as urgent response to the new context of aggressive tax planning and global corporate tax avoidance (OECD, 2013). The OECD (2015) identified 15 measures (see Box 16.1 below) to counter international tax evasion. The implementation of the 2015 plan has allowed changes to be made at the level of domestic tax laws, exchange of information, transfer pricing guidelines as well as at the level of tax treaties (as shown in OECD, 2020).

BOX 16.1 BEPS ACTIONS

Action 1: Addressing the Challenges of the Digital Economy

Action 2: Neutralising the Effect of Hybrid Mismatch Arrangements

Action 3: Designing Effective Controlled Foreign Company Rules

Action 4: Limiting Interests Deductions and other Financial Payments

Action 5: Countering Harmful Tax Practices – *Minimum standard*

Action 6: Preventing Tax Treaty Abuse – *Minimum standard*

Action 7: Preventing the Artificial Avoidance of Permanent Establishment Status

Actions 8–10: Aligning Transfer Pricing Outcomes with Value Creation

Action 11: Measuring and Monitoring BEPS

Action 12: Mandatory Disclosure Rules

Action 13: Country-by-Country Reporting – *Minimum standard*

Action 14: Dispute Resolution Mechanisms – *Minimum standard*

Action 15: Developing a Multilateral Instrument to Modify Bilateral Tax Treaties

Source: https://www.oecd.org/tax/beps/about/ accessed 23 April 2023.

In essence, the BEPS project seeks to achieve three main objectives (OECD, 2017a): (i) coherence in the global corporate tax regime (ii) substance of the economic activities to be considered for tax purposes (iii) and transparency. The minimum standards are subject to peer review to ensure implementation in a given timeframe. The legacy of the harmful tax competition season is visible in the BEPS focus on the 'substance' of economic activity (as opposed to mere on-paper presence) and global tax transparency. In 2022, the framework included 141 countries and 14 observers. Regional and international organisations play an important role through co-ordinated actions to support the implementation of the project, especially in developing countries.

The project has been observed with both interest and criticism by university researchers and tax experts. The critical observations point out the inconsistency from the theoretical and practical perspectives, especially with regard the adoption of the value creation principal in the Actions 8–10 for the allocation of taxing rights between source and residence countries (see Herzfeld, 2017; Devereux and Villa, 2018; Hey, 2018; Schön, 2019). Its enforcement is also questioned, since compliance with the minimum standards is in the hands of peer review, whilst for other actions it seems to some observers just a matter of good faith (Christians, 2016).

Two-pillar solution to address the challenges arising from digitalisation
As mentioned, the digitalisation of the economy was a push factor of the proposed BEPS Action plan and Action 1 was dedicated to address this issue. Digital companies rely on data and intangibles. They can make profit within a jurisdiction at large scale without nexus (permanent establishment in the sense of the current international tax system). This has ultimately posed serious questions on the allocation of the tax base – between source and residence countries (OECD, 2015). Whilst some countries launched unilateral measures to protect their tax base targeting the digital industry (the Digital Service Tax for example), the OECD has always been, naturally, in favour of a multilateral approach (OECD, 2021c). Through the Inclusive Framework Task Force on Digital Economy, the OECD has proposed two approaches: new allocation rules in the digital era (Pillar one) and the establishment of global minimum corporate tax rate (Pillar two). Yet again, the support of the G20 has been the necessary condition for the OECD to play this role and make these proposals.

On the other side of the Atlantic, the Biden administration announced its commitment to a rise in corporate tax within the US and a global minimum tax to prevent profit shifting to low-tax countries. This accelerated the works already in progress on the Two-Pillar reform amid unprecedented global health conditions after the outbreak of the Covid-19 pandemic. The economic analysis and impact assessment conducted by the secretariat in 2019 were followed by the report on the Blueprint of Pillar One and Pillar Two done by the inclusive framework in 2020 and a series of public consultations. The Two-Pillar Solution was finally signed by the Inclusive Framework Members in October 2021 except for four members: Nigeria, Kenya, Pakistan, and Sri Lanka. The solution implies the following equilibrium between two priorities of the Biden administration: the removal of existing Digital Services Taxes and the decision not to levy new ones (the giant internet-based US companies would be damaged by new levies) as well as the global minimum corporate tax (to curb aggressive profit shifting and global tax avoidance).

The Pillar 1 recognises the limits of the allocating regime based on the arm's length principle and the physical presence as a nexus test in the jurisdictions where the activities are conducted. It, therefore, aims at allocating some of the multinationals' profits to market jurisdictions where goods and services are used or consumed (Avi-Yonah, 2021). This follows the three-fold formula of 'user contribution, marketing intangibles and significant economic presence' (Schön, 2019). The profit share to be allocated is 25 per cent of the residual profit, defined as profit in excess of 10 per cent of revenue (see more OECD, 2021c).

Pillar 2, introduced the global minimum tax at a rate of 15 per cent as an attempt to reduce 'the race to the bottom'. Developing countries worry about the impact of the new rules on their tax revenues, considering the difference between the proposed global corporate tax rate and the (higher) average rate in the low- and middle-income countries.

THE OECD RESOURCES

The OECD bureaucracy is impressive for expertise and resources (Schmidtke, 2019). By producing revenue statistics, knowledge and technical expertise, as well as orchestrating fora with delegates from member states and beyond, the OECD sees the tax world in its own ways (Sharman 2012). For tax policy, the OECD relies on the personnel formed by officials from the member states governments, but it has also cultivated a relationship with some of the finest scholars in global tax networks (Porter and Webb, 2008). The secretariat of the Committee on Fiscal Affairs has shown entrepreneurship and capacity to learn. Entrepreneurship refers to the capacity to launch new projects and the skilful exploitation of windows of opportunity. Learning is evidenced by the capacity to readjust the target – when the harmful tax competition agenda did not seem to sustain momentum. The Committee's work is facilitated by the Centre of Tax Policy and Administration which, as a specialised secretariat for the Committee, co-ordinates the work of the Committee's different bodies, builds consensus, carries out analysis and provides statistical information (OECD, 2021a; Kudrle, 2010).

Over the years, in addition to the packages and reforms cited above, the organisation has developed statistical tools and data sets. It established the Global Revenue Statistics Database which constitutes the framework of the OECD's work with other countries to produce reliable revenue information and comparative data (OECD, 2021a). The OECD has also engaged in capacity-building programmes within low- and medium-income countries. Exchange of information, whether on request or automatic, requires huge IT infrastructures and well-trained officers. The role of the organisation includes technical assistance and learning opportunities for officers in partnership with other international organisations such as the International Monetary Fund, the United Nations and the World Bank. In 2020, more than 4,200 officials from 155 jurisdictions and nine international organisations benefited from training and 70 developing countries benefited from technical assistance (OECD, 2021a).

DISCUSSION AND CONCLUSIONS

The OECD has shaped the international tax order by leveraging its own knowledge, global knowledge networks, the financial and political power of decisions taken by its member states, and its presence alongside the most important governance fora in the world, including the G20. Importantly, historically the Paris-based organisation has been an ally of the United Nations and the European Union, especially the European Commission. Its voice, therefore, is amplified by the concert of other powerful voices, as shown by the events that led to the decision on a global minimum corporate tax. The UN Secretary-General appointed a new committee of tax experts for the period 2021–25 with the ultimate goal of combating illicit financial flows and strengthening domestic revenue mobilisation capacities in developing countries.[2] This can be yet again another case where the two organisations complement each other, instead of competing with each other.

Critics question the fact that the US' financial contribution to the OECD's budget makes it objectively hard to act in neutral ways (Carroll and Kellow, 2011; Porter and Webb, 2008). Some have argued that the OECD policy reforms and visions of tax governance do not originate at the Château de la Muette. OECD ideas may come from elsewhere, arguably in US circles (Kudrle, 2010; see also Eden and Kudrle 2005; Rixen, 2008). However, our account has shown that the OECD and the US administrations did not always see eye to eye. And if the OECD

---

[2]   https:// www .un .org/ development/ desa/ financing/ post -news/ secretary -general -appoints -25 -members-un-tax-committee accessed 23 April 2023.

were simply an amplifier for US ideas, it would not have credibility – government officers and global tax networks would look directly to the US instead of going to Paris. Another critical issue is legitimacy. Calls for an increased role of the UN Tax Committee in international tax affairs draw on the argument that the UN is more inclusive than the OECD club. In Paris, the response has been to orchestrate initiatives targeting jurisdictions beyond the OECD member states always in concert with other international organisations (the EU and UN) and the G20. For the future, it looks unlikely that the OECD role in global tax policies will be substituted by another organisation, whilst the ambitious policies on the agenda can be carried out only by international organisations and global fora moving together with shared goals.

REFERENCES

Avi-Yonah, R. (2021). 'The International Tax Regime at 100: Reflections on the OECD's BEPS project.' *University of Michigan Law & Econ Research Paper*, No. 21-020.

Carroll, P. and A.J. Kellow (2011). *The OECD: A Study of Organisational Adaptation.* Cheltenham: Edward Elgar Publishing.

Christians, A. (2016). 'BEPS and the New International Tax Order,' *BYU L. Rev* 1603.

Cockefield, A.J. (2006). 'The Rise of The OECD as Informal "World Tax Organisation" Through National Responses to e-Commerce Tax Challenges. *Yale Journal of Law and Technology,* 8, 136–87.

Devereux, M. and J. Vella (2018). 'Value Creation as the Fundamental Principle of the International Corporate Tax System.' *European Tax Policy Forum Policy Paper.* https://papers.ssrn.com/sol3/papers.cfm?abstract_id=3275759

Eccleston, R. (2013). *The Dynamics of Global Economic Governance: The Financial Crisis, the OECD, and the Politics of International Tax Cooperation.* Edward Elgar Publishing.

Eden, L., and T.R. Kudrle (2005). 'Tax Havens: Renegade States in the International Tax Regime?' *Law and Policy*, 27:1, 100–127.

Eilstrup-Sangiovanni, M. and J.C. Sharman (2022). *Vigilantes Beyond Borders: Transnational NGOs as Enforcers of International Law.* Princeton University Press.

Hearson, M. (2020). 'The International Political Economy of Global Tax Governance.' In Ernesto Vivares (ed), *The Routledge Handbook to Global Political Economy: Conversions and Inquiries,* (pp. 673–90) Routledge.

Hey, J. (2018). '"Taxation where Value is Created" and the OECD/G20 Base Erosion and Profit Shifting.' *Bulletin for International Taxation*, 72, 203–8.

Herzfeld, M. (2017). 'The Case against BEPS – Lessons for Coordination.' *University of Florida Levin College of Law Research Paper* No. 18-3.

Kleinbard, D.E. (2011). Stateless Income. *Florida Tax Review*, 11, p. 699.

Kudrle, T.R. and L. Eden (2003). 'The Campaign Against Tax Havens: Will It Last? Will it Work?' *Stanford Journal of Law, Business and Finance*, 9, 37–68.

Kudrle, T.R. (2010). 'Tax Policy in The OECD: Soft Governance Gets Harder.' In K. Martens and A.P. Jakobi (eds). *Mechanisms of OECD Governance, International Incentives for National Policy-Making?* Oxford University Press, (pp. 75–97).

OECD. (1998). Harmful tax Competition, An Emerging Global Issue. Paris: OECD Publications.

OECD. (2000). Towards Global Tax Co-operation, Progress in Identifying and Eliminating Harmful Tax Practices. https://www.oecd.org/tax/harmful/2090192.pdf accessed 6 November 2022.

OECD. (2002). Agreement on Exchange of Information on Tax Matters. https://www.oecd.org/ctp/exchange-of-tax-information/2082215.pdf accessed 20 November 2022.

OECD. (2004). The OECD's Project on Harmful Tax Practices: Progress Report. https://www.oecd.org/tax/beps/oecd-harmful-tax-practices-project-2004-progress-report.pdf accessed 20 November 2022.

OECD/Global Forum. (2009). Tax Co-Operation 2009: Towards a level playing field. https://www.oecd.org/tax/exchange-of-tax-information/taxco-operation2009towardsalevelplayingfield-2009assessmentbytheglobalforumontransparencyandexchangeofinformation.htm accessed 20 November 2022.

OECD. (2011a). Better Policies for Better Lives, the OECD at 50 and Beyond. https://www.oecd.org/about/47747755.pdf accessed 20 November 2022.

OECD. (2011b). Global Forum on Transparency and Exchange of Information for Tax purposes; Tax Transparency 2011: Report on Progress. https://bfsb-bahamas.com/international/064167700.pdf accessed 20 November 2022.

OECD. (2013). Action Plan on Base Erosion and Profit Shifting. https://www.oecd.org/ctp/BEPSActionPlan.pdf accessed 20 November 2022.

OECD. (2014). Standard for Automatic Exchange of Financial Accounts Information in Tax Matters. OECD Publications: Paris.

OECD. (2015). Action Plan on Base Erosion and Profit Shifting. OECD Publications, Paris. https://www.oecd.org/ctp/BEPSActionPlan.pdf accessed 6 November 2022.

OECD. (2015). OECD/G20 Base Erosion and Profit Shifting Project, BEPS Project Explanatory Statement, 2015 Final Reports. Paris: OECD Publications. https://www.oecd.org/ctp/beps-project-explanatory-statement-9789264263437-en.htm accessed 10 November 2022.

OECD. (2017a). Inclusive Framework on BEPS, Progress Report July 2016–June 2017. https://www.oecd.org/tax/bcps/beps-inclusive-framework-progress-report-june-2016-july-2017.htm Paris: OECD Publications.

OECD. (2017b). Model Tax Convention on Income and Capital: Condensed Version. Paris: OECD Publications. https://www.oecd.org/ctp/treaties/model-tax-convention-on-income-and-on-capital-condensed-version-20745419.htm accessed 10 November 2022.

OECD. (2020). OECD/G20 Base Erosion and Profit Shifting Project: Tax Challenges Arising From Digitalisation- Report on Pillar Two Blueprint. Paris: OECD Publications. https://www.oecd.org/tax/beps/tax-challenges-arising-from-digitalisation-report-on-pillar-two-blueprint-abb4c3d1-en.htm accessed 10 November 2022.

OECD, (2021a) OECD Work on Taxation. https://www.oecd.org/tax/centre-for-tax-policy-and-administration-brochure.pdf accessed 10 November 2022.

OECD. (2021b) Addressing the Tax Challenges Arising from the Digitalisation of the Economy. https://www.oecd.org/tax/beps/brochure-addressing-the-tax-challenges-arising-from-the-digitalisation-of-the-economy-july-2021.pdf accessed 6 November 2022.

OECD. (2021c). Statement on a Two-Pillar Solution to Address the Tax Challenges Arising from the Digitalisation of the Economy. https://www.oecd.org/tax/beps/statement-on-a-two-pillar-solution-to-address-the-tax-challenges-arising-from-the-digitalisation-of-the-economy-october-2021.htm accessed 6 November 2022.

OECD. (2021d). Developing Capacities in Times of Covid-19, 2021 Global Forum capacity Building Report. https://www.oecd.org/tax/transparency/documents/2021-Global-Forum-Capacity-Building-Report.pdf accessed 6 November 2022.

OECD. (2022). *OECD Transfer Pricing Guidelines for Multinational Enterprises and Tax Administrations*. OECD Publications: Paris.

Owens, J. (2011). 'Liable to No Tax.' Paper for the 65th Congress of the International Fiscal Association, Paris. http://www.oecd.org/ctp/48694722.pdf accessed 6 November 2022.

Picciotto, S. (1992). *International Business Taxation, A Study in the Internationalization of Business Regulation*. Cambridge University Press Cambridge.

Porter, T. and M. Webb (2008). 'Role of the OECD in the Orchestration of Global Knowledge Networks.' In R. Mahon and S. McBride (eds). *The OECD and Transnational Governance*, UBC Press, 43–59.

Radaelli, C.M. (1997) *The Politics of Corporate Taxation in the European Union. Knowledge and International Policy Agendas*. London, Routledge.

Radaelli, C.M. (1998). 'Game Theory and Institutional Entrepreneurship: Transfer Pricing and the Search for Coordination in International Tax Policy.' *Policy Studies Journal* 26(4): 603–19.

Radaelli, C.M. (1999). 'Harmful Tax Competition in the European Union: Policy Narratives and Advocacy Coalitions.' *Journal of Common Market Studies* 37(4): 661–82.

Radaelli, C.M. (2003). 'The Code of Conduct Against Harmful Tax Competition: Open Method of Coordination in Disguise?' *Public Administration* 81(3): 513–31.

Radaelli, C.M. and U.S. Kraemer (2008). 'Governance Arenas in EU Direct Tax Policy.' *Journal of Common Market Studies* 46(2): 315–36.

Rixen, T. (2008) *The Political Economy of International Tax Governance*, Palgrave Macmillan, 2008.

Sharman, J.C. (2006). *Havens in a Storm: The Struggle for Global Tax Regulation.* Ithaca: Cornell University Press.

Sharman, J.C. (2012). 'Seeing Like the OECD on Tax.' *New Political Economy* 17:1, 17–33.

Schmidtke, H. (2019). *The Politics of Global Tax Governance*, NY New York, Routledge.

Schön, W. (2019), 'One Answer to Why and How to Tax the Digitalized Economy,' *Max Planck Institute for Tax Law and Public Finance*, Working Paper 2019-10.

Tanzi, V. (1999). 'Is there a Need for a World Tax Organisation?' In R. Assaf and S. Efraim, *The Economics of Globalization. Policy Perspectives from Public Economics*, Cambridge University Press, (pp. 176–86).

United Nation Economic Commission for Africa (UNECA). (2021). Institutional Architecture to Address Illicit Financial Flows. https://repository.uneca.org/handle/10855/43826 accessed 6 November 2022.

United Nations. (2017). Model Double taxation Convention between Developed and Developing Countries. https://www.un.org/esa/ffd/wp-content/uploads/2018/05/MDT_2017.pdf accessed 6 November 2022.

Webb, M. (2004). Defining the boundaries of legitimate state practice: norms, transnational actors and the OECD's project on harmful tax competition, *Review of International Political Economy* 11:4, 787–827.

Wells, B. and C.H. Lowell (2013). 'Income Tax Treaty Policy in the 21st Century: Residence vs. Source.' *Columbia Journal of Tax Law*, 5:1, 1–39.

17. Economic policy

George Papaconstantinou[1]

1. INTRODUCTION: ECONOMIC POLICY AS THE CORE MISSION OF THE OECD

The centrality of economic policy in the OECD mission is apparent in the Organization's name and founding documents. Article 1 of the Convention establishing the OECD states its aims as:

> to promote policies designed: (a) to achieve the highest sustainable economic growth and employment and a rising standard of living in Member countries, while maintaining financial stability, and thus to contribute to the development of the world economy; (b) to contribute to sound economic expansion in Member as well as non-member countries in the process of economic development; and (c) to contribute to the expansion of world trade on a multilateral, non-discriminatory basis in accordance with international obligations. (OECD, 1960)

Article 1 points to the main 'tenets' that guide OECD economic analysis and policy prescription: the pursuit of growth as a means for higher living standards, underpinned by 'sound' (in other words fiscally responsible and sustainable) policies for economic expansion, in a multilateral environment grounded on expanding trade and interconnectedness. This is reinforced in Article 2 of the Convention which commits Member States to 'promote the efficient use of their economic resources', 'encourage research', 'pursue policies designed to achieve... internal and external financial stability', 'reduce or abolish obstacles to the exchange of goods and services and current payments and maintain and extend the liberalisation of capital movements'.

In this sense, the Convention establishing the OECD to replace the OEEC places squarely the Organization's work of evaluation, peer-review, advice, and coordination of economic policy within the prevailing post-WWII paradigm. This is centred around a belief in open markets, price stability, an orientation towards growth as a paramount policy goal, and the adoption initially of a broadly speaking Keynesian outlook to economic policy (for an analysis of the goals and early history of the OECD see also Chapter 2 in this volume). In the 60 years that followed, the OECD followed this paradigm but adapted its analysis and policy delivery tools to the evolution of the dominant economic thinking and policy agenda.

In this context, this chapter offers a critical analysis of OECD economic policy. Section 2 examines the structures, institutions and working methods for the delivery of the Organisation's economic analysis and policy advice. Section 3 focuses on the work on internationally comparable data, statistics and indicators that underpin it. Section 4 distinguishes between macroeconomic analysis and policy, and the increasingly prevalent work on structural policy. Section 5 discusses the evolution of OECD economic thinking and the gradual incorporation in its work

---

[1] The author is grateful for conversations with senior OECD management that have helped in the elaboration this chapter, though the final content and views expressed here cannot be ascribed to them.

of issues that were absent from the initial design as well as new issues that have emerged since 1961. Concluding remarks are in Section 6.

2.   STRUCTURES, METHODS AND OUTPUTS

The structure of work on economic policy at the OECD follows the same pattern as with other policy topics treated by the Organisation: Committee work with representatives of Member States, operating on the basis of work undertaken by the Secretariat. Today, economic analysis and policy work is conducted in many parts of the OECD Secretariat and is elaborated in a number of its Committees. Nevertheless, two Committees serve exclusively economic policy: the Economic and Development Review Committee (EDRC); and the Economic Policy Committee (EPC). Each is composed of one member per country plus representatives from the European Commission, the International Monetray Fund (IMF) and the Bank of International Settlements (BIS).

2.1   The Main OECD Economic Policy Committees

The EDRC (established in 1961) examines the country economic surveys prepared by the OECD Secretariat, following a dialogue between Committee, Secretariat and officials from the examined country; approval is unanimous, and publication is under EDRC responsibility following this peer review process. The process is built-in to the Organisation's work method and is underpinned by the statutory requirement for Member States to keep the OECD informed of significant changes in its economic policy (see Permanent Representation of the Republic of Poland to the OECD, 2019 for a view of EDRC work by its Chairman).

The surveys have evolved over time. Their intital focus was on macroeconomic developments and policies; today however, they place a clear emphasis on structural policies and their impact on overall economic performance, in a manner that distinguishes them from similar country work undertaken by other organisations such as the IMF. This focus on structural policies involves a wide range of areas: labour markets, innovation, digital policies, human capital, financial markets, environmental policies, social security, taxation, health care, public spending. Surveys typically contain one or more chapters focusing on such policies.

The EPC focuses on horizontal macroeconomic policy issues, as well as on structural reforms. Its mandate 'to contribute to balanced and sustainable economic growth with due attention to social and environmental consequences' has as mid-level objectives 'to promote responsible structural, fiscal and monetary policies and financial stability' (OECD, 2022a). In this context, it guides the work and strategic priorities of the OECD Economics Department in assessing fiscal, monetary, financial and structural policies and their linkages, while paying particular attention to global spill-over effects. Its members are high-level officials and historically, the role of EPC Chair has been assigned to the Chair of the US Council of Economic Advisers, a clear nod to the influence of the OECD's largest economy (see Permanent Representation of the Republic of Poland to the OECD, 2019 for a view of EPC work by its Chairman).

EPC work is channelled through a number of Working Parties (WP). The influential WP1 on Macro-economic and Structural Policy Analysis brings together national experts to discuss the cross-country analysis produced by the OECD Economics Department at a technical level. The analysis relates to structural surveillance and extends to macroeconomic issues subsequently dealt with in the Economic Outlook's special chapter(s). WP1 reports to the EPC on control of demand and inflation, the role of fiscal and monetary policy, supply-side policies, public expenditure and revenue decisions, financing and analysis of major expenditure programmes.

Next to WP1, WP3 on Policies for the Promotion of Better International Payments Equilibrium brings together top officials at Deputy Minister of Finance and deputy Central Bank governor level, and focuses on the effect on international payments of monetary, fiscal and other policy measures. Participation is restricted to G10 countries, but a debriefing session is organised for all interested OECD members, and the OECD Chief Economist reports on WP3 activities as they relate to international payments equilibrium at the start of each EPC meeting. The focus is mainly on the policy responses called for by ongoing economic developments and risks, notably as they relate to international imbalances (OECD, 2008).

Finally, the Working Party on Short-Term Economic Prospects (STEP) brings together national forecasters and is focused on a more systematic exchange of the preliminary set of detailed macroeconomic projections prepared by the Secretariat in the context of the preparation of the OECD Economic Outlook (OECD, 2022a). It is a process that builds on and feeds into national forecasts, including for budget purposes in some Member countries. By allowing cross-checking of data and comparing forecasts, it is also aimed at improving the quality and credibility of the projections that ultimately appear in the OECD Economic Outlook.

2.2   The OECD Economics Department

In the OECD Secretariat, the work servicing these Committees and their WPs is undertaken by the Economics Department. It is headed by the OECD Chief Economist, in recent years often also acting as a Deputy Secretary-General and thus having wider coordinating responsibilities. Importantly for the influence of the Organisation, the OECD Chief economist also participates in the G20, deputising the OECD Secretary General and taking part in the deliberations of G20 Finance Ministers. Two Directors assist the Chief Economist, one for each of the two ECO branches: the Country Studies (CS) branch and the Policy Studies (PS) branch. The former is organised around groups of countries and its work is geared around the production of the country reviews (reviews of OECD Members and some non-members occur over a two-year cycle); the latter around policy themes with the work reflected in flagship OECD publications such as the Economic Outlook or Going for Growth, as well as in more research-oriented publications and working papers.

The two branches interact regularly in both the production of the annual country surveys and the work of the flagship publications; the OECD-wide Economic Outlook projections for example are 'built-up' from country-level projections of the country desks, while the country Economic surveys make use of horizontal policy research and international benchmarking comparisons, as well as expertise from other OECD Departments in their 'special' chapter.

2.3   The Flagship Publications

The *OECD Economic Outlook* (EO) and *Going for Growth* (GfG) are the flagship publications of the OECD Economics Department, focusing on macroeconomic and structural policies respectively. While the aspects covered are influenced by the demand from Members as expressed in EPC and EDRC, they are the outlets where the Secretariat itself can put forward its analyses of economic developments and reform needs. The twice-yearly EO provides a general assessment of the macroeconomic situation across the OECD, followed by sections on the macro developments in all OECD and selected non-Member economies. Its forecasts rely heavily on expert judgement from a range of different models (a global macro model; now-casting models; a trade model; models to determine potential output; and national forecasts by Country Desks) with forecasts subjected to repeated peer review.

Given the abundance of macroeconomic projections from other institutions as well as private sources, the role and impact of the Economic Outlook has declined over time. Hence the recent introduction of Interim Economic Outlooks during Covid-19 (see section 5 below), meant to better track economic developments in real time. In addition, internal OECD assessments of the forecasting track record suggest that while current year GDP growth forecasts tend to outperform naïve forecasts, the track record of one-year-ahead forecasts is less impressive (Turner, 2018). Perhaps more accurately, they are projections rather than forecasts, meant to describe 'scenarios', inform the debate and ideally elecit a policy response.

Going for Growth is the other OECD flagship publication relating to economic policy. First published in 2005, it inaugurated a new form of benchmarking surveillance, complementing the OECD's long-standing country- and sector-specific surveys. Its analysis and policy recommendations rely on structural policy indicators with a link to economic performance; these serve to 'gauge to what extent GDP divergence reflects differences in the effectiveness of public policies rather than in tastes and societal choices' (OECD, 2006). Starting initially with core microeconomic policy issues such as product market regulation, retirement schemes and labour force participation, it expanded to innovation policy as a major determinant of growth, and gradually to include a much wider range of structural issues and policies that underpin economic performance (see section 4 below).

2.4   Economic Analysis and Policy Across the OECD

Economists work and deliver economic analysis and policy recommendations across a number of OECD Directorates in addition to the Economics Department (Tax Policy and Administration; Financial and Enterprise Affairs; Employment, Labour and Social Affairs; Environment; Science, Technology and innovation; Trade and Agriculture – to name but a few). Their relationship with the Economics Department has not always been easy; in the past, 'economic policy' was narrowly limited to macroeconomic performance and a limited set of structural underpinnings relating to product and labor market functioning and efficiency.

The Economics Department has not always been receptive to 'non-traditional' approaches to economic thinking prevalent in other OECD Departments. As however the set of topics that interest economic policy makers has broadened to include the determinants of growth, issues of sustainability and increasingly of inclusion (see section 5 below), with macroeconomic policy losing its erstwhile centrality, ECO faced a progressive loss of authority. Power shifted away from it and its work was often eclipsed in terms of public attention from high-profile work in other OECD Directorates and policy areas. In order to adjust to this new environment and be better able to tackle structural and longer-term issues, the Economics Department has reorganised its work around 'workstreams' such as productivity, financial markets, labour markets, inequality, labour, green issues. It also re-oriented its work to include the examination of longer-term issues and trends (e.g., Guillemette and Turner, 2018).

As a corollary, the relationship between the Economics Department and the other OECD departments necessarily became more symbiotic. In this new multipolar environment, while the Economics Department continues to pride itself as the centre of OECD economic policy analysis, it in fact increasingly acts as a hub, cooperating with others, incorporating extensive work done elsewhere, and relying on external expertise. In addition, its funding has suffered; unlike other OECD departments that have increasingly relied on 'voluntary contributions' outside the normal OECD budget, ECO funding has continued to rely on the official contributions of Member States through the so-called Part 1 budget which has been stagnating.

3.   DATA AND STATISTICS

Evidence-based economic analysis and policy recommendations cannot exist without the underpinning of robust and internationally comparable data. Developing and standardising statistical concepts and assembling large sets of internationally comparable quantitative data for use in analysis, indicators and benchmarking is thus a core mission of the OECD. Its Committee on Statistics and Statistical Policy (CSSP) is a gathering of Chief Statisticians from OECD countries with as aim to 'provide civil society with reliable, internationally comparable statistical information' by overseeing the OECD's statistical policy and the broad range of statistics the OECD collects (OECD, 2018). The CSSP is assisted by a number of specialised Working parties (on National Accounts, International Trade Statistics, International Investment Statistics, Financial Statistics).

The CSSP has a consultative role to other Committees regarding their statistical needs and also develops and oversees measurement guidelines, methodologies and standards in specific statistical areas. It has thereby also played a role in new international statistical developments, by helping tackle measurement in new policy areas (from wellbeing and all things digital to green and inclusive growth) as well as taking forward statistical policy issues in non-traditional but increasingly important areas, for example, the use of commercial and big data or tackling disinformation (see Permanent Representation of the Republic of Poland to the OECD, 2019 for a view of CSSP work by its Chairman). Most of such work however tends to be initiated in other Committees before being taken up by the CSSP.

Within the OECD Secretariat, this work is undertaken by the Statistics and Data Directorate (SDD), headed by the OECD Chief Statistician. The OECD however has a disaggregated system of statistics with a number of Directorates collecting their own data, within which SDD acts as generator of the largest bulk and as coordinator of all OECD data, providing governance and tools for corporate data management, an OECD data quality framework and support for data skills development. Broadly speaking, SDD data work falls into three categories: traditional macroeconomic data underpinning economic policy analysis; newer data sets typically developed outside national statistical offices that buttress macro policy analysis; and data addressing broader policy issues increasingly embedded also in economic policy analysis (e.g., inequality, inclusion, distribution, digital transformation, and green transition).

For decades, the bread and butter for the SDD has been its macroeconomic data and indicators collected by national statistical offices. Internationally comparable time series data collected directly from national authorities or indirectly from Eurostat for EU countries and indicators built on these were reproduced in OECD databases and statistical publications. The *Main Economic Indicators* (OECD, 2022b) is a prime example. It covers quarterly national accounts, consumer prices, business surveys, retail sales, industrial production, construction, total employment, unemployment rates, interest rates, money and domestic finance, foreign finance, foreign trade, and balance of payments for OECD countries and non-Member economies. It is extensively used for the preparation of the OECD Economic Outlook and has been the main flagship statistical publication of the Organisation over decades.

3.1   New Directions in Data and Statistics Work

During the last decade however there has been a fundamental change in OECD data and statistics work. Digitalisation has significantly enriched the data sources available for OECD analysts (such as administrative micro data, webscraping, geospatial data, and social media data) adding to the well-established official statistics sourced typically from National Statistical Offices. Accordingly, to harness the new opportunities, but also to address the issues of data quality, the SDD has defined an OECD Smart Data Strategy (OECD, 2022c), now a constituent feature of OECD data and statistics, also aimed as a possible blueprint for National Statistical Offices as they develop their own strategies in the face of the new digital environment.

These new directions for OECD data and analysis are evident in the use of micro-level data that have been increasingly used alongside macro and sectoral data. These are either sourced from the commercial sector or from administrative sources and their use requires handling confidentiality issues. Arguably in this respect the pandemic has acted as accelerator for their use in order to better monitor GDP shifts. Together with work on breaking down national accounts data on income, consumption, savings into household income groups, such data have been used for more timely and granular information on economic developments and allow a better tracking of current economic activity.

Other significant work has pushed the boundaries of data and statistics for economic analysis in several directions. Regarding productivity measurement, the *Compendium of Productivity Indicators* (OECD, 2021a) presents a comprehensive overview of recent and longer-term trends in productivity levels and growth in OECD and non-OECD countries. The *Guidelines on Measuring Trust* (OECD, 2017) provide international recommendations on collecting, publishing and analysing trust data, to encourage their use by National Statistical Offices (NSOs). Recent work based on the OECD Wealth Distribution database provides a review of patterns of wealth inequality (Balestra and Tonkin, 2018). Other important work links economic and environmental data for the first time, with the ability to assign emissions to specific industries, while the *Measuring Distance to the SDG Targets* study (OECD, 2022d) provides a tool and methodology to assess the distance countries need to travel to meet SDGs. In all these cases, the resulting work represents collaboration across OECD Directorates.

Perhaps most importantly, the new directions are also evident in a number of publications and efforts that use quantitative evidence to better understand and track well-being, beyond GDP measurement (for an analysis of GDP and wellbeing measurements see Deaton and Schreyer, 2021). The report by the Stiglitz-Sen-Fitoussi Commission (Stiglitz et al., 2009), launched at a high political level, triggered a whole workstream at the OECD with regard to measurement beyond GDP in terms of scope or disaggregation. A series of *How's Life?* reports followed, presenting evidence from indicators covering both current wellbeing outcomes and resources for future wellbeing. The contents of the 2020 edition (OECD, 2020a) are indicative: they cover income and wealth, housing, work and job quality, health, knowledge and skills, subjective well-being, safety, work-life balance, social connections, civil engagement, as well as various aspects of capital (economic, natural, human, social).

4.   MACROECONOMIC AND STRUCTURAL POLICY

Part of the attraction of the OECD has been its function of creating international networks in various policy domains; put another way, it has managed to 'socialise bureaucrats' in its Member States into identifying and learning from best practice (Carroll and Kellow, 2011). Except that in the economic policy domain, there are many other opportunities for doing so, especially in the context of institutions that have more immediate political and financial impact than the OECD. The European Union economic policy officials for example meet and exchange regularly in the various European Council formations, such as the Eurogroup or Ecofin. Outside Europe, IMF Article 4 consultations carry the added weight of 'lender of last resort' and are arguable followed by markets very carefully (hence are important to governments).

In this environment, the OECD has struggled to find its space. Its macroeconomic projections and analyses are published alongside many other similar projections from public and private bodies; they carry the Organisation's good name and weight but are not distinct in terms of approach or message (though they have evolved in recent years – see section 5 below). In turn, the importance of the country reviews varies: they are less consequential for the large OECD countries (the OECD Economic Survey of the US or Germany have rarely made headlines) than for the smaller OECD Member States or for the countries that aspire to be members for the OECD club. For these, the reviews have been sort of a rite of passage. But even in those cases, at a time of crisis, the policy analyses emanating from the IMF, the Commission or even from rating agencies tend to carry more weight and have more of an impact.

4.1   The Shift to Structural Policy

The OECD's response to being in this increasingly crowded 'policy analysis space' has been to move decidedly to focus more on structural reforms. As a first approximation, one could interpret this shift of focus to structural issues as a corollary of economic thinking moving from demand-side to supply-side policies in the context of the dominance in economic thinking and policy advice of international organisations such as the OECD of the 'Washington consensus' (Williamson, 2002). Structured around fiscal discipline, competitive exchange rates, trade and foreign investment liberalisation, privatisation and deregulation, it downplays the role of fiscal and monetary policy for short-run economic stabilisation and instead champions supply-side reforms that make for more efficient product, labour, and financial markets.

Indeed, the indicators used in the first edition of the *Going for Growth* reports (OECD, 2005) to motivate policy advice relating to structural reforms are indicative: minimum wages and labour cost, replacement rates for unemployed, the average tax wedge on labour, employment protection legislation, coverage of collective bargaining agreements, state control of business operations, barriers to entrepreneurship, business entry, trade and foreign investment, etc. Over the years, the framework and approach evolved away from an exclusive focus on reforms to improve labour productivity and labour utilisation, to incorporate the importance of safeguarding social cohesion by including indicators regarding inequalities of income and opportunities as well as poverty, as well as by including environmental sustainability as an additional dimension in the framework to identify policy priorities for individual countries.

Arriving at country-specific structural reform recommendations in this framework involves an approach combining quantitative and qualitative assessment. The methodology that has been developed involves outcome and policy indicators matched into pairs for each of the three broad Going for Growth dimensions (growth, inclusion, and sustainability). These pair links (currently about 450), developed based on academic and applied OECD research, are then used in order to benchmark economies against the OECD average. Qualitative judgement is then used to select the top priorities, which is then peer-reviewed before publication (OECD, 2021b).

4.2   The Limits of Structural Policy Recommendations

This is an ambitious and robust framework which however inevitably over time tends to end up repeating recommendations that are also produced elsewhere. It also suffers from a number of weaknesses. One is in assessing the effect of reforms by estimating the impact of structural interventions on macroeconomic variables and overall performance. The results of existing models that involve strong simplifications of structural relationships are not always useful. To complement this more standard analysis, the OECD has increasingly relied on using micro-level data in addition to its macro and sectoral data and indicators, as it has done in research in productivity carried out jointly with the Directorate of Science, Technology and Innovation. Another issue related to impact is the follow-up of reforms; while there is a reform tracker database, there is a lack of systematic follow-up and analysis of what seems to have succeeded and what not (and why), with the associated learning (Ekholm and Padoan, 2020).

Other issues that arise in the context of this increasing focus on structural policy are less in the sphere of methodology and more in the realm of political economy. In many cases the broad parameters of required reforms in particular countries are well-known. What is lacking is the detail to make these effective, and this touches upon the functioning of government, and more broadly of institutions (including the political system, parties, parliament, and relations with civil society). Also lacking is analysis on how reforms can be packaged and communicated to be made more effective and acceptable, including by addressing distributional issues and compensating those losing out from the changes. Finally, a robust system of monitoring reform efforts and even more importantly assisting their implementation is also key. To the extent that OECD structural policy recommendations do not touch upon these issues, their relevance and usefulness is reduced (though recent work has attempted to go in this direction, for example by examining perceptions and attitudes to climate policies).

5.   MOVING WITH THE TIMES

The avid reader of OECD economic output who is comparing today's reports and publications with those of a few decades back will find some similarities but many differences. Rigorous, evidence-based analysis, grounded on internationally comparable data and indicators, filtered through peer review and benchmarking continue to be the name of the game. But the substance, tone and positioning are very different.

The changes can first be traced to what one would call the OECD macroeconomic policy paradigm. Often criticised as being the high priest of the pursuit of a 'neoliberal agenda' of tight money, cuts in expenditures and restrain in wage increases (Gill, 1991), it is true that OECD macroeconomic policy analysis and advice has been squarely within the prevailing macroeconomic paradigm and has broadly followed it. It gradually moved from the early Keynesian phase of the 1960s and 1970s to reflect the monetarist revolution and the rise of rational expectations in macroeconomics with its associated reluctance to use fiscal tools for short-run stabilisation, in a transformation that was punctuated by the publication during a period of economic stagflation of the McCracken report (McCracken, 1977). While the report has had more than one interpretation (e.g., Lucas, 1979), it is generally seen as ushering an era of supply-side policies (Gayon, 2017).

National representatives to international organisations and to their committees reflect national priorities and views and only track the evolving debate in economic literature with a lag. OECD policy analysis and advice thus largely reflects the debate on economic policy in the Member States. Hence during the Eurozone crisis the OECD continued to generally preach for austerity policies, even as the mainstream economic literature had evolved in its understanding of the roots of the crisis in financial markets regulatory failure. All this however changed during the pandemic. The OECD was very vocal in supporting an activist fiscal policy, putting focus on the demand side of the economy, with higher concern for social issues, a position also reflected in the participation of the Organisation in the G20 (OECD, 2020b).

This recent shift in the macroeconomic policy stance advocated by the OECD should be seen in conjunction with the gradual departure in OECD economic thinking from a narrow understanding of economic policy around the pursuit of economic efficiency linked to market functioning, to incorporate in turn a number of issues: first, those relating to the importance of knowledge and technology for long-term growth; then, the link between environmental concerns and sustainable growth; and finally the goal of inclusiveness and social cohesion.

5.1   Knowledge and Technology for Growth

Pursuing policies conducive for long-term economic growth has been at the core of the OECD mission from the outset. 'Encouraging research' was understood even in the 1960s as being one of the factors important for growth alongside productivity and factor utilisation, but it took some time for the OECD to fully integrate innovation and technology into its economic analysis. The *Structural Adjustment and Economic Performance* (OECD, 1987) report and its follow-ups *Technology and Productivity: The Challenge for Economic Policy* (OECD, 1991) and *Technology and the Economy: the Key Relationships* (OECD, 1992) squarely placed innovation and technology at the core of the economic growth process, with implications for supply-side policies to boost productive potential, from basic research to innovation and the facilitation of technology diffusion (Godin, 2003).

Since those early publications, the work linking technology and human capital, all things digital and the economy has exploded at the OECD, typically as collaborative initiatives involving a number of OECD Directorates. With it has come a realisation that core tenets of neoclassical economics (scarcity, rivalry, diminishing returns) do not necessarily hold in an environment where knowledge and technology embody characteristics of public goods. This work is today evident in a number of policy-oriented research initiatives and publications; amongst these: the *Going Digital* horizontal project and series of reports (OECD, 2019a), the OECD global forum on productivity, the work on the implications of AI on work, and productivity and skills.

5.2   Environmental Concerns and Sustainable Growth

The second major departure has been the integration of environmental issues and sustainability into economic policy. While the OECD Environment Directorate has long worked on these issues, it is only relatively recently that green growth has become a core OECD concern in economic policy, starting with a 2009 OECD Ministerial declaration on Green Growth and *Towards Green Growth* report (OECD, 2011a; see also Chapter 14 of this volume).

Since then, work has multiplied in a number of directions. Green growth has been part of country policy surveillance, links between fiscal policy and green growth have been explored, empirical work has examined the economic impacts and distributional aspects of environment policies, while other work has focused on green finance and investment, and on links of green growth with innovation or trade. The *Going For Growth* structural reform agenda for OECD Member countries for example includes recommendations on addressing climate and pollution, increasing pricing of environmental externalities, investing in green infrastructure and removing or reforming agricultural subsidies. In the OECD distribution of policy priorities for advanced economies, environment-related ones rank third (together with a set of labour market policies), following policies for product market regulation, competition and trade, and those for education and skills (OECD, 2021b). This has also been feeding into surveys, and more recently in a coherent way, as with the decarbonisation framework (OECD, 2022f).

5.3   Incorporating Issues of Inclusiveness and Social Cohesion

The third major departure relates to inclusion. The OECD has moved away from the long-prevailing tenet that economic policy analysis and prescriptions by the Organisation should be limited to efficiency issues, with redistributive issues left to politicians. Starting with landmark reports such as *Divided We Stand – Why Inequality Keeps Rising* (OECD, 2011b), *Making Inclusive Growth Happen* (OECD, 2014) and *In It Together: Why Less Inequality Benefits All* (OECD, 2015), issues relating to income and wealth inequality and social cohesion have progressively moved to become more central in the OECD economic policy agenda. Long the purview of Directorates such as Employment, Labour and Social Affairs, they have now been 'mainstreamed' into OECD economic policy outputs, while also a new dedicated Centre on Well-being, Inclusion, Sustainability and Equal Opportunity has been created.

What is common to all three of these – digital, green and to some degree inclusion – is that the work has been 'horizontal', meaning it has used the policy breadth of the OECD to analyse a complex issue in a multidisciplinary way. Few other research organisations or even OECD Member governments themselves can do this. This one of the notable OECD advantages that it needs to continue to refine.

5.4   Adapting the Institutional Setup

Institutionally speaking, this gradual broadening of the economic policy approach spans the tenure of a number of OECD Secretary-Generals, though it became more pronounced during the time of Angel Gurría (2006–2021). It was during his tenure that issues of inequality, inclusivity, gender, social cohesion and increasingly resilience became more central to the Organisation's work. It should be expected that this new direction – more in sync with broader developments, including in other international organisations – is to a large extent embedded now in the OECD and will continue also under the tenure of his successor, Mathias Cormann.

Perhaps the most emblematic initiative in this direction is the ambitious *New approaches to economic challenges* project that attempted to create a 'new growth narrative' based on a examining the relationship between growth, human wellbeing, a reduction in inequalities and environmental sustainability, with associated frameworks of economic theory and analysis (including the implications of advances such as the behavioural revolution and bounded rationality), and approaches to policy that include a wider set of policy and institutional reforms to achieve social and economic goals (OECD, 2019b). While innovative in its approach and an important tool to open up OECD thinking, the initiative struggled to deliver operational policy recommendations and to become accepted as part of the regular OECD programme of work.

5.5   Responding to Crises

A final issue relates to the response of the OECD to the most recent crises: the Covid-19 pandemic and the Ukraine war. The Organisation exhibited its more recently acquired agile character in advocating early and forcefully for a more activist economic policy encouraging governments to spend in order to protect people and businesses and face the economic and social costs associated with the pandemic. In addition, it adapted its output to a rapidly shifting economic environment that required more timely delivery of its products. In this vein, an Interim Economic Outlook was launched in March 2020 by the Chief Economist (with two such interim reports complementing the regular Economic Outlook publications), making the OECD first movers in drawing attention to the economic impact of the crisis (OECD, 2020b).

The Economic Department work programme was adapted to address Covid-19 issues and produced a number of Covid-19-related policy briefs, developed a COVID policy tracker of countries' announcements of fiscal, monetary and policy responses, and a special Covid-19 recovery edition of Going for Growth. A weekly GDP tracker developed with the Statistics and Data Directorate during the pandemic was aimed to dispose of higher frequency data than the official quarterly GDP, and fits squarely into the general quest by policy makers for more granular (and timely) data, going beyond aggregates. A similar effort of timely analysis was underway also with regard to the economic consequences of Ukraine war, including tracking the impact of sanctions (OECD, 2022e).

6.   CONCLUDING REMARKS

OECD economies have weathered a series of crises in the last decades. From the global financial crisis and the Eurozone crisis to the Covid-19 pandemic and the war in Ukraine with its associated economic fallout, these crisis episodes have forced policy makers to reassess their policy prescriptions, learn from past mistakes, and invent new policy tools and methods. They have done so against the background of a number of old and new challenges that transcend these crises and that require new approaches: the digital technologies and their implications for the transformation of economies and societies; the impact of climate change and of an accelerating environmental crisis; new patterns of global economic interdependence; and widening income and wealth inequality that puts a stress on societal cohesion and undermines the trust in democratic systems and open economies.

In this context, the role of an organisation such as the OECD is to examine, assess, analyse, compare, and advise its Member States and civil society at large on the best available policy options that can be used to face up to these challenges. Since its creation 60 years ago, it has sought to do so by assembling and working on internationally comparable quantitative data and indicators, through a combination of evidence-based analysis, peer review, benchmarking and expert judgement. Its committees, as well as within the OECD Secretariat the Economics Department, together with all the other OECD Directorates dealing with economic issues, have produced an impressive amount of quality work in this regard. Moreover, they have evolved together with economic analysis and with the nature of the problems at hand, in the process enriching their analytical frameworks, underlying data, and policy advice.

Looking ahead, the ability of OECD economic analysis and policy advice to remain relevant rests on a number of factors. First among these is to continue refining and extending their analytical tool-kit based on a conceptual framework that blends efficiency goals with concerns about sustainability and inclusion. Second, to be able to back it up with increasingly timely and granular quantitative evidence that tracks the multi-dimensional changes that are under way. Third, to be able to translate this analytical framework and data into practical advice that improves people's lives, not just in their member countries but beyond these. And finally, to do so in an environment where, in addition to conversing with governments, they can directly interact with and influence civil society in all its manifestations.

REFERENCES

All websites accessed 23 April 2023.

Balestra, Carlotta and R. Tonkin (2018), 'Inequalities in household wealth across OECD countries: Evidence from the OECD Wealth Distribution Database', Statistics and Data Directorate Working Paper No. 88, Paris: OECD.

Carroll, Peter and A. Kellow (2011), *The OECD – A Study of Organisational Adaptation,* Edward Elgar Publishers.

Deaton, Angus and P. Schreyer (2021), 'GDP, Wellbeing and Health: Thoughts on the 2017 Round of the International Comparison Program', Review of Income and Wealth.

Ekholm, Karolina and Pier Carlo Padoan (2020), 'Note on reviewing work at the Economics Department of the OECD', mimeo, 26 January.

Gayon, V. (2017). 'Debating International Keynesianism: The Sense of the Acceptable and the Neoliberal Turn at the OECD.' *Annales. Histoire, Sciences Sociales, 72*(1), 113–56. doi:10.1017/ahsse.2018.21.

Gill, Stephen (1991), *American Hegemony and the Trilateral Commission*, Cambridge: Cambridge University Press.

Godin, B. (2003), 'The New Economy: What the Concept Owes to the OECD', Project on the History and Sociology of S&T Statistics Working Paper No. 21.

Guillemette Y. and D. Turner (2018), 'The Long View: Scenarios for the World Economy to 2060', Economic Policy Paper No. 22, Paris: OECD.

Lucas, Robert E. Jr. (1979), 'Paul McCracken et al., 'Towards Full Employment and Price Stability: A Report to the OECD by a Group of Independent Experts,' June 1977: A Review', Carnegie-Rochester Conference Series on Public Policy 11: 161–68.

McCracken, Paul et al. (1977), Towards Full Employment and Price Stability: A Report to the OECD by a Group of Independent Experts, Paris: OECD.

OECD (2022a), *On-Line Guide to OECD Intergovernmental Activity*, Paris: OECD.

OECD (2022b), *Main Economic Indicators* series, Paris: OECD.

OECD, (2022c), *OECD Smart Data Strategy*, Paris: OECD.

OECD (2022d), *The Short and Winding Road to 2030: Measuring Distance to the SDG Targets*, OECD Publishing, Paris, https://doi.org/10.1787/af4b630d-en.

OECD (2022e), *OECD Economic Outlook, Interim Report – Economic and Social Impacts and Policy Implications of the War in Ukraine*, March, Paris: OECD.

OECD (2022f), 'A Framework to Decarbonise the Economy', OECD Economic Policy Paper No. 31, February.

OECD (2021a), *OECD Compendium of Productivity Indicators*, Paris: OECD, https://doi.org/10.1787/f25cdb25-en.

OECD (2021b), *Going for Growth 2021:Shaping A Vibrant Recovery,* Paris: OECD.

OECD (2020a), How's Life? 2020: Measuring Well-being, OECD Publishing, Paris, https://doi.org/10.1787/9870c393-en.

OECD (2020b), *OECD Economic Outlook, Interim Report – Coronavirus: The World Economy at Risk*, March, Paris: OECD.

OECD (2019a), *Going Digital: Shaping Policies, Improving Lives*, Paris: OECD.

OECD (2019b), 'Beyond Growth: Towards a New Economic Approach', Report of the Secretary-General's Advisory Group on a New Growth Narrative, OECD: Paris.

OECD (2018), 'Proposed Extension of the Mandate of the Committee on Statistics and Statistical Policy', COM(2018)123, Paris: OECD.

OECD (2017), *OECD Guidelines on Measuring Trust*, Paris: OECD, https://doi.org/10.1787/9789264278219-en.

OECD (2015), *In It Together: Why Less Inequality Benefits All*, OECD Publishing. http://dx.doi.org/10.1787/9789264235120-en.

OECD (2014), *Making Inclusive Growth Happen*, Paris: OECD.

OECD (2011a), *Towards Green Growth*, Paris: OECD.

OECD (2011b), *Divided We Stand – Why Inequality Keeps Rising*, Paris: OECD.

OECD (2008), Proposed Renewal of the Mandate of the Economic Policy Committee, C(2008)21, Paris: OECD.

OECD (2006), *Going for Growth: Structural Policy Priorities and Indicators in OECD Countries*, Paris: OECD.

OECD (2005), *Going for Growth: Structural Policy Priorities and Indicators in OECD Countries*, Paris: OECD.

OECD (1992), *Technology and the Economy: the Key Relationships*, Paris: OECD.

OECD (1991), *Technology and Productivity: The Challenge for Economic Policy*, Paris:OECD.

OECD (1987), *Structural Adjustment and Economic Performance*, Paris: OECD.

OECD (1960), *Convention on the Organisation for Economic Cooperation and Development*, Paris: OECD.

Permanent Representation of the Republic of Poland to the OECD (2019), *Inside the OECD: Committees and their Chairs,* Scholar Publishing House, Warsaw.

Stiglitz, J., J-P Fitoussi and A. Sen (2009), Report by the Commission on the Measurement of Economic Performance and Social Progress, Paris.

Turner, David (2018), 'The Use of Models in Macroeconomic Forecasting at the OECD,' World Scientific Book Chapters, in: Peter Pauly (ed.), *Global Economic Modeling A Volume in Honor of Lawrence R. Klein*, Ch 3, 30–48, World Scientific Publishing Co. Pte. Ltd.

Williamson, John (2002), 'Did the Washington Consensus Fail?' Outline of Remarks at CSIS. Washington DC: Institute for International Economics, November 6.

PART IV

THE IMPACT ON DOMESTIC POLICIES

18. Australia: Varieties of policy impacts

Peter Carroll

In deciding to apply, successfully, for membership of the OECD in 1970, the Australian government was not only hoping to gain the benefits of membership, it was deciding, in effect, to accept a variety of constrains on a wide range of its policies (yet, not all of its agreements are binding on all of its members, see Carroll and Kellow, 2011). More than 50 years later, we can appraise the impact of the OECD on Australia by leveraging the concepts of policy learning, capacity, content and process. We will focus on the case of OECD tax policy to explore matters in more depth. Throughout, we will draw in part, upon Kellow and Carroll (2017) and Carroll and Kellow (2011, 2021). Kellow and Carroll (2017) in particular, provides a book-length study of Australia's relationship with the OECD and the latter's impact on Australian policy.

CONTEXT

The outputs of the OECD are collectively arrived at, so that any examination of the impact of these outputs on its members' policies is, in considerable part, an examination of the outputs of their interactions. The statistics it collects are, for example, for the most part collected in collaboration with the members, who retain ownership of the data. Similarly, its analyses of the collected data undertaken, for the most part, by its Secretariat, are conducted with the active and continuous involvement of member governments, who subject them to rigorous peer review. Its many conventions, decisions, recommendations and declarations are developed and approved with the active and continuous involvement of member governments. As argued by Carroll and Kellow (2011, p. 5), the 'ownership' of the OECD by its member countries is what makes its work of much higher value to them, with a significant, though varying, impact on their domestic policy.

THE ACCESSION PROCESS AND AUSTRALIAN POLICY

The OECD's accession process for Australia involved the detailed examination by the organisation of a wide range of existing Australian policies to help ensure that they complied with existing OECD agreements. As was the case with all its members, some exceptions and reservations were permitted, usually with the caveat that they would be gradually withdrawn to bring policies into line with OECD agreements in the future, notably with the OECD's Code of Liberalisation of Capital Movements and Code of Liberalisation of Current Invisible Operations.

The initial impact on policy thus took place during the accession process. Only one area caused protracted difficulties, when the Secretariat indicated two issues of concern in relation to shipping and the OECD Invisibles Code, with Australian policy being allegedly inconsistent with the Code by discriminating in favour of Australian flag carriers and by restricting competition, as well as regulating prices and competition. However, following further analysis and discussion, up to the level of Cabinet, during which it was noted that both the USA and France practiced extensive flag discrimination, it was agreed by the OECD's Invisibles Committee that this was not the case and that a number of Australian reservations to the Code were acceptable (Carroll and Kellow, 2011).

On accession Australia specified a number of exceptions and reservations to the Code of Liberalisation of Capital Movements for its then foreign investment policy. In following years, encouraged in part by the periodic OECD reviews of members' situations in relation to the Code, it gradually removed these exceptions, so that by 1999 it had liberalised the scope of its foreign investment policy and all of the restrictions on access to the Australian financial market, excepting that relating to the issue in Australia of bearer securities by foreign governments. Similarly, the Code's recommendation that members avoid new or more restrictive exchange restrictions on the movement of capital or the use of non-resident owned funds, was fully met in the 1980s, when all exchange controls were dismantled.

In summary, accession resulted in no initially significant changes to Australian domestic policy, but it did involve:

1. A detailed review of all relevant Australian policy by OECD and Australian officials, a review that used existing OECD agreements as the main criteria for evaluation.
2. An endorsement of much of Australian economic and trade policy as it existed in the early 1970s.
3. Subjecting Australian policy to regular OECD reviews that acted as an ongoing incentive for government to work towards a variety of agreed, policy objectives. It should be noted that a range of other factors not associated with the OECD were, of course, also important in bringing about policy change, not only the incentives posed by OECD review mechanisms.

THE IMPACT ON POLICY LEARNING, POLICY CAPACITY AND POLICY PROCESSES

In the decades since Australia joined the OECD in 1971, the organisation has had a varying though continuing impact on domestic policy. In this section that impact is examined in relation to policy learning, policy capacity and policy process.

Policy Learning, Analysis and Advice

All of the Australian public servants interviewed for this study, without exception, indicated that the major reason for their continuing, if varying, participation in OECD committees and working groups was that of policy learning, in one form or another. All, bar one, also felt that the aim of policy learning had been achieved, though to varying extents, and that it was a more or less continuous process. Similarly, the bulk of the members of the OECD's Secretariat interviewed felt that the opportunity for policy learning in a cross-national and cross-cultural context was the primary value the organisation offered to its members.

In the remainder of this section a selection examples of the OECD's impact on policy learning are presented. The first is the Australian Industries Assistance Commission (now the Productivity Commission) analysis of the economic effects of varying trade liberalisation scenarios, using a modification of the WALRAS model developed earlier by the OECD (the analysis was commissioned by the Department of Foreign Affairs and Trade, ABARE 1985, 1988, Stoeckel, 1985 and Industry Commission, 1991).

The head of the Industry Development and International Branch within the Department of Health and Ageing's Policy and Strategy Group, who noted to the Secretary that the OECD provided useful health data on a range of countries and that, in particular, its peer analysis process could provide a regular evaluation of Australia's health policies in a 'fairly confidential and non-threatening environment', with evaluations published only with the consent of the country concerned (Kellow and Carroll, 2017, p. 310). Similarly, a number of senior officials within the Department of Science, Education and Training, stressed the value of the PISA educational data and the reputation of OECD statistics for comparisons. Whitnall and Pitts (2019) of the Australian Bureau of Agricultural and Resource Economics and Sciences, drew heavily upon comparative OECD data to examine trends in meat consumption. Consultants Ernst and Young (EY, 2019), also drew heavily upon OECD data in developing a government report regarding innovation in agriculture. In turn, the Department of Agriculture, Water and the Environment in considerable part based its new National Agricultural Innovation Agenda on the Ernst and Young report (Littleproud, 2020)

Policy Learning and Policy Modification: The Case of Privacy

Policy learning has also led to changes to Australian policy and legislation. In 1980 the OECD issued the 'Guidelines on the Protection of Privacy and Transborder Flows of Personal Data' (1980). It had decided to address the problems of diverging national legislation regarding the topic and in 1978 instructed a Group of Experts to develop Guidelines on basic rules governing the transborder flow and the protection of personal data and privacy, in order to facilitate the harmonisation of national legislation and prevent member states from introducing incompatible and conflicting laws for the defence of privacy. The aim was to reach agreement on a broad set of fundamental principles to protect personal data that reduce pressure to regulate or control international data flows.

Eight basic principles were established, providing a framework that enabled members to exercise a considerable degree of discretion in any legislation they implemented regarding privacy. The Expert Group was under the chairmanship of an Australian, the Honourable Mr Justice Kirby. The Australian Law Reform Commission (ALRC) had begun work on privacy in 1976, although its report was not published until 1983, and Justice Kirby was chair of the Commission from 1978 to 1980 (Australian Law Reform Commission, 2010).

Given the roles played by Justice Kirby in the OECD and ALRC, as well as the mounting concern for privacy in the face of rapidly expanding information technology, it is not surprising that the Australian Privacy Act, 1988, drew substantially on the OECD Guidelines. Its preamble, for example, indicates that Australia is a member of the OECD, that its governing Council had recommended that the legislation of members take into account the privacy principles set out in the 1980 OECD Guidelines and that Australia had expressed its intention to participate in the recommendation. Further, the eight privacy principles in the OECD Guidelines, were the foundation for the 11 Information Privacy Principles contained in the Privacy Act, 1988 (Australian Law Reform Commission, 2010).

While the Australian government thus endorsed the OECD Guidelines, in line with the discretion afforded by the OECD Guidelines, the Privacy Act, 1988, unlike the Guidelines, exempted a wide range of organisations from its coverage and was confined to the public sector, although the Privacy Commissioner established by the Act was to encourage the private sector to observe the OECD Guidelines.

In summary, the OECD has been, and continues to be, a valuable source of comparative data and learning, the analysis of which has led, at times, to the modification of both policy and legislation in Australia, notably where Australia has become a signatory to an OECD Convention and the issue addressed by a convention requires collective action by members (and, increasingly, by non-members) to be effective. However, as the Bribery Convention and Privacy Guidelines indicate, the policy and legislation adopted are not always fully in line with OECD recommendations, nor are they always enforced with any great enthusiasm.

Capacity Building for Policy

Developing policy capacity often requires and builds on policy learning. The use of ideas, concepts, guidelines, recommendations and agreements developed by the OECD is a common feature of the reports of government review bodies in Australia, helping to improve its policy capacity. Improvements to the federal government's regulatory impact statement system, for example, followed the acceptance of many of the recommendations made by the Taskforce on Regulation. The Taskforce had used the OECD's seven principles of regulatory design as the base from which to: one, compare the quality of Australian regulation; two, help it estimate the cost of regulation for Australian business; three, as a source of endorsement as to the value of regulatory impact systems; and four, to support its case as to the need for regular reviews of regulation (Taskforce on Regulation, 2006, pp. 8, 14, 172).

In relation to chemicals, Australia improved the efficiency of its capacity to assess and regulate the use of chemicals by participating in the OECD's 'Mutual Acceptance of Data' (MAD) system, which harmonises national approaches to the regulation of chemicals. MAD consists of a set of OECD Council decisions, notably the Guidelines for the Testing of Chemicals and the Principles of Good Laboratory Practice. In summary, Australian regulators when undertaking the assessment of products containing chemicals, can now accept relevant test data developed by other signatories to MAD, confident that it meets Australian testing standards, thus reducing the need to undertake the tests in question (OECD, 2021). The OECD has estimated that the use of MAD saves governments and the chemicals industry approximately €309 million per annum.

The OECD and Australian Policy Processes

As well as its impact on policy learning and capacity, the OECD has also had a range of impacts on Australian policy processes. This is most obvious in relation to government reviews of policy, which have to take into consideration any relevant or potential OECD agreements, decisions, standards and conventions to which Australia has become, or is likely to become, a signatory. This can range from needing to inform the OECD as to likely and actual changes to policy, to subjecting Australian policies to regular peer review and the recommendations that result from such reviews, especially as regards the implementation and enforcement of agreements to which Australia is a signatory, in effect, adding an extra stage or level to domestic policy processes.

In 2010, for example, the Global Forum on Transparency and Exchange of Information (EOIR) for Tax Purposes evaluated Australia in a combined review against the 2010 Terms of Reference for both the legal implementation and enforcement of the EOIR standard as well as its operation in practice. Australia was found to be largely compliant, although a number of recommendations for changes to the processes being utilised were recommended and accepted (OECD, 2017a).

Another example are the reports of the OECD Working Group on Bribery that evaluate and make recommendations on the implementation and enforcement efforts of signatories, such as Australia, to the OECD Anti-Bribery Convention, which established legally binding standards to criminalise bribery of foreign public officials in international business transactions. Australia has been subject to four phases of monitoring by the Working Group and has adopted most of its recommendations for improvements to its enforcement processes (OECD, 2017b).

THE OECD AND AUSTRALIAN TAX POLICY: A CASE STUDY

In this section we provide a case study of the impact of the OECD on Australian tax policy, to illustrate at greater length what can be its significant and continuing impact. The increasing, global influence and success of the OECD in developing tax policies (see Chapter 16 in this volume) and processes provides Australia with the opportunity and the incentive to participate in, and exert influence upon, those policies and, as a result, their likely impact on policy. Without membership it is unlikely that Australia, as a middle power, would have the ability to significantly shape international tax policy. Moreover, as Bentley noted (2003), if Australia is to be a player within the OECD in tax matters, then its government needs to largely align its tax policies with those recommended by the OECD. As the following examples illustrate, this has largely been the case.

The OECD's role in the development of international tax policy began with Council's adoption in 1963 of a Recommendation concerning the avoidance of double taxation, urging its members when concluding or revising bilateral tax conventions, to conform to this 'Draft Double Taxation Convention on Income and Capital', as interpreted by an increasing number of Commentaries. This title was modified in 1992, to become the 'Model Tax Convention on Income and Capital' (hereinafter MTC), to indicate that the Convention dealt with a range of issues, not only the elimination of double taxation but the prevention of tax evasion and avoidance, transfer pricing and non-discrimination.

The MTC has since been subject to ongoing revision and Australia has lodged a number of reservations to the MTC, both on its accession and, over time, withdrawing some reservations and entering new ones (a detailed history of the reservations and withdrawal of reservations made by Australia up to 2017 can be found in the OECD's 'Model Tax Convention on Income and on Capital', (full version, 2017c). Indeed, Australia's increasing tax treaty network is now largely based on the ever-evolving MTC, including, for example, its adoption of the 1995 OECD Transfer Pricing Guidelines for Multinational Enterprises and Tax Administrations.

The Guidelines have been highly influential in determining the Australian Tax Office's (ATO) approach to, and interpretation of, Australia's transfer pricing legislation, which is based closely on the OECD guidelines (see, e.g., Paragraph 1.5 of Taxation Ruling 98/11,

Dirkis, 2013). The alignment was made even closer and more explicit in 2013 by a modification of legislation, following Justice Middleton's ruling that the 1995 OECD's Transfer Pricing Guidelines for Multinational Enterprises and Tax Administrations could not be used by the ATO in interpreting Division 13 of the Income Tax Assessment Act 1936 (Dirkis, 2013). The modification ensured that the Guidelines could be used for such purposes of interpretation.

However, OECD recommendations regarding tax are not always adopted by Australia. In regard to the proposal that led to the OECD's Convention on Mutual Administrative Assistance in Tax Matters 1988, for example, following a meeting of the ATO, Treasury, Foreign Affairs and Trade, and Prime Minister and Cabinet, the advice was not to support the proposal, but to monitor its development and leave open the question of becoming a member at a later date. (Kellow and Carroll, 2017, pp. 223–4). The Convention aimed to facilitate administrative cooperation between states in the assessment and collection of taxes, the exchange of information, including automatic exchange, and the recovery of foreign tax claims.

In 1988 the Australian Treasurer announced that the government had decided not to become a signatory to the Convention. The ATO, in particular, felt that adopting the Convention might adversely impact the new Tax File Number system being introduced in Australia as a means of improving the integrity of the tax system. Neither Treasury nor the Department of Foreign Affairs and Trade were convinced, however, as to the ATO's position and, following nearly several years of further discussion, the Cabinet eventually agreed to the signing of what had by then become an amended Convention, in November 2011 (Kellow and Carroll, 2017, pp. 223–4).

Australia has been increasingly concerned with the rising incidence of tax avoidance and evasion and their adverse impact on tax revenues, using its membership of the OECD's Committee on Fiscal Affairs and its subcommittee, Working Party No. 8 on Tax Avoidance and Evasion, to help address those concerns and argue for reforms. Its concern has been focused on multinational corporations (MNCs), generally large in size and highly profitable, with operations that cross state boundaries and generate streams of foreign income, especially those in the information technology, pharmaceutical and energy sectors. MNCs, as with most firms, attempt to minimise their corporate income tax and are able to exploit differences in tax rates and rules in the countries in which they operate, moving profits from high-tax to low-tax countries, notably those described as tax havens, to reduce the tax they pay, commonly known as base erosion and profit shifting or BEPS.

A number of MNCs operate via wholly-owned subsidiaries in Australia and, until recently, were required to make only minimal disclosures regarding their operations, structuring their finances to reduce their tax liabilities in Australia (McClure, Lanis, Govendir 2016). The result has been, as with most developed countries: one, an erosion of the Australian tax base and loss of potential corporate income tax revenue (the corporate income tax rate in Australia, at 30 per cent, is relatively high); two, the distortion of competition and investment decisions as MNCs have a competitive advantage unavailable to domestic firms; three, the adverse impact of international tax competition from at least the 1980s as countries reduced corporate tax rates and offered a variety of 'tax holidays'.

The OECD has estimated that there were annual, global losses brought about by BEPS of between $US 100 to $US 240 billion dollars (OECD, 2015). Moreover, Australia is dependent on corporate income tax revenue to a greater extent than most OECD members and its corporate tax base is highly concentrated, with the largest 20 firms paying more than 40 per cent of total corporate income tax paid, so BEPS is of particular concern.

The global financial crisis (GFC) provided a massively increased stimulus to address the erosion of national tax bases, with governments rapidly increasing their debt to provide support for struggling economies, debt that meant that the increasing loss of corporate income tax revenue was felt more severely. The GFC provided the OECD with an opportunity to further promote the tax avoidance work it had already been pursuing, but which had lacked substantive political support from leaders. In 2004–08, in particular, it had developed an internationally agreed tax standard, supported by the G20 Finance Ministers, that required the exchange of information on request in all tax matters for the administration and enforcement of domestic tax law.

OECD officials recognised the GFC as an opportunity to further drive its tax work and, at the end of the April 2009 G20 summit in London, it issued a 'Progress Report to its members on the jurisdictions Surveyed by the OECD Global Forum in Implementing the Internationally Agreed Tax Standard' (OECD, 2009). The Report identified jurisdictions that had committed to, but not yet implemented the tax standard and jurisdictions that had not committed to the standard, with the resulting loss of tax revenues at a time when governments could ill afford such losses. It was a bold move, given that the Report noted that several OECD members, being Luxembourg, Switzerland, Austria and Belgium, together with Singapore and Chile, the Cayman Islands, Liechtenstein and Monaco, either had not implemented the tax standard, or had not committed to it.

The publication of the Report enhanced the reputation of the OECD, especially with the G20 members, the latter requesting it undertake further tax work, notably the 2012 request from the G20's Finance Ministers that the OECD develop an Action Plan to address BEPS, which was completed in 2013 (OECD, 2013). This move was strongly supported by Australia, which also helped ensure that, as host of the G20 heads of government summit in Australia in 2014, the plan had a prominent place on its agenda. Representatives from over 60 countries then undertook further work that resulted in the 2015 BEPS Final Reports of 13 reports covering an agreed 15 Actions that would be pursued by members and an increasing number of non-members (OECD, 2015).

Actions 5, 6, 13 and 14 were adopted as 'minimum standards', core measures that countries committed to implement in a coordinated manner and that would deal with issues where no action by some countries would have resulted in negative spill-overs on others (Carroll and Kellow, 2021). In addition, the OECD/G20 Inclusive Framework on BEPS was established in 2016 to implement the BEPS measures (OECD, 2016). The extent of the Australian government's concern regarding tax avoidance can be seen in its establishment of a Tax Avoidance Taskforce in 2016, provided with $679 million funding, with an additional funding of $AUS1 billion in the 2019–20 Budget (ATO, 2016).

Australia committed to addressing BEPS and, to date, has implemented recommendations relating to BEPS Actions 2, 5, 8–10, 13, 14 and 15 (ATO, 2019). These have taken the form of:

1. the Treasury Laws Amendment (Tax Integrity and Other Measures No. 2) Act 2018,
2. Schedules 1 and 2 introduced a new Division 832 of the International Tax Administration Act, 1997 and the necessary amendments to give effect to the OECD Hybrid Mismatch rules.
3. Signing the Multilateral Convention to Implement Tax Treaty Related Measures to Prevent BEPS (MLI) in 2017 (BEPS Action 15), that will modify 32 of Australia's tax treaties

to implement integrity provisions to protect those treaties from being exploited and to improve tax treaty related dispute resolutions mechanisms.

4. Agreeing to mandatory arbitration in relation to tax treaty related disputes.
5. In 2018, updating its mutual agreement procedures (MAP) guidance to implement recommendations in BEPS Action 14.
6. Withdrawing its Taxation Ruling TR 2000/16 Income tax: international transfer pricing and profit reallocation adjustments, relief from double taxation and the Mutual Agreement Procedure.
7. Updated PCG 2017/2 Simplified transfer pricing record keeping options in January 2019, which implemented the BEPS Actions 8–10 transfer pricing simplification recommendation for low value-adding intragroup services.
8. Fully implementing Country-by-Country Reporting (BEPS Action 13), including from 2018, the exchange of the reports with partner jurisdictions via the OECD Common Transmission System.

Several OECD members were reluctant to agree to the necessary actions and progress was very slow for several years, especially regarding BEPS Action 1: Address the Digital Economy. Hence, Australia (in October 2020) and the UK, among others, were keen to see more rapid progress and announced that they would develop unilateral, interim taxes on digitalised services, Australia doing so within the context of its International Cyber and Critical Tech Engagement Strategy. However, when progress at the OECD later improved, following the change of US policy under the new Biden administration, the Australian government announced it would discontinue this work and, in October 2021, 136 jurisdictions (including Australia) out of the 140 members of the Inclusive Framework joined the G20/OECD 'Statement on a Two-Pillar Solution to Address the Tax Challenges Arising from the Digitalisation of the Economy' (G20/OECD, 2021).

In brief summary, the Statement is based on a 'two pillar solution' to the tax challenges posed by the increasingly digitalised, global economy. Pillar One will reallocate approximately $US125 billions of MNC profit to market jurisdictions on an annual basis but, to Australia's benefit, excluded the financial services and natural resources sectors from its coverage. Pillar Two introduces a global minimum corporate tax rate set at 15 per cent that will apply to MNCs with revenue above EUR750 million, estimated to generate approximately $US150 billion in addition, annual, global tax revenues.

CONCLUSION

The OECD has had a continuing, though variable impact on several areas of Australian policy, an impact that varies in its extent and depth, both by policy area and over time. In considerable part, the variable impact derives from the often-considerable discretion afforded by OECD agreements and conventions as to how they should be implemented by members and, increasingly, non-members. While the impact may be variable, there is little doubt that the work of the OECD is highly valued by Australian policy makers, as suggested by the 2021 appointment of a Matthias Cormann as its Secretary-General. Corman held a range of ministerial appointments in the Australian government from 2013 to 2020. As illustrated in this chapter, the OECD impact on tax policy has been increasing and significant, in large part because successive Australian governments have worked continuously within the OECD, along with several other members, to persuade members and, increasingly, non-members, of the need for a range of global tax policy developments and related agreements.

The fact that they are intergovernmental and multilateral in nature means that OECD agreements usually increase the effectiveness of members' policies beyond that which could be achieved on a unilateral or bilateral basis. If only Australia and New Zealand, for example, had agreed to a minimum corporate tax rate of 15 per cent, it would have had little or no impact on the profit shifting activities of MNCs. Pillar Two, in contrast, introduces a global minimum corporate tax rate set at 15 per cent that will apply to the largest MNCs, and is supported by 136 countries, severely restricting such profit shifting. Further, it is easier and less expensive to gain agreement on such policies within the context of an international organisation than it is on a bilateral basis. Similarly, the cost of gaining comparative data and sound analysis for policy development, a major OECD activity, is far less expensive when undertaken on a multilateral, intergovernmental basis.

REFERENCES

ABARE. (1985). 'Agricultural Policies in the European Community.' *ABARE Policy Monograph No. 2*, AGPS.

ABARE. (1988). 'Japanese Agricultural Policies.' *ABARE Policy Monograph No. 3*, AGPS.

ATO. (2016). *Tax Avoidance Taskforce*. Retrieved 11/2/2021 from https://www.ato.gov.au/general/tax-avoidance-taskforce/.

ATO. (2019). *Base Erosion and Profit Shifting*. Retrieved 11/2/2021 from https://www.ato.gov.au/business/international-tax-for-business/in-detail/base-erosion-and-profit-shifting/.

Australian Law Reform Commission. (2010). 'Development of Current Australian Privacy Principles.' Retrieved 11/2/2021 from https://www.alrc.gov.au/publication/for-your-information-australian-privacy-law-and-practice-alrc-report-108/18-structural-reform-of-the-privacy-principles/development-of-current-australian-privacy-principles/.

Barker, C. (2019). Australia's implementation of the OECD Anti-Bribery Convention. *Parliamentary Library, Research Paper Series, 2019–20*. Retrieved 11/2/2021 from https://parlinfo.aph.gov.au/parlInfo/download/library/prspub/6300407/upload_binary/6300407.pdf

Bentley, D. (2003). 'Influence from the Shadows: the OECD, The Shape of Domestic Tax Policy and Lessons for Federal Systems.' *Revenue Law Journal, vol 13 no. 1*, 128–46.

Carroll, P. and A. Kellow (2021). *The OECD: A Decade of Transformation 2011 to 2021* (1st edn) De Gruyter.

Carroll, P. and A. Kellow (2011). *The OECD: A Study of Organisational Adaptation* (1st edn) Edward Elgar.

Commonwealth of Australia. (1999). *Making Transparency Transparent: An Australian Assessment*. Retrieved 22/4/2023 from https://treasury.gov.au/sites/default/files/2019-03/full.pdf.

Dirkis, M. (2013). 'On the Eve of the Global Response to BEPS: Australia's New Transfer Pricing Rules. *Revenue Law Journal, vol 23* (1).

EY. (2019). *Agricultural Innovation — A National Approach to Grow Australia's Future*. A report commissioned and published by the Australian Government Department of Agriculture and Water Resources. Retrieved 22/4/2023 from https://www.awe.gov.au/sites/default/files/sitecollectiondocuments/agriculture-food/innovation/full-report-agricultural-innovation.PDF.

G20/OECD. (2021). *Statement on a Two-Pillar Solution to Address the Tax Challenges Arising from the Digitalisation of the Economy*. Retrieved 11/2/2021 from https://www.oecd.org/tax/beps/statement-on-a-two-pillar-solution-to-address-the-tax-challenges-arising-from-the-digitalisation-of-the-economy-july-2021.pdf .

Industry Commission. (1991). *SALTER A General Equilibrium Model of the World Economy Volume 2 Gains from Global Trade Liberalisation: An Illustrative Application of SALTER*.

Kellow, A. and P. Carroll (2017). *Middle Powers and International Organisations: Australia and the OECD* (1st edn). Edward Elgar.

Littleproud, D. (2020). *SENATE QUESTION NO. 1868*. The answer to a question in the Australian Senate from Senator Sterle to The Hon. David Littleproud, MP, Minister for Agriculture, Drought and Emergency Management on 26 August 2020. Retrieved 22/4/2023 from https://parlwork.aph.gov.au/api/senate/questions/76142/Attachments/a5b35afd-de13-43cf-a4bd-3f34de3c392b/0.

McClure, R., Lanis, R., Govendir, B. (2016). 'Analysis of Tax Avoidance Strategies of Top Foreign Multinationals Operating in Australia: An Expose.' Retrieved 27/10 2021 at https://web-tools.uts.edu.au/projects/detail.cfm?ProjectId=PRO16-1368).

OECD. (1980). *Guidelines on the Protection of Privacy and Transborder Flows of Personal Data*. Retrieved 11/2/2021 from https://www.oecd.org/sti/ieconomy/oecdguidelinesontheprotectionofprivacyandtransborderflowsofpersonaldata.htm.

OECD. (2009). *Progress Report on the Jurisdictions Surveyed by the OECD Global Forum in Implementing the Internationally Agreed Tax Standard*. Retrieved 11/2/2021 from https://www.oecd.org/tax/exchange-of-tax-information/42497950.pdf.

OECD. (2013). *Action Plan on Base Erosion and Profit Shifting*. Retrieved 11/2/2021 from https://www.oecd.org/ctp/BEPSActionPlan.pdf.

OECD. (2015). *OECD/G20 Base Erosion and Profit Shifting Project, Explanatory Statement 2015 Final Reports*. Retrieved 11/2/2021 from www.oecd.org/tax/beps-explanatory-statement-2015.pdf.

OECD. (2016). *OECD/G20 Inclusive Framework on BEPS*. Retrieved 11/2/2021 from https://www.oecd.org/tax/beps/flyer-inclusive-framework-on-beps.pdf.

OECD. (2017a). *Global Forum on Transparency and Exchange of Information for Tax Purposes: Australia 2017 (Second Round): Peer Review Report on the Exchange of Information on Request*. Retrieved 11/2/2021 from https://www.oecd.org/australia/global-forum-on-transparency-and-exchange-of-information-for-tax-purposes-australia-2017-second-round-9789264280069-en.htm.

OECD. (2017b). *Implementing the OECD Anti-Bribery Convention – Australian Phase 4 Monitoring Report*. Retrieved 11/2/2021 from https://www.oecd.org/daf/anti-bribery/australia-oecdanti-briberyconvention.htm.

OECD. (2017c). *Model Tax Convention on Income and on Capital 2017 (Full Version)*. Retrieved 11/2/2021 from https://www.oecd.org/tax/model-tax-convention-on-income-and-on-capital-full-version-9a5b369e-en.htm.

OECD. (2021). *Mutual Acceptance of Data (MAD)*. Retrieved 11/2/2021 from https://www.oecd.org/env/ehs/mutualacceptanceofdatamad.htm.

Stoeckel, A. (1985). 'Intersectoral Effects of the CAP: Growth, Trade and Unemployment.' *ABARE Occasional Paper No. 95*, AGPS.

Taskforce on Regulation. (2006). *Rethinking Regulation: Report of the Taskforce on Reducing Regulatory Burdens on Business*. Report to the Prime Minister and the Treasurer, Productivity Commission. Retrieved 22/4/2023 from https://www.pc.gov.au/research/supporting/regulation-taskforce.

Whitnall, T. and N. Pitts (2019). 'Global Trends in Meat Consumption.' *Agricultural Commodities, 9(1)*, 96–99.

19. Mexico: From the diffusion of ideas to the making of policy changes

Fabiola Perales-Fernández and Mauricio I. Dussauge-Laguna

INTRODUCTION

Mexico has been a member of the Organisation for Economic Co-operation and Development (OECD) since 1994. Throughout these years, reform ideas, 'best practices', and policy recommendations from the OECD have significantly influenced policymaking processes in Mexico in a variety of ways. Mexican officials have become aware of international trends, learned about policy innovations in other jurisdictions, and adopted policy models to advance (or to legitimise) institutional changes. Thus, OECD membership has been a powerful trigger for policy and institutional transformations in the Mexican public administration. At the same time, the diffusion of international policy ideas has sometimes faced important challenges when being implemented in the Mexican public sector. There have been experiences of institutional simulation, partial adoption of policy principles, and policy reversals, all of which have shown that policy transfer processes from international organisations to national governments are not straightforward.

Drawing on OECD reports, official documents from the Mexican government, secondary sources, and our own previous research and experience as federal public servants, we present an analysis of how the OECD has informed and influenced policy and institutional changes in Mexico during the past three decades. We first present an overview of Mexico's accession process to the OECD and the reasons behind it. We then provide an analysis of the ways in which the OECD has exerted its influence on Mexico's public sector. We finally zoom in to a discussion on 'better regulation', an area in which the Mexican government is considered an international leader, precisely as a result of how Mexican officials have learned from the experience of the OECD and its member countries.

Our discussion is mainly informed by the literature on policy diffusion and transfer, particularly with regards to the way in which international organisations spread ideas and influence changes in national jurisdictions (Stone, 2004; Biermann and Siebenhüner, 2009; Pal, 2012; see also Chapter 15 in this volume). However, we also take very much into account the political and institutional restrictions to policy changes that commonly surround cross-national learning processes (Dussauge-Laguna, 2012; 2013).

MEXICO'S ACCESSION TO THE OECD

On 18 May 1994, Mexico formalised its entry into the Convention for the Organisation for Economic Co-operation and Development (OECD), thus becoming its 25th country member. Mexico's accession to the OECD was significant in various ways: the Organisation had not accepted new member countries since 1973 (Flores, 1994; Signoret, 2005; Paz, 2005), and Mexico was the first developing country to gain OECD membership (Schricke, 1994). This signalled the Organisation's move to approach the Latin America region (Paz, 2005). Because of its liberalisation reforms during the 1980s and 1990s, Mexico had become an interesting case from which to learn about how to avoid recurrent economic crises and how to avoid adverse consequences from the latter for the international economic system (Paz, 2005).

Accessing the OECD was one of the most important foreign policy actions for the Mexican government to insert Mexico into the global economy (Flores, 1994). By becoming a member of one of the world's leading international organisations in economics and finance, allowed Mexico to adapt its economy to the new priorities of the international agenda. Policymakers expected that OECD membership would generate confidence in the Mexican economy, lower risk rating and thus credit with lower financial costs, and a better international image to attract foreign investment (Flores, 1994).

From the OECD's perspective, Mexico's accession was a recognition of its remarkable process of economic reform (Schricke, 1994). Furthermore, the way Mexican policymakers had behaved during pre-accession assessments was a sign that Mexico had 'discovered' the OECD culture (Schricke, 1994, p. 5): they had demonstrated Mexico could embrace transparency in government processes, had the willingness to provide explanations and justifications, and could exercise self-criticism and pay attention to feedback resulting from the traditional OECD peer review mechanisms (Schricke, 1994).

Mexico's accession to the OECD also represented the possibility of opening horizontal dialogues with the world's top economies (Paz, 2005). For the Mexican government, joining the OECD was akin to enrolling in the 'best pragmatic university in the world' (Paz, 2005, p. 49). Mexican officials were convinced the OECD would facilitate cross-national learning and the implementation of effective public policies. Moreover, some scholars thought that the evaluation of public policies would be normalised through the social pressure that the OECD would exercise with its comparative methods, which 'could help, on a domestic level, to ensure that the activities of Mexican officials were regularly monitored' (Paz, 2005: 49–50). In sum, Mexico's accession to the OECD represented the entrance to international fora for learn the know-how and evaluate public policymaking continuously (Signoret, 2005).

This Mexico-OECD relationship grew over time. The federal administrations that followed that of President Carlos Salinas de Gortari (who had managed Mexico's accession) was keen to reinforce its links. According to Jorge Castañeda, Mexico's Secretary of Foreign Affairs from 2000 to 2003, the Mexican governments kept: 'a very active stance that attempted to promote Mexico's participation in international organisations' (Castañeda, 2006, p. 219). Indeed, in June 2006, José Angel Gurría (former Minister of Finance of Mexico) was appointed Secretary-General of the OECD and remained in the office during the following 15 years. During this time (2006–21), Mexico's relationship with the Organisation got closer. This becomes clearer once one considers that, under Gurría's leadership, the OECD produced 118 of the 141 technical studies[1] on Mexico (84 per cent). Conversely, Gurría also seems to have used his relationship with Mexico to bring the OECD closer to Latin America countries.

---

[1]   These documents were found in the online data base of the OECD repository iLibrary, as well as in the OECD's website selecting Mexico microsite. The documents identified were published until April 2022.

For instance, Chile, Colombia, and Costa Rica formalised their accession to the OECD during his tenure.

Table 19.1   *Studies elaborated by the OECD on Mexico per presidential term*

President	Number of studies	Percentage
Carlos Salinas de Gortari (1988–1994)	1	1%
Ernesto Zedillo Ponce de León (1994–2000)	10	7%
Vicente Fox Quezada (2000–2006)	13	9%
Luis Felipe Calderón Hinojosa (2006–2012)	24	17%
Enrique Peña Nieto (2012–2018)	68	48%
Andres Manuel Lopez-Obrador (2018–2024)	25	18%
Total OECD's studies	141	100%

Source: Elaborated with information of OECD-iLibrary, Mexico's microsite in OECD webpage.

Since Mexico's accession, OECD reports and studies (see Table 19.1 above) have touched on a variety of topics, from Agricultural and Fisheries Policies to Taxation. However, 53 per cent of the documents have been written about Economic Surveys, Competition Policy, Education Policies, and Public Governance (mainly Regulatory Policy, Public Procurement and Territorial Reviews). Another interesting feature is that 48 per cent of the OECD studies were published during President Enrique Peña Nieto's administration. This seems to have happened for two reasons. For the OECD, the so-called 'structural reforms' enacted by Peña Nieto offered both the opportunity to advance the organisation's own structural reforms narrative (OECD, 2010), and to closely study an interesting case of reforming country[2]. For the Mexican government, many of these reports represented a welcome opportunity to showcase and legitimise its reformist agenda, which was 'aimed at modifying the national economic structure' (Cárdenas, 2016, p. 111), and promoted 'free markets, economic competition, the fight against monopolies and the promotion of foreign investment' (ibid., p. 111).

Lastly, it is important to note how Mexico has engaged in the Organisation's activities over time. According to information provided by the Mexican Ministry of Foreign Affairs,[3] in 2022 Mexican officials were taking part in 44 committees and 115 working groups which covered the whole range of issues studied by the OECD. Likewise, the foreign ministry pointed out that Mexico holds a vice-chairmanship in four committees: Budget, Consumer Policy, Digital Economy Policy, and the Governing Board of the Development Centre.

THE OECD'S INFLUENCE ON POLICY AND INSTITUTIONAL CHANGES IN MEXICO

The strong relationship that has emerged between the OECD and the Mexican government throughout the years has allowed the former to exert a significant influence on the latter's policy and institutional reforms. This influence has taken various forms. The OECD has played the role of promoter of ideas or technical adviser at various times, as it has done in other

---

[2]   See 13 structural reforms in https://www.gob.mx/conamed/documentos/13-reformas-transformad oras accessed 23 April 2023.
[3]   Request for information number 330026822000845.

jurisdictions (Pal, 2012). Moreover, the Organisation's comparative reports have also fulfilled a broader role in informing academic debates and public discussions. On the other hand, policy advice and reform inspiration coming from OECD recommendations have not always succeed in the short run. Furthermore, some have been derailed or have been even reversed with the passage of time.

The first way in which the OECD has influenced Mexican government practices has been through the constant diffusion of ideas, which in turn have informed the making of federal policies. One clear example is that of administrative reform policy (Huerta, 2006; Pardo, 2008; Dussauge-Laguna, 2013). Since the mid-1990s, the Mexican government (and its Ministry for Public Administration in particular) became engaged in the various OECD committees and activities under the rubric 'public management' and 'governance'. As a result, the string of public sector modernisation programmes produced in the past three decades in Mexico (starting with President Ernesto Zedillo's famous *Programa de Modernización de la Administración Pública, PROMAP 1995–2000*) have clearly reflected broader OECD reform topics: performance management, transparency, e-government, quality of services, better regulation, etc. (see OECD, 1995, 2005a; Pal, 2012; Vicher, 2018). Thus, reform ideas and policies originated in OECD countries (and disseminated through several OECD reports) have permeated Mexican reform programmes, bureaucratic jargon, and administrative practices.

In some cases, policy approaches promoted internationally by the OECD have even led to paradigmatic shifts in certain policy sectors. For instance, in the field of science and technology, the OECD's influence has been key for Mexico to transition toward an 'innovation'-driven model (Valdés, 2022). Throughout three decades, Mexican officials met with OECD experts and drew inspiration from the OECD's Oslo Manual (OECD, 2005b) and related reports about topics such as how to involve private actors in scientific and technological activities, how to link innovation and economic growth, and how to assess and measure public sector-led innovations. As a result, the OECD's science and technology 'innovation model' was slowly transferred to Mexico, as shown by the ideas contained in the *Programa Especial de Ciencia, Tecnología e Innovación* (Special Program of Science, Technology, and Innovation) of 2008 and 2014, and the institutional framework introduced by the Science and Technology Law of 2002 (see Valdés, 2022; Cabrero *et al.*, 2022).

In other cases, the link between OECD policy recommendations and significant institutional changes in Mexico has been particularly clear. A good example is provided by the reforms of the telecommunications policy sector in the 2010s (OECD, 2012, 2017a; Mariscal, 2020). Among many other things, the OECD analysis of the telecommunications sector noted the lack of competition, the limitations of existing regulations, and the lack of independence that the regulatory agency (*Comisión Federal de Telecomunicaciones, COFETEL*) had vis-à-vis its parent Ministry of Communications and Transportation (OECD, 2012). The Organisation offered a set of recommendations in its report, which were then included as part of the 'structural reforms' introduced by President Peña Nieto in 2013–14. The new legal framework for the telecommunications sector introduced new concepts to strengthen competition dynamics (e.g. asymmetrical regulations); eliminated legal features that had previously undermined the powers of the regulator (e.g. the '*doble ventanilla*' principle, which allowed private actors to challenge and bypass regulatory decisions by approaching the ministry instead of *COFETEL*); and gave formal independence to the regulator by creating a constitutionally autonomous regulatory agency, the *Instituto Federal de Telecomunicaciones* (*IFT*, Federal Telecommunications Institute; see OECD, 2017a.) Alternatively, the OECD has sometimes provided policy advice which has contributed to 'fine-tune' (Dussauge-Laguna, 2013) ongoing policy changes. For instance, also as part of Peña Nieto's 'structural reforms', the government of Mexico introduced significant changes in the energy sector. These included legal reforms to allow for deeper and broader participation of private actors, and the redesign of the energy sector's governance framework. The institutional status and regulatory powers of the *Comisión Reguladora de Energía* (*CRE*, or Energy Regulatory Commission) and the *Comisión Nacional de Hidrocarburos* (*CNH*, or National Hydrocarbons Commission) were strengthened, and a new *Agencia de Seguridad, Energía y Ambiente* (*ASEA*, or Security, Energy, and Environment Agency) was established (Elizondo and Dussauge-Laguna, 2018). In response to these changes, the OECD produced a series of studies which analysed each of these regulatory agencies and assessed the potential challenges posed by the new framework (OECD, 2017b, 2017c, 2017d, 2017e). The Organisation's recommendations about how to improve joint performance and strategic planning were taken into account by the heads of these regulatory agencies when they set in motion an inter-agency coordination mechanism (Elizondo and Dussauge-Laguna, 2018).

Yet another way in which the OECD has influenced policymaking in Mexico and, along the way, broader academic and public debates, has been the use of benchmarks and comparisons. Perhaps the best example of this has been the application of the OECD's Programme for International Student Assessment (PISA). Since 2000, the PISA examinations have been applied periodically to measure the ability of Mexican students on reading, math, and scientific knowledge and skills (Márquez, 2017; Villanueva, 2018). Results from PISA have been used by government officials to assess education policy and inform policy proposals. This was particularly the case with the former *Instituto Nacional de Evaluación para la Educación* (*INEE*, or National Institute for the Evaluation of the Education, terminated in 2019), but remains partly true for its successor the *Comisión Nacional para la Mejora Continua de la Educación* (*MEJOREDU*, or National Commission for the Continuous Improvement of Education) and its parent Ministry of Education. More broadly, results from PISA are commonly discussed by education specialists and in the media. Indeed, data from PISA and other OECD comparative studies and rankings are often used by political actors and civil society organisations to criticise government policies and engage in blame-games and calls for accountability (see also Chapter 13 in this volume).

A final way in which the OECD has influenced policy developments in Mexico is by providing a valuable tool for 'selling' and advancing specific reforms. An interesting case is that of performance-based budgetary reforms introduced during the 2000s (Dussauge-Laguna, 2013). While important institutional changes had taken place in the early 2000s to establish a federal monitoring and evaluation system, officials from the Ministry of Finance had had a hard time getting approval from senior officials and legislators to establish a broader results-oriented budgetary system. They thus invited key politicians to join them at the OECD's Senior Budget Officials meetings so that they could learn about ongoing international debates on the subject. This gave officials a means to persuade politicians about the relevance of changing the budget law to strengthen the performance orientation of the budgetary system. In addition, Mexican officials later requested an OECD review of the new system to increase its political and bureaucratic legitimacy (OECD, 2009a).

While the previous discussion shows that the OECD's influence on Mexico has been profound, the depth and stickiness of such influence have also varied across policy areas and across time. First, the OECD is obviously not the only ideational player in Mexico: The World

Bank, the Inter-American Bank, national universities, and a growing number of think tanks have also actively participated in national policy debates with an international perspective. Therefore, it is not always easy the tease out which and how policy and institutional changes have originated in (or have been informed by) OECD recommendations, or whether they have resulted from other sources or broader epistemic consensus. Second, some of the changes discussed above have led to significant administrative, institutional, and legal transformations, but it remains unclear how much they have also transformed daily government routines and operations. This has been the case in the government modernisation agenda and some areas of the telecommunications reform. Third, presidential interest on different topics has been variable, and hence the OECD's relative influence has been weaker at some points (or not as long-lasting as initially expected). For instance, while PISA results were strongly debated within government institutions between 2000 and 2018, the current López-Obrador admin-istration does not seem to care much about such comparative exercises. Similarly, while the OECD backed performance-based budgeting reforms were a topic on the agenda of President Felipe Calderón's administration, it lost much of its relevance during the Peña Nieto's administration.

Last but not least, recent policy reversals, in areas such as the energy sector or science and technology, show that the political relevance of OECD policy recommendations can always be subject to contestation. In contrast to OECD 'best-practices' on regulatory gov-ernance, the López-Obrador administration has followed a centralised approach to regulatory policy, in which the Ministry for Energy is expected to exert political control over formally semi-autonomous regulatory agencies. Similarly, both the president and the head of the science and technology agency currently favour a nationalist, government-centred model of scientific development, which has been framed as exactly the opposite to the 'neoliberal' innovation-led model sponsored by the OECD.

THE OECD'S INFLUENCE ON BETTER REGULATION POLICY

To better understand how the OECD has influenced specific policy areas, we now turn to a brief analysis of 'better regulation'. Mexico joined to the OECD after having completed an extended regulatory reform with the aim to transform the economy, from an inward-looking economy to an open and market-based economy (OECD, 1999). This meant that, from 1982 to 1997, over 90 per cent of the national legal framework was reformed to reduce state interven-tionism and enhance market mechanisms (OECD, 1999).

Mexico fully embraced OECD's regulatory policy principles as a means to support its efforts to modernise the state (OECD, 1999). In turn, the Mexican government's work has received continuous support from the OECD.[4] The following paragraphs describe how the OECD has influenced the development of better regulation policies, institutions, and tools in Mexico. We followed similar categories of analysis of diffusion ideas to those used in the previous section. However, we added some variations that further show the complexity of this story of mutual learning and cooperation.

---

[4]   On sub-national level issues, Mexican regulatory policy has also been influenced by the World Bank through the Doing Business. On international regulatory cooperation, Mexican regulatory policy has also been influenced by multilateral organisations as APEC, the WTO and free trade agreements.

First of all, following the OECD's dissemination of regulatory ideas and best practices, Mexico has adopted at least four highly relevant better regulation tools: the Regulatory Impact Assessment (RIA), formally adopted in 1996 (with amendments in subsequent years); competition assessment analysis; risk analysis; and ex-post RIA (adopted in 2012–2013). Mexican officials have learned about the importance of these tools thanks to the OECD's recommendations and technical reports. These tools are the basis of the regulatory review system in Mexico. They are the engine of the regulatory policy, as they allow scrutiny ex ante of the government's reasons for the selected regulatory mechanisms, but they also help observe how regulations have worked during their implementation.

Moreover, with the support of regulatory experts from the Organisation, officials at the *Comisión Nacional de Mejora Regulatoria* (*CONAMER*, National Commission for Better Regulation) and its predecessor the *Comisión Federal de Mejora Regulatoria* (*COFEMER*, or Federal Commission for Better Regulation) have acquired the know-how to design and implement them in accordance with national characteristics. For example, in 2012 and 2013, extensive training was conducted by the OECD for federal government officials on risk analysis and competition assessment. That has facilitated the implementation of these tools in the RIA.

The Mexican government's better regulation policy has been also influenced by the OECD through the latter's peer review exercises. In 1999, 2004 and 2014, OECD assessed Mexico's Regulatory Policy. In these reports,[5] the OECD reviewed the progress in implementing the Regulatory Policy and its tools and provided some policy recommendations. The most important one was creating an oversight body in charge of managing the Regulatory Policy (COFEMER from 2000 to 2018, and then CONAMER from 2018 to this date), public consultation mechanisms, regulatory transparency, and regulatory policies at the sub-national level. These recommendations were adopted and developed over time by the Mexican government, with significant implications for the structure of administrative law and bureaucratic procedures.

Another way in which the OECD has influenced Mexico's regulatory policy has been through the transfer of specific policy innovations, which are then tested in the Mexican administrative system. In 2010, the OECD Report *Cutting Red Tape: Why is Administrative Simplification so Complicated? Looking Beyond 2010* emphasised the importance of measuring administrative burdens to streamline administrative simplification exercises. The standard cost model (SCM) was the measurement tool recommended to cope with this problem. The SMC had been designed by an OECD member country (the Netherlands) in 2004 and some European countries had already implemented it showing signs of the tool's usefulness. Thus, at the end of 2010, the Mexican government decided to import the SMC methodology and attempt the first measurement of administrative burdens on federal procedures. Later, Mexican officials took the challenge to innovate and produce their own application. Instead of recurring to surveys to the public, as in the original model from the Netherlands, Mexican official developed an administrative burden calculator algorithm with the parameters of the SCM. With this tool, the Mexican government has calculated, at least once, the administrative burden of federal and state paperwork.

The Mexican government, however, has not only been an 'importer' of regulatory policy ideas from the OECD, but has slowly become an OECD diffusion partner, promoting better

---

[5]   (OECD, 1999), (OECD, 2004) (OECD, 2014).

regulation tools among Latin American countries. Mexican officials have accompanied the OECD on international missions to Argentina, Brazil, the Dominican Republic, Chile, Costa Rica, Colombia, El Salvador, and Peru, either as peer reviewers or to showcase their own good practices. Given the country similarities in political, social, and cultural aspects, as well as in the type of legal systems (civil law), Mexico is usually perceived as a credible example which other nations can follow. Until 2011, Mexico was the only country in the Latin American region with a functioning RIA system and a fully developed set of better regulation tools. The OECD recognised this and fostered a win-win partnership. The OECD gained a partner which would help reduce the policy adoption gap in the region. In turn, Mexico increased its international reputation on this area, something that was also helpful in domestic terms: its regulatory policy tools were validated and their adoption at the sub-national level was facilitated. This was particularly relevant as it was not until 2018 that better regulation became a national policy established in the constitution, and hence mandatory for all public sector bodies in the country.

The transfer of OECD regulatory policies and ideas to Mexico has gained broader international visibility in recent years, as the country has not only learned from abroad but also seems to have outperformed other national governments. At the end of 2015, the OECD launched its first Regulatory Policy Outlook, which studies regulatory policy tools in a comparative perspective across OECD member economies. In the three editions of the report (2015, 2018, and 2021), Mexico has stood out among the top performers in the three main OECD Regulatory Governance indicators: stakeholder engagement; Regulatory Impact Assessment; and ex-post evaluation.

Given the above, the better regulation Mexico experience shows an example in which the OECD has greatly influenced institutional changes via multiple policy transfer mechanisms, such as best regulatory practices and technical recommendations. The OECD has been an effective disseminator of policy ideas and, at the same time, Mexican officials have been capable of both learning from their peers and introducing innovations to adapt regulatory tools to their own country's features.

However as in the case of other policy areas described above, the implementation of better regulation policies and tools has also faced some setbacks and delays. In fact, it currently is far from being a priority of the López-Obrador administration. Recent political dynamics have questioned the value of such a policy, the agency in charge (*CONAMER*) has been politically captured, and better regulation procedures are being ignored or manipulated on a regular basis. For instance, in the past four years, *CONAMER* has applied the regulatory review process with significant discretion to favour policies that are of high interest to the current government. There have been cases of regulations suspended by the judiciary branch because of transgressing administrative processes of better regulation, specifically, in energy sector (El Financiero, 2020; Garrigues, 2021; Mexico, 2021). Similarly, in 2022 the Federal Economic Competition Authority (*COFECE*) publicly denounced *CONAMER* for suspending unilaterally the collaboration agreement for joint review of regulations, something which could affect economic competition (Forbes, 2022; El Universal, 2022). The early review of regulations from an economic competition perspective was suggested by the OECD in 2009 through the Recommendation of the Council on Competition Assessment, and it was formally implemented starting on 2013 with the cooperation of both institutions. Those examples put into question the temporal reach of the OECD's influence and the durability of its policy ideas.

CONCLUSIONS

This chapter has provided an overview of the relationship between the OECD and Mexico. After describing why the Mexican government joined this international Organisation, we discussed a few diffusion and transfer mechanisms by which the OECD has influenced policymaking and institutional change processes in Mexico in several policy fields. We then discussed the case of 'better regulation' policy to further illustrate how the OECD performs its various roles: from promoting policy ideas and models, to advising specific changes. We also showed that Mexican officials have not only learned from OECD technical reports, peer reviews, and personal exchanges. On the contrary, the Mexican government has also used its membership at the OECD to gain political support for some reform proposals, increase its international reputation, or facilitate the dissemination of policies at the subnational level.

The influence of the OECD has been notorious in a multiplicity of policy areas in Mexico. In the field of better regulation, Mexican policies have been particularly and consistently receptive to the OECD's advice for a continuous period of at least 23 years. Indeed, the Mexican experience has become an international benchmark and Mexico has even become a partner of the OECD in diffusing better regulation ideas and know-how across Latin America. Therefore, the Mexican experience is interesting for better understanding how an international organisation such as the OECD pursues its mission, how policy ideas travel internationally, and how national settings condition (both temporally and institutionally) diffusion and transfer processes.

The chapter has also shown that the OECD's ideational power and policy influence cannot be taken for granted. Throughout time, national adherence to benchmarks, models, and policies varies, as one would expect. However, there also seems to be particular moments in which the legitimacy of well-established OECD principles is put into question, and countries like Mexico start to willingly depart from the Organisation's recommended practices (e.g., regarding innovation in science and technology, educational standards, or regulatory principles broadly speaking). This poses a challenge to the OECD as a merely 'technical' body and begs the question of how to analyse, measure, review, and report on member countries which simply do not seem to care about the Organisation's agenda.

Should the OECD warn about the risks Mexico is facing by not following its policy advise? How should these concerns be included in high level communications, reports, or policy indicators? How to report impartially on legal and policy developments when the political factors simply obscure any technical considerations? These are not easy questions, but they will certainly need to be answered in years to come.

REFERENCES

Biermann, F. and B. Siebenhüner (eds) (2009). *Managers of Global Change: The Influence of International Environmental Bureaucracies*. MIT Press.

Cabrero, E., V. Carreón and M. Guajardo (2022). *México frente a la sociedad del conocimiento*. Siglo XXI-CIDE.

Castañeda, J.G. (2006). Un recorrido por la política exterior de México. Entrevista con Jorge G. Castañeda. Norteamérica, *Revista Académica del CISAN-UNAM*, vol. 1, no 02.

Cárdenas Gracia, J. (2016). *El modelo jurídico del neoliberalismo*. México, Instituto de Investigaciones Jurídicas de la Universidad Nacional Autónoma de México (UNAM).

Cofemer. (2012). Implementación del Modelo de Costeo Estándar: Lecciones y Experiencias de México. Comisión Federal de Mejora Regulatoria (Cofemer) de México https://conamer.gob.mx/varios/adjuntos/01.11.2012/Mexico_Modelo_de_Costeo_Estandar.pdf accessed 23 April 2023.

Dussauge-Laguna, M.I. (2012). On the Past and Future of Policy Transfer Research: Benson and Jordan revisited. *Political Studies Review*, 10(3), 313–24. https://doi.org/10.1111/j.1478-9302.2012.00275.x accessed 23 April 2023.

Dussauge Laguna, M.I. (2013). *Cross-national policy learning and administrative reforms: the making of 'management for results' policies in Chile and Mexico (1990–2010)* [Doctoral dissertation, London School of Economics and Political Science].

Elizondo, A. and M.I. Dussauge-Laguna (2018). *ASEA. Una nueva institución del Estado mexicano*. ASEA-CIDE-PIRCE. Agencia de Seguridad, Energía y Ambiente de México. https://www.gob.mx/asea/documentos/asea-un-nuevo-modelo-de-institucion-del-estado-mexicano accessed 23 April 2023.

Flores, V. D. (1994). El ingreso de México a la OCDE. Comercio Exterior (México). http://revistas.bancomext.gob.mx/rce/magazines/360/22/RCE16.pdf accessed 23 April 2023.

Huerta, O. (2006). *Understanding International Transfer Agents of Policy Transfer: The Case of the OECD and Mexican Administrative Reform* [Doctoral dissertation, University of York].

Information request number 330026822000845. Mexico's National Transparency Platform. https://www.plataformadetransparencia.org.mx accessed 23 April 2023.

Mariscal, J. (2020). A Tale of Two Reforms: Telecommunications Reforms in Mexico. *Telecommunications Policy*, 44(7), 101942. https://doi.org/10.1016/j.telpol.2020.101942 accessed 23 April 2023.

Márquez, A. (2017). A 15 años de PISA: resultados y polémicas. *Perfiles educativos*, 39(156), 3–15.

México. (1994a). Decreto de promulgación de la Convención de la Organización de Cooperación y Desarrollo Económicos. Published in the Diario Oficial de la Federación on July 5, 1994. Retrieved July 15, 2022, from http://dof.gob.mx/nota_detalle.php?codigo=4710963&fecha=05/07/1994.

México. (1994b). Decreto de promulgación del Acuerdo entre el Gobierno de los Estados Unidos Mexicanos y la Organización de Cooperación y Desarrollo Económicos sobre Privilegios e Inmunidades de la Organización en los Estados Unidos Mexicanos. Published in the Diario Oficial de la Federación on July 5, 1994. Retrieved July 15, 2022, from http://www.dof.gob.mx/nota_detalle.php?codigo=4710971&fecha=05/07/1994.

México. (1994c). Decreto de promulgación de la Declaración del Gobierno de los Estados Unidos Mexicanos sobre la aceptación de sus obligaciones como miembro de la Organización de Cooperación y Desarrollo Económicos. Published in the Diario Oficial de la Federación on July 5, 1994. Retrieved July 15, 2022, from http://dof.gob.mx/index.php?year=1994&month=07&day=05.

México. (2003). Decreto por el que se aprueba el Programa de Mejora Regulatoria 2001–2006. Published in the Diario Oficial de la Federación on Juanuary 17, 2003. Retrieved July 13, 2022, from http://www.ordenjuridico.gob.mx/Publicaciones/Compilacion/1065.pdf.

México. (2021). ACUERDO por el que se deja insubsistente el Acuerdo por el que se emite la Política de Confiabilidad, Seguridad, Continuidad y Calidad en el Sistema Eléctrico Nacional. publicado en el Diario Oficial de la Federación el 15 de mayo de 2020. Published in the Diario Oficial de la Federación on March 4, 2021. Retrieved July 13, 2022, from https://www.dof.gob.mx/nota_detalle.php?codigo=5612716&fecha=04/03/2021#gsc.tab=0.

OECD. (1995). *Governance in Transition: Public Management Reforms in OECD Countries*. OECD Publishing.

OECD. (1999). OECD Reviews of Regulatory Reform: Regulatory Reform in Mexico 1999, OECD Reviews of Regulatory Reform, OECD Publishing, Paris, https://doi.org/10.1787/9789164180315-en accessed 23 April 2023.

OECD. (2004). OECD Reviews of Regulatory Reform: Mexico 2004: Progress in Implementing Regulatory Reform, OECD Reviews of Regulatory Reform, OECD Publishing, Paris, https://doi.org/10.1787/9789264017528-en accessed 23 April 2023.

OECD. (2005a). Modernising Government: The Way Forward? OECD Publishing, Paris, https://doi.org/10.1787/9789264010505-en accessed 23 April 2023.

OECD. (2005b). *Oslo Manual*. OECD-Eurostat.

OECD. (2009a). *OECD Journal on Budgeting, Volume 2009 Supplement 1: OECD Review of Budgeting in Mexico*, OECD Publishing, Paris, https://doi.org/10.1787/budget-v9-sup1-en accessed 23 April 2023.

OECD. (2009b). Recommendation of the Council on Competition Assessment. OECD/LEGAL/0376. http://legalinstruments.oecd.org accessed 23 April 2023.

OECD. (2010). *Making Reform Happen*. OECD Publishing.

OECD. (2012). *Estudio de la OCDE sobre políticas y regulación de telecomunicaciones en México*. OECD Publishing, Paris, https://doi.org/10.1787/9789264166790-es accessed 23 April 2023.

OECD. (2014). *Regulatory Policy in Mexico: Towards a Whole-of-Government Perspective to Regulatory Improvement*, OECD Reviews of Regulatory Reform, OECD Publishing, Paris, https://doi.org/10.1787/9789264203389-en accessed 23 April 2023.

OECD. (2015). *OECD Regulatory Policy Outlook 2015*. OECD Publishing, Paris. http://dx.doi.org/10.1787/9789264238770-en accessed 23 April 2023.

OECD. (2017a). *Estudio de la OCDE sobre telecomunicaciones y radiodifusión en México 2017*. OECD Publishing, Paris, https://doi.org/10.1787/9789264280656-es accessed 23 April 2023.

OECD. (2017b). *Impulsando el desempeño de los órganos reguladores en materia energética en México*. OECD Publishing, Paris, https://doi.org/10.1787/9789264272996-es accessed 23 April 2023.

OECD (2017c). *Impulsando el desempeño de la Comisión Reguladora de Energía de México*. OECD Publishing, Paris, https://doi.org/10.1787/9789264280960-es accessed 23 April 2023.

OECD. (2017d). *Impulsando el desempeño de la Comisión Nacional de Hidrocarburos de México*. OECD Publishing, Paris, https://doi.org/10.1787/9789264280908-es accessed 23 April 2023.

OECD. (2017e). *Impulsando el desempeño de la Agencia de Seguridad, Energía y Ambiente de México*. OECD Publishing, Paris, https://doi.org/10.1787/9789264280991-es accessed 23 April 2023.

OECD. (2018). *OECD Regulatory Policy Outlook 2018*. OECD Publishing, Paris. https://doi.org/10.1787/9789264303072-en accessed 23 April 2023.

OECD. (2020). *The OECD at 60: 60 Years of Consensus Building*. OECD Publishing, Paris, https://doi.org/10.1787/afb7f6a8-en accessed 23 April 2023.

OECD. (2021). *OECD Regulatory Policy Outlook 2021*. OECD Publishing, Paris, https://doi.org/10.1787/38b0fdb1-en accessed 23 April 2023.

OECD. (2022). Recommendation of the Council for Agile Regulatory Governance to Harness Innovation, OECD/LEGAL/0464. https://legalinstruments.oecd.org/en/instruments/OECD-LEGAL-0464 accessed 23 April 2023.

Pal, L. (2012). *Frontiers of Governance: The OECD and Global Public Management Reform*. Springer.

Pardo, M. (2008). *La modernización administrativa en México, 1940–2006*. El Colegio de México.

Paz, Ü.I. (2005). El Ingreso de México a la OCDE y el inicio de la relación doble. In Zomosa (2005) *La participación de México en la OCDE: 1994-2002*. México: El Colegio de Mexico. pp. 25–70 (46 pages). https://doi.org/10.2307/j.ctvhn09qs.4 accessed 23 April 2023.

Signoret, A.Z. (2005), Introducción. In *La participación de México en la OCDE: 1994–2002* (1st ed., Vol. 147, pp. 13–24). El Colegio de Mexico. https://doi.org/10.2307/j.ctvhn09qs.3 accessed 23 April 2023.

Schricke, C. (1994), Mexico, 25th member of the OECD. Organisation for Economic Cooperation and Development. The OECD Observer, 1994, no 188, p. 4.

Stone, D. (2004). Transfer Agents and Global Networks in the 'transnationalization' of Policy. *Journal of European public policy*, *11*(3), 545–66. https://doi.org/10.1080/13501760410001694291 accessed 23 April 2023.

Valdés, I. (2022). Cambios en la política de ciencia, tecnología e innovación: transferencia de la política en México entre 1988 y 2018 [Doctoral dissertation. FLACSO México].

Vicher, D. (2018). *La Organización para la Cooperación y el Desarrollo Económico (OCDE) y la reforma de la administración pública*. Tirant LoBlanch/INAP, México.

Villanueva, A. (2018). La influencia de organismos internacionales en el diseño de políticas públicas nacionales: el papel de la OCDE en la creación del Servicio Profesional Docente en México [MSc Thesis. FLACSO México].

Blogs and Newspapers

Garrigues (2021) Mexico: Federal judge declares the unconstitutionality of the Reliability, Security, Continuity and Quality Policy for the National Electric System. Published on February 23, 2021.

Link: https://www.garrigues.com/es_ES/noticia/mexico-juez-federal-declara-insubsistencia-politica -confiabilidad-seguridad-continuidad accessed 23 April 2023.

El Financiero (2020). Greenpeace obtains permanent suspension against Sener and Cenace measures limiting renewables. Published on June 24th, 2020. Link: https://www.elfinanciero.com.mx/ economia/greenpeace-obtiene-suspension-definitiva-contra-medidas-de-sener-y-cenace-que-limitan -a-renovables/?outputType=amp accessed 23 April 2023.

El Universal (2022). To avoid competition recommendations, Conamer cancels agreement with Cofece. Published on June 24, 2020. Link: https://www.eluniversal.com.mx/cartera/para-evitar -recomendaciones-en-materia-de-competencia-conamer-cancela-acuerdo-con-cofece accessed 23 April 2023.

Forbes (2022). Conamer terminates collaboration agreement with Cofece; impacts on competition warned. Published on April 30, 2022. Link: https://www.forbes.com.mx/conamer-corta-convenio-de -colaboracion-con-cofece-advierten-impactos-en-competencia/ accessed 23 April 2023.

20. Brazil: Cooperation, policy transfer and resistance

Osmany Porto de Oliveira

INTRODUCTION

On 25 January 2022 the Brazilian ambassador, delegate at the OECD, Carlos Marcos Condezey posted in his twitter account an image with a champagne saying 'day to celebrate'.[1] On that day, the OECD had officially informed that the Council had decided to open accession discussions with Brazil and five other candidates.[2] In the meantime, the French Ministry of Foreign Affairs rapidly released a note stating that the country would pay particular attention to ensure that candidates achieve progress in different areas, such as the fight against deforestation and climate change, among others. These events are an illustrative snapshot of the current scenario of the relations between the OECD and Brazil, which involve a high level of cooperation in different areas, policy transfers in order to meet the organization standards and faces the resistance of certain members, such as France.[3]

In this chapter I discuss the relationship between the OECD and Brazil. Their interactions date back to the beginning of the 1990s, when the country sent a mission to the OECD headquarters in Paris to learn more and start to approach the organization. The past 30 years of cooperation have been marked by important events: the rapprochement followed different rhythms, being more or less intense according to the attitudes and preferences of the Brazilian governments. In the remainder, we shall address three questions: how have the relations between Brazil and the OECD evolved? Which conditions led the country to start the accession process? Which forces facilitated and constrained the process? Specifically, I will focus on three dimensions of the engagement of Brazil with the OECD. These are foreign policy and international cooperation, policy transfer and political resistance.

We shall mobilize different literatures to process-trace and interpret the relations between Brazil and the OECD. First, we shall consider studies on international relations, in particular, scholars interested in foreign policy who understand and analyse this phenomena as a public policy (Allison and Zelikow, 1999). There is a growing scholarship focusing on the different domestic determinants of foreign policy – thus promoting more integration between public policies and international relations studies. The engagement of Brazil with the OECD is embedded in a dual relationship involving both foreign policy and public policies. As a matter of fact, if on the one hand, diplomats are those in charge with the formal relations with the OECD, on the other hand, the organization is a powerful agency promoting the adoption of its vast array of policy models, from anti-corruption measures to environmental standards. Besides that, the

---

[1]   https://twitter.com/CarlosCozendey/status/1486106639392518159, consulted 7 February, 2022.
[2]   The other five candidates were Argentina, Bulgaria, Croatia, Peru and Romania.
[3]   https://www.diplomatie.gouv.fr/en/french-foreign-policy/development-assistance/news/article/oecd-opening-of-accession-negotiations-26-jan-22, consulted 22 February, 2022.

adoption of the OECD policy instruments involves bureaucrats and political authorities, from the most different sectors and governmental organizations, who play an active role in the peer reviewing processes (see Chapter 9 in this volume), among other activities.

Policy transfer studies is the second field we shall mobilize (Dolowitz and Marsh, 2000; Hadjiisky et al., 2017; Porto de Oliveira, 2021) to capture the mechanisms of adoption of policy from elsewhere. Policy transfer studies analyse the harmonization and adherence of policies from the OECD acquis, which is a condition of access the organization. This literature also brings into the discussion the role of resistance in adopting policies from abroad (Pal, 2019). Here this concept is deployed to refer to the resistance of different agents who have been opposing the Brazilian access to the OECD.

As mentioned, we shall process-trace the trajectory of the Brazilian engagement with the OECD. We shall do that by drawing on data from official documents, specialized literature and media. A process-tracing technique allows us to analyse and outline the different moments of the Brazilian relationship, identifying key events along this path. The chapter is divided in three parts, following this introduction, and a conclusion. The first part introduces the evolution of the cooperation between Brazil and the OECD, detailing the specificities of each government in the past 30 years. The second, discusses the recent road towards accession. The third, informs about the different opponents to the Brazilian candidacy.

THREE DECADES OF COOPERATION

The relations between the OECD and Brazil have grown gradually since the 1990s. Before that, the most notable exchange was when the organization created the Steel Committee in 1978. Given the Brazilian relevant share of the global market, the OECD invited Brazil to participate. However, at that time the invitation did not interest Brazil (Pinto, 2000, p. 97). This changed a decade later with the end of dictatorship, the promulgation of a democratic constitution, and the Presidential elections.

Throughout the 1980s, there were different informal contacts between the organization and Brazil. The relationship was not significant until the Brazilian Mission to the OECD in June 1991 (Pinto, 2000, p. 97). The mission had different purposes, among these to better understand the *modus operandi* of the OECD and identify means of participation in the organization's different institutions. Brazil formally presented a letter expressing the interest in increasing the collaboration with the organization (Pinto, 2000, p. 98). The academic literature and official documents present the relationship between Brazil and OECD in as an evolutionary linear process, often ignoring the different political positions and contexts in Brazil. However, each Brazilian administration had different types of engagement with the organization. I will discuss in this section the relationship between Brazil and the OECD, following the different changes that occurred in the past governments.

The politics in Brazil were turbulent in the early 1990s. The elected President Fernando Collor de Mello was impeached in 1992 and Itamar Franco assumed as interim. A strong neo-liberal agenda was imposed on Latin America in the 1990s, when the 'Washington Consensus' was a paradigm for the region, preaching *inter alia* the privatization of national enterprises. The next elections took place in 1994, when Fernando Henrique Cardoso from the centre-right Brazilian Social Democracy Party (*Partido da Social Democracia Brasileira* – PSDB) won. He was President for two terms (1995–2003). His administration was characterized by monetary policies, and the introduction of a new Brazilian currency called 'Real'. New Public Management principles and state reforms started to be introduced during his government. He also intensified the process of privatizations of state companies. From 1995 on, these processes gave new impetus to the relations between the OECD and the Brazilian government. Different high-level visits occurred at that time (Pinto, 2000, p. 111). Brazil joined the Steel Committee in 1996, after years of discussion since 1992 (Pinto, 2000, pp. 101–102; Godinho, 2018, p. 189).[4] By the end of the 1990s Brazil was participating in several other committees (Godinho, 2018, p. 190). The relationship between Brazil and the OECD enhanced even further in 1999 when a specific program was created for the country and Brazil also started to be invited to all OECD Ministerial meetings (Thorstensen and Gullo, 2018, p. 19).

In 2003 the government of the left-wing Workers Party (*Partido dos Trabalhadores – PT*) Luiz Inácio Lula da Silva (from now on Lula) began, whose administration was marked by social policies on the domestic level, meanwhile a series of actions for building a post-liberal world order was implemented on the international level. Different actions were carried out for this purpose, such as building international coalitions, with the G21 at the World Trade Organizations, boosting relations among the rising powers (Hussain, 2004), with the BRICS (Brazil, Russia, India, China and South Africa), and investing in South-South Cooperation (SSC) projects. During this period Brazil developed a portfolio of successful public policies in different areas, in particular to fight against hunger and poverty. These programs have spread all over the world, through different dynamics of policy transfers, leading the country to a global role in exporting social policy innovations (Porto de Oliveira, 2020). It was also during Lula's administrations that Brazil witnessed a commodities boom, giving a momentum of economic prosperity and growth.

The OECD was interested in the rapprochement with Brazil, among other rising powers. Angél Gurría, at that time the OECD Secretary-General, visited the country at different times. However, this did not seem as an aspiration for Brazil and the topic of OECD was not a priority in the foreign policy agenda (Sanchez, 2008, p. 20). In fact, it was Lula's understanding that if Brazil joined the 'club of the rich' it would end the country's representativeness among developing nations.[5] In spite of the divergences, during Lula's administration a few important steps were made within the rapprochement with the OECD. In 2003, a national contact point was established, promoting OECD the directives for multinational corporations (Ministério da Fazenda, 2003). A crucial step was made with the OECD Council Resolution on 'Enlargement and Enhanced Engagement' adopted in 2007, through which the organization invited Brazil, with other countries (China, India, Indonesia and South Africa), to become 'Key Partners', as well as beginning to strengthen relations with a view to a possible membership and created mechanisms that facilitated the participation of these countries in the OECD bodies.[6]

Further crucial steps of engagement with the OECD were taken by Dilma Rousseff who had an agenda more focused on domestic politics than her predecessor. In 2013, Brazil became

---

[4]   Brazil has historically been a crucial player in this sector, currently it is the ninth producer in the world, according to the World Steel Association. However, Brazil conditioned the entry to the steel committee on the conclusion of the process of privatization of the national steel industry and after a wide domestic consultation it was finally verified the interest of the country to be part of the Committee (Pinto, 2000, p. 101).

[5]   https://www.bbc.com/portuguese/internacional-58826796, consulted 7 February, 2022.

[6]   https://www.oecd.org/brazil/oecdcouncilresolutiononenlargementandenhancedengagement.htm, consulted 18 February, 2022.

1991	1996	2003	2007	2015	2017	2022
Brazilian Mission to the OECD	Brazil joins the Steel Committee	National Contact Point is Created	Enhanced Enlargement	Signature of the Cooperation Agreement	Brazil request the accession	OECD Council invites Brazil for acession

Source: Author.

Figure 20.1   *Timeline of Brazilian relations with the OECD*

vice-chair of PISA and two years later a cooperation agreement between Brazil and the OECD was signed. The agreement led to the development of a two-year (2016–17) program of work 'designed to support Brazil in advancing its reform agenda and informing its public policies' (OECD, 2018, p. 6). Among the activities we can mention a number of policy reviews in different areas, including an 'innovation policy review to help Brazil reflect and build on the OECD Innovation Strategy', an expenditure review with focus on health. [7] The program also foresees the increase of the participation of Brazil in different OECD bodies, in particular in committees on competition and tax policies. [8] According to Angél Gurría the purposes of the program were not only for Brazil to adopt the OECD 'best practices', but also to shape these.[9]

Rousseff was impeached in 2016, after a complicated political process, which led to power the interim President Michel Temer of the centre Party of the Brazilian Democratic Movement (*Partido do Movimento Democrático Brasileiro* – PMDB). In his administration a different route in foreign policy was implemented, by focusing on the relations between the so-called 'traditional partners' (e.g., the United States, Europe and Japan) (Serra, 2018). The official demand to access the OECD was requested in 2017. The following government of the far-right President Jair Bolsonaro from the Liberal Party (*Partido Liberal* – PL) started in 2019. The accession to the OECD was a priority. The government aspires, with the accession, to legitimize the adoption of neoliberal policies, get international recognition, as a member of the OECD, and attract foreign investments. The government created a specific body, the Council Brazil-OECD, within the political and strategic coordination for the preparation to the accession. The Council is coordinated by the Brazilian Presidential Chief of Staff Minister and composed by the of the General Secretary of the Presidency of the Republic, the Chief Minister of the Government Secretary, the Ministry of Economy and the Ministry of Foreign Relations. The Brazilian strategy to access the OECD involves three axes: first, the campaign towards receiving the formal invitation to the accession; second, the progressive rapprochement to the OECD thematic committees; the alignment with the OECD best practices, which consisted of anticipating the adherence of the organization's acquis in order to try to reduce the

---

[7]   https://www.oecd.org/brazil/launch-of-brazil-oecd-programme-of-work-2016-2017.htm, consulted 21 February, 2022.

[8]   https://www.oecd.org/brazil/launch-of-brazil-oecd-programme-of-work-2016-2017.htm, consulted 21 February, 2022.

[9]   https://www.oecd.org/brazil/launch-of-brazil-oecd-programme-of-work-2016-2017.htm, consulted 21 February, 2022.

time for accession (Gomes et al., 2021, p. 23). In the next section, the accession process will be discussed, with specific focus on the adoption of OECD instruments by Brazil.

POLICY TRANSFERS: A PATHWAY TOWARDS ACCESSION?

With the government of Dilma Rousseff, the relationship between the OECD and Brazil grew significantly. It was also clear from the part of the OECD the intent of making Brazil adopting OECD's best practices, such as it was stated in the 2016–17 Work Programme. I will discuss in this section the stages for accession and the progress Brazil made with the adherence of the OECD acquis, which is related to circa 260 legal instruments of the organization. The policy transfer of the acquis is a condition for accession even if there is some margin for negotiation with the committees on the adherence of parts of these legal instruments (Cozendey, 2019, p. 55), the alignment with the OECD standards and practices is a crucial element in the evaluation of the candidate country for accession by the commission. In order to ensure the adherence of the acquis, the OECD prepares peer reviews, produces reports and recommendations for countries in the different sectors, such as in the case of environment, as will be discussed later in this section.

The road to the OECD accession is complex, with several stages and peer reviews (see also Chapter 18 on the Australian accession process). It takes a long time to become a member and there is no deadline for completion of this process.[10] In the case of Colombia, for example, one of the most recent Latin American members,[11] the process began in 2013, followed by a five-year accession path, becoming officially a member in 2020.[12] The enlargement of OECD had different groups of accession (see the Chapter 2 for a historical account of the organization).

According to the OECD, 'each country follows its own accession process and is assessed independently'.[13] A specific report (OECD, 2017, p. 6) establishes a framework for the accession. There are different procedures to be accomplished along the road for accession. Brazil presented a formal request in 2017, as mentioned in the previous section. The request was evaluated by the Council, which decided to open discussions for the Brazilian accession on 25 January 2022, within a group of other six countries. A few months later, on 10 June, 2022, the Roadmap for the OECD Accession Process of Brazil was adopted by the Council at ministerial level (OECD, 2022).

The roadmap is prepared for each country individually, setting the terms, conditions and process for accession. Along the process the country will be submitted through in-depth evaluation by the OECD technical committees (26 in the case of Brazil), in an extensive variety of public policy sectors. In the case of Brazil, policy areas identified by the Council were: 1. Structural reform; 2. Open trade and investment; 3. Inclusive growth; 4. Governance; 5. Environment, biodiversity and climate change; 6. Digitalization; 7. Infrastructure (OECD,

---

[10] https://www.oecd.org/newsroom/oecd-takes-first-step-in-accession-discussions-with-argentina-brazil-bulgaria-croatia-peru-and-romania.htm, consulted 10 February, 2022.

[11] Costa Rica completed the accession in 2021.

[12] https://www.oecd.org/newsroom/global-oecd-welcomes-colombia-as-its-37th-member.htm, consulted 10 February, 2022.

[13] https://www.oecd.org/about/document/enlargement.htm, consulted 10 February, 2022

2022, p. 4). The evaluation considers the alignment of the country with the standards, policies and practices of the organization.[14] During this process OECD can request modifications and adjustments in the country's legislation in order to meet the acquis of the organization. The country can also demand to negotiate the OECD requests on specific domains (Conzedey, 2019, p. 55). Each committee provides the Council with a formal opinion.

The adherence of shared values of the organization is also a 'fundamental requirement for membership' (OECD, 2022, p. 2). Among the values shared by the OECD members are 'the preservation of individual liberty, the values of democracy, the rule of law and the protection of human rights', as well as the 'commitment to promote sustainable and inclusive economic growth and their goals to tackle climate change, including halting and reversing biodiversity loss and deforestation'.[15]

Technical reviews will begin after the submission of an Initial Memorandum by Brazil, which is expected to be sent by the end of September. After that information-gathering and in-depth analysis will be started by OECD committees (OECD, 2022, p. 5). Once the reviews are concluded, on the basis of the committee's assessment a unanimous decision to invite the candidate country to become a member will be taken by the Council.

At the moment of writing this chapter Brazil is preparing the Initial Memorandum. As mentioned previously the country made the accession a high priority. In the forum of Davos, 2019, Bolsonaro explicitly mentioned in his speech that the country was going to 'seek to better integrate Brazil into the world by mainstreaming international best practices, such as those adopted and promoted by the OECD'.[16] These agents have made an intense effort to align the Brazilian legislation and public policies to the OECD instruments. In Figure 20.2 below we can observe that in 1997 Brazil had adhered to 11 of the OECD instruments. This rate does not raise significantly in the following years. In 2016 the country adopted to 20 more instruments, completing 31 instruments, that is, adhering to 20 instruments in 19 years. After the country made the formal request to become a member the number of adhered instruments grew vertiginously, with 30 new instruments between 2017 and 2018, reaching 100 in 2021.[17] Today, Brazil is the candidate country for accession, as well as the key partner, with the highest number of adhered instruments. The participation of Brazil in the OECD committees also increased and 39 studies and reviews were ongoing or had been concluded by 2019 (Gomes et al., 2021, p. 23).

There are however challenges in a few areas for Brazil to align with the OECD acquis. These are in particular the tax and financial, navy industry and, especially, environment. The recent OECD report 'Evaluating Brazil's progress in implementing Environmental Performance Review recommendations and promoting its alignment with OECD core acquis on the environment', released in 2021, pointed several challenges to the country. The purpose of the report was to evaluate the alignment of the country with 23 OECD instruments related to the environment. It recognized that Brazil made improvements in some areas in line with

---

[14] Ibid.

[15] Ibid.

[16] https://www.gov.br/mre/en/content-centers/speeches-articles-and-interviews/president-of-the-federative-republic-of-brazil/speeches/discurso-del-presidente-de-la-republica-jair-bolsonaro-durante-la-sesion-plenaria-del-foro-economico-mundial-davos-suiza-22-de-enero-de-2020, consulted 14 February, 2022.

[17] https://www.gov.br/casacivil/pt-br/assuntos/noticias/2021/maio/ocde-brasil-atinge-100-instrumentos-aderidos, consulted 14 February, 2022.

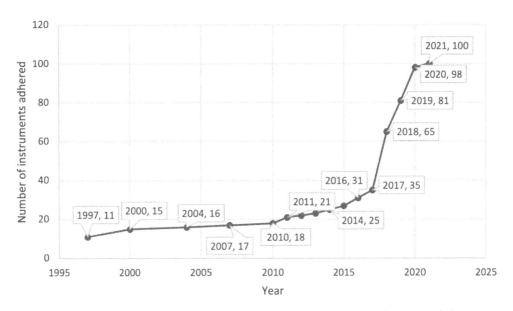

Note: See https://www.gov.br/casacivil/pt-br/assuntos/noticias/2020/dezembro/brasil-adere-a-mais-instrumento
s-da-ocde-1, consulted 7 February, 2022.
Source: Prepared by the author, based on official documents of the Brazilian Government.

Figure 20.2   *Evolution of adherence of OECD instruments by Brazil*

OECD and international principles, meanwhile in others it falls behind the organization standards (Labuhn and Mazur, 2021, p. 6). The report highlights that significant efforts are required
to meet the OECD instruments and practices. A wide range of areas requiring improvement
are mentioned in the document, such as the periodic environmental information management;
monitoring and controlling pesticides in water bodies; managing solid waste; fighting against
deforestation with stringent measures; and implementation of the polluter-pays principle. This
issue is also detailed in the roadmap for accession, where the environmental policy committee
presents 22 requests for adjustments, improvements or implementation of public policies
(OECD, 2022, pp. 15–17). The environmental issue is particularly sensitive for France, which
has been a major opponent to the Brazilian accession to the organization, as will be described
in the next section.

THE POLITICS OF INTERNATIONAL POLICY RESISTANCE

The process of acceptance for the Brazilian candidacy for accession was neither technical
nor automatic. In fact, the country had to build support to the accession approval of the
Commission, especially with the United States (US). During the government of Bolsonaro,
Brazil increased exponentially the adoption of OECD instruments, at the same time the
country faced direct opposition from global civil society and the government of France. In
this section it will be discussed the international dynamics of resistance to accession. First the

support from the US will be outlined and then the quarrels with civil society and France will be described.

The decision to invite a country for the accession process at the OECD must be taken by all members unanimously. According to Cozendey (2019, p. 56) in 2017 during the evaluation of candidates for accession there were distinct positions among the members of the OECD. Europeans supported the beginning of the accession process for all six candidates, which included three members from the European Union, meanwhile the US was cautious regarding the expansion of the organization (Cozendey, 2019, p. 57). The US demanded that only one country should be approved and endorsed the candidacy of Argentina (Cozendey, 2019, p. 57). The US has been against the enlargement of the OECD dating back to the Obama administration, fearing that the expansion could impact the homogeneity of the organization, as well as its operational capacity (Mello, 2020, p. 13).

The support of the US for Brazil would come years later. Even if there was an ideological alignment between the two far-right leaders Trump and Bolsonaro, the support for the OECD was not taken for granted. Trump suggested that the US would have supported the Brazilian candidacy. However, it took some time until the country made it official in 2019. As a matter of fact, Brazil had to make some concessions to get the support from the Trump administration. In order to ensure the support, Bolsonaro agreed to make different commercial concessions in benefit for the US.[18] The major concession was related to the renounce to the status of developing country in the World Trade Organization (WTO), which gives special rights to these countries. According to the WTO developing countries have the following special provisions: longer time periods for implementing agreements and commitments, measures to increase trading opportunities for developing countries, provisions requiring all WTO members to safeguard the trade interests of developing countries, support to help developing countries build the capacity to carry out WTO work, handle disputes, and implement technical standards and provisions related to least-developed country (LDC) Members.[19]

The support from the US was not enough to ensure the acceptance for the Brazilian candidacy for accession. A resistance movement from international civil society was organized. In January, 2021, the Human Rights Watch (HRW) sent a letter to the Representatives of Member States the OECD, with accusations against Bolsonaro's policies in the Amazon region. The letter targeted the Environment Policy Committee, which was reviewing the Brazilian status at that time. The HRW requested the disqualification of Brazil for an upgrade, which is an important step towards the accession, insofar as it can accelerate the process of adhesion for the environmental guidelines. The letter, included a long report showcasing the environmental consequences of the Brazilian policies and argued that the Bolsonaro administration had actively worked against the objectives of the Committee's mandate and 'sabotaged Brazil's environmental law enforcement agencies, falsely accused civil society organizations of environmental crimes and sidelined them from policymaking, and sought to undermine Indigenous rights'.[20] According to *Folha de São Paulo*, one of the major Brazilian newspapers, after the OECD received the letter, the upgrade of the Brazilian status, was removed from the com-

---

[18]   https://www.bbc.com/portuguese/internacional-50009155, consulted 14 February, 2022.
[19]   https://www.wto.org/english/tratop_e/devel_e/dev_special_differential_provisions_e.htm, consulted 14 February, 2022.
[20]   https://www.hrw.org/news/2021/02/06/letter-amazon-and-its-defenders-organisation-economic-cooperation-and-development, consulted 22 February, 2022.

mittee's agenda. Again, later that year, in May, a group of over 60 civil society organizations delivered a letter to Mathias Cormann, current Director-General, to denounce the backsliding on human rights, as well as on environmental issues, showing their concerns with the Brazilian accession to the OECD.[21]

Resistance did not come only from the international civil society. The French government was also an important opponent to the Brazilian candidacy for accession, especially due to the environmental issue. This is related to a broader process, regarding episodes of tension between Bolsonaro and Macron, the President of France, about environmental issues. A particular moment was during the G-7 summit, held in Biarritz in 2019. After huge fires in the Amazon, globally broadcast by international media, the President of France proposed that this topic should be a priority for the G-7 meeting. Bolsonaro in his turn accused Macron of being colonialist, by attacking an internal issue of Brazil.[22] The environmental topic became an impasse also for the ratification of the Agreement between Brazil and the European Union.

In January 2022 when the OECD made public that the accession was approved for six new countries, including Brazil, the French Ministry of Foreign Affairs released a note stating that;

> At the request of France and its partners, the OECD Secretary General sent a letter to the candidate countries requesting that they commit to adhering to the values and priorities outlined in the OECD's 60th anniversary Vision Statement as well as the policy conclusions that were adopted last year at the ministerial level meeting of the Council of the OECD.[23]

The note continued stressing that France was going to 'pay particular attention to ensuring that all of the candidates achieve significant, concrete, measurable progress on the ground in several priority areas, especially with regard to the fight against deforestation and climate change, the protection of biodiversity' among others.[24]

The environment is currently among the most serious hindrances for the Brazilian accession, as mentioned in the previous section. The French government revealed that it will not approve the Brazilian access the OECD without a significant change in the country's legislation and practices related to the protection of the environment. International civil society also showed their power to persuade, by directly accusing the Brazilian behaviour in the environmental committee. These are expressions of international political resistance dynamics to the candidacy of assessment of Brazil to the OECD, which reveals that in this case domestic sectoral policies and international relations are intrinsically intertwined in a complex political game, involving distinct governmental and non-governmental agents.

CONCLUSION

This chapter traced the evolution the relations between Brazil and the OECD, until the recent release of the roadmap for accession. It has argued that different dynamics were present during

---

[21] https://www.conectas.org/en/noticias/organizations-warn-oecd-of-brazils-backsliding-on-human-rights-and-environmental-safeguards/, consulted 22 February, 2022.

[22] https://twitter.com/jairbolsonaro/status/1164667767242596354, consulted 26 February, 2022.

[23] https://www.diplomatie.gouv.fr/en/french-foreign-policy/development-assistance/news/article/oecd-opening-of-accession-negotiations-26-jan-22, consulted 22 February, 2022.

[24] Ibid.

this process, namely, cooperation, transfer and resistance. The interactions between Brazil and the OECD have followed different rhythms, according to the presidents in power and the foreign policy political projects on their agenda. The chapter discussed the different moments of a 30-year cooperation, from the first mission in 1991 until the approval for the accession in 2022.

Along this process Brazil engaged with several OECD committees and progressively adhered to the organization's best practices and standards. The adoption of the organization's acquis is a condition for the accession. The chapter outlined the road to accession and the increase in the number of legal instruments adopted by Brazil. This process was discussed under the lens of policy transfer. Finally, the chapter informs that the accession is not a technical and automatic process. Instead, it involves politics, as was showed by the episodes of diplomatic actions for building support with the US, the protesting from international civil society and the watchdog role performed by France.

The domestic politics in Brazil has also ben shown to be crucial for the intensity of the engagement with the OECD. During the governments of PT, the country tended to engage with the organization at a slower pace. Becoming a member of the OECD was not at the top of PT's foreign policy agenda. This changed when right wing forces came into power, especially, during the government of Bolsonaro. With Presidential elections this year, the future of relations between Brazil and OECD is still to be revealed. Investigating the policy and political dimensions of such engagement is a key step towards a better understanding a broader phenomenon, such as the interplay between Global South countries and the OECD.

REFERENCES

Allison, G., and Zelikow, P. (1999). *Essence of Decision: Explaining the Cuban Missile Crisis*. Longman. https://books.google.com.br/books/about/Essence_of_Decision.html?id=aSk3ek0t54EC& redir_esc=y consulted 24 April 2023.

Cozendey, C.M. (2019). O pedido de acessão do Brasil à OCDE: onde estamos. *Cadernos de Política Exterior*, *5*(8), 49–74.

Dolowitz, David P. and Marsh, D. (2000). Learning from Abroad: The Role of Policy Transfer in Contemporary Policy Making. *Governance*, *13*(1), 5–24.

Godinho, R. de O. (2018). *A Ocde Em Rota De Adaptação Ao Cenário Internacional*. 323.

Gomes, M.B., Florêncio, P. de A. e L., de Souza Lima, O.C., Brant Wolff, S.C. and Torres Amaral, R.R. (2021). Brasil Na Ocde. *Boletim de Economia e Política Internacional*, *28*, 9–27. https://doi.org/10.38116/bepi28art1 consulted 24 April 2023.

Hadjiisky, M., Pal, L.A. and Walker, C. (2017). *Public Policy Transfer: Micro-Dynamics and Macro-Effects*. Edward Elgar Publishing.

Hussain, I. (2004). After Cancún: G21, WTO, and Multilateralism. *Journal of International and Area Studies*, *11*(2), 16.

Labuhn, B. and Mazur, E. (2021). *Evaluating Brazil's progress in implementing Environmental Performance Review recommendations and promoting its alignment with OECD core acquis on the environment* (p. 76). OECD.

Mello, F. de C. (2020). The OECD enlargement in Latin America and the Brazilian candidacy. *Revista Brasileira de Política Internacional*, *63*(2), e011. https://doi.org/10.1590/0034-7329202000211 consulted 24 April 2023.

OECD. (2017) 'Report of the Chair of the Working Group on the Future Size and Membership of the Organization to Council: Framework for the Consideration of Prospective Members'.

OECD. (2018). *Active with Brazil*. OECD.

OECD. (2022). *Roadmap for the OECD Accesssion Process of Brazil*. OECD.

Pal, L.A. (2019). Policy Transfer and Resistance: Proposals for a New Research Agenda. Em Porto de Oliveira, Osmany, Osorio Gonnet, Cecilia, S. Montero and C.K. da S. Leite (Orgs.), *Latin America and Policy Diffusion: From Import to Export* (p. 183–201). Routledge.

Portaria do Ministério da Fazenda, Nº 92—2003 (2003).

Pinto, D.F. de S. (2000). *OCDE: Uma visão Brasileira*. IRBr-FUNAG.

Porto de Oliveira, O. (2020). Brazil Exporting Social Policies: From Local Innovation to a Global Model. *Journal of Politics in Latin America*, 1–23. https://doi.org/10.1177/1866802X19889757 consulted 24 April 2023.

Porto de Oliveira, O. (2021). A Prelude to Policy Transfer Research. In *Handbook of Policy Transfer, Diffusion and Circulation* (p. 1–24). Edward Elgar Publishing.

Sanchez, M.R. (2008). O Brasil e a OCDE: uma aproximação pelas bordas. *Textos Cindes*, *4*, 30.

Serra, J. (2018). *Discurso do ministro José Serra por ocasião da cerimônia de transmissão do cargo de ministro de estado das Relações Exteriores. Brasília, 18 de maio de 2016*. https://www.gov .br/mre/pt-br/centrais-de-conteudo/publicacoes/discursos-artigos-e-entrevistas/ministro-das-relacoes -exteriores/discursos-mre/discurso-do-ministro-jose-serra-por-ocasiao-da-cerimonia-de-transmissao -do-cargo-de-ministro-de-estado-das-relacoes-exteriores-brasilia-18-de-maio-de-2016 consulted 24 April 2023.

Thorstensen, V. and Gullo, M.F. (2018). O Brasil na OCDE: membro pleno ou mero espectador? *CCGI - Working Paper Series*, *8*(479), 30.

21. Kazakhstan: In search of international legitimacy

Colin Knox and Saltanat Janenova

INTRODUCTION

Kazakhstan is in Central Asia which is geographically located with Russia to the north and China to the south-east. The region has a population of 73m people and comprises the five post-Soviet countries of Kazakhstan, Kyrgyzstan, Tajikistan, Turkmenistan and Uzbekistan. The two most populous countries are Uzbekistan and Kazakhstan with 34.2m and 18.8m people respectively. Kazakhstan is the most developed in the region largely due to its hydrocarbon resources, strong domestic demand, and foreign direct investment. It is now classified as a middle-income country which enjoys significant economic freedom with a GDP per capita of 9,106 current US$, and Tajikistan the poorest (GDP 863 US$) (Kazakevitch, 2020; World Bank, 2021). All five countries are defined as 'consolidated authoritarian regimes' based on democracy scores which rate: national and local governance, the electoral process, independent media, civil society, judicial framework, and corruption (Freedom House, 2021).

Kazakhstan is not yet a member of the OECD but has long-standing ambitions to join the organisation dating back as far as 2008. This aspiration is part of a wider agenda aimed at international approbation and includes Kazakhstan's strategic goal to become one of the top 30 developed countries by 2050. Kazakhstan is a participatory member of the United Nations and a member of the Organisation for Security and Cooperation in Europe (OSCE). It chaired the OSCE in 2010 and has been a member of NATO's Partnership for Peace since 1994. All of this is part of Kazakhstan's agenda to become a recognised and respected member of the international community, notwithstanding its Soviet legacy and enduring authoritarian rule (O'Connor et al., 2021).

This chapter will chart Kazakhstan's involvement with the OECD from its origins through to its ongoing collaboration with several ministries. It will consider the roadmap which the OECD has set for the government of Kazakhstan to achieve membership, and the impact this partnership has had in one key area of collaboration – supporting effective public governance. We benchmark Kazakhstan against Estonia, a post-Soviet country, and through the theoretical lens of isomorphism examine whether policy changes have simply between adopted in principle with significant gaps between OECD proposals and their implementation. Finally, the chapter will question whether the marginal progress in international governance metrics which Kazakhstan has made while working with the OECD can been directly attributed to this partnership.

ORIGINS OF AND WORK WITH THE OECD

Kazakhstan's cooperation with the OECD began through the Eurasia Competitiveness Programme (ECP) which was launched in 2008. It comprised 13 countries in Eastern Europe, South Caucasus and Central Asia. The overall aim of this programme was to attract investment, increase competitiveness, and build private entrepreneurship in Eurasia. Constituent countries were encouraged to develop policies which would improve the business climate for foreign investment using OECD standards and tools. Specifically, the Central Asia programme (a constituent element of the ECP) comprised Afghanistan, Kazakhstan, Kyrgyzstan, Mongolia, Tajikistan, Turkmenistan and Uzbekistan. Typical projects carried out under this initiative included analytical work, capacity-building activities, monitoring and implementing public sector reforms. Country specific work was peer-reviewed at the OECD Eurasia Competitiveness Roundtable. The programme also organised an annual event (OECD Eurasia Week) as a means of strengthening relations between countries in the region and the OECD. Through sharing experiences or best practice, the aim was to improve competitiveness and attract foreign direct investment.

Building on this initial cooperation, Kazakhstan was invited in 2011 to participate in the Steering Committee of the Eurasian Competitiveness Programme on the condition that it became a donor to the programme, amounting to €800,000. In 2015 Kazakhstan signed a County Cooperation Agreement for the period 2015–2018 which allowed it to adopt OECD standards, strengthen institutions, and build capacity for policy reforms. Then Prime Minister of Kazakhstan, Karim Massimov, said at the signing of the agreement 'the introduction of OECD best practices in our policies is a prerequisite for strengthening our role in a global economy' (Massimov, 2015: 2).

These programmes are seen as helping countries to move closer to OECD standards and policy recommendations, providing an anchor for policy reforms (Peru and Morocco adopted similar reform programmes). As part of the Kazakhstan country programme the OECD conducted 30 reviews and capacity-building projects. It helped Kazakhstan upgrade its partnerships in seven OECD bodies, and to adhere to 33 legal instruments (e.g.: Recommendation of the Council on *Gender Equality in Education, Employment and Entrepreneurship* (2016); and, the Recommendation of the Council on *Regulatory Policy and Governance* (2017)). Kazakhstan has also been active in promoting OECD approaches and policy recommendations in the wider Central Asia region, most notably on multilateral tax initiatives and work on trade and transport connectivity (OECD, 2019).

The impact of this collaboration over several years was captured in an OECD publication entitled *Enhancing Competitiveness in Central Asia* (OECD, 2018) which charted economic growth in the region but highlighted the risks of over-reliance on minerals, exports and remittances, and the importance of reforms in governance, connectivity and the business environment. The report noted: 'Each of the country case studies presented here is the result of a country-specific project carried out by the OECD, hand-in-hand with the governments of Kazakhstan, Kyrgyzstan, Mongolia, Tajikistan, Uzbekistan' (2018: 3). This highlights the role which the OECD sees itself playing: *primus inter pares* in developing countries interested in reforms aimed at meeting OECD standards.

Working with the OECD required ongoing collaboration structures within the Kazakhstan government. The formal mechanism is a Coordinating Council chaired by the Prime Minister of the Republic of Kazakhstan. The Ministry of National Economy takes the lead role supported by ministerial teams from across the various public policy priority areas: tax policy; education and innovation; social development and skills; investments and transport; green economy; corruption and integrity; public administration; competition; SMEs and corporate governance; and agriculture. Each team, headed by a Vice Minister, develops a strategy to work with OECD committees and bodies, provides support for OECD missions in Kazakhstan and suggests new activities or projects to expand co-operation (Kazakhstan Economic Research Institute, 2021).

The sheer scale of ambition to join the OECD for a developing country like Kazakhstan is captured by the fact that by the end of the Country Cooperation Programme in 2018, the OECD made 535 recommendations in an implementation road map arising from Kazakh officials participating in 34 working agencies of the OECD. Then Minister of National Economy, Timur Suleimenov, suggested Kazakhstan was 'close to OECD membership' in 2017 and noted:

> Economic interdependence is ever more prevalent...This reality means that cooperation between nations, whether through bilateral or multilateral platforms, is ever more important. Kazakhstan, as an active member of the international community, has been actively striving to learn from developed nations by partnering with countries and international organisations. Our cooperation with the Organisation for Economic Cooperation and Development (OECD) has been especially noteworthy. (Suleimenov, 2017: 1)

Yet the collaboration between Kazakhstan and the OECD did not progress well or quickly enough. A multilateral review conducted by the OECD in 2016 suggested Kazakhstan needed deep structural reforms including a mixture of economic diversification, greater efforts to privatise, and tighter environmental regulation (OECD, 2016). Kazakhstan's early hopes of accession to the OECD by early 2017 were dashed. Undeterred, the most recent collaboration efforts involve a Memorandum of Understanding between the Government of Kazakhstan and the OECD for the period 2019–22. Key priorities for future cooperation include productivity and regulation, reform and privatisation of state-owned enterprises, implementing sustainable development goals (SDGs), and tourism development. The most recent development is a National Action Plan aimed at bringing country policies to OECD standards and preparing an application to join the organisation in 2025. The action plan was described by First Deputy Prime Minister, Alikhan Smailov, as a way 'to give a new impetus to a long-term partnership with the OECD' with a hint of exasperation that the journey to membership was taking much longer and proving more expensive than expected (Smailov, 2021:1).

IMPACT OF OECD-KAZAKHSTAN PARTNERSHIP WORKING

Given the number of policy areas in which the Kazakhstan government works with the OECD, assessing the impact of this collaboration over more than 13 years is a difficult proposition. For example, there is research which looks at the role of the OECD in several policy areas: social security, education, labour rights, economic innovation, and agriculture (Mukhamadiyeva et al., 2017; Sarmurzin et al., 2021; Zhetpisbayev et al., 2017; Saiymova et al., 2018). Much of this research considers Kazakhstan's efforts in adopting OECD standards to the field of social welfare through legislation aimed at meeting the needs of those with disabilities, in poverty, retired, and social security guarantees for the family and the child. In the area of education reforms, the OECD produced a plethora of research reports which led directly to

Kazakhstan adopting the International Student Assessment (PISA) test although with limited impact on student learning outcomes. Kazakhstan has also attempted to unify its labour laws such that they are consistent with those in OECD countries aimed at improving fraught problems of labour relations. This work is part of a wider strategy to adopt international human rights standards in a country known for frequent breaches. The OECD has promoted the diversification of the Kazakhstan economy away from its heavy reliance on the oil and gas sector and problems associated with the Dutch disease to knowledge-based innovations in the nanotechnology sector. Usefully, the OECD produced a 'taking stock' report entitled *Reforming Kazakhstan: progress, challenges and opportunities* (2017) which reflected on the achievements under the Country Programme and the way forward. The OECD concluded that it 'stands ready to work with Kazakhstan on the polices needed to deliver clean, inclusive and sustained growth over the decades to come' (OECD, 2017: 3). While the report claimed significant achievements arising from the OECD-Kazakhstan government partnership to date, it made four key recommendations: supporting effective governance; building a competitive and open economy; strengthening higher education, employment and social inclusion; and fostering green growth.

We select *one* of these areas, supporting effective public governance, for more detailed scrutiny to assess the extent to which there has been progress arising from the OECD's work in Kazakhstan.

The OECD made the following recommendations in 2017 set out in Table 21.1.

Table 21.1   OECD supporting effective public governance in Kazakhstan

Public governance	• Better allocate roles and responsibilities to ensure efficient functioning of the government.
	• Introduce new tools for risk management and policy evaluation.
	• Encourage 'public-facing' cultural change in the public sector.
	• Strengthen local governance capacity to improve accountability and resource management.
	• Allow local government greater fiscal flexibility.
	• Allow direct elections of local representatives.
	• Build stronger advisory functions at the central level to support local public institutions.
Public sector integrity	• Reinforce legal and institutional frameworks supporting integrity and enable their enforcement.
	• Promote greater transparency and include all non-governmental stakeholders in fighting corruption.
Open government	• Adopt a clear definition of open government.
	• Ensure proper implementation of the access to information law.
	• Further improve e-governance with increased mobile and user.
	• Access to information and tools.
	• Consult with all stakeholders at all levels to ensure better buy-in and ownership of policies.

Source: OECD (2017: 15).

How has Kazakhstan, in partnership with the OECD, responded to these challenges: public governance; public sector integrity; and, open government?

Public Governance

The overall response to improving public governance came in the form of a new model of public administration approved by the decree of the President of Kazakhstan in February 2021. Reflecting the call by the OECD for the public sector to be much more 'public-facing' through a cultural change in the public sector, the decree has the rather long title *The Concept of Public Administration Development in Kazakhstan until 2030: building a 'human-centred' model – People First*.

The decree notes:

> The current model of public administration, based on the administrative and control form of inter-action between the state and its citizens, does not fully meet the expectations of the population. As a result, there is a need for the formation of a service and 'human centred' model of public administration, where the main values are citizens and their well-being. (Kazakhstan Presidential Administration, 2021: 3)

The new public administration model outlined several tasks, central to which was the 'transition to proactive public services based on the needs of citizens'. The route to achieving this goal is, according to the new model, through two projects: the development of legislation to expand and remove barriers in the provision of public services, and simplification of the processes of obtaining public services.

This approach demonstrates important characteristics of how changes take place in a post-Soviet authoritarian country. Kazakhstan's public administration system is highly legalistic. To make even the smallest of changes from pre-existing arrangements requires a new law or legal amendments to current laws. This is a legacy of the Soviet Union which Kazakhstan has found difficult to elude. Inevitably this makes the process of change slow, and developing legislation can become an end goal rather than a means to an end. Bluntly, 'dyed in the wool' officials believe that the act of changing the law automatically translates into policies which create a citizen-centric state.

In terms of the second project, simplification of the processes of obtaining public services has relied on a significant transition from face-to-face public services provision to e-government (Bhuiyan, 2011; Knox and Janenova, 2019a). Kazakhstan has achieved remarkable success in this regard. The UN e-government development index (2020) shows Kazakhstan ranked in 29th place (just below Canada and Ireland) from over 190+ countries, up from 39th place in 2018. This index is a composite measure of three important dimensions of e-government: provision of online services, telecommunication connectively, and human capacity (United Nations, 2020). The new public administration model sets a goal to deliver at least 90 per cent of public services in electronic format by 2030. All of this is very laudable. However, many of the business processes which underpin these services remain replete with excessive bureaucratic documentation, the end result being to make inefficient systems faster but no less ineffective (Knox and Janenova, 2019b; Suleimenova et al., 2019). In addition, many public services such as the provision of heath care, education and social welfare depend on human interaction and officials working in these sectors are poorly trained and badly paid.

To give two examples of e-government services now available to the citizens of Kazakhstan:

I. Issuance of certificate for the right to manage small-size vessels, and
II. State registration of a pledge (deregistration) of tractors and self-propelled chassis and mechanisms made on their base, trailers for them, including trailers with mounted special equipment, self-propelled, agricultural, land-reclamation and road-building machines and mechanisms, as well as special off-road vehicles.

That said, there has been a steady improvement in public services provided by ministries (see Figure 21.1: higher scores represent better public services). We include Estonia as a comparator since it is ranked 29th in the UN Human Development Index (an aspiration for Kazakhstan), is also a post-Soviet country and pioneer of internet governance and democracy. Note the decline in public services during the Covid pandemic.

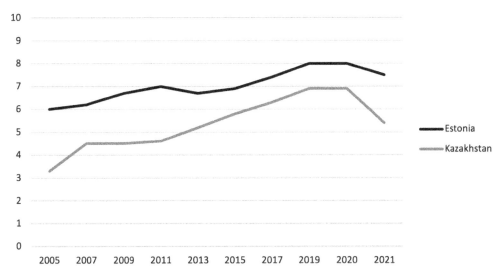

Note: Public Services – The provision of health, education, and sanitation services, among others, are key roles of the state. Includes pressures and measures related to policing, criminality, education provision, literacy, water and sanitation, infrastructure, quality healthcare, telephony, internet access, energy reliability, roads.
Source: Fund for Peace (2021) and Dahlberg et al., 2021.

Figure 21.1   *Public services*

Public Sector Integrity

The OECD made two recommendations to strengthen public sector integrity in Kazakhstan: reinforce legal and institutional frameworks supporting integrity and enable their enforcement; and promote greater transparency and include all non-governmental stakeholders in fighting corruption (see Table 21.1 above). We offer two examples to illustrate how Kazakhstan, working with the OECD, has responded to these recommendations: ethics commissioners and public councils.

In a bid to improve public sector integrity, the Kazakhstan government introduced an ethics code in 2015 based on international principles which governed civil servants' behaviour (Hossain et al., 2020). The code attempts to build trust between the citizen and state officials by preventing unethical behaviour in various work circumstances: at the workplace, relations between colleagues, superiors and subordinates, and importantly, outside the workplace. In other words, the ethics code defined the standards of behaviour expected from public officials (Janenova and Knox, 2020). In a bid to enforce these standards a new position of ethics commissioner was created in 2016 for all central and local government bodies. Initially these were part-time positions allocated amongst existing employees but after 18 months became full-time permanent posts. The impact of these system-wide ethics' enforcer has been minimal for several reasons. First, they had responsibility without power. Any breach of ethics has to be reported to their superiors who are more interested in protecting their organisations against negative press coverage. Second, they were perceived as whistle-blowers, anathema within a bureaucratic system which operates on strong principles of patronage, loyalty and kinship. Third, trying to monitor, arbitrate and enforce ethical standards outside the workplace was not only problematic but intrusive on the personal lives of officials (Pelizzo and Knox, 2021).

The second example is the introduction of public councils in 2016 which were set up as autonomous and independent bodies to hold state organisations to account and highlight corrupt activities (Sullivan, 2018; Yuvitsa, 2021). Public councils comprised two-thirds representatives from NGOs and members of the public, and one-third from state or local government representatives. They had three mechanisms to hold state bodies to account: monitor; hold a public meeting; or conduct a public examination of public bodies to assess how well they provided services to citizens. This initiative (established by law) offered the potential for active involvement of civil society in the state decision-making process. A formative evaluation of work of public councils showed limited impact. Their remit was advisory and consultative which meant that public bodies could, and did, ignore their findings. Because civil society is weak in Kazakhstan or many NGOs depend on government contracts for their survival, the idea of having an independent voice proved futile. Public councils had no budgets and therefore depended on members funding their own activities. Rather than acting as a guarantor of state transparency and accountability, public councils became a toothless tiger (Knox and Janenova, 2018). If we look at international metrics on corruption, one aspect

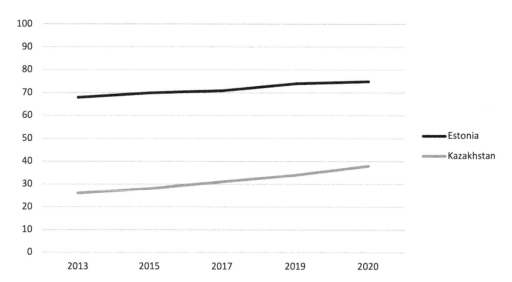

Note: Corruption Perceptions Index. Scale of 0-100 where a 0 equals the highest level of perceived corruption and 100 equals the lowest level of perceived corruption.
Source: Transparency International – Corruption Perceptions Index and Dahlberg et al., 2021.

Figure 21.2   Corruption perceptions index

of public sector integrity, Kazakhstan shows a modest improvement but is well below Estonia (see Figure 21.2).

Open Government

The third priority area identified by the OECD was that Kazakhstan should adopt open government principles and practice. The Kazakhstan government responded with five main electronic platforms to promote greater citizen inclusion in the decision-making process. The *Open Data* portal was introduced under the Law on Access to Information (2015) which requires public bodies to place publicly available data on-line (Kassen, 2017); the *Open Legislation* portal publishes draft bills, laws and standards of public services and permits; the *Open Dialogue* portal provides an opportunity for citizens to interact with government through blogs, internet conferences and polls; the *Open Budgets* portal permits citizens access to statistics on state finances and spending; and, the *Government Assessment* portal allows people access to government agencies' effectiveness ratings, and to express public opinions on their performance (EGov, Kazakhstan, 2021).

All of the above suggests a willingness on the part of the Kazakhstan government to be open, transparent and accountable. However, an evaluation of the open government initiatives suggests a number of flaws. The *Open Legislation* website is replete with legalese, largely impenetrable to the average citizen and therefore attracts limited public attention. This is not to suggest apathy on the part of the public who have voiced their concerns via social media on important legal changes to issues such as an increase in the state retirement age for women, mandatory health insurance, and a radical overhaul of pension entitlements. Similarly with *Open Budgets*. Promises that government bodies would publish their budgets have been met irregularly and in a format which defies comprehension by the average citizen. There is often a lot of meaningless financial data with limited or no explanatory narrative. *Open Dialogue* is entirely dependent on the willingness of ministers or senior officials to build on-line rapport with citizens. These 'conversations' or exchanges tend to be heavily moderated or screened by gatekeepers. In short, there is evidence of bureaucratic obstruction by officials who see open government as disrupting the status quo, particularly opportunities to engage in patronage, nepotism and corruption. This has led some researchers on this topic to describe Kazakhstan as having 'half-open' government or the trappings of transparency with a very different reality on the ground (O'Connor et al., 2019). Thus far Kazakhstan has been unwilling to join the *Open Government Partnership* (OGP), a global initiative comprising governments and civil society of around 80 countries which began in 2011 with the aim of promoting transparency, participation, inclusiveness and accountable governance (Open Government Partnership, 2021). Membership of OGP would require the government of Kazakhstan to make an open government declaration, create actions plans in consultation with civil society organisations, and commit to independent and public evaluation of their progress towards meeting those plans. This appears a step too far for Kazakhstan. Overall, Kazakhstan has shown a marginal decline in the quality of government until 2017 (see Figure 21.3) but a significant improvement since then, most likely related to e-government services.

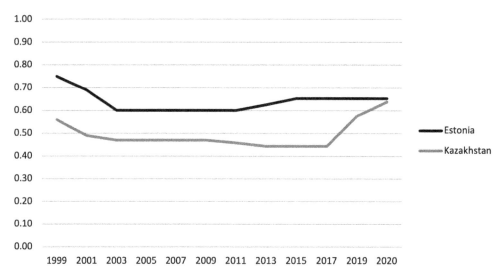

Note: The mean value of the ICRG variables 'Corruption', 'Law and Order' and 'Bureaucracy Quality', scaled 0-1. Higher values indicate higher quality of government.
Source: International Country Risk Guide (ICRG) and Dahlberg et al., 2021: Indicator of Quality of Government.

Figure 21.3   Quality of government

DISCUSSIONS AND CONCLUSION

Looking at the ongoing changes resulting from the OECD-Kazakhstan government partnership, there remain several limitations in terms of the overall goal to become one of the top 30 developed countries by 2050. The OECD has been unable to promote change on several systemic issues concerning public governance, some of which are remnants of Soviet rule, and others characteristics of an authoritarian regime.

Policy documents such as the *People First* model, aimed at improving interactions between citizens and government, are preoccupied with processes, structures and outputs. Kazakhstan is fixated on functional reviews, rearranging the responsibilities of ministries, creating semi-state bodies, or state institutions with special designation approved by the President. This results in a hugely fragmented system of governance predicated on vertical accountability to the President rather than citizen centricity. The Kazakhstan polity is also characterised by frequent ministerial churn which means constant policy changes when new ministers eschew the policies of their predecessors who leave no institutional memory. Policy evaluation does not feature given the brevity of a minister's term of office. Ministers arrive in new positions with an entourage of trusted advisers selected for their loyalty rather than their competency to fulfil a public services mandate.

All systemic changes in governance arrangements are rooted in legislation which can become a straitjacket that limits innovation and risk taking. The success which Kazakhstan has achieved in e-government obscures its neglect of business processes which underpin e-services and those key functions where human capacity is less developed (health, education, social welfare). Claims to have adopted the principles and practice of open government can be seriously challenged. Certainly, the machinery of open government exists but the practice is far from open, evidenced by officials either impeding requests for information or divulging it in a format which is largely incomprehensible. The involvement of the third sector as a possible stakeholder which could hold government to account is limited given the weak capacity of independent NGOs. International metrics (Figures 21.1–21.3 above), even where there is a marginal improvement in government performance, cannot establish a causal link resulting from the OECD partnership. Such changes (the counterfactual) may have happened in any case.

The experience of the OECD-Kazakhstan government partnership may be a good example of isomorphic mimicry (DiMaggio and Powell, 1991) where the government has simply adopted those changes promoted by the OECD. This has led to 'empty mimicry' where countries 'adopt the visible trappings of reforms…without actually implementing them to achieve their intended functions' (Brinkerhoff and Brinkerhoff, 2015: 224, citing Krause, 2013; Andrews et al., 2017). The problem with reading-across best practices of OECD countries to developing countries is that they ignore context – Kazakhstan is a post-Soviet authoritarian state with a significant legacy of that era. Pritchett et al. (2010: 1) described isomorphic mimicry as the 'technique of failure' because governments adopt changes 'that are successful elsewhere to hide their actual dysfunction'. Going further, Krause (2013: 3) argued that developing countries can indulge in gaming with international institutions and, in the extreme, have no intentions of implementing externally promoted reforms which he described as 'institutional ventriloquism'.

This suggestion of empty mimicry and a modest improvement in international metrics, despite a long-standing partnership with the OECD, not surprisingly, is rejected by Kazakhstani officials who argue that it is all about media perceptions:

> Many OECD countries are unaware of current reforms in Kazakhstan; they have a negative bias rather than a professionally neutral view. We need to build a more positive image of Kazakhstan. We are not providing the correct information to the media. There is a perception of Kazakhstan as a former Soviet Union country, a 'stan' country. When OECD countries came to Almaty in November (2017) for Eurasia week, they could see significant differences between media news and reality. (Cited in Knox, 2021: 129)

So why then does the Kazakhstan government engage with and spend significant funds working with the OECD if it is merely 'empty mimicry'? In its bid to achieve international legitimacy, inextricably linked to becoming one of the top 30 developed countries, the Kazakhstan government sees membership of the OECD as an important part of their global strategy. Hence, we witness all the rhetoric of the OECD reform agenda but only partial implementation. Even though key strategic documents (such as *People First*) herald significant OECD-style changes, these can be thwarted by officials whose vested interests may be damaged as a result of their implementation – open government, for example, could expose corruption. Notwithstanding the implementation deficit, Kazakhstan is becoming impatient with the OECD as the proposed date of application for membership (2025) looms large. Kazakhstan might be described as adopting a Janus-faced approach to public sector reforms: the outward impression to the OECD and international community that one is embracing its recommendations (tick-box style) and the inward reality that some of these changes are merely tokenistic. Radical reforms may challenge the status quo and disrupt political stability. A strong and independent NGO sector could, for example, build on ethnic and political tensions and mobilise against the state as witnessed in neighbouring Kyrgyzstan with the 'tulip revolution' in 2010 and, more recently, violent unrest following the presidential elections in 2020. Given Kazakhstan's long association with the OECD and its 'apprenticeship' in working with and within various OECD committees, the government is now exerting strong pressure to be admitted as a member. It has 'paid its dues', seemingly adopted OECD reforms, and yearns for the international legitimacy that membership would bestow. All that remains is an OECD entry pass to the global community.

REFERENCES

Andrews, M., Pritchett, L. and Woolcock, M. (2017) Looking Like a State: The Seduction of Isomorphic Mimicry. In *Building State Capability: Evidence, Analysis, Action* (pp.29–52) Oxford University Press.

Bhuiyan, S.H. (2011) Trajectories of e-government Implementation for Public Sector Service Delivery in Kazakhstan. *International Journal of Public Administration*, 34(9), 604–15.

Brinkerhoff, D. and Brinkerhoff, J. (2015) Public Sector Management Reform in Developing Countries: Perspectives Beyond NPM Orthodoxy. *Public Administration and Development*, 35, 222–37.

Dahlberg, S., Sundström, A., Holmberg, S., Rothstein, B., Alvarado Pachon, N. and Dalli, C.M. (2021) The Quality of Government Basic Dataset, Version Jan21. *University of Gothenburg: The Quality of Government Institute*, 10.

DiMaggio, P. and Powell, W. (1991) *The New Institutionalism in Organizational Analysis*. Chicago, IL: University of Chicago Press.

EGov. Kazakhstan (2021) What is Open Government? Accessible at https://egov.kz/cms/en/articles/communications/open_gov accessed 23 April 2023.

Freedom House (2021) Democracy Under Siege accessible at: https://freedomhouse.org/report/freedom-world/2021/democracy-under-siege accessed 23 April 2023.

Fund for Peace (2021) Fragile States Index. Accessible at: https://fragilestatesindex.org accessed 23 April 2023.

Hossain, F., Kumasey, A.S., Rees, C.J., and Mamman, A. (2020) Public Service Ethics, Values and Spirituality in Developing and Transitional Countries: Challenges and Opportunities. *Public Administration and Development*, 40(3), 147–55.

International Country Risk Guide (ICRG) accessible at: https://www.prsgroup.com/explore-our-products/international-country-risk-guide/ accessed 23 April 2023.

Janenova, S. and Knox, C. (2020) Combatting Corruption in Kazakhstan: A Role for Ethics Commissioners? *Public Administration and Development*, 40(3), 186–95.

Kazakevitch, G. (2020) 'A Taxonomy of Post-communist Economies after 30 years of Reforms'. In A. Akimov and G. Kazakevitch (eds), *30 Years since the Fall of the Berlin Wall: Turns and Twists in Economies, Politics, and Societies in the Post-Communist Countries* (pp. 13–29). Springer.

Kazakhstan Economic Research Institute (2021) Kazakhstan and OECD. Accessible at: https://economy.kz/en/OESR/Kazahstan_i_OESR/ accessed 23 April 2023.

Kassen, M. (2017) Open Data in Kazakhstan: Incentives, Implementation and Challenges. *Information Technology & People*.

Kazakhstan Presidential Administration (2021) *The Concept of Public Administration Development in Kazakhstan until 2030: building a 'human-centred' model – People First*. Office of the President, Nur-Sultan.

Knox, C. and Janenova, S. (2018) Public Councils in Kazakhstan: A Case of Emergent Participative Democracy? *Central Asian Survey*, 37(2), 305–21.

Knox, C. and Janenova, S. (2019a) The e-government Paradox in Post-Soviet Countries. *International Journal of Public Sector Management*, 32(6), 600–615.

Knox, C. and Janenova, S. (2019b) Public Management Reforms: One-Stop Shops to Digital Government. In *Oxford Research Encyclopedia of Politics*, Oxford University Press.

Knox, C. (2021) Development Evaluation in Authoritarian States: A Case from Kazakhstan. *Development Policy Review*, *39*(1), 121–34.

Krause, P. (2013) *Of Institutions and Butterflies: Is Isomorphism in Developing Countries Necessarily a Bad Thing?* Background Note. London: Overseas Development Institute.

Massimov, K. (2015) OECD bolsters relationship with Kazakhstan – Signs Kazakhstan Country Programme Agreement accessible at: https://www.oecd.org/newsroom/oecd-bolsters-relationship -with-kazakhstan-signs-kazakhstan-country-programme-agreement.htm accessed 23 April 2023.

Mukhamadiyeva, G.N., Mukaldyeva, G., Karasheva, Z.T., Khamzin, A.S., Buribayev, Y.A., and Khamzina, Z.A. (2017) Modernization of Social Security System Legal Regulation in Kazakhstan: Experience and Standards of the OECD Members Implementation. *Journal of Advanced Research in Law and Economics*, *8*, 2498.

O'Connor, K., Janenova, S. and Knox, C. (2019) Open Government in Authoritarian Regimes. *International Review of Public Policy*, *1*(1: 1), 65–82.

O'Connor, K., Knox, C., and Janenova, S. (2021) Bureaucrats, Authoritarianism, and Role Conceptions. *Review of Public Personnel Administration*, *41*(2), 358–83.

OECD (2016) *Multi-dimensional Review of Kazakhstan: Volume 1. Initial Assessment*, OECD Development Pathways, OECD Publishing, Paris, https://doi.org/10.1787/9789264246768-en accessed 23 April 2023.

OECD (2017) *Reforming Kazakhstan: progress, challenges and opportunities*. OECD Publishing, Paris. https://www.oecd.org/eurasia/countries/OECD-Eurasia-Reforming-Kazakhstan-EN.pdf accessed 23 April 2023.

OECD (2018) *Enhancing Competitiveness in Central Asia*, Competitiveness and Private Sector Development, OECD Publishing, Paris, https://doi.org/10.1787/9789264288133-en accessed 23 April 2023.

OECD (2019) Making OECD Standards and Policies Count on a Global Scale. Report by the Secretary General to Ministers on OECD Global Relations. Accessible at: https://www.oecd.org/mcm/2019/ documents/C-MIN(2019)11.en.pdf accessed 23 April 2023.

Open Government Partnership (2021) About Open Government Partnership. Accessible at: https://www .opengovpartnership.org/about/ accessed 23 April 2023.

Pelizzo, R. and Knox, C. (2021) 'Sobriety, Human Dignity and Public Morality': Ethical Standards in Kazakhstan. *Public Money & Management*, 1–9.

Pritchett, L., Woolcock, M. and Andrews, M. (2010) Capability Traps? The Mechanisms of Persistent Implementation Failure. *Center for Global Development Working Paper*, 234.

Saiymova, M., Yesbergen, R., Demeuova, G., Bolatova, B., Taskarina, B., Ibrasheva, A. and Saparaliyev, D. (2018) The Knowledge-based Economy and Innovation Policy in Kazakhstan: Looking at Key Practical Problems. *Academy of Strategic Management Journal*, *17*(6), 1–11.

Sarmurzin, Y., Amanzhol, N., Toleubayeva, K., Zhunusova, M. and Amanova, A. (2021) The Impact of OECD Research on the Education System of Kazakhstan. *Asia Pacific Education Review*, 1–10.

Smailov, A. (2021) Government Discusses Issues of Cooperation between Kazakhstan and OECD, 12 October. Accessible at: https://primeminister.kz/en/news/ukimette-kazakstannyn-eydu-men -yntymaktastygynyn-maseleleri-talkylandy-1293345 accessed 23 April 2023.

Suleimenov, T. (2017) Kazakhstan is getting closer to OECD membership. *EURACTIV Media network*, 19 October.

Suleimenova, G., Kapoguzov, E., Kabizhan, N. and Kadyrova, M. (2019) Performance Evaluation of the Government Agencies of Kazakhstan. *The NISPAcee Journal of Public Administration and Policy, XI*, 2, 171–98.

Sullivan, C.J. (2018) Kazakhstan at a Crossroads. *Asia Policy*, *13*(2), 121–36.

Transparency International – Corruption Perceptions Index. Accessible at: https://www.transparency .org/en/cpi/2020/index/nzl accessed 23 April 2023.

United Nations (2020) E-Government Development Index. Accessible at: https://publicadministration .un.org/egovkb/en-us/About/Overview/-E-Government-Development-Index accessed 23 April 2023.

World Bank (2021) Kazakhstan Country Report accessible at https://www.worldbank.org/en/country/ kazakhstan accessed 23 April 2023.

Yuvitsa, N. (2021) Local Government and Self-government in the CIS and Kazakhstan. *Journal of Public Policy and Administration*, *5*(3), 84.

Zhetpisbayev, B.A., Baisalova, G.T., Shadiyev, K.K., Khamzin, A.S., Buribayev, Y.A. and Khamzina, Z.A. (2017) Legal Support of the Process of Kazakhstan Accession to the OECD: Potential for Improving Quality of Individual's Labour Rights Regulation. *Journal of Advanced Research on Law and Economics*, *8*, 2292.

PART V

EMERGING ISSUES

22. Public governance

Leslie A. Pal

The GOV directorate at the OECD is responsible for 'public governance', which it defines as supporting countries 'to ensure that the way they are governed and the way policies are designed and delivered supports democracy and fosters prosperity for all' (OECD, 2021c: 98). Put this way, it conceivably embraces almost everything about government, governance and public policy, from political party competition and public administration ('the way they are governed'), to economic, social and environmental policies ('the way policies are designed and delivered'), to labour markets, trade, investment, science and technology ('fosters prosperity for all'). It could be a directorate about everything.

Obviously, it is not. The evolution and constraints of its mandate have been determined by several factors. One is the origins and inspiration of the OECD itself – it was designed to be about *economic* cooperation and development, and in its early days (the 1960s; see Chapter 2 in this volume) there was no concept of 'governance' in the broad sense that we understand it today, and even the link between effective public administration and economic prosperity was underappreciated. An early challenge was simply to establish public management (the predecessor to GOV was PUMA) as a legitimate focus for the OECD. Another constraint was how far the definition of 'public management' or 'public governance' should go. It was an unwritten rule that the OECD should be silent about the political affairs of its member states, it could not applaud or condemn governments themselves, or political systems as such (though the rhetorical commitment was always to democracy and public participation, even when member states were thinly veiled autocracies, as Portugal, Spain, and Turkey were in the early days). So 'public governance' had a hard limit in focusing on 'management' – on public administration. In light of these constraints, public governance effectively came to mean public management.

Governance, in the sense of the importance of well-functioning public institutions, increasingly came to be seen after the 1990s as a key ingredient in political stability as well as in economic success (Arndt and Oman, 2008; World Bank, 1983, 1997). The core business of the GOV directorate was secured (especially with the extensive work required to support the EU-accession of former Soviet central and eastern European states), but no bureaucracy can subsist only on its core business. It has to renew and refresh, and expansion of mandate after 2000 had to deal with the constraints of being 'a-political' and not trenching on other policy areas already staked out by other directorates. The result has been a jumbled mix of building on the early core (e.g., integrity and anti-corruption in public administration), expanding into niches (e.g., gender mainstreaming, justice administration, innovation), and leveraging 'horizontal' fields like sustainability (see Chapter 25 on the concept of sustainable development). Moreover, the work on the core is often marked by statements of the obvious (central government agencies should be more coherent and coordinated), or misplaced approbation (celebrating government 'innovation' against the backdrop of the stunning ineptitude in tackling COVID). The work on the niches is just that, niches. The bigger picture on the fractured fortunes of western governance, pandemic-inspired securitization, or the rise of authoritarian brands of democracy, is completely absent. Whereas 30 years ago the OECD could be seen as leading global debates on governance and public management, today it is eclipsed by Davos, the Think 20 (a loose international network of think tanks supporting the G20 in solving global challenges), and the better public policy schools.

This chapter traces the history of the institutional and conceptual foundations of public governance within the OECD, with illustrations of its contemporary applications.

ORIGINS AND EVOLUTION OF PUBLIC GOVERNANCE IN THE OECD[1]

As Article 1 of its 1961 founding Convention states, the OECD was created to promote polices to achieve economic growth and employment, and to contribute to 'sound economic expansion' and particularly to the expansion of world trade. This was part of a broader postwar 'neoliberal' project to support and protect the expansion of global trade and investment (Schmeltzer, 2016; Slobodian, 2018), and if there was any appreciation of appropriate governance and policies, it was with respect to economic policy and efficient management of the economy. In 1961 there was no directorate for governance, or indeed any focus at all on what we now conventionally assume to be the core capacities of government. However, after the experience of re-building postwar western European governments and economies, the drafters of the OECD Convention appreciated the challenges of development for less advanced economies. To support this cooperation and to provide guidance, the OECD in 1961 incorporated a Development Assistance Committee (DAC, which continues to coordinate donor efforts in official overseas development aid, see Chapter 12 in this volume), and a Technical Cooperation Committee (TECO). TECO was designed to provide technical economic advice, but more importantly to manage development projects that had been held over from the OECD's predecessor, the Organisation for European Economic Cooperation (OEEC, created in 1947 to manage the Marshall Plan). Under the OEEC, a suite of operational grants grew through the 1950s for southern Italy, Greece, Turkey, Yugoslavia, Spain, Iceland and Portugal. Italy and Iceland 'graduated' from this assistance by the mid-1960s, and the OECD (through TECO) found itself supporting the rest with programs in economic planning, agriculture, and industry; science; education; institutes of statistics; civil service management; irrigation, fruit and vegetable production; and even sheep-breeding.

TECO was held in low regard in the newly created OECD, partly because it was about unfocused and scattered 'operations' and technical assistance (which had a tinge of development work with poor countries, whereas the OECD's membership at the time comprised the richest and most developed economies on earth), and its 'clients' were either military dictatorships or autocracies (even while being members of the OECD). For these reasons, TECO was almost disbanded in the early 1970s, but was saved by a combination of the collapse of its client regimes between 1971 and 1975 and their imperfect conversion to democracies, and a re-focusing of 'technical cooperation' on public administration. Greece, Spain, Portugal and Turkey suddenly needed to rebuild their states as fully functioning, democratic members of the OECD. The OECD could oblige by supporting their public administrative capacities,

---

[1]   This section draws on Pal (2012: chapt. 2).

ones that cut across single ministries (e.g., agriculture), and which would in any case be the natural partners of other, subject-area focused directorates in the OECD. The emerging 'clients' for a reinvented TECO would be centres of government, such as cabinet offices, public service commissions and training institutes, audit agencies, ministries of finance and treasuries. To build its expertise and stake its ground, TECO held its first international symposium on public management in Madrid in February 1979. Conferences and symposia on governance and administration today happen almost monthly somewhere on the planet, but this was a first effort and unique in supporting the notion – radical at the time – that there were universal principles and practices of effective and efficient public management which could (carefully) be transferred and copied around the world. This is now the OECD's well-worn trademark of 'good (amended from 'best') practices' and 'lessons learned'. The 1979 symposium launched a unique research program and projects around so-called 'horizontal' public management themes: 'TECO produced a remarkable and pioneering series of publications on service delivery, well anticipating – and probably stimulating – national reviews of service standards and the importance of citizen-centred services' (Pal, 2012: 42). These efforts were sufficiently successful that by 1991 TECO (which had been merely a 'committee' in OECD parlance) was transformed into a directorate on Public Management (PUMA), the first new directorate created in the OECD since its founding. Just as crucial, it was now acknowledged that economic development (the core focus of the OECD), depended crucially on efficient and effective public management. A 1991 report entitled 'Serving the Economy' asserted that surveys of public management across OECD members showed a shared understanding of common problems, as well as broadly similar directions of change and reform (OECD, 1991). The theme of 'common challenges' and 'common directions of reform' was to become the foundation of the OECD's role as diagnostician, advisor, and institutional therapist. The report went on to describe the vital contributions of the public sector to economic development:

> The public sector, acting on behalf of political authorities, affects every part of the economy and society. Its effectiveness conditions, to a large extent, economic development and sustains political and social cohesion. The public sector is responsible for the legal and administrative environment in which private business activity takes place. It affects production decisions and costs through a myriad of regulatory controls, services, transfers, taxes and tax reliefs. It alters patterns of demand by redistributing income. It is also a large purchaser in the private economy and thereby affects overall resource allocation. It influences national economic efficiency, the rate of technological and organisational innovation, the direction and speed of structural adjustment, and the cost, to users, of unpriced resources like the environment. (OECD, *Serving the Economy Better* (1991): 7; as cited in Pal (2012: 43))

PUMA's focus thus became public management reform in aid of better economic performance, a focus on the contribution of sound management of human and financial resources in the public sector, efficient regulatory regimes, informed (today we would say 'evidence-based') decision-making, and enhanced coordination and capacity in the 'centres of government'. The transition from TECO to PUMA occurred (and was partly driven by) the collapse of the former Soviet republics in central and Eastern Europe in 1988–89 (principally Hungary, Poland, East Germany, Czechoslovakia, Bulgaria, and Romania), and then by the collapse of the Soviet Union itself in 1991. The OECD as such had no mandate for Europe, but it was clear that eventually some or all of the central and Eastern European states would seek EU accession. To prepare them, the EU (as primary funder) and the OECD jointly sponsored an OECD initiative, housed in PUMA, called SIGMA (Support for Improvement in Governance and

Management), with programs initially for Bulgaria, the Czech and Slovak republics, Hungary, Poland and Romania. SIGMA was the first program in the OECD to use the term 'governance', and it focused on several key areas: policy-making capacity (including the quality of legislation, financial management); cohesion and coordination in centres of government; rule of law; and creation of a neutral, efficient, competent, and ethical public service.

By 1995, through a combination of this internal organizational evolution, its global networks of experts and researchers, and its on-the-ground experience in public sector reform, the OECD achieved a prominent and leading role in global debates on public management. It needs to be noted that the OECD had been one of the first international organizations into the 'governance' field, and certainly in the field of public management (almost helping to define it as a global community of debate and discussion). Moreover, at the time, it was extremely difficult to know what other governments were doing or how their public sectors were organized, and the OECD had the advantage of being able to draw on data supplied by its members, the richest and most 'advanced' in the world. Not surprisingly, its scope and influence were somewhat exaggerated in the scholarly literature (Hansen, Salskov-Iversen and Bislev, 2002; Premfors, 1998, 2006; Sahlin-Andersson, 2000), particularly its leadership in a public sector reform movement or agenda known as 'new public management' (Barzelay, 2001; Christensen and Laegreid, 2001; Lane, 2000). PUMA/OECD published two leading reports on 'modernizing' public management, the first in 1995 entitled *Governance in Transition* (OECD, 1995), and again in 2005, entitled *Modernising Government* (OECD, 2005) that cemented its reputation for leading debates, but also highlighted its approach to, and definition of, 'public governance'.

Governance in Transition was surveying a bleak landscape of collapsed empire (the Soviet Union), fiscal crisis, economic turbulence and falling public trust. It argued that the global pressures for change were so deep and radical that only deep and radical change in public management institutions would suffice to meet the challenge. In this, the OECD was calling for profound (NPM-styled) reform of traditional public bureaucracies. It called for a focus on performance and results, efficiency in delivery and quality of service, and decentralization. The report described reforms in the following areas: devolution of authority; performance and accountability measures; competition and choice among services; human resources management; information technology; regulation; and central coordination. It claimed to see a broad trend among its member states (the survey was anchored in member state experiences) toward this new-styled NPM governance, and it encouraged and supported that development.

Modernising Government in 2005 was similar in tone but emphasized different themes and in some respects signalled reversals and re-thinking. The Soviet collapse was now history, but new crises had taken its place: budget pressures, continued declines in public trust, higher demands for public services, technology. The public sector across the OECD had to continue to reform, but in a more nuanced and less mechanistic and managerial way. Organizational culture mattered; ethics mattered; collaboration with civil society mattered; openness, transparency and accountability mattered. There was greater acceptance of the influence of context on modernizing agendas, that the lessons of reform had to be applied carefully and calibrated to national needs and traditions. This emphasis on context and different national paths in the reform journey echoed the new emphasis in the OECD as of 2000 on outreach and expansion (OECD, 2000). This was tied to the appointment of a new Secretary-General, Donald Johnston, in 1996.

As part of an internal housekeeping and re-focusing exercise under Johnston, PUMA's role and scope was changed so that eventually, in 2002, it became the GOV directorate, mandated to support Johnston's agenda of enhanced engagement with non-OECD countries, and the eventual accession of new members. As a result, GOV had to consciously define its accession criteria, and thereby what it meant by the public sector, public management, and ultimately, good governance. This yielded a 2007 report on the 'Building Blocks' of public sector governance. The 'building blocks' consisted of: (1) budget practices and procedures; (2) human resource management; (3) integrity in the public sector; (4) internal and external reporting; (5) e-government readiness; (6) centre of government; (7) management of regulatory quality; and (8) multilevel governance. Each of these was elaborated with technical goals as well as with a sketch of institutional arrangements to achieve them. As an example, the fourth building block of 'internal and external reporting: open government' had the goals of transparency, accessibility, responsiveness, and inclusiveness. Institutional arrangements to achieve these goals included laws on access to information, publication of annual reports, client or service charters, e-government arrangements to ensure 24/7 access, tools and procedures for public consultation, and provision of incentives for people to interact with government. Each building block was accompanied by equally if not more elaborate benchmarks (OECD, 2007).

By roughly 2010, the result of the evolution described above was what we might call a 'core' of public governance preoccupations and priorities for the GOV directorate and its associated committees: (1) at the highest and most abstract (and difficult to define precisely) a commitment to liberal democracy and capitalist market economy, (2) the building blocks (and attendant requirements) of budgets, centres of government, human resources, integrity and accountability, regulatory quality, multilevel governance, and e-government, (3) anti-corruption in taxation and regulation, and general integrity in the public sector and in the public sector-private market interface, (4) transparency, openness and collaboration with the general public and stakeholders. This is a mix of the anatomical and procedural features of governments (e.g., central agency coherence, quality of taxation and regulation), quality indicators (e.g., values such as integrity, ethics, and openness), and connections to civil society and market actors (collaboration and consultation). Note what was left out: the military, the courts and rule of law, substantive policy areas such as social policy, education, or the environment (which are under other directorates), and the 'political' – that is, constitutions, elections, and political parties. All of these could plausibly be listed under 'public governance' but for organizational and prudential reasons, were not part of the GOV portfolio circa 2010.

This conventional, core mandate continued to evolve over the next decade, abetted by a trio of rationales. The first is the potential scope of the master concept of governance itself. To the extent that 'governance' is necessarily part of the GOV mandate in some broader systemic sense (i.e., the governance of the nation), it can also apply to the governance of sub-sectors and of policies and programs. And so, the GOV directorate can legitimately pose questions about the governance of health care or climate change. The second is the 'quality' of governance, which can be a channel for ethical and representational considerations, well beyond efficiency and effectiveness narrowly defined. Hence, GOV can pose questions about the quality of consultations, the quality of representation of minorities and hence of discrimination, the quality of political representation, and the quality of 'access' to public sector institutions. The third concept is 'results' of public sector governance, as expressed by citizen satisfaction, but also in empirical outcomes such as social and economic inequality.

PUBLIC GOVERNANCE: CORES, NICHES, AND HORIZONTALS

GOV's self-defined 'flagship of OECD work on public governance' is *Government at a Glance* (OECD, 2021b), and it illustrates the range of preoccupations that come under the mandate of 'how public administrations function and perform'. Its own summary of the contents shows the interpolation of what we called the 'core' with the expanded foci that come from governance, quality, and results:

> The 2021 edition includes indicators on public finances and public employment, the latter with a special focus on the representation of different gender and age groups in public administrations and the political sphere. Data on government processes include budgeting practices, strategic human resources management, regulatory policy, public procurement, digital government, and responsibilities of centres of government including on public communication. New process indicators for this edition cover public sector integrity, infrastructure governance, and open government. Indicators of government results include trust in public institutions, political efficacy, inequality reduction, and measures of access to, responsiveness, quality of, and citizen satisfaction with education, health and justice sectors. (OECD, 2021b: 3)

In the opening 'editorial', the Director of GOV naturally refers to the pandemic as the biggest shock that OECD countries had undergone since World War II, and notes that one of the biggest lessons of the crisis 'is that governments will need to respond to future crises at speed and scale while safeguarding trust and transparency – and, indeed, the very underpinnings of democracy' (OECD, 2021b: 5). Quick mention is made of trust, transparency, and resilience, with a pivot to climate change as an element of pandemic economic recovery funds and the need for greater 'green governance.' Maintaining trust and transparency is the rationale for examining three new areas in *Government at a Glance*: (1) mis-information and dis-information; (2) fairness, inclusion and diversity in the public sector workforce and in lobbying legislation; (3) planning, foresight and data sharing in preparation for future crises. The report's 14 chapters expressed this combination of 'core' public governance in the sense of core public administration – chapters on public finance, public employment (with heavy emphasis on gender equality, understood as the representation of women), centres of government, budgeting, human resource management, regulatory governance, public procurement, open government, and digital government – and the newer emphases, with chapters on 'governance of infrastructure', 'public sector integrity' (anti-corruption and lobbying), and results (a chapter on 'core government results' which includes trust, income redistribution, and rule of law; and a chapter on 'serving citizens' with sections on access to education, health care, and justice).

Government at a Glance represents an evolving 'core' of public governance preoccupations in the OECD, but the work of GOV also includes niches and horizontal fields, fuelled by the expansionary rationales mentioned above, not to mention the increasing competition in the governance field from other international organizations like the G20 and the World Bank. Three illustrative 'niches' are gender mainstreaming, public sector innovation, and mis-information.

The OECD's work on gender-mainstreaming is anchored in its 2015 *Recommendation of the Council on Gender Equality in Public Life* (OECD, 2016). Tellingly, the title refers to 'public life' and not to 'public administration' or even to 'public management'. Even as a recommendation (without the full force of international law), it has lofty ambitions. It encourages a 'whole of society' approach to addressing gender stereotypes, and encourages women to participate in politics, something that goes well beyond the traditional boundaries of 'public administration'. Gender-sensitive programs and policies are recommended throughout government, with accompanying statistics and indicators to support implementation and monitoring. 'Gender equality institutions' are to be placed at the 'highest possible level' of government, and gender-based budgeting is to be introduced. Independent institutions such as 'Independent Commissions, Supreme Audit Institutions, Ombuds Offices,' and advisory bodies should have strengthened capacity 'to monitor the implementation of gender equality strategies, integrate gender issues in policy-making, and facilitate regular reporting, audits and measurement'. Parliaments and parliamentary committees are called upon to support gender equality by integrating gender perspectives into their practices, legislation and budgets. The *Recommendation* goes yet further into the political realm by suggesting 'gender diversity' in parliamentary bodies, and including 'disclosure requirements, quotas, voluntary targets, parity laws, alternating the sexes on the party list and linking gender ratios in political parties to their access to public funding'. Building on the *Recommendation*, the OECD has extended its scope to the justice system (in a program of work on Gender Equality in Judiciary) and to work with MENA region parliaments.

The OECD launched its Observatory on Public Sector Innovation (OPSI) in 2013, and in principle it represents a sharp alternative to the bad old days of NPM. Instead of a book of standard recipes inspired by alleged private sector efficiency, OPSI curates hundreds of contributions of cases by member states and others under dozens of categories, from anti-corruption to blockchain and service design. In good OECD fashion, it offers toolkits, primers, country studies, and trends reports. The crowning achievement over a five-year period of consultations and incremental agreements (another signature OECD technique of starting with kernels of ideas and ending up – often years later – with legal instruments and global standards) is the *Declaration on Public Sector Innovation*. The adherents are mostly the OECD members themselves, but they have embraced five principles and associated actions (it should be noted that the OPSI is also funded by the European Union Horizon 2020 program). The principles are to: (1) embrace and enhance innovation within the public sector; (2) encourage and equip public servants to innovate; (3) cultivate partnerships; (4) support exploration, iteration and testing; and (5) diffuse lessons and share practices (OECD, 2019a).

Among the most recent additions to the public governance portfolio has been work on reinforcing democracy through combatting mis-information. The dark backdrop to this initiative was the Trump presidency, the attack on the Washington Capitol in January 2021, and more recently, vaccine hesitancy and resistance during the pandemic. In this the OECD is simply catching up to wider public angst on the quality of democracy in the social media age, and to initiatives undertaken by other international organizations (the UN General Assembly in September 2021, for example, had a 'Summit for Information and Democracy'). But it is also building on its own earlier work on trust in public institutions. Several reports have been produced, including *Enhancing Public Trust in COVID-19 Vaccination: The Role of Governments* (OECD, 2021a), *Governance Responses to Disinformation: How Open Government Principles Can Inform Policy Options* (Matasick, Alfonsi and Bellantoni, 2020), and *Combatting COVID-19 Disinformation on Online Platforms* (OECD, 2020). A more synoptic report was due for publication at the end of 2021, *International Report on Public Communication: The Global Context and the Way Forward*. With these reports, GOV finds itself commenting on health policy communication, social media, and what it calls 'information ecosystems.' All of these come under the wider umbrella of 'Reinforcing Democracy.'

The prime example of 'horizontal' work on public governance is the program on Policy Coherence for Sustainable Development (PCSD). Like its work on gender equality in public life, this initiative is also grounded in a legal instrument, the *Recommendation of the Council on Policy Coherence for Sustainable Development* (OECD, 2019b). The 17 *Sustainable Development Goals* (SDGs) are part of the UN's *Agenda 2030*, an ambitious set of international commitments agreed to unanimously at the UN in 2015, encompassing almost every conceivable policy area. In principle they are 'indivisible', and so require a 'whole of government' approach. Adherents are encouraged to develop a strategic vision for integrated achievement of the SDGs, and in particular 'so that commitment to PCSD outlives electoral cycles and changes in government, cabinet compositions or government programmes.' GOV helpfully has produced toolkits for self-assessment, guides on strengthening institutional mechanisms, and compendia of good practices.

CONCLUSIONS

Public governance in the first 30 years of the OECD's existence coalesced somewhat narrowly around public administration, the sound management of human and financial resources, central agency coordination, effective regulatory and taxation regimes, reporting and accountability, and e-government. There was a tacit agreement that the OECD obviously was committed to liberal democracy, but since some of the early OECD members (e.g., Spain, Turkey) were less than liberal and less than democratic, the directorates responsible for public governance avoided commentary on the political and social sphere (parties, elections, human rights, equality). The various directorates (TECO, PUMA, and then GOV) in that period had a singular advantage in access to member states, their data and their prestige, as well as the convening power of an international organization in the pre-internet age.

In the last 30 years, the definition of public governance has expanded considerably, if somewhat incoherently, in the OECD. Public administration has been expanded to embrace 'governance', and 'governance' has been framed to include the management and delivery of services such as health, education, and justice. Expanding on the high-level commitment to liberal democracy, public governance expanded to include the 'quality' of governance, in terms of equity, diversity, and inclusion, the holy trinity of contemporary cosmopolitan liberalism. And the early emphasis on performance, which originally was about internal efficiency of public sector workers and managers, has come to include the results of key public services such as health and education, as well as access to those services and even to the justice system.

The OECD's public governance portfolio now consists of the original public management core (or building blocks), an assorted mix of niches (gender, justice, innovation, misinformation), and some horizontal 'policy coherence' flagships such as the PCSD. It once tiptoed around the political, but now forthrightly proclaims on political party financing, judicial appointments, and information ecosystems. Ironically, while the mandate and scope of public governance in the OECD has expanded considerably in the last 30 years, the portfolio is less coherent and the OECD is less prominent as a leader in international debates. It no longer has a monopoly on data, and even *Government at a Glance* is not much more than an aggregation of readily available sources. Its framing of gender equality in the binaries of biological assignment seems quaint in an age of fluid identities and intersectionality. The G20 easily musters more intellectual capital through its 'Think20' engagement group than the OECD directorate can mobilize internally (Pal, 2020; Pal and Spence, 2021). The most cited policy tracker on government responses to COVID-19 did not come from the OECD, but from Oxford's Blavatink School of Public Policy (Blavatnik School, 2020). And on some of the most challenging governance issues of our time – authoritarianism, the surveillance state, the appalling incompetence of most governments in the face of the pandemic ('innovations' in ineptitude), the possible rise of a 'Beijing model' of governance – GOV is sadly silent.

REFERENCES

Arndt, C. and Oman, C. (2008). *The Politics of Governance Ratings*. Working Paper MGSoG/2008/WP003. Maastricht: Maastricht University, Maastricht Graduate School of Governance.

Barzelay, M. (2001). *The New Public Management: Improving Research and Policy Dialogue*. Berkeley: University of California Press.

Blavatnik School. (2020). *Coronavirus Government Response Tracker*. Available at: https://www.bsg.ox.ac.uk/research/research-projects/coronavirus-government-response-tracker accessed 24 April 2023.

Christensen, T. and Laegreid, P. (2001). New Public Management: The Effects of Contractualism and Devolution on Political Control. *Public Management Review, 3*(1), 73–94.

Hansen, H.K., Salskov-Iversen, D. and Bislev, S. (2002). Discursive Globalization: Transnational Discourse Communities and New Public Management. In M. Ougaard and R. Higgott (Eds.), *Towards a Global Polity* (pp. 107–24). London: Routledge.

Lane, J.-E. (2000). *New Public Management*. London: Routledge.

Matasick, C., Alfonsi, C. and Bellantoni, A. (2020). Governance Responses to Disinformation: How Open Government Principles can Inform Policy Options. *OECD Working Papers on Public Governance, 39*. doi:https://doi.org/10.1787/d6237c85-en accessed 24 April 2023.

OECD. (1991). *Serving the Economy Better*. Occasional Papers on Public Management. Paris: OECD.

OECD. (1995). *Governance in Transition: Public Management Reforms in OECD Countries*. Paris: OECD.

OECD. (2000). *Governance Outreach Initiative: Progress Report and Next Steps*. Paris: OECD.

OECD. (2005). *Modernising Government: The Way Forward*. Paris: OECD.

OECD. (2007). *A General Procedure for Future Accessions*. Paris: OECD.

OECD. (2016). *Recommendation of the Council on Gender Equality in Public Life*. Paris: OECD. Available at: http://dx.doi.org/10.1787/9789264252820-en accessed 24 April 2023.

OECD. (2019a). *Declaration on Public Sector Innovation*. Paris: OECD. Available at: https://oecd-opsi.org/publications/oecd-declaration-on-public-sector-innovation/ accessed 24 April 2023.

OECD. (2019b). *Recommendation of the Council on Policy Coherence for Sustainable Development*. Paris: OECD. Available at: https://www.oecd.org/governance/pcsd/recommendation-on-policy-coherence-for-sustainable-development-eng.pdf accessed 24 April 2023.

OECD. (2020). *Combatting COVID-19 Disinformation on Online Platforms*. Paris: OECD. Available at: https://www.oecd.org/coronavirus/policy-responses/combatting-covid-19-disinformation-on-online-platforms-d854ec48/ accessed 24 April 2023.

OECD. (2021a). *Enhancing Public Trust in COVID-19 Vaccination: The Role of Governments*. Paris: OECD. Available at: https://www.oecd.org/coronavirus/policy-responses/enhancing-public-trust-in-covid-19-vaccination-the-role-of-governments-eae0ec5a/ accessed 24 April 2023.

OECD. (2021b). *Government at a Glance 2021*. Paris: OECD. Available at: https://www.oecd-ilibrary.org/docserver/1c258f55-en.pdf?expires=1634984917&id=id&accname=guest&checksum=F960BF421CCCDB5B8DDDF8E328DFD062 accessed 24 April 2023.

OECD. (2021c). *Secretary-General's Report to Ministers, 2021*. Paris: OECD. Available at: https://www.oecd-ilibrary.org/docserver/8cd95b77-en.pdf?expires=1632564512&id=id&accname=guest&checksum=6FA0A9C4E9C623494A773004F6AF0731 accessed 24 April 2023.

Pal, L.A. (2012). *Frontiers of Governance: The OECD and Global Public Management Reform.* Houndmills, Basingstoke: Palgrave Macmillan.

Pal, L.A. (2020). Twilight of hegemony: The T-20 and the defensive re-imagining of global order. In P. Dutkiewicz, T. Casier, and J.A. Scholte (eds), *Hegemony and World Order: Reimagining Power in Global Politics* (pp. 148–63). London: Routledge.

Pal, L.A. and Spence, J. (2021). Defending the Realm: Knowledge Networks, Regime Maintenance and Policy Transfer. In O.P. d. Oliveira (ed), *Handbook of Policy Transfer, Diffusion and Circulation* (pp. 237–56). Cheltenham: Edward Elgar.

Premfors, R. (1998). Reshaping The Democratic State: Swedish Experiences in a Comparative Perspective. *Public Administration, 76*(1), 141–59.

Premfors, R. (2006). Modernising Government: The Way Forward: A comment. *International Review of Administrative Sciences, 72*(3), 333–35.

Sahlin-Andersson, K. (2000). Arenas as standardizers. In N. Brunsson and B. Jacobsson (eds), *A World of Standards* (pp. 100–13). Oxford: Oxford University Press.

Schmeltzer, M. (2016). *The Hegemony of Growth: The OECD and the Making of the Economic Growth Paradigm.* Cambridge: Cambridge University Press.

Slobodian, Q. (2018). *Globalists: The End of Empire and the Birth of Neoliberalism.* Cambridge, MA: Harvard University Press.

World Bank. (1983). *World Development Report.* New York: World Bank and Oxford University Press.

World Bank. (1997). *World Development Report 1997: The State in a Changing World.* Washington, DC: World Bank.

23. Good governance

B. Guy Peters

Although it began its existence as an economically oriented organization, the Organization for Economic Cooperation and Development has become a major institution in the pursuit of 'good governance'. Like many other international organizations seeking to promote economic growth, and effective markets, the OECD has learned that markets do not emerge and function on their own, they require an effective state. For example, the World Bank began as early as 1991 to consider the importance of 'good governance' for its operations (Nanda, 2006), and other organizations have followed.

The importance of good governance for economic development is very clear and direct. The state must create and enforce a legal framework for the functioning of economic activity, e.g., contracts, and must also enforce competition laws. Markets are to some extent natural, but they also must be institutionalized by the state (Greif, 2006) if they are to be able to provide the open and fair competition central to the concept of a market. In addition, the state functions as the representative of market actors in numerous international fora that are important for firms within the country.

The development of a concern with governance, and especially good governance, can be seen as the result of a functional process analogous to that of international integration. Advising on economic development could go only so far without recognizing that a properly functioning economy requires good economic law and regulations. But those laws and regulations are going to be successful only to the extent that they can be enforced by an effective public bureaucracy. Further, it is especially important to reduce levels of corruption within that bureaucracy, and government in general. And finally, the market can function much better with healthy and well-educated and well-trained workers.

While we are all in favour of good governance,[1] this is something of a slippery concept. There have been numerous attempts to define the concept, with one of the better coming from Henk Addink (2019, 16):

> Good governance is not only about the proper use of the government's powers in a transparent and participative way, it also requires a good and faithful exercise of power. In essence, it concerns the fulfilment of the three elementary tasks of government: to guarantee the security of persons and society; to manage an effective and accountable framework for the public sector; and to promote the economic and social aims of the country in accordance with the wishes of the population.

For the OECD and other international organizations the latter two elements of this definition have been the most important. First, good governance is about the capacity of citizens (and perhaps other international actors) to hold the country's government accountable for its

---

[1]   As Merilee Grindle said, 'who can be in favor of bad governance?'

actions. This has increasingly implied that some form of democracy is assumed to be a component of good governance, although the degree of consolidation of the democracy is variable.[2]

This second criterion of accountability also implies that good governance involves limiting corruption in the public sector itself, as well as in the conduct of business within the economy. One of the major emphases in good governance for the OECD and other international organizations has been to control corrupt practices in both the public and private sectors (see also Chapter 24 on corruption in the context of the OECD activities concerning public governance reform). As important as controlling corruption may be, it remains a very significant challenge for the national governments as well as for the international organizations (World Bank, 2021).

The third criterion for good governance to some extent represents the ultimate goal of the OECD. As an organization founded to help promote the recovery of European economies at the end of World War II, it has been principally concerned with economic modernization and advancement. Beginning with that almost exclusively economic portfolio, it has moved on to become extensively involved in social affairs such as labour policy, social and health policy, and education. The OECD now has a very broad focus on the performance of states, and the multiple policies that they must pursue to meet economic and social goals for their societies.

The apparent 'mission creep' of the OECD has been geographical as well as functional. While originally having only European members, a first set of reforms in 1961 added non-European members such as Canada and Australia. The collapse of the Soviet Union in the early 1990s led to a significant expansion involving countries such as Czechia, Estonia and Poland. The OECD has also begun to add middle-income countries such as Colombia, Chile and Costa Rica. With a more diverse membership now, involving countries with recent histories of 'bad governance' issues of good governance are becoming more important for the organization. Membership in OECD has been seen as one means of solidifying the commitment of countries to good governance and to market economies.

With a few notable exceptions, the role of the OECD has been that of the 'good cop' when promoting economic and institutional change among its members and the world more generally.[3] While organizations such as the International Monetary Fund have played the role of 'bad cop', and have had the capacity to impose potentially stringent requirements of countries, the OECD has tended to engage more in persuasion and in documenting best practice. The OECD has been described as club of rich countries, and to some extent it is, but as is true in most clubs the members want to conform, and to be seen as being worthy of being members of the club.

ACTIVITIES BY THE OECD PROMOTING GOOD GOVERNANCE

For an organization nominally devoted to economic development, the OECD has had, and continues to have, a large and expanding portfolio of activities that are associated with promoting good governance. Like many international organizations that work to promote market economies, there has been the realization that markets need strong and effective states if they are to have well-functioning markets. Further, the outputs of those markets have to contribute

---

[2]   The OECD, e.g., has members such as Hungary in which democracy is far from complete by most measurements of that concept.

[3]   The most notable exception is its involvement with SIGMA and the vetting of potential member countries for membership in the EU (see below).

to the well-being of citizens if the market economies, and the democratic politics that sustain them, are to survive. The *development* of the OECD's interventions into good government demonstrates both the *development* of the organization and the *development* of challenges to that good governance agenda.

PUMA–The Public Management Committee

Perhaps the first major effort of the OECD in good governance was the Public Management Committee, or PUMA, formed in 1990. This organization represented a response from OECD to a conference held in Madrid in 1979 that emphasized the importance of thinking about governance within the member countries (Pal, 2007). As the name implies, this section within OECD was charged with improving public management within the member nations. Good governance is a broad concept, but many of the goals of good governance can be at least improved upon, if not attained, through improving the quality of public bureaucracies.

PUMA began its existence during the height of interest in New Public Management (see Hood, 1991) and the widespread advocacy of managerialist solutions to the problems of governance. Stated perhaps too broadly, the managerialist approach to the public sector wanted to import many of the methods and structures of the private sector into the public sector, and tended to assume that the 'old fashioned' ideas of public administration did not produce effective and efficient governance.

Much of PUMA's work balanced the ideas of New Public Management (NPM)) with more conventional ideas of public administration. This approach reflected perhaps the need to balance the ideas of NPM that were popular in most of the Anglo-American countries, and some of the Nordic countries, with the traditional bureaucratic models that were more prevalent in Continental Europe. While functioning as a locus for discussion and collaboration, and bringing together a wide range of actors interested in making public sectors more effective. PUMA did not fall prey to the dogmatism that was characteristic of many organizational advocates of NPM (see De Francesco and Guaschino, 2020). This difference in strategy was in part because it tended to be more a meeting of relative equals rather than a wealthy donor organization imposing its agenda on the dependent recipients.

As Leslie Pal (2007) has pointed out (see also his chapter in this volume), the work of PUMA in its early years was encapsulated in several major publications that had a significant impact on public administration and regulatory policy tools (see De Franesco and Radaelli's chapter) in the member countries and beyond. Perhaps most notable was the 1995 publication *Governance in Transition* that presented a broad program for administrative improvements, some driven by NPM ideas and some more familiar to students of public administration. The comprehensive nature of the reforms described, and advocated, in this and in subsequent documents coming from PUMA were widely discussed and provided something of a standard of good practice against which to compare public administration in the member countries.

PUMA has now become the Governance Committee GOV of OECD, and the name change reflects its movement away from concentrating on just public administration to a broader vision of the tasks and responsibilities of governing contemporary states. Some of the enhanced conception of governance will be discussed below, e.g., the concern with strategic management. However, as is perhaps even more obvious for SIGMA, the Governance Committee is largely incapable of addressing political problems and the managerial and policymaking weaknesses of elected governments. No government would stand for being lectured by the international bureaucrats of a nominally unaccountable international organization.

SIGMA

While the Public Management Committee of OECD was directed at the then member states of the organization, SIGMA was directed at the newer members, and continues to function for countries that remain outside the OECD and the European Union (EU). SIGMA (Support for Improvement of Government Management) was founded in 1992 as a joint venture between the EU and OECD, and at present is funded largely by the EU. Originally this program was directed at ensuring that the countries emerging from decades of domination by the Communist party and the Soviet Union would be ready to become members of the EU. It was also available to assist countries such as Cyprus and Malta that had not been under Soviet domination, but which did not have governance systems capable of meeting the requirements of the EU.

Although connected with PUMA, SIGMA appeared less interested in NPM as it advised candidate countries about membership in the EU. One option the organization might have chosen in dealing with the countries of Central and Eastern Europe was to press for a rapid movement to the NPM style, with more decentralized administration, market-based personnel systems, and accountability based on performance management. That sort of pressure for reform was not uncommon for countries receiving aid from the World Bank and other international donors (see Schick, 1998).

What SIGMA did prepare was a set of documents espousing standards for the candidate countries if they wanted to be accepted for membership. Not only did the economies of these countries need to be functioning reasonably well before being admitted to the EU, but so too did the administrative apparatuses of the governments. The standards that SIGMA used for promoting reforms, and assessing the effectiveness of the reforms can be placed into four groups: Rule of Law, Openness and Transparency, Accountability, and Efficiency (see Pereto and Freiben, 2007).

Many of the criteria used by SIGMA were, as noted, very traditional, but reflected the need to build something like a Weberian public administration before considering the possibilities of dismantling it in favor of the concepts of the NPM. The experiences of communist style administration, and administration under the Nazi regime before that in many of the countries, meant that a formal, legal system of administration, and an equally legalistic set of administrative ideas, needed to be created before the fourth of the criteria could be pursued to the extent that it might be under NPM.

The criteria that SIGMA put forward for public administration and good governance during the first round of accession in the 1990s continue to be used, and have been expanded. SIGMA is still working with countries in the Western Balkans, as well as Turkey and Ukraine, who are seeking possible admittance. The criteria being used continue to stress basic principles of good administration, but have to some extent moved more in the managerialist direction. Some of those managerialist ideas, such as performance management, have become part of the canon for good public administration.

Several other comments should be made about the role of SIGMA in preparing the candidate countries for accession. The first is that while there was a great deal of attention to public administration, and to the courts, there was very little given to the political institutions. There was a basic criterion of being a functioning democracy, but much less attention was given to the capacity of ministers to be effective leaders and policymakers.[4] A second point is that some of the bureaucracies of the member states in the EU would have had some difficulty in meeting the standards being imposed on the candidate countries.

In summary, SIGMA played a major role in the expansion of the EU, and continues to be important as candidate countries continue to pursue EU membership. This program has been a major contribution to good governance in Europe, assisting countries without recent histories of accountable and effective governance toward a more promising future. That task is not, however, without its weaknesses. As already noted, less attention has been paid to the political side of 'good governance' than to the administrative side. The weaknesses on the political side may be seen, perhaps, in the extent of democratic backsliding in some of the accession countries (Hajnal and Boda, 2021; Mazur, 2021), changes that have certainly had less to do with public administration than the political leadership.

Budgeting and Financial Management

The public budget reflects the priorities of governments, expressed in whatever monetary unit the country may utilize. The budget therefore is a central element in any attempt to provide good governance, and must be considered from both a macro and a micro perspective. At the macro level, the principal question is one of balancing income and expenditure, and fiscal management. The question at the micro-level is how much to spend for each of the various programs of government, and then making the desired spending for those programs match the macro-level.

The OECD has made several significant contributions to improving public budgeting and fiscal management. One has been simply through providing information on public spending and taxation, and doing so in directly comparative formats. This information has been of a great deal of use for scholars, but it also has been useful for member countries who can see that their fellow members are doing and what policy lessons might be drawn from the information. This role as a source of information has been especially helpful in areas such as tax expenditures (Kraan, 2006) and tax evasion that are difficult to calculate in a truly comparable manner.

The information on budgeting and financial management provided by the OECD goes beyond the extensive collections of data available. For example, the Public Management and Budget division provides extensive analyses of best practices in budgeting, and has been engaged in examining methodologies such as green budgeting and gender budgeting that go well beyond the usual financial management aspects of budgets. These developments demonstrate that budgeting is an essential component of a broader 'good governance' agenda for both the OECD and its member countries.

As well as the general diffusion of information about best practices in budgeting, the Public Management and Budget division also works with individual countries to help improve their practices in this area. For example, there are extensive country reviews of budgeting in member states, which provide not only a comprehensive assessment of performance but also policy recommendations for improving practice. This division also works with parliaments to

---

[4]   In fairness there was a good deal of attention given to the offices of presidents and prime ministers as the principal political figures in these countries.

improve the capacity of legislative bodies in the member states to hold the executive account-able for spending, and also to enhance the role of the legislature in budgeting.

The final point to make about the role of the OECD in budgeting and finance is to stress the importance of the *OECD Journal of Budgeting*. Contemporary political science and even contemporary policy studies have moved away from any significant concern with the budget process in governing. This is extremely unfortunate because, as already noted, the budget is a statement of priorities, and the process by which it is made is therefore a fundamental politi-cal process The OECD journal provides a home for scholars and practitioners who continue to have an interest in the allocation of funds in the public sector.

Strategic Management

The concern with the public budget leads on to another of the points of emphasis in the OECD's pursuit of good governance, being a concern with strategic management in the public sector. Unlike budgeting, however, strategic management is an extremely important topic in contemporary discussions of the public sector. The disjuncture between the two strands of research and practice is, however, very unfortunate. The budgetary process is a crucial element of any attempt to develop a more strategic perspective on governance, and these two strands of thinking should be closely linked.

Some of the arguments about the importance of strategy for governing have gone beyond simply strategic management to thinking about a strategic state (see Paquet, 2001). This approach has emphasized coordination as central to all the activities of governing, with strategy being coordination with greater foresight (see also Peters, 2015). This conception of the strategic state has also emphasized social learning, and the capacity of the state to adapt to a changing environment as it pursues its basic goals. While this approach may anthropo-morphize the state to an excessive degree, it does point to the challenges of pursuing broad strategies in a world of rapid social, political and technological change.

As they have developed strategic management activities of the OECD have included several dimensions. One is the mainstream issue of encouraging thinking about longer terms issues facing the public sector – and the countries they serve – and devising means of enabling gov-ernments to deal with those issues. The recognition that significant 'wicked problems' such as climate change and food insecurity now confront almost all countries has made thinking more strategically essential for all governments, no matter how wealthy. The OECD has developed several major documents on strategic management, that have been used to promote the ideas among the member governments.

The 'strategic foresight' (OECD, 2019) implied in the above paragraph can be extended to think about 'strategic agility' on the part of governments. Strategic agility (Doz and Kosonen, 2010) was originally developed to shape the future behaviour of businesses, but the practice can also be used to shape the behaviours of governments. The strategic element of the term involves having clear plans for the future, based in part on foresight about the likely future state of relevant variables. The agility component implies building in shorter term information gathering, combined with on-going assessment of the means for reaching the longer-term goals. Maintaining such a strategic governance arrangement is, of course, especially difficult in democratic regimes in which successive governments may wish to alter even the basic goals being pursued (MacKenzie, 2021).

As well as advocating for longer-term thinking about public policies and governance, the OECD has been active in developing a community among member governments that is concerned with this very important issue in governance. The members of this community meet from time to time and share a great deal of information about how to improve policymaking for the long-run and how to 'future proof' policymaking. While some of the discussions of longer-range planning can appear excessively optimistic, at a minimum this community does promote getting policymakers to think beyond the next election, or the next performance evaluation.

Finally, the OECD's work on strategic management for good governance has included work on risk management. Governments have always been confronted with risk, but over the past several decades they have begun to confront and analyze risk more directly (Murray and Evang, 2022). The OECD has been playing its role in improving risk management, through mechanisms such as the High Risk Forum and on-going work on the nature of evolving crises (see Baboon, 2013) the organization has been able to enhance the capacity of governments to understand and prepare for the crises that they must inevitably encounter.

EDUCATION, LABOUR, HEALTH, AND SOCIAL POLICY

The final area in which the OECD has attempted to impart the values and practices of good governance has been in several major policy areas that touch on economic policy. In these policy domains the concerns have been less with issues such as accountability and transparency and more about the actual quality of the services being delivered. For economic development, and the continuing prosperity of already affluent countries public programs such as education, health and labour markets must function effectively, and the OECD has gradually expanded its activities to have a significant role in these policy domains.

The role of the OECD has been most visible in education, with the development of the PISA (Programme for International Student Assessment) program that judges the quality of educational outcomes in a number of countries, including some that are not members of the OECD (see Grek and Lingard's chapter in this volume on PISA). The program involves testing 15-year-old students in mathematics, science and reading, using primarily standardized testing. This testing exercise is supported by OECD expert evaluations of individual national educational systems for the member nations. Although controversial (especially in countries that score poorly), PISA has been a driver for improving educational performance since its inception (Breakspear, 2012).

The involvement of OECD in labour market policies and health policies are perhaps less visible, but the organization is still a major player in these policy domains. In labour market policy promoting active labour market policy has been one of the major emphases of the OECD (2021). Rather than relying on unemployment insurance to support the unemployed, these programs involve retraining and concentrated efforts to get unemployed individuals ready for new jobs, and placed in those jobs. This active approach is advocated as performing better for both the economy as a whole and the individuals who are unemployed.

A healthy workforce is also an important component of economic performance. Further, given that health is one of the most expensive, if not the most expensive, program of governments attempting to understand and improve the performance of health systems is even more a crucial part of good governance. As is true for labour market policy, the OECD is involved in health policy primarily through promoting best practices and in making information on health care and policy readily available. And, just as it cooperates with the International Labor Organization and the EU on labor market policy, the OECD cooperates with the World Health Organization on health policy.

THE CHALLENGES TO GOOD GOVERNANCE

The OECD and its various components involved with good governance have had a good deal of success since the organization began its activities in this domain. While there have been numerous contributions the work of SIGMA in Central and Eastern Europe perhaps stands out. As already discussed, by preparing these former communist regimes to be able to implement the *acquis* of the EU appeared to have made a significant contribution to solidifying the place of these countries in the 'family' of democratic regimes.

Contemporary challenges to the perpetuation of that family, both in the CEE countries and elsewhere, appear to threaten the perpetuation of good governance in a number of OECD countries. The fiscal challenge to high levels of spending for social programs, and other public programs, has been apparent for some time, and became more apparent after the 2009 fiscal crisis. There was some reversal of the retrenchment of programs during the COVID pandemic in order to prevent economic recession, but the underlying fiscal challenge to good governance remains.

In addition to the fiscal challenge, the most obvious challenge here is the rise of illiberal versions of populist politics that undermine the rule of law, and often other elements of the good governance agenda (Bauer et al., 2021). It is important to note here that populist regimes not only emphasize individual leadership over formal constitutional procedures, they also undermine institutions such as a career, neutral civil service and autonomous courts that have been important components of good governance. Contemporary illiberal governments also tend to have much higher levels of corruption than do other developed political systems.

Populist politics, as well as fiscal constraints, may also undermine other aspects of a broad understanding of good governance. The OECD has been important in measuring and promoting some areas of social policy, notably health policy, and governments have been tending to lessen their commitments to those policies. In part this has come through attempts to eliminate eligibility of migrants for some policies, and constraining benefit growth for all recipients. The latter policy choices may be driven more by the budget than by a loss of commitment to good governance, but the changes do represent real losses for citizens.

Finally, even in non-populist regimes, there appears to be an increasing politicization of the public service, and of governance more generally. A neutral civil service has long been considered a central feature of good governance,[5] but many contemporary politicians are attempting to develop public services, or at least segments of public services, that are more committed to the policy goals of the government of the day. This politicization is evident even in countries that long have been considered to be models of good governance (Cooper, 2021). The OECD continues to advocate for the classical conception of the career service, while not directly questioning the politicization of public bureaucracies.

---

[5]   This point may be exaggerated at times, however, and patronage may be able to deliver some benefits for governments and their citizens. See Panizza, Peters and Ramos (2022).

SUMMARY AND CONCLUSIONS

The work of the OECD on good governance goes well beyond the emphasis on the rule of law, anti-corruption, and an effective public service that has been central to this concept for many scholars and organizations. This expansive view of good governance may be in part because the OECD has had the luxury of working almost entirely with consolidated democracies that already have basically effective governments. It can assume many of the basics for good governance are already in place in those systems, and can then go beyond to advocate mechanisms for improving the performance of those already high-performing governments.

This expansive view of good governance also helps to demonstrate that this concept is not just a simple set of procedures and the enforcement of rules. It involves governments (along with their allies in the private sector), actually delivering high-quality services. Further, as the world of policy and governance becomes ever more complex, those services need to be compatible and coordinated, and also related to other sweeping public policies, such as the Sustainable Development Goals coming from the United Nations. These developments require not only competence, but also a clear strategic sense of how best to govern, and for what purposes, and also how to integrate a range of important goals for governance.

REFERENCES

Addink, G.H. (2019), *Good Governance: Concept and Context* (Oxford: Oxford University Press).

Baboon, C. (2013) *Strategic Crisis Management* (Paris: Organization for Economic Cooperation and Development), OECD Risk Management Working Paper 23.

Bauer, M.S., B.G. Peters, J. Pierre, K. Yesilkagit and S. Becker (2022) *Democratic Backsliding and Public Administration* (Cambridge: Cambridge University Press).

Breakspear, S. (2012), The Policy Impact of PISA: An Exploration of the Normative Effects of International Benchmarking in School System Performance', *OECD Education Working Papers*, No. 71, (Paris: OECD).

Cooper, C.A. (2021) The Politicization of the Bureaucracy Across and Within Administrative Traditions, *International Journal of Public Administration* 44, 56–77.

De Francesco, F. and E. Guaschino (2020) Reframing Knowledge: A Comparison of OECD and World Bank Discourse on Public Governance Reforms, *Policy and Society* 39, 113–28.

Doz, Y.L. and M. Kosonen (2010) Embedding Strategic Agility: A Leadership Model for Accelerating Business Model Renewal, *Long-Range Planning*, 43, 370–82.

Greif, A. (2006) *Institutions and the Path to the Modern Economy: Lessons from Medieval Trade* (Cambridge: Cambridge University Press).

Hajnal, G. and Z. Boda, (2021) Illiberal Transformation of a Government Bureaucracy in a Fragile Democracy: The Case of Hungary, in M.S. Bauer, B.G. Peters, J. Pierre, K. Yesilkagit and S. Becker (eds). *Democratic Backsliding and Public Administration* (Cambridge: Cambridge University Press).

Hood, C. (1991) A Public Management for All Seasons?, *Public Administration* 69 (1) 3–19.

Kraan, D. (2006), Off-budget and Tax Expenditures, *OECD Journal on Budgeting*, 4, 121–42.

MacKenzie, M.K. (2021) *Future Publics: Democracy, Deliberation and Future-regarding Collective Action* (Oxford: Oxford University Press).

Mazur, S. (2021) Public Administration in Poland in a Time of Populist Drift, in M.S. Bauer, B.G. Peters, J. Pierre, K. Yesilkagit and S. Becker (eds). *Democratic Backsliding and Public Administration* (Cambridge: Cambridge University Press).

Murray, J. and I, Evang. (2022) *Conceptualizing Risk Assessment and Management Across the Public Sector* (Bingley: Emerald).

Nanda, V.P. (2006). The 'Good governance' Concept Revisited. *The Annals of the American Academy* 603, 269–83.

OECD (2019) *Strategic Foresight for Better Policies* (Paris: Organization for Economic Cooperation and Development).

OECD (2021), *Active Labour Market Policy Measures to Mitigate the Rise in (long-term) Unemployment – A Summary of Country Responses to the OECD-EC Questionnaire*, (Paris: OECD).

Pal, L.A. (2007) Inversions Without End: The OECD and Global Public Management Reform, Paper presented at Global Governance Workshop, Carleton University, Ottawa, Canada, January 1–19.

Panizza, F.E., B.G. Peters and C.Ramos (2022) *Patronage Appointments in Latin American Central Administrations* (Pittsburgh: University of Pittsburgh Press).

Paquet, G. (2001) The New Governance, Subsidiarity and the Strategic State, in *Governance in the 21st Century* (Paris: Organization for Economic Cooperation and Development).

Pereto, F.C. And A. Freiben (2007) The European Administrative Space and Sigma Assessments of EU Candidate Countries, *Hrvatska Javna Uprava* 7, 51–59.

Peters, B.G. (2015) *Pursuing Horizontal Management: The Politics of Public Sector Coordination* (Lawrence: University Press of Kansas).

Schick, A. (1998) Why Most Developing Countries Should Not Try New Zealand's Reforms, *World Bank Research Observer* 13, 123–31.

World Bank (2021) Combating Corruption (Washington, DC: World Bank), October 19 https://www.worldbank.org/en/topic/governance/brief/anti-corruption accessed 24 April 2023.

24. Cyber security
Anthony J. S. Craig

INTRODUCTION

In May 2022, the President of Costa Rica announced that his country was 'at war' with a group of cyber criminals who had disabled 27 government institutions and were demanding a multi-million-dollar ransom be paid (BBC, 2022). The Central American state – which had become the latest and 38th member of the Organisation of Economic Co-operation and Development (OECD) a year earlier – declared the incident a national emergency and set out a series of measures to build cyber security capacity.

Stories like this have become commonplace in the 21st century and reflect the fact that cyber threats are now a major national and economic security threat. In response, most countries have now published a national cyber security strategy, a national incident response team (CSIRTs), and many are developing a military capability to engage in cyber operations (Craig, 2020). International organisations like the OECD also have a clear interest in promoting cyber security capacity to protect the economic and social benefits that the internet brings to its members and partners.

The internet creates opportunities and challenges in at least three areas which overlap with the work of the OECD – economic growth, democratic governance, and digital inequalities. Digital technology creates opportunities in each of these areas, yet also enables malicious cyber activities which undermine progress. By exploring the academic debates and research in these areas, this chapter underlines the importance of cyber security to the OECD's key interests and workstreams. Defining its role in cyber security and building the cyber security capacity of its members and of the international community more widely should be a priority for the OECD in the digital age.

As a topic of academic research, cyber security is interdisciplinary and can be investigated from multiple levels of analysis (Ramirez and Choucri, n.d., p. 2216). For example, computer science may look at how to protect computer systems at a technical level, while the social sciences may investigate the broader implications of cyber threats and inform policies for their mitigation. This chapter is written mainly through the lens of International Relations (IR). In this sub-discipline of political science, there are growing theoretical and empirical studies aiming to build a body of knowledge on cyber conflict between global actors and its consequences for international security.

Its traditional focus on market liberalisation and economic growth might suggest the issue of cyber security is not one of the main policy areas for the OECD, but the issue is in fact highly relevant. While not specifically addressing cyber security, the OECD has increased its work on digital issues, opting for the term 'digital' rather than 'cyber' security, which they suggest captures not only the technical but also the social and economic aspects of the concept (OECD, n.d.).

After a brief overview of the OECD and its work on cyber security, this chapter discusses the academic debates and empirical evidence in the field of cyber security as they relate to three of the OECD's main goals: economic prosperity, promoting democratic values, and reducing inequalities through the provision of data and statistics. This discussion can help policy makers understand the issue of cyber security from an international political perspective and highlight areas for progress in the OECD's digital security work.

CYBER SECURITY AND THE OECD

Cyber security has been defined as the 'measures to protect the operations of a computer system or the integrity of its data from hostile action' (Kello, 2013, p. 18). Hostile actions in cyberspace encompass the use of digital technologies by state or non-state actors to engage in espionage, sabotage, or subversion (Rid, 2013, p. 10).

The OECD's overarching goal is to 'promote policies that will improve the economic and social well-being of people around the world' (OECD, 2011). The OECD's interest in cyber security is naturally centred around this aim. For this reason, some commentators have noted that the OECD tends to emphasise the economic opportunity from digital technology rather than the security risks associated with them (Lewis J.A., 2014, p. 568). The OECD has nevertheless published policy advice on cyber security, with one of its earliest sets of guidance released in 1992 (OECD, 1992). The stated aim of the OECD in digital security is to 'develop and promote policies that strengthen trust without inhibiting the potential of information and communication technologies (ICTs) to support innovation, competitiveness and growth' (OECD, n.d.). Security is thus seen as important insofar as it protects economic development.

In a 2011 report the OECD addressed the controversial concept of 'cyber war' which featured warnings from academic experts against the exaggeration or hyping of cyber threats (Sommer and Brown, 2011). This reflected the broader academic and policy debate at that time between those (mainly policy makers) who envisioned cyber war as something real and pressing, characterised by catastrophic attacks disabling critical infrastructure (Clarke and Knake, 2010), and scholars who were highly sceptical of its severity (Gartzke, 2013; Lindsay, 2013) and its validity as a concept (Rid, 2013).[1]

The empirical record shows that cyber incidents have been increasing in number over time (Valeriano, Jensen and Maness, 2018, p. 67). However, a general consensus has been established that cyber incidents fall well below the severity associated with traditional military conflict. Rather than replace more effective forms of warfighting, digital technology enables new avenues for conflict and competition that fall between peace and war (Whyte and Mazanec, 2019, p. 150).

The OECD engages in three digital security workstreams – enhancing the security of IT products, managing vulnerabilities, and advising businesses how to respond to attacks. Two groups have been set up to help on these initiatives: the Global Forum on Digital Security for Prosperity, and the Working Party on Security in the Digital Economy (OECD, n.d.). The Global Forum on Digital Security for Prosperity provides an opportunity for stakeholders to share their experience of cyber security governance and discuss how to ensure socio-economic progress in the face of digital threats. The Working Party on Security and Privacy in the Digital Economy (SPDE) is made up of experts from the OECD member and partner countries, the

---

[1] For an overview of this debate see Lango (2016).

technical community, civil society, and businesses, and provides recommendations to policy makers and businesses, meeting twice a year.

Since the OECD is primarily concerned with the economic and social facet of cyber security, less focus is placed on other areas like arms control, national defence, and diplomacy. Instead, the organisation targets its policy recommendations towards issues like improving digital skills, improving the security of digital products and services, and creating partnerships between government and business.

ECONOMIC INTERESTS AND CYBER THREATS

The internet has transformed the structure of the global economy, especially among OECD members and partners which represent around 80 per cent of world trade and investment (OECD, n.d.). According to one review of the literature, most studies show that increased broadband usage in a country is associated with higher levels of GDP per capita (Minges, 2015). The positive effect of the internet on economic development could be explained through at least three mechanisms. First, the internet provides information both to businesses about customers they would not have otherwise been able to reach, and to customers about available products and services. Second, by making financial transactions cheaper and faster the internet reduces economic costs and raises productivity. Thirdly, the internet enables innovation and fosters new economic activity such as tech start-ups (World Bank, 2016, pp. 42–46).

Despite these economic benefits, global internet dependence gives rise to cyber security threats – some of which undermine the goals of economic progress that are central to the OECD's aims. The transnational flow of data, facilitated by advances in digital technology (including cloud computing, the internet of things, and social media), is not only an economic resource, but a potential threat to national and human security, as highlighted in the 2021 UN Digital Economy report (United Nations, 2021, p. 3). Against the backdrop of the COVID-19 pandemic, cross-border digital flows increased by 35 per cent in 2020 (United Nations, 2021, p. 17). This has increased the opportunity for malicious actors to employ techniques that harm the confidentiality, integrity, or availability of data – the classic triad of information security – for their economic or political aims (Singer and Friedman, 2014, pp. 34–35).

A distinction is often made between politically motivated cyber operations and financially motivated acts of cyber-crime. Cyber-crime causes economic damage by forcing firms to 'redistribute resources' to mitigate the threat, leaving them with less to spend on innovation. Cyber-crime is estimated to have cost the global economy up to $6 trillion in 2021 (Morgan, 2020), yet it is very difficult to estimate the cost of intellectual property theft and such estimates vary widely (Lewis and Baker, 2013, pp. 6–7). Loss of revenue can occur if a company's services are taken offline due to a cyber incident such as a Denial of Service (DDoS)[2] attack and because of the subsequent harm to the business' reputation (Whyte and Mazanec, 2019, p. 195).

Research has helped us understand the impact of cyber incidents. Agrafiotis et al (2018) conducted a systematic search of news articles and databases to develop a typology of the harms

---

[2]   A DDoS attack is a type of cyber operation in which the computer system being targeted is overloaded with multiple data requests sent from a network of computers (botnet) leaving it unable to function (Singer and Friedman, 2014, p. 44).

caused by cyber-attacks which are categorised into physical/ digital, economic, psychological, reputational, and social/societal type harms. As the 2011 hack of Sony shows, economic harm was incurred through the theft of confidential customer information from databases, leading to misuse of customers' credit cards and compensation from the company. Sony were forced to take their services offline resulting in financial loss and had to spend resources on replacing systems to resolve the incident. Sony's share price subsequently dropped, with the incident estimated to have cost the company $171 million dollars. The Sony incident is believed to have been carried out by North Korean military and intelligence agencies, which were also allegedly behind the 2016 Bangladesh bank heist (BBC, 2021). This shows how well-resourced and determined state actors, not only criminal groups, are engaged in cyber-crime operations.

At the more extreme end of the economic harm caused by digital threats, scholars have argued that cyber espionage can alter a country's overall power in the international system (Whyte, 2015). Computer Network Operations (also known as Offensive Cyber Operations) can be categorised into Computer Network Attack (CNA) and Computer Network Exploitation (CNE). CNA is a deliberate act to destroy, damage, or change the information held in computer systems and their networks, including the physical systems to which they are linked. CNE on the other hand are non-destructive acts which instead aim to obtain or steal confidential information from computer systems (Lin, 2010).

Cyber espionage is a type of CNE and has been defined as 'an attempt to penetrate an adversarial system for purposes of extracting sensitive or protected information' (Rid, 2013, p. 81). Valeriano, Jensen and Maness (2018) argue cyber espionage is aimed at producing 'bargaining benefits between rival states engaged in long-term competition'. China is accused of many intrusions into the networks of foreign governments and companies for espionage purposes dating back to at least 2003 (Lindsay and Cheung 2015, pp. 58–59) including information relating to the designs of the American fighter jet, the F-35. Empirical studies suggest it is the most widespread form of cyber operation in the international system (Rid, 2013, p. 82; Valeriano, Jensen and Maness, 2018, p. 18).

A state's international power is underpinned by its ability to incentivise continued technological innovation which ensures it can maintain the economic power to remain on the cutting edge of military capabilities (Whyte, 2015, p. 108; Buzan and Herring, 1998, p. 30). Cyber espionage which results in the theft of intellectual property can 'dramatically offset the ability of a nation or bloc to leverage an innovative edge in international competitions' (Whyte, 2015, p. 109). Countries at the forefront of technological innovation like the United States (US) lose their competitive advantage over other countries leading to loss of revenue which can harm future innovation.

Cyber espionage is very difficult to prevent. Its clandestine character makes it especially difficult to attribute to a specific actor, although there has been a significant body of literature on developing models for achieving attribution (Rid and Buchanan, 2014; Egloff, 2020). Cyber espionage is also considered an act that falls in the grey area between peace and war. Espionage has been a normal part of statecraft for thousands of years, and digital technology has simply provided more opportunities for these activities to occur. According to the Tallinn Manual – the guidance developed by experts on the laws pertaining to cyber conflict – cyber espionage is not unlawful (NATO CCDCOE, 2017). The international community therefore faces great challenges in developing diplomatic solutions to prevent cyber espionage and the theft of intellectual property.

This problem is confounded by the lack of global governance and regulation over cyber security (Stevens, 2017). This reflects the non-hierarchical nature of internet governance where non-state actors and private companies have a major role in managing cyber security, making it difficult to establish a top-down system of control (Mueller, Schmidt and Kuerbis, 2013, p. 95). Nye (2014, p. 5) points out that 'over the past 15 years, the advances in [cyber] technology have far outstripped the ability of institutions of governance to respond'. As a result, there are few mechanisms at the global level to prevent cyber-attacks. The Budapest convention on cyber-crime which seeks to align each members' cyber-crime laws is one of the few international agreements in this area (Clough, 2014).

It is in this context that the idea of cyber norms has emerged among academics and policy makers. A norm is 'a collective expectation for the proper behaviour of actors with a given identity' (Katzenstein, 1996, p. 5) and some scholars argue that if aggressive cyber activity can be made socially unacceptable or taboo in the international community, greater stability might be achieved (Stevens, 2012; Finnemore and Hollis, 2016; Nye, 2016/2017). There have already been efforts in this area including the bilateral agreement in 2015 between the US and China for the cessation of cyber espionage (Brown and Yung, 2017) and the 2015 meeting of the UN Group of Government Experts which set out principles of responsible state behaviour in cyberspace (United Nations, 2015).

While we may not be in a 'cyber war', the academic literature makes clear the urgency of the cyber threat and the importance of developing diplomatic solutions. Given their economic harms, limiting cyber-crime and espionage should be at the forefront of the OECD's cyber security policy. Yet, by focusing more on the promotion of internet connectivity worldwide, the OECD has perhaps been slow to engage fully in the security dimension of the internet. The organisation does appear to be increasing its efforts like publishing guidance on risk management and capacity building (OECD, 2015; OECD, 2019). These are suitable approaches given the difficulty in preventing cyber-attacks and espionage. Nonetheless there is room for the OECD to further expand its digital security strategy into areas like norms and international agreements.

DEMOCRACY AND HUMAN RIGHTS IN CYBERSPACE GOVERNANCE

The OECD is committed to a 'pluralist democracy based on the rule of law and the respect of human rights, adherence to open and transparent market economy principles and a shared goal of sustainable development' (OECD, 2013, p. 2). The links between democracy and economic development could help explain the OECD's dedication to this style of governance. For example, there is evidence that democracy can lead to economic growth indirectly by enabling and promoting favourable levels of human capital, economic freedom, inflation, and political stability (Baum and Lake, 2003; Doucouliagos and Ulubaşoğlu, 2008).

Since the early days of the World Wide Web, the OECD's cyber security policy has reflected democratic commitments. A 1992 report states that the 'security of information systems should be compatible with the legitimate use and flow of data and information in a democratic society' (OECD, 1992). However, the OECD faces great challenges in protecting these values against the misuse of internet technology. The internet can simultaneously promote and undermine democracy. The Arab Spring showed how social media can help pro-democratic forces to organise against their governments (Wolfsfeld, Segev and Sheafer, 2017). Yet these same governments can harness digital technology to undermine freedoms in the name of national security. Cyber attacks also threaten democratic processes within OECD countries themselves. According to one news article, half of OECD countries that held national elections in 2018 were targeted (France 24, 2019).

Democratic values of openness and pluralism are relevant in academic debates about internet (or cyberspace) governance, defined as the 'development and application by Governments, the private sector, and civil society, in their respective roles, of shared principles, norms, rules, decision-making procedures, and programmes that shape the evolution and use of the Internet' (WGIG, 2005). Western democracies associate themselves with the multi-stakeholder model of internet governance. Under this model, responsibility for developing technical standards, rules, and norms is spread among non-state actors like private companies, civil society, and the technical community, as well as nation states (DeNardis, 2014, pp. 226–227; Whyte and Mazanec, 2019, p. 40). Proponents argue that the multi-stakeholder model can strengthen democratic values of openness and pluralism by allowing the participation of a wider range of societal voices in the governance process (Dutton, 2016).

Some scholars have critiqued the multi-stakeholder model, however. They argue against those who view the model as a value in and of itself without a clear exposition of how it can further goals such as security and openness (DeNardis, 2014, p. 229). They point out that the model's proponents have also failed to recognise that it is not always the most appropriate approach across all issue areas, and that there is a need for a more fine-grained understanding of different governance approaches (DeNardis and Raymond, 2013). Others have taken issue with its US-centrism, arguing that it serves US hegemonic and market interests, reflected in the predominance of US multinational tech companies in the international system (Carr, 2015).

Despite these debates, the OECD certainly favours a more decentralised form of cyberspace governance since it promotes social and economic freedoms. Yet the policies of some governments to regulate and control internet content place these democratic ideals under threat. Authoritarian regimes like Russia and China see a free and open internet as a threat to their national security and values and tend to favour a state-centric approach where national governments maintain sovereignty over internet policy within their borders (Inkster, 2016, p. 120). Internationally, they favour agreements to be reached multilaterally through the UN rather than by private actors. Despite the limitations of the multi-stakeholder model, the internet governance policies pursued by the authoritarian countries are characterised by repression, censorship, and surveillance.

Academic studies have uncovered the prevalence of cyber repression and the methods used to silence dissent in certain countries. Governments can censor information and limit freedom of speech in several ways. For instance, King, Pan and Roberts (2013, 2017) conducted a study of social media posts in China which shows how the Chinese government deletes posts on topics that could stir collective action and fabricates internet content to distract citizens. Threats to democracy also come from the global proliferation of software used for surveillance purposes to regimes with poor human rights records, as tracked by Citizen Lab – an interdisciplinary research group based at the University of Toronto (Marczak and Scott-Railton, 2016; Diebert, 2016). According to Diebert (2015), the growth of digitial connectivity in the Global South, and the Snowdon revelations which have diverted attention towards the behaviour of Western states, have enabled a resurgence of cyber repression amongst authoritarian regimes.

These issues have increased the call among some scholars to shift cyber security studies away from national cyber security perspectives and towards human centred security. Diebert (2018) outlines policies to move toward a world where citizens can take back control of their personal data, where access to information online is universal regardless of political system, and human rights are protected.

Despite its self-declared dedication to human rights and democracy, and its promotion of internet freedoms to less developed countries and social groups (OECD, 2018a), the OECD engages very little in these broader political debates over the governance of cyberspace. The OECD's economic cooperation with China (a non-member partner of the OECD), for instance, has grown closer over time (OECD, 2018b). Given China's alleged human rights violations both off and online, this relationship suggests that the OECD tends to place economic interests above those of human security.

DIGITAL DIVIDES AND CYBER CAPACITY BUILDING

The third priority for the OECD discussed in this chapter is the supply of statistics on digital development to help reduce disparities between countries. The OECD is dedicated to reducing global inequalities and this concern has moved into cyberspace, particularly in relation to the 'digital divide'. At an international level, the digital divide refers to the gap between countries with high levels of access to internet technology (e.g., smartphones and broadband) and those with less access (Norris, 2001, p. 4). For example, one study suggests OECD member countries have more than twice the number of broadband subscriptions per capita than the world average (OECD, 2021).

To help promote development, part of the OECD's work is in providing trustworthy data and statistics on its members' capacities in digital technology. The OECD is well known for providing a rich level of data on the economic, technological, and social progress of its member states, rivalling other data providers such as the World Bank. These statistics serve an important role in helping to set and meet standards and enabling countries to monitor their development.

One of the problems with discussions on the digital divide is that the concept emphasises access to technology but overlooks the gap in cyber security capacities between developed and less developed countries (Schia, 2017). This is a transnational problem since states with weak cyber security infrastructure or legal systems are more likely to be vectors for cyber threats and to harbour cyber criminals (Haner and Knake, 2021). Some researchers have investigated the causes of disparities in national cyber security capacity like Calderaro and Craig (2020) who find that a country's scientific and technical expertise is a robust predictor of its cyber security preparedness, using indicators from the International Telecommunications Union as a metric. Data is therefore important not only for identifying digital divides, but for understanding their drivers.

The OECDs Directorate for Science, Technology, and Innovation collects data on several indicators (OECD, n.d.). These relate mainly to ICT development including mobile subscriptions, investment in ICT, broadband infrastructure, the size of the ICT industry, and employment in this sector. However, like the academic discussion, the security aspect of digital capabilities is lacking from the OECD's data provision. To address the economic and social harms previously discussed, an understanding of countries' abilities to protect their economies and societies from cyber threats is needed.

The measurement of cyber capacity will of course differ depending on the theoretical perspective taken. Among international security researchers, the approach to understanding cyber capacity usually takes a state-centric focus with an emphasis on cyber capability as contributing to military power (Craig, 2020; Valeriano, Jensen and Maness, 2018; Smeets, 2018). Research in this area often deals with the mechanisms by which a state can successfully deter aggression from another state or a non-state actor (Nye, 2016/2017; Harknett and Nye, 2017; Stevens, 2012).

The concept of cyber power has also been developed within this literature. For Nye (2011, p. 123) this is the ability to 'obtain preferred outcomes through use of the electronically interconnected information resources of the cyber domain' - by hard means (e.g., DDoS attacks and malware infections), or soft means (e.g., information campaigns). The concept of the cyber weapon has developed as a concept closely synonymous with malware and other computer-based technologies designed to inflict harm (Rid and McBurney, 2012; Herr, 2013). Developing the concept of capacity into the more intangible areas, Stevens (2017) adopts Barnett and Duvall's (2005) typology of power to the cyber domain and argues that cyber power can be operate via direct coercion, or through institutions, social structures, or the shaping of narratives.

Gathering precise data on a country's capacity to engage in military or intelligence cyber operations is exceedingly difficult given the low shelf-life and 'transitory' nature of cyber weapons (Smeets, 2018). A government's arsenal of zero-day vulnerabilities will also be kept secret or will otherwise become obsolete. This creates challenges in advancing our understanding of this aspect of cyber capacity. One way forward is to look for proxy indicators for measuring the capacity to carry out cyber operations such as the presence of military cyber units (Craig, 2020; Voo et al, 2020). An even less direct proxy for cyber power includes an index based on internet infrastructure and knowledge capital (Valeriano, Jensen and Maness, 2018, p. 60). The lack of quantitative research in international cyber security could be down to the perception that data is inherently difficulty to collect in the cyber domain due to government secrecy, or the scepticism of many IR scholars to the significance of cyber security in global politics (Kello, 2013, pp. 9–11).

An alternative area of literature is focused much less on cyberwarfare and instead deals with cyber capacity more holistically as the resilience of societies against cyber security threats based on policies, laws, organisations, technologies, or cooperative arrangements in a country. This area has a prescriptive emphasis in that it is interested in promoting policies that can better prepare less developed states, broader society, and individual users to cope with cyber threats, known as capacity building (Dutton et al, 2019).

Dutton et al (2019, p. 281) define cybersecurity capacity as the 'supportive environment for enabling cybersecurity' based on incident management, culture, knowledge and skills, strategy, technical standards, legal frameworks, and enforcement. Several cyber capacity indices have been developed by think tanks and international organisations including the International Telecommunications Union's Global Cybersecurity Index (ITU, 2020) which gauges each country's cyber readiness across five dimensions: legal frameworks, technical capacity, organisational capacity, cyber capacity building, and cooperation.

Existing work by the OECD in internet related statistics includes the Digital Government Index, helping to track the use of digital technology in governance (OECD, 2020a).

Nevertheless, the OECD could contribute further to bridging global cyber capacity divides through expanding its statistical work into the security aspect of digital technology. As discussed in this section, the military aspect of cyber security is of increasing interest in academic discussions. While precise data on cyber operations or malware is very challenging to obtain, more work could be done on developing metrics that would allow policy makers to understand the proliferation of cyber weapons and the security implications of this process. More data indicators on the development of norms and international agreements would also be beneficial as these provide potential mechanisms for a reduction in cyber conflict.

CONCLUSION

When seen in the context of academic discussions and research, the OECD's activities in cyber security are relatively narrow in range. Emphasis is placed on the economic opportunities of the internet, while cyber security policies are mainly focused on risk management. Furthermore, despite its commitment to democratic rights, the OECD does not appear to promote the human side of cyber security as robustly as it could.

The role of the OECD in cyber security will surely continue to evolve and expand given the growing importance of the internet to the economies and societies of OECD members. While the OECD has not traditionally focused on security issues in international politics, the relevance of cyber security to the OECD's interests is clear. Cyber technology has major implications for the economy, for democracy, and development.

The organisation is certainly engaged in tackling issues concerning digital technology and governance, yet there is opportunity for further work in a wider range of cyber security policies and in a greater emphasis on human rights online. Perhaps the area where the OECD can make the biggest difference to the development of cyber security capacity globally is in expanding its provision of statistical indicators not only on ICT development but on threats and the capability to manage them. Helping to build cyber security capacity in the international system provides a path forward towards a more secure cyberspace.

BIBLIOGRAPHY

Agrafiotis, I., Nurse, J.R., Goldmsith, M., Creese, S. and Upton, D. (2018). A Taxonomy of Cyber-harms: Defining the. *Journal of Cybersecurity*, 1–15.

Barnett, M. and Duvall, R. (2005). Power in International Politics. *International Organization*, 59(1), 39–75.

Baum, M.A. and Lake, D.A. (2003). The Political Economy of Growth: Democracy and Human Capital. *American Journal of Political Science*, 47(2), 333–47. Retrieved from https://onlinelibrary.wiley .com/doi/10.1111/1540-5907.00023 accessed 24 April 2023.

BBC. (2021, June 21). The Lazarus Heist: How North Korea almost pulled off a billion-dollar hack. *BBC News*. Retrieved from https://www.bbc.co.uk/news/stories-57520169 accessed 24 April 2023.

BBC. (2022, May 18). President Rodrigo Chaves says Costa Rica is at war with Conti hackers. *BBC News*. Retrieved from https://www.bbc.co.uk/news/technology-61323402 accessed 24 April 2023.

Brown, G. and Yung, C.D. (2017, January 19). Evaluating the US-China Cybersecurity Agreement, Part 1: The US Approach to Cyberspace. *The Diplomat*. Retrieved from https://thediplomat.com/2017/01/ evaluating-the-us-china-cybersecurity-agreement-part-1-the-us-approach-to-cyberspace/ accessed 24 April 2023.

Buzan, B. and Herring, E. (1998). *The Arms Dynamic in World Politics*. London: Lynne Reinner.

Calderaro, A. and Craig, A.J. (2020). Transnational Governance of Cybersecurity: Policy Challenges and Global Inequalities in Cyber Capacity Building. *Third World Quarterly*. Retrieved from https://www.tandfonline.com/doi/abs/10.1080/01436597.2020.1729729 accessed 24 April 2023.

Carr, M. (2015). Power Plays in Global Internet Governance. *Journal of International Studies*, 43(2), 640–59. Retrieved from https://journals.sagepub.com/doi/abs/10.1177/0305829814562655 accessed 24 April 2023.

Clarke, R.A. and Knake, R.K. (2010). *Cyber War: The Next Threat to National Security and What to Do About It*. New York: Ecco.

Clough, J. (2014). A World of Difference: The Budapest Convention on Cybercrime and the Challenges of Harmonisation. *Monash University Law Review*, 698–736.

Craig, A.J. (2020). *Capabililty and Conflict in the Cyber Domain: An Empirical Study*. Cardiff University.

Deibert, R. (2018). Toward a Human-Centric Approach to Cybersecurity. *Ethics and International Affairs*, 32(4), 411–24. Retrieved from https://www.cambridge.org/core/journals/ethics-and-international-affairs/article/toward-a-humancentric-approach-to-cybersecurity/4E8819984202A24186BB0F52E51BC1E4 accessed 24 April 2023.

DeNardis, L. (2014). *The Global War for Internet Governance*. New Haven: Yale University Press.

DeNardis, L. and Raymond, M. (2013). Thinking Clearly about Multistakeholder Internet Governance. Paper Presented at Eighth Annual GigaNet Symposium. Retrieved from https://papers.ssrn.com/sol3/papers.cfm?abstract_id=2354377 accessed 24 April 2023.

Diebert, R. (2015). Cyberspace Under Siege. *Journal of Democracy*, 64–78. Retrieved from https://muse.jhu.edu/article/586479 accessed 24 April 2023.

Diebert, R. (2016). What an MRI of the Internet Can Reveal. Netsweeper in Bahrain. Citizen Lab. Retrieved from https://deibert.citizenlab.ca/2016/09/what-an-mri-of-the-internet-can-reveal-netsweeper-in-bahrain/ accessed 24 April 2023.

Diebert, R. (2018). Toward a Human-Centric Approach to Cybersecurity. *Ethics and International Affairs,* 411–24.

Doucouliagos, H. and Ulubaşoğlu, M. A. (2008). Democracy and Economic Growth: A Meta-Analysis. *American Journal of Political Science*, 52(1), 61–83. Retrieved from https://www.jstor.org/stable/25193797?refreqid=excelsior%3Afc2f9103bbe7be63065f12529eb95761 accessed 24 April 2023.

Dutton, W.H. (2016). Multistakeholder Internet Governance? In World Development Report (p. 15).

Dutton, W.H., Creese, S., Shillair, R. and Bada, M. (2019). Cybersecurity Capacity: Does it Matter? *Journal of Information Policy*, 9, 280–306.

Egloff, F. J. (2020). Public Attribution of Cyber Intrusions. *Journal of Cybersecurity*, 1–12.

Finnemore, M. and Hollis, D.B. (2016). Constructing Norms for Global Cybersecurity. *The American Journal of International Law*, 110(3), 425–79. Retrieved from https://www.iilj.org/wp-content/uploads/2017/01/Finnemore-Hollis-Constructing-Norms-for-Global-Cybersecurity.pdf accessed 24 April 2023.

Fischerkeller, M.P. and Harknett, R.J. (2017). Deterrence is Not a Credible Strategy for Cyberspace. Foreign Policy Research Institute, 381–93.

France 24. (2019, August 4). Leap in cyber attacks against elections in OECD countries: Canada. France 24. Retrieved from https://www.france24.com/en/20190408-leap-cyber-attacks-against-elections-oecd-countries-canada accessed 24 April 2023.

Gartzke, E. (2013). The Myth of Cyberwar: Bringing War on the Internet Back Down to Earth. *International Security*, 38(2), 41–73.

Haner, J. K. and Knake, R. (2021). Breaking Botnets: A Quantitative Analysis of Individual, Technical, Isolationist, And Multilateral Approaches to Cybersecurity. *Journal of Cybersecurity*, 1–15.

Harknett, R.J. and Nye, J.S. (2017). Correspondence: Is Deterrence Possible in Cyberspace. *International Security*, 42(2).

Herr, T. (2013). PrEP: A Framework for Malware and Cyber Weapons. *The Journal of Information Warfare*, 13(1).

Inkster, N. (2016). *China's Cyber Power*. London: Routledge.

ITU. (n.d.). Global Cybersecurity Index. Retrieved December 2019, from https://www.itu.int/en/ITU-D/Cybersecurity/Pages/global-cybersecurity-index.aspx.

ITU. (2020). Global Cybersecurity Index 2020: Measuring commitment to cybersecurity. International Telecommunications Union. Retrieved from https://www.itu.int/dms_pub/itu-d/opb/str/D-STR-GCI .01-2021-PDF-E.pdf accessed 24 April 2023.

Katzenstein, P.J. (1996). *The Culture of National Security: Norms and Identify in World Politics*. New York: Colombia University Press.

Kello, L. (2013). The Meaning of the Cyber Revolution: Perils to Theory and Statecraft. *International Security*, 38(2), 7–40.

King, G., Pan, J. and Roberts, M.E. (2013). How Censorship in China Allows Government Criticism but Silences Collective Expression. *American Political Science Review*, 107(2), 1–18.

King, G., Pan, J. and Roberts, M.E. (2017). How the Chinese Government Fabricates Social Media Posts for Strategic Distraction, Not Engaged Argument. *American Political Science Review*, 484–501.

Lango, H. (2016). Academic Approaches to Cybersecurity. In K. Friis and J. Ringsmose (eds), *Conflict in Cyber Space: Theoretical, strategic and legal perspectives*. London: Routledge.

Lewis, J.A. (2014). National Perceptions of Cyber Threats. *Strategic Analysis*, 38(4). Retrieved from https://www.tandfonline.com/doi/full/10.1080/09700161.2014.918445 accessed 24 April 2023.

Lewis, J. and Baker, S. (2013). *The Economic Impact of Cybercrime and Cyber Espionage*. Washington DC: Center for Strategic and International Studies.

Lin, H.S. (2010). Offensive Cyber Operations and the Use of Force. *Journal of National Security Law and Policy*, 63, 63–86.

Lindsay, J.R. (2013). Stuxnet and the Limits of Cyber Warfare. *Security Studies*, 22(3), 365–404.

Lindsay, J.R. and Cheung, T.M. (2015). From Exploitation to Innovation: Acquisition, Absorption, and Application. In J.R. Lindsay, T.M. Cheung and D.S. Reveron (eds.), *China and Cybersecurity: Espionage, Strategy, and Politics in the Digital Domain* (pp. 51–86). New York: Oxford University Press.

Marczak, B. and Scott-Railton, J. (2016). The Million Dollar Dissident: NSO Group's iPhone Zero-Days used against a UAE Human Rights Defender. *Citizen Lab and Lookout Security*. Retrieved from https://citizenlab.org/2016/08/million-dollar-dissident-iphone-zero-day-nso-group-uae/ accessed 24 April 2023.

Minges, M. (2015). Exploring the Relationship Between Broadband and Economic Growth. Background Paper prepared for the World Development Report 2016: Digital Dividends. Retrieved from https://documents1.worldbank.org/curated/en/178701467988875888/pdf/102955-WP-Box394845B -PUBLIC-WDR16-BP-Exploring-the-Relationship-between-Broadband-and-Economic-Growth -Minges.pdf accessed 24 April 2023.

Morgan, S. (2020, 11 13). Cybercrime To Cost the World $10.5 Trillion Annually By 2025. *Cybercrime Magazine*. Retrieved from https://cybersecurityventures.com/hackerpocalypse-cybercrime-report -2016/ accessed 24 April 2023.

Mueller, M., Schmidt, A. and Kuerbis, B. (2013). Internet Security and Networked Governance in International Relations. *International Studies Review*, 15(1), 86–104.

NATO CCDCOE. (2017). *Tallinn Manual 2.0 on the International Law Applicable to Cyber Operations*. Cambridge: Cambridge University Press.

Norris, P. (2001). *Digital Divide: Civic Engagement, Information Poverty, and the Internet Worldwide*. Cambridge: Cambridge University Press.

Nye, J.S. (2011). *The Future of Power*. New York: PublicAffairs.

Nye, J.S. (2014). *The Regime Complex for Global Cyber Activities. Global Commission on Internet Governance*. Chatham House.

Nye, J.S. (2016/2017). Deterrence and Dissuasion in Cyberspace. *International Security*, 41(3), 44–71.

OECD. (1992). Guidelines for the Security of Information Systems. Organisation for Eocnmic Co-operation and Development. Retrieved from https://www.oecd.org/sti/ieconomy/oecdguidelin esforthesecurityofinformationsystems1992.htm accessed 24 April 2023.

OECD. (2011). Better Policies for Better Lives: The OECD at 50 and beyond. Retrieved from https:// www.oecd.org/about/47747755.pdf accessed 24 April 2023.

OECD. (2013). Roadmap for the Accession of Colombia to the OECD Convention. Organisation for Economic Co-operation and Development. Retrieved from https://one.oecd.org/document/ C(2013)110/FINAL/en/pdf accessed 24 April 2023.

OECD. (2015, August 17). Recommendation of the Council on Digital Security Risk Management for Economic and Social Prosperity. Retrieved from OECD Legal Instruments: https://legalinstruments .oecd.org/en/instruments/OECD-LEGAL-0415 accessed 24 April 2023.

OECD. (2018a). Active with the People's Republic of China. Retrieved from https://www.oecd.org/ global-relations/active-with-china.pdf accessed 24 April 2023.

OECD. (2018b). Bridging the Digital Gender Divide: Include, Upskill, Innovate. Retrieved from https:// www.oecd.org/digital/bridging-the-digital-gender-divide.pdf accessed 24 April 2023.

OECD. (2019, December 11). Recommendation of the Council on Digital Security of Critical Activities. Retrieved from OECD Legal Instruments: https://legalinstruments.oecd.org/en/instruments/OECD -LEGAL-0456 accessed 24 April 2023.

OECD. (2020a). Digital Government Index: 2019 results. In OECD Public Governance Policy Paper, No. 3. Paris: OECD Publishing.

OECD. (2020b). Discover the OECD: Better Policies for Better Lives. Organisation for Economic Co-operation and Development. Retrieved from https://www.oecd.org/general/Key-information -about-the-OECD.pdf accessed 24 April 2023.

OECD. (2021). Bridging connectivity divides. In OECD Digital Economy Papers, No. 315. Paris: OECD Publishing.

OECD. (n.d.). Digital Security. Retrieved 1/31, 2022, from Website of the Organisation for Economic Co-operation and Development: https://www.oecd.org/digital/ieconomy/digital-security/ accessed 24 April 2023

OECD. (n.d.). Directorate for Science, Technology, and Innovation. Retrieved 1/31, 2022, from Website of the Organisation for Economic Co-operation and Development: https://www.oecd.org/sti/ accessed 24 April 2023.

OECD. (n.d.). Our global reach. Retrieved 1/31, 2022, from Website of the Organisation for Economic Co-operation and Development: https://www.oecd.org/about/members-and-partners/ accessed 24 April 2023.

OECD. (n.d.). Who we are. Retrieved 1/31, 2022, from Homepage of the Organisation for Economic Co-operation and Development: https://www.oecd.org/about/ accessed 24 April 2023.

Ramirez, R., and Choucri, N. (n.d.). Improving Interdisciplinary Communication With Standardized Cyber Security Terminology: A Literature Review. IEEE Access, 4, 2216-2243. Retrieved from https://ieeexplore.ieee.org/abstract/document/7437356 accessed 24 April 2023.

Rid, T. (2013). *Cyber War Will Not Take Place*. London: C Hurst & Co Publishers Ltd.

Rid, T. and Buchanan, B. (2014). Attributing Cyber Attacks. *Journal of Strategic Studies*, 38(1-2), 4–37. Retrieved from https://www.tandfonline.com/doi/abs/10.1080/01402390.2014.977382 accessed 24 April 2023.

Rid, T. and McBurney, P. (2012). Cyber Weapons. *The RUSI Journal*, 157(1), 6–13. Retrieved from https://www.tandfonline.com/doi/full/10.1080/03071847.2012.664354 accessed 24 April 2023.

Schia, N.N. (2017). The Cyber Frontier and Digital Pitfalls in the Global South. *Third World Quarterly*, 821–37. Retrieved from https://www.tandfonline.com/doi/full/10.1080/01436597.2017.1408403 accessed 24 April 2023.

Singer, P.W. and Friedman, A. (2014). *Cybersecurity and Cyberwar: What Everyone Needs to Know*. New York: Oxford University Press.

Smeets, M. (2018). A Matter of Time: On the Transitory Nature of Cyberweapons. *The Journal of Strategic Studies*, 41(1–2), 6–32. Retrieved from https://www.tandfonline.com/doi/pdf/10.1080/ 01402390.2017.1288107?needAccess=true accessed 24 April 2023.

Smeets, M. (2018). Integrating Offensive Cyber Capabilities: Meaning, Dilemmas, and Assessment. *Defence Studies*, 395–410.

Sommer, P. and Brown, I. (2011). Reducing Systemic Cybersecurity Risk. Organisation for Economic Co-operation and Development. Retrieved from https://www.oecd.org/gov/risk/46889922.pdf accessed 24 April 2023.

Stevens, T. (2012). A Cyberwar of Ideas? Deterrence and Norms in Cyberspace. *Contemporary Security Studies*, 33, 148–70.

Stevens, T. (2017). Cyberweapons: Power and the Governance of the Invisible. *International Politics*, 55, 482–502.

United Nations. (2015). Group of Government Experts on Developments in the Field of Information and Telecommunications in the Context of International Security. United Nations.
United Nations. (2021). Digital Economy Report. Geneva: United Nations Conference on Trade and Development.
Valeriano, B., Jensen, B. and Maness, R.C. (2018). *Cyber Strategy: The Evolving Character of Power and Coercion.* New York: Oxford University Press.
Voo, J., Hemani, I., Jones, S., DeSombre, W., Cassidy, D., and Schwarzenbach, A. (2020). National Cyber Power Index 2020: Methodological and Analytical Considerations. Belfer Center for Science and International Affairs, Harvard Kennedy School. Retrieved from https://www.belfercenter.org/sites/default/files/2020-09/NCPI_2020.pdf accessed 24 April 2023.
WGIG. (2005). Report of the Working Group on Internet Goverance. Retrieved from http://www.wgig.org/docs/WGIGREPORT.pdf accessed 24 April 2023.
Whyte, C. (2015). Power and Predation in Cyberspace. *Strategic Studies Quarterly*, 100–18.
Whyte, C. and Mazanec, B. (2019). *Understanding Cyber Warfare: Politics, Policy, Strategy.* London: Routledge.
Wolfsfeld, G., Segev, E. and Sheafer, T. (2017). Social Media and the Arab Spring: Politics Comes First. *The International Journal of Press/Politics*, 18(2), 115–37.
World Bank. (2016). How the Internet Promotes Development. In World Development Report 2016: Digital Dividends. Washington DC: World Bank. Retrieved from https://documents1.worldbank.org/curated/en/896971468194972881/pdf/102725-PUB-Replacement-PUBLIC.pdf accessed 24 April 2023.

25. Sustainable development

Ulrike Zeigermann

INTRODUCTION

This chapter analyses how the OECD has both reacted to and shaped global debates on sustainable development through its work, strategic orientation and structure. Is sustainability merely a rhetoric without any substantial meaning or can we observe tangible operational processes indicating a mainstreaming of sustainability goals – as formulated in the 2015 Sustainable Development Goals (SDGs) – within the OECD?

The year 2022 was important for such reflection because it celebrated the 50th anniversary of the 1972 Stockholm Conference and the 30th anniversary of the 1992 Rio 'Earth Summit'. The Stockholm Conference marks the starting point for the international debate on the relationship between environmental problems, social well-being and economic growth. It also revealed conflicting interests of OECD countries and developing countries, that are persisting until today in global sustainability governance. The latter considered that environmental problems were the result of industrialization and therefore mainly a responsibility of OECD countries rather than a global responsibility. Furthermore, there was the fear that environmental policies would negatively affect the potential of (developing) countries to attain better living conditions. This controversial debate also characterized the 1992 Rio Earth Summit, which marks, nonetheless, the beginning of today's global environmental regime. Drawing on the 1987 Report of the World Commission on Environment and Development, the Rio Declaration highlighted that sustainable development – defined as a 'development that meets the needs of the present without compromising the ability of future generations to meet their own needs' (WCED, 1987, p. 41) – required new forms of decision-making, production and lifestyle in order to balance and integrate economic, social and environmental concerns and sustaining human life on the planet. The declaration was revolutionary at the time, bringing forth a new debate across governments and international organizations on how to achieve intergenerational justice and ecological preservation through sustainability governance. As such, the Earth Summit fostered a new orientation of the OECD towards the assessment and translation of sustainability norms in its member states.

The different controversies continue to determine the standards used for analysing efforts towards achieving sustainability goals and developing corresponding policies at the national and international level, 50 – respectively 30 – years after the beginning of international negotiations on sustainability. With the OECD as an international organization whose main purpose has been to provide knowledge and advice to inform policies (OECD, 1960, Art. 1), this chapter studies how the OECD has positioned itself in the controversial debate about (a) the responsibilities of developing countries vs. OECD countries for achieving sustainable development; (b) conflicting economic and environmental interests; and (c) the role of today's generations and future generations in sustainability politics. The focus is on dynamics in the OECD over the decade since 2012, when the process to develop a post-2015 framework for sustainable development was launched.

The qualitative analysis of documents on the structure, work programme and strategy of the OECD in this chapter shows that the new vision of the organization formulated at the occasion of the 60th anniversary of the organization in 2021, the OECD Action Plan on the Sustainable Development Goals and the strategy of Secretary-General Mathias Cormann, who was appointed in June 2021, are generally in line with the principal value of promoting economic growth, as already outlined in the Convention to the OECD. At the same time, OECD concepts were revised and new initiatives emerged in the context of the global debates on a post-2015 sustainable development agenda. They mark incremental, yet important changes in the work of the OECD that reflect its new strategic orientation. Furthermore, while the focus of the OECD is on the well-being of today's generations, it is remarkable that the notion of future generations has become more and more important in official OECD documents. It also comes with a shifting orientation of its work towards necessary transformations in OECD countries for sustainable development and a strengthened partnership with the United Nations and external stakeholders beyond the exclusive club of member countries.

THE OECD IN GLOBAL SUSTAINABLE DEVELOPMENT GOVERNANCE

The end of World War II marked the beginning of a new era with an international institutional architecture around the United Nations to promote international cooperation and problem-solving. In 1960, as part of this new international architecture, the Convention on the Organisation for Economic Co-operation and Development was signed. Its Article 1 defined economic development and *sustainable economic growth* as the main objectives of the OECD. The same year, a group of countries forming the Development Assistance Group expressed the objective to consult on their economic assistance to 'less developed' countries. In the newly-created OECD, this group was integrated as the Development Assistance Committee, known ever since as the DAC and often labelled synonymous with the OECD (Bracho et al., 2021). Since its beginnings, the OECD has thus promoted development in terms of economic expansion, increasing human prosperity (including through development assistance), employment and growth, including through efficient and effective international assistance for developing countries (see also Chapter 12 in this volume).

This understanding of development was challenged only some years after the creation of the OECD, including by the Director-General for Scientific Affairs at the OECD – Alexander King – who co-founded the Club of Rome in 1968. In 1972, the Club of Rome published the influential report *The Limits to Growth* questioning the economic orthodoxy that earth would provide the necessary resources for continuing trends in population growth, industrialization, the consumption and production of economic goods and services, and environmental damages (Meadows et al., 1972). In the same year, the Stockholm Declaration and Action Plan for the Human Environment defined the first international principles linking economic growth with social issues and with the protection and improvement of the human environment. The environment was hereby declared a major international concern and base for human well-being and economic development (Art. 2).

Sustainability governance has since attempted to steer human societies towards sustainable development bringing forth approaches that consider social, economic and environmental issues in a holistic, balanced and long-term vision. Accordingly, the 1992 Rio Declaration on Environment and Development proclaimed that human beings, who are at the centre of concerns for sustainable development, are entitled to a healthy and productive life in harmony with nature (Principle 1) and that the 'right to development must be fulfilled so as to equitably meet developmental and environmental needs of present and future generations' (Principle 3). In the following years, an international environmental regime emerged around the notion of sustainability in order to promote intra- and intergenerational justice without overstraining critical 'planetary boundaries' (Steffen et al., 2015).

International organizations, like the OECD, have always been active players in global sustainability governance. As formalized intergovernmental bureaucracies with a legal standing and substantive focus of operations (Weiss and Wilkinson, 2018), they coordinate and entrench in international frameworks the integration of environmental, social and economic aspects for sustainable development (Breitmeier, 1997; Peterson, 1997). In that context, the OECD increasingly linked economic questions to various issues and policy fields; expanded its global reach from originally 20 industrialized countries to 38 member countries and diverse partnership programs around the globe; and established its research, data and tools for analysis as its main source of power for international policy diffusion and agenda-setting (Lehtonen, 2007; OECD, 2022a; Ougaard, 2010). The OECD can thus be seen as an important actor in international sustainability governance that is both influencing and influenced by global sustainability goals (Zeigermann, 2020a and 2020b; Zeigermann and Böcher, 2019).

At the same time, scholars have repeatedly criticized that a substantial political response to today's ecological problems – that have the potential to threaten human fate on earth (IPCC, 2022) and that come with growing global economic and social inequality (Chancel et al., 2022) – is still missing in global sustainability governance (Hayden et al., 2019). Hence, it remains unclear to what extent international organizations, like the OECD, actually converge around sustainability principles in an international environmental regime.

This chapter studies how the OECD has both reacted to and shaped global the 2030 Agenda for Sustainable Development, that marks an important international milestone for sustainability governance as it defined a new universally recognized set of 17 SDGs. This requires an analysis of how the OECD has positioned itself in regard to a number of key debates that have affected global sustainability governance since its beginnings: First, scholars have confirmed that every significant environmental summit, multilateral agreement, or global environmental institution has been challenged by issues related to North-South inequity and justice (Okereke, 2019). Second, fundamental contradictions between goals for social well-being through economic growth and environmental protection continue to characterize the debate on sustainable development (Higgs, 2019; Princen, 2019). Third, despite attempts to consider and represent current and future generations (Lawrence, 2019), contemporary governance and institutions are defined by a massive bias for current generations (Setälä, 2022). The following section will study the OECD structure, work programme and strategy between 2012 and 2022 that are considered to be affected by and determining these debates on sustainable development.

KEY DEVELOPMENTS IN THE OECD RELATED TO SUSTAINABILITY DEBATES

North-South Sustainability

At the Rio+20 Conference on Sustainable Development, the international community launched a process to develop the post-2015 development agenda and SDGs, which build upon but improves the Millennium Development Goals (MDGs). The OECD participated as an observer in related UN General Assembly debates and contributed to the Rio+20 Conference, including through analyses, reports and four side-events (OECD, 2012a). It promoted especially its green growth strategy and related toolkits. In a session on global dialogue on sustainability and inclusion OECD Secretary-General noted: 'Let me stress that in developing countries, even more than elsewhere, accompanying measures are needed for green growth to be inclusive.' (Gurría, 2012b). This statement reflects the OECD approach to North-South responsibilities for sustainable development at the Rio+20 Conference. It illustrates that the strategy and work of the OECD was shaped by the existing development framework, i.e., the MDGs. The MDGs defined an agenda around eight goals that were based on the OECD DAC International Development Goals agreed by Development Ministers in the 1996 'Shaping the 21st Century Strategy' (OECD DAC, 1996). The MDGs were, however, criticized for their focus on actions in developing countries (mostly in the South) although industrialized countries (mostly in the North) have been the greatest emitters of greenhouse gases and – through their economic activities and defined standards – origin of global inequalities and the exploitation of natural resources (Meadowcroft et al., 2012). The emphasis of the OECD on activities in developing countries can thus be explained by the importance attributed to international development cooperation in the DAC (Bracho et al., 2021). Yet, it remains controversial considering demands from developing countries and the new OECD Strategy on Development, which was launched in the same year (OECD, 2012b) and presented as a 'new thinking [that] moves away from paternalistic policies [i.e., defined by countries in the North for countries in the South], shifting up a gear to more holistic and coherent ones' (Gurría, 2012a).

In the following years, the 2012 OECD Strategy on Development not only brought about changes in the rhetoric of the organization, but also new developments in the institutional structure and orientation of the OECD. Most importantly, knowledge sharing and policy coherence for development were defined as two central pillars of the strategy (OECD, 2012b). They required new activities and internal monitoring to ensure that the work of different directorates and departments in the OECD is not contradictory and as such undermining development efforts through incoherence (Zeigermann, 2020a). They also required a new approach towards the OECD contribution to global processes and cooperation with multiple stakeholders. Following this new framework and the activities of transnational '*passeurs*' who pushed and integrated global sustainability norms within the organization, a cross-OECD task team was created to contribute to the UN-led post-2015 process (Zeigermann, 2020b). Furthermore, new initiatives were set up to support global efforts beyond original OECD activities. Initiatives include notably the Global Knowledge Partnership on Migration and Development starting its first phase of work in 2013, as well as the four-year PISA for Development initiative (2014–2018), and the Multi-dimensional Country Reviews to assess development efforts in countries in the South in a holistic way beyond economic growth (OECD, 2014a).

With the agreement of the 2030 Sustainable Development Agenda, the OECD had to foster its collaboration with other international organizations and partners from civil society and economy because the SDGs promise to *leave no one behind*, putting sustainable development in motion globally. Accordingly, the OECD intended to facilitate reporting on sustainability goals building on existing OECD tools and data (OECD, 2015a, p. 14). It noted therefore in its Action Plan on the SDGs 'Country and regional coverage of OECD datasets and knowledge varies, and continues to expand. In some policy areas, the Organisation's expertise remains focused on OECD countries and Key Partners. Nevertheless, evidence and expertise in many policy areas now covers a much larger number of countries' (OECD, 2016a, p. 4). This highlights the interest – and need – of the organization to engage further in inter-organizational cooperation and activities beyond the original partners. This new approach of the OECD is also reflected in new work programs and standards promoted by the different directorates. For instance, the framework for total official support for sustainable development (TOSSD) is a new standard for monitoring diverse resources flowing into developing countries for their contribution to sustainable development (OECD, 2021c), that builds on previous initiatives for mobilizing resources for sustainable development (OECD, 2014b).

To summarize, the processes for developing a post-2015 development agenda were marked by the recognition of limitations of the MDGs, an opening towards UN processes and the integration of diverse stakeholder groups and countries beyond original OECD partners. These changes are not only reflected in the organizations' strategies but also in its diverse work programmes, legal instruments and in its structure. They were aligned with the SDGs and have increasingly considered the responsibilities of OECD countries for sustainable development.

Economic, Social and Environmental Sustainability

In January 2012, the Secretary-General of the OECD Angel Gurría explained: 'In today's world, well-being is no longer a choice between a growing economy and a cleaner planet; it is about both' (Gurría, 2012a). This statement highlights the strategic orientation pursued by the OECD since the Rio+20 Conference on Sustainable Development. It refers to an approach for linking the economic, social and environmental dimensions of sustainable development. Three main concepts promoted by the OECD over the last decade describe that approach. They were also integrated in the vision for the OECD for the next decade at the occasion of the 60th anniversary of the organization (OECD, 2021b).

First, there is the notion of policy coherence for development that was reframed into *policy coherence for sustainable development* in order to ensure equality and justice principles as outlined in the 2030 Agenda (Morales, 2016; Zeigermann, 2020a). It describes a framework to assess how diverse policies might influence the achievement of the SDGs and to revise policies and institutions accordingly in order to ensure an integrated and coherent approach in implementing the SDGs (OECD, 2016b). The second concept is *resilience*. It covers the ability of countries to cope with complex environmental vulnerabilities, uncertainty and systematic threats to economic and social prosperity (Linkov et al., 2018). The OECD has promoted the concept through a multidisciplinary approach of different directorates and initiatives ranging from projects for addressing conflict and fragility over the governance of critical risks, the Covid-19-pandemic, cities, infrastructure requirements for the future, and recently also biodiversity and climate disasters. The third concept is *inclusive and green growth*. With growing inequality in the aftermath of the global financial crisis 2007, the OECD started, with its

Green Growth Declaration in 2009, to develop new frameworks linking economic recovery with social cohesion and trust in institutions. The OECD defines green growth as 'fostering economic growth and development, while ensuring that natural assets continue to provide the resources and environmental services on which our well-being relies' (OECD, 2011, p. 9). With the 2011 OECD Green Growth Strategy and the 2012 OECD Strategy on Development, the concept of inclusive green growth was increasingly connected to sustainable development (OECD, 2015b, 2016c). In that context, the Green Growth Knowledge Partnership as well as the annual meeting of the Green Growth and Sustainable Development Forum were introduced to facilitate the exchange among participants from diverse countries, policy fields and disciplines and to identify policy tools linking economic opportunities, with social well-being of diverse groups in and across societies, and environmental concerns. These three concepts characterizing the work and strategy of the OECD towards sustainable development highlight the organization's focus on integrated frameworks that were increasingly broadened towards the environmental dimension of human well-being and prosperity.

The report for the 2014 Meeting of the OECD Council at Ministerial Level stressed: 'The OECD will continue to support processes under certain UN conventions, in particular the UN Framework Convention on Climate Change (UNFCCC) efforts to secure a new global climate deal in 2015.' (OECD, 2014a, p. 8). Accordingly, the OECD contributed to the 2015 Paris Agreement and participated in the following Conferences of Parties (COP) to the UNFCCC to discuss OECD research, knowledge-sharing and policy advice to support climate mitigation and adaptation. Two important points are worth noting: First, at the 2015 COP, the focus was still on the nexus of climate change and efforts for climate adaptation, finance and transitions in developing countries. The 2021 DAC Declaration on a new approach to align development cooperation with the goals of the Paris Agreement on Climate Change (OECD DAC Chair, 2021) confirmed the need to support developing countries in their efforts to tackle climate change. However, it also highlighted the need for OECD countries to foster their engagement towards zero net emissions. The OECD DAC thus started to integrate climate change into development cooperation while other directorates have worked towards the reduction of greenhouse gas emissions in OECD countries. Second, initiatives for environmental management and climate action by the OECD are understood as initiatives that support *sustainable economic development* and *prosperity* (cf. OECD, 1960, 2022c). Accordingly, to contribute to the implementation of the SDGs, OECD work increasingly seeks to foster human well-being by balancing socio-economic progress with concerns for natural resources and climate change. These initiatives go beyond GDP growth but remain people-centred and, as such, limited in regard to the protection of natural resources and ecosystems.

To conclude, with the OECD stating that it 'supports countries in developing and using environmental and green growth indicators and in achieving environment-economy integration over time' (OECD, 2022c), this long-term vision has already brought incremental changes through new strategies and tools. The OECD approach for linking the economic, social and environmental dimensions of sustainability is therefore best captured by the concept of 'weak sustainability'. Weak sustainability postulates the optimal allocation of scarce resources because green growth with technological progress is assumed to generate necessary solutions to tackle climate change but also because natural capital and reproducible manufactured capital are considered substitutable (Dietz and Neumayer, 2007; Ekins et al., 2003). In a context of increasing critique of this concept and a changing international discourse towards a 'strong sustainability' recognizing the multidimensional interactions between the natural environment and human well-being and the importance of critical natural capital that cannot be substituted, the OECD has, however, not only extended its activities for climate action (e.g., with the International Programme for Action on Climate launched in 2021) and for considering the '*inequalities-environment nexus*' (OECD, 2021d) but also started reflections for approaches '*Beyond Growth*' (OECD, 2020a) in the New Approaches to Economic Challenges (NAEC) initiative. We can thus observe important strategic and structural developments in the OECD and in its work in light of the SDGs.

Intergenerational and Intragenerational Sustainability

The critical sustainability question of future generations was only recently taken up by the OECD, while the questions of intragenerational justice between people of the same generation and intergenerational justice between people of different living generations have been important areas of work for decades, including notably through the OECD's work on youth employment and education. With SDG 4, inclusive and equitable quality education for all was recognized as an important area for sustainable development. At that time, the OECD had already established its soft power in education, and successfully diffused its standards for quality education and its recommendations for lifelong learning (Bieber and Martens, 2011; Jakobi and Martens, 2007). Since the beginnings of the OECD, education was considered an important investment in sustainable economic growth (Jakobi and Martens, 2007, p. 253). With its regular evaluation of knowledge and competencies of young people in reading, mathematics and science with the Programme for International Student Assessment (PISA), the organization of meetings to discuss best practices and challenges in education policies across participating countries and the promotion of policy frameworks, the OECD has become a key player in the field (see also Chapter 13 in this volume). It fosters education policies that support gender equality in education, equal access and opportunity for marginalized groups and children from poor backgrounds in the sense of intragenerational justice. In addition, the OECD had already defined a first *Youth Action Plan* in 2013. With its new Investing in Youth series, it started to offer country reviews with detailed assessments of education, employment and social policies, and recommendations on the school-to-work transition. These developments indicate efforts in regard to inter- and intragenerational sustainability of today's generations.

After the adoption of the 2030 agenda, it took some time until the notion of intergenerational justice between today's and future generations was picked up by the OECD. One of the early examples include the 2016 Secretary-General's Report to Ministers discussing the water-food-energy nexus in regard to the needs of future generations (SG OECD, 2016, p. 57). It was mainly with the global school strikes organized in the spring of 2019 in most OECD countries that the topic gained importance in the organization. These protests brought forth discussions on how to support governments in designing and implementing policies to empower youth and promote intergenerational justice. Accordingly, the OECD published a first report on *Governance for Youth, Trust and Intergenerational Justice* (OECD, 2020b), updated the Youth Action Plan (OECD, 2021a), proposed consultations with 30 young people from 20 OECD countries and launched the policy paper *Delivering for Youth: How Governments Can Put Young People at the Centre of the Recovery* (OECD, 2022b). These initial activities indicate a new area of action of the OECD that is aligned with its efforts to promote sustainable development and the SDGs. At the same time, any substantial work is still missing and only the future will show how the vision formulated by member states at the occasion of the 60th anniversary of the OECD will be implemented in the following years (OECD, 2021b).

This section has shown that mainstreaming the concerns of young and future generations in the work and structure of the organization has been a difficult task but that the OECD has been successful in its work on education. First initiatives are undertaken to consider future generations in governance. Yet, there remains a bias towards current generations.

CONCLUSIONS

The analysis of key developments in the OECD in regard to three main sustainability debates has shown that there have been incremental – yet important – changes in the work, strategy and structure of the OECD in order to promote sustainable development. These changes come with a greater alignment of its expertise and services with the global SDG framework. In other words, the OECD that has for many years provided its work mainly to member countries and that defined international standards – e.g., for governance, education or development assistance – has started to link its data, tools and services to global sustainability norms. It can be argued that the OECD has hereby given up some of its soft power. At the same time, it has also contributed to defining new standards for measuring and implementing SDG targets.

We have seen that the OECD is undergoing a process of mainstreaming the SDGs. However, while the organization was quick to change its rhetoric and develop strategies to promote policy coherence for sustainable development, it is not surprising that different OECD directorates have different understandings and priorities for implementing the 2030 Agenda because there are diverse interactions and trade-offs between the SDGs (McGowan et al., 2019; Nilsson et al., 2018). This is reflected in the position of the OECD regarding North-South sustainability, the relationship between the economic, social and environmental dimensions of sustainability, and the debate about intergenerational and intragenerational justice. As a result, elements of a substantial response to existential sustainability problems can be seen in recent developments of the OECD but we are at a critical juncture. The implementation of the new vision of the OECD for the next decade (OECD, 2021b) and the leadership of the new Secretary-General Mathias Cormann will show if and to what extent its work will make the OECD an important actor in the necessary global transformation for effective sustainable development governance.

REFERENCES

Bieber, T. and Martens, K. (2011). The OECD PISA Study as a Soft Power in Education? Lessons from Switzerland and the US. (Report). *European Journal of Education, 46*, 101.

Bracho, G., Carey, R., Hynes, W., Klingebiel, S. and Trzeciak-Duval, A. (2021). *Origins, Evolution and Future of Global Development Cooperation: The Role of the Development Assistance Committee (DAC)*. Deutsches Institut für Entwicklungspolitik (DIE).

Breitmeier, H. (1997). International Organizations and the Creation of Environmental Regimes. In O.R. Young (ed.), *Global Governance: Drawing Insights from the Environmental Experience* (pp. 87–114). MIT Press.

Chancel, L., Piketty, T., Saez, E., and Zucman, G. (2022). *World Inequality Report*. World Inequality Lab. https://wir2022.wid.world accessed 27 April 2023.

Dietz, S., and Neumayer, E. (2007). Weak and Strong Sustainability in the SEEA: Concepts and Measurement. *Ecological Economics, 61*(4), 617–626.

Ekins, P., Simon, S., Deutsch, L., Folke, C. and De Groot, R. (2003). A Framework for the Practical Application of the Concepts of Critical Natural Capital and Strong Sustainability. *Ecological Economics*, *44*(2–3), 165–185.

Gurría, A. (2012a, January 20). *Towards a Positive Legacy of a Terrible Crisis*. https://www.oecd.org/general/towardsapositivelegacyofaterriblecrisis.htm accessed 27 April 2023.

Gurría, A. (2012b, June 20). *Remarks by Angel Gurría, OECD Secretary-General*, delivered at the Rio+20 Earth Summit, Session on Global Dialogue on Sustainability and Inclusion. https://www.oecd.org/greengrowth/globaldialogueonsustainabilityandinclusion.htm accessed 27 April 2023.

Hayden, A., Fuchs, D. and Kalfagianni, A. (2019). Introduction: Critical and Transformative Perspectives on Global Sustainability Governance. In *Routledge Handbook of Global Sustainability Governance*. Routledge.

Higgs, K. (2019). Growth and Development. In *Routledge Handbook of Global Sustainability Governance*. Routledge.

IPCC. (2022). *Climate Change 2022: Impacts, Adaptation and Vulnerability. Contribution of Working Group II to the Sixth Assessment Report of the Intergovernmental Panel on Climate Change*. Cambridge University Press.

Jakobi, A.P. and Martens, K. (2007). Diffusion durch internationale Organisationen: Die Bildungspolitik der OECD. In K. Holzinger, H. Jörgens, and C. Knill (eds), *Transfer, Diffusion und Konvergenz von Politiken* (pp. 247–270). VS Verlag für Sozialwissenschaften.

Lawrence, P. (2019). Representation of Future Generations. In *Routledge Handbook of Global Sustainability Governance*. Routledge.

Lehtonen, M. (2007). Environmental Policy Integration Through OECD Peer Reviews: Integrating the Economy with the Environment or the Environment with the Economy? *Environmental Politics*, *16*(1), 15–35.

Linkov, I., Trump, B.D., Poinsatte-Jones, K., Love, P., Hynes, W. and Ramos, G. (2018). Resilience at OECD: Current State and Future Directions. *IEEE Engineering Management Review*, *46*(4), 128–135.

McGowan, P.J.K., Stewart, G.B., Long, G. and Grainger, M.J. (2019). An Imperfect Vision of Indivisibility in the Sustainable Development Goals. *Nature Sustainability*, *2*(1), 43–45.

Meadowcroft, J., Langhelle, O. and Rudd, A. (2012). *Governance, Democracy and Sustainable Development: Moving Beyond the Impasse*. Edward Elgar Publishing.

Meadows, D.H., Meadows, D.L., Randers, J. and Behrens, W.W. (1972). *The Limits to Growth: A Report for the Club of Rome's Project on the Predicament of Mankind* (1st edn). Universe Books.

Morales, E.S. (2016). *Aligning Policy Coherence for Development to the 2030 Agenda*. OECD Publishing.

Nilsson, M., Chisholm, E., Griggs, D., Howden-Chapman, P., McCollum, D., Messerli, P., Neumann, B., Stevance, A.-S., Visbeck, M. and Stafford-Smith, M. (2018). Mapping Interactions Between the Sustainable Development Goals: Lessons Learned and Ways Forward. *Sustainability Science*, *13*(6), 1489–1503.

OECD. (1960). *Convention on the Organisation for Economic Co-operation and Development*. OECD.

OECD. (2011). *Towards Green Growth*. Organisation for Economic Co-operation and Development. https://www.oecd-ilibrary.org/environment/towards-green-growth_9789264111318-en accessed 27 April 2023.

OECD. (2012a). *OECD and Rio+20* (p. 12). OECD. https://www.oecd.org/greengrowth/50276858.pdf accessed 27 April 2023.

OECD. (Ed.). (2012b). *OECD Strategy on Development*. OECD Publishing. http://www.oecd.org/pcd/OECD%20Development%20Strategy.pdf accessed 27 April 2023.

OECD. (2014a). *Looking Ahead to Global Development Beyond 2015: Lessons Learnt from the Initial Implementation Phase of the OECD Strategy on Development. C-MIN(2014)13* [Report for the Meeting of the OECD Council at Ministerial Level, 6-7 May 2014]. OECD.

OECD. (2014b). *Development Co-operation Report 2014. Mobilising Resources for Sustainable Development*. Organisation for Economic Co-operation and Development. http://www.oecd-ilibrary.org/content/book/dcr-2014-en accessed 27 April 2023.

OECD. (2015a). *Supporting the Post-2015 Agenda or Sustainable Development. The Role of the OECD and its Members. C/MIN(2015)13* [Report for the Meeting of the OECD Council at Ministerial Level, 7 May 2015]. OECD.

OECD. (2015b). *Better Policies for Development 2015 Policy Coherence and Green Growth: Policy Coherence and Green Growth.* OECD Publishing.

OECD. (2016a). *Better Policies for 2030 An OECD Action Plan on the Sustainable Development Goals [C(2016)166/REV2].* OECD.

OECD. (2016b). *A New Framework for Policy Coherence for Sustainable Development.* OECD. https:// doi.org/10.1787/9789264256996-6-en accessed 27 April 2023.

OECD. (2016c). *Policy Coherence and Green Growth.* OECD. https://doi.org/10.1787/9789264256996 -9-en accessed 27 April 2023.

OECD. (2020a). *Beyond Growth: Towards a New Economic Approach.* Organisation for Economic Co-operation and Development. https://www.oecd-ilibrary.org/economics/beyond-growth_33a25ba3 -en accessed 27 April 2023.

OECD. (2020b). *Governance for Youth, Trust and Intergenerational Justice: Fit for All Generations?* Organisation for Economic Co-operation and Development. https://www.oecd-ilibrary.org/ governance/governance-for-youth-trust-and-intergenerational-justice_c3e5cb8a-en accessed 27 April 2023.

OECD. (2021a). *OECD Youth Action Plan. Building blocks for future.* OECD. https://www.oecd.org/ gov/youth-and-intergenerational-justice/OECD-Youth-Action-Plan.pdf accessed 27 April 2023.

OECD. (2021b). *Trust in Global Co-operation The Vision for the OECD for the Next Decade. [C-MIN_2021_16-FINAL.en].* OECD. https://www.oecd.org/mcm/MCM_2021_Part_2_[C -MIN_2021_16-FINAL.en].pdf accessed 27 April 2023.

OECD. (2021c). *What is TOSSD -Total Official Support for Sustainable Development.* https://www .tossd.org/what-is-tossd/ accessed 27 April 2023.

OECD. (2021d). *The Inequalities-Environment Nexus: Towards a People-Centred Green Transition.* OECD. https://doi.org/10.1787/ca9d8479-en accessed 27 April 2023.

OECD. (2022a). *About the OECD - OECD.* https://www.oecd.org/about/ accessed 27 April 2023.

OECD. (2022b). *Delivering for Youth How Governments Can Put Young People at the Centre of the Recovery.* OECD. https://read.oecd-ilibrary.org/view/?ref=1131_1131487-xd5bm4h5h8& title=Delivering-for-Youth-how-governments-can-put-young-people-at-the-centre-of-the-recovery accessed 27 April 2023.

OECD. (2022c). *OECD and the Sustainable Development Goals: Delivering on Universal Goals and Targets.* https://www.oecd.org/dac/sustainable-development-goals.htm accessed 27 April 2023.

OECD DAC. (1996). *Shaping the 21st Century: The Contribution of Development Co-operation.* OECD. https://www.oecd.org/dac/2508761.pdf accessed 27 April 2023.

OECD DAC Chair. (2021). *OECD DAC Declaration on a New Approach to Align Development Cooperation with the Goals of the Paris Agreement on Climate Change. DAC/CHAIR(2021)1/FINAL.* OECD DAC. https://one.oecd.org/document/DAC/CHAIR(2021)1/FINAL/en/pdf accessed 27 April 2023.

Okereke, C. (2019). North-South Inequity and Global Environmental Governance. In *Routledge Handbook of Global Sustainability Governance.* Routledge.

Ougaard, M. (2010). The OECD's Global Role: Agenda-setting and Policy Diffusion. In *Mechanisms of OECD Governance.* Oxford University Press.

Peterson, M.J. (1997). International Organizations and the Implementation of Environmental Regimes. In O. R. Young (Ed.), *Global Governance: Drawing Insights from the Environmental Experience* (pp. 115–152). MIT Press.

Princen, T. (2019). The Mining Dilemma. In *Routledge Handbook of Global Sustainability Governance.* Routledge.

Setälä, M. (2022). Inclusion, Participation and Future Generations. In *The Routledge Handbook of Democracy and Sustainability.* Routledge.

SG OECD. (2016). *Secretary-General's Report to Ministers 2016.* OECD. https://www.oecd-ilibrary .org/docserver/sg_report-2016-en.pdf?expires=1682586627&id=id&accname=guest&checksum=FE 6C09BA7275212DF81425E3E99B24ED accessed 27 April 2023

Steffen, W., Richardson, K., Rockström, J., Cornell, S.E., Fetzer, I., Bennett, E.M., Biggs, R., Carpenter, S.R., Vries, W. de, Wit, C. A. de, Folke, C., Gerten, D., Heinke, J., Mace, G.M., Persson, L.M., Ramanathan, V., Reyers, B. and Sörlin, S. (2015). Planetary Boundaries: Guiding Human Development on a Changing Planet. *Science, 347*(6223), 1259855.

WCED. (1987). *Report of the World Commission on Environment and Development: Our Common Future*. Oxford University Press.

Weiss, T.G. and Wilkinson, R. (2018). From International Organization to Global Governance. In *International Organization and Global Governance* (2nd edn). Routledge.

Zeigermann, U. (2020a). *Transnational Policy Entrepreneurs: Bureaucratic Influence and Knowledge Circulation in Global Cooperation*. Palgrave Macmillan.

Zeigermann, U. (2020b). Quand les passeurs passent par les organisations internationales. Les acteurs transnationaux dans la politique publique globale du développement durable. *Revue française de science politique* 2020/5 (Vol. 70). pp. 575–593.

Zeigermann, U. and Böcher, M. (2019). Challenges for Bridging the Gap Between Knowledge and Governance in Sustainability Policy – The Case of OECD 'Focal Points' for Policy Coherence for Development. *Forest Policy and Economics*, 102005.

Index